Gertrude
Stein
in Pieces

RICHARD BRIDGMAN

NEW YORK
OXFORD UNIVERSITY PRESS
1970

Grateful acknowledgment is given to the following for permission to reprint:

The Baltimore Museum of Art for quotes from Gertrude Stein's manuscript, *The Value of College Education for Women.*

Crown Publishers, Inc., for quotes from *Journey Into the Self*, edited by Edmund Fuller. Copyright 1950 by the Estate of Leo D. Stein, Deceased.

Holt, Rinehart and Winston, Inc., for six brief excerpts from *What Is Remembered* by Alice B. Toklas.

Alfred A. Knopf, Inc., for excerpts from *The Flowers of Friendship*, edited by Donald C. Gallup.

Random House, Inc., for quotes from the following copyrighted works of Gertrude Stein: *Portraits and Prayers, Everybody's Autobiography, Ida A Novel, Wars I Have Seen, The Geographical History of America, Lectures in America, The Autobiography of Alice B. Toklas, Three Lives*, and *Selected Writings of Gertrude Stein.*

Annette Rosenshine for her description of Alice B. Toklas from her autobiography *Life Is Not a Paragraph.*

The Bancroft Library of the University of California at Berkeley for quotes from the diaries of Amelia Stein and from Roland E. Duncan's interview with Alice Toklas.

Gertrude Stein Collection, Collection of American Literature, Yale University Library, for unpublished Gertrude Stein material.

Gertrude Stein Estate for quotes from *Brewsie and Willie* and *Last Operas and Plays.*

Yale University Press for quotes from Gertrude Stein's *Four in America* and from the eight volumes included in their *Yale Edition of the Unpublished Writings of Gertrude Stein.*

TO HENRY NASH SMITH

ACKNOWLEDGMENTS

Frederick Anderson and Stephen Orgel, two exemplary friends, invariably improved the manuscript with their sensible and pointed questions. Better still, they suggested specific revisions which, after five years in Gertrude Stein's company, I could no longer generate myself.

Donald C. Gallup, the literary executor of Gertrude Stein's estate, kindly provided answers to a number of questions, as did Norman Holmes Pearson. The staff of the Beinecke Rare Book and Manuscript Library of Yale University where the Stein Papers are housed—in particular Mrs. Anne Whelpley—responded to my requests with patience and alacrity.

Dr. Thomas B. Turner, formerly Dean of the Medical Faculty of the Johns Hopkins School of Medicine and currently its Archivist, was very helpful, not only in locating Gertrude Stein's academic records, but also in conveying a sense of the period when she studied there.

James D. Hart, who has long devoted his efforts to assembling materials about Gertrude Stein in the Bancroft Library of the University of California was always generous in sharing his knowledge. Tevis Jacobs provided such legal assistance as made a portion of my research possible. Matthew Carney obligingly acted as my Paris agent.

Other assistance was furnished by Elizabeth Petroff who drafted the original version of the chronology and did other laborious jobs of research; by Susan Ensign and Irene Smookler who did the groundwork for the index of Gertrude Stein's autobiographical works; by Robert Hirst who typed the manuscript with the intelligent scrupulosity it required; by Noel Perrin; and by Marianne Richter.

I also wish to acknowledge the many years of encouragement that my parents, Max and Corinne Bridgman, have given me.

Two institutions benevolently provided the time this study required: the University of California with a Humanities Research Fellowship (as well as with miscellaneous funds) and the John Simon Guggenheim Memorial Foundation which, by its award of a Fellowship for 1968–1969, enabled me to bring the project to a close.

CONTENTS

KEY TO ABBREVIATIONS

ABT *The Autobiography of Alice B. Toklas*
A&B *Alphabets and Birthdays*
AFAM *As Fine As Melanctha*
B&W *Brewsie and Willie*
BTV *Bee Time Vine*
CAP *Composition As Explanation*
EA *Everybody's Autobiography*
FIA *Four in America*
GHA *The Geographical History of America, or The Relation of Human Nature to the Human Mind*
G&P *Geography and Plays*
GMP *Matisse Picasso and Gertrude Stein*
GSFR *Gertrude Stein First Reader*
HTW *How To Write*
LCA *Lucy Church Amiably*
LGB *A Long Gay Book*
LIA *Lectures in America*
LO&P *Last Operas and Plays*
MMW *Many Many Women*
MOA *The Making of Americans*
MR *Mrs. Reynolds*
NOTY *A Novel of Thank You*
O&P *Operas and Plays*
P&P *Portraits and Prayers*
PL *Painted Lace*
RAD *Gertrude Stein: Form and Intelligibility: The Radcliffe Themes*
SIM *Stanzas in Meditation*
SW *Selected Writings of Gertrude Stein* (Modern Library edition)
TATA *Things As They Are*

TB	*Tender Buttons*
TWO	*Two: Gertrude Stein and Her Brother*
UK	*Useful Knowledge*
WAM	*What Are Masterpieces*
WIHS	*Wars I Have Seen*
WIR	Alice Toklas, *What Is Remembered*
YCAL	The Gertrude Stein Collection, Yale Collection of American Literature

NOTE ON DOCUMENTATION

The titles of Gertrude Stein's books are normally abbreviated according to the list above. Other quotations will be identified parenthetically in the text by the author's last name and, if necessary, a short title, with full information available in the bibliography. Whenever quotations appear successively from a single source, page references alone will be cited in the text after the source has been identified once.

Certain of Gertrude Stein's works not easily available in the original edition such as *Tender Buttons* and *Composition As Explanation* are keyed to the Modern Library *Selected Writings of Gertrude Stein*.

The quotations from Gertrude Stein preserve the vagaries of her punctuation and spelling. For example, in her letters she customarily shortened the prefix "ex-" to "x," as in "xcited," and she rarely enhanced her French with accent marks, so that Cézanne appears as "Cezanne" in her titles and quotations.

In the absence of other evidence, postmarks have been used to date Gertrude Stein's letters.

INTRODUCTION

~∴. "The idea of modern composition
is to keep it up that is all."
 ("I Can Feel The Beauty")

Reading Gertrude Stein at length is not unlike making one's way
through an interminable and badly printed game book. As a result,
few of her critics have had the patience, let alone the time, to acquaint
themselves with anything like the whole of her work. In the course of
summarizing her position in the world of letters, Edmund Wilson admitted that he had not read the whole of *The Making of Americans*
and moreover declared himself uncertain whether it was possible to
do so (*Axel's Castle*, 239). The predictable consequence of this reluctance—or inability—to become familiar with the full range of Gertrude Stein's writing is that informed discussion of her has been sparse
and confined to a few titles. And, while in a modest way her reputation
continues to flourish, her literary identity remains ambiguous. Was she
a venturesome leader of the avant-garde? An arrogant self-publicist
who achieved notoriety by abusing the legitimate experimentation of
modern art? An eccentric graced with the random perceptions of a
child? No answer can be advanced with any confidence so long as the
legacy of her mind, forbidding in bulk and perplexing in manner, remains unknown. The present book then is a preliminary inventory of
Gertrude Stein's literary estate.

Until recently, even if a person were willing to read all of Gertrude
Stein's work, troublesome obstacles stood in the way. Because her compositions often appeared in fugitive periodicals, some of them remained
virtually unobtainable. She did gather some of her shorter pieces in
volumes like *Geography and Plays* and *Useful Knowledge,* but since the
contents of such collections were carefully selected, they are unreliable
models of Gertrude Stein's actual development. Furthermore, at the
time of her death, a good portion of her writing had not yet appeared

in print. Not until 1958 did Yale University Press complete its eight-volume edition of her unpublished manuscripts. Only then, and with the help of the chronological list in the *Yale Catalogue*,* could her pieces be read in the approximate order in which they were composed.

Except in its account of Gertrude Stein's early years before she had fully committed herself to verbal expression, this study is not a biography, but rather a descriptive reading of her work. I have tried to acquaint myself responsibly with Gertrude Stein's character and the facts of her life. But how essential such information is for an appreciation of her art remains a moot question. Donald Sutherland has argued that even if it is often possible to make a shrewd guess at Gertrude Stein's subject in one of her lyric flights, to do so is "really a temptation and a distraction from the actual aesthetic object" ("Preface: The Turning Point," *SIM*, xii). In theory, the virtues of purely formal appreciation are strong. It is true that one is moved by the poetry of such characteristic moderns as Rimbaud and Pound long before one rationally comprehends it, supposing one ever does. Even then, it is questionable whether the knowledge acquired fundamentally changes the original response to the poem.

Consider, as an instance, "Thank You," a minor piece Gertrude Stein composed in 1913. It reads in its entirety:

> Thank you thank you thank you I'll be there. Thank you. I'll be there. Thank you. Thank you. A good time in knee grows hands. (*BTV*, 43)

Virgil Thomson informs us that this piece quotes the English suffragette, Sylvia Pankhurst, "who when released from arrest on her promise to reappear for trial had said to the magistrate, 'Thank You, I'll be there.'" After she failed to appear as promised, she explained that "The word 'there' had not, in her mind, as she said it, meant the courtroom" (*BTV*, 43. The story is also told in *WIR*, 62–63). Familiarity with this historic example of semantic relativism does illuminate "Thank You" slightly. In particular, the identification suggests a significance for the pun "knee grows hands," inasmuch as Sylvia Pankhurst interested herself in Ethiopian affairs throughout her life.†

Gertrude Stein herself insisted upon the irrelevance of annotation.

---

* *A Catalogue of the Published and Unpublished Writings of Gertrude Stein* is an invaluable resource, compiled in 1941 by Robert Bartlett Haas and Donald C. Gallup. Its fourth part lists all of Gertrude Stein's writings by date of composition. Appendix C of the present book provides a revised key to that chronological register.
† See David Mitchell, *The Fighting Pankhursts, passim*.

Discussing a verbal portrait she had done of Georges Hugnet, she declared that it did not matter who Hugnet was or what he had done. "All that was necessary was that there was something completely contained within itself . . . and moving . . ." (*LIA*, 202). She did not hold consistently to this position, however, but frequently interrupted her private utterances to comment upon them or to hint at their subject; and in a few important instances, she deliberately revised her elliptical art in the direction of comprehensibility.

In the study that follows, Gertrude Stein's own explications of her career are treated as emerging out of her experimental period rather than—as she sometimes implied was the case—predetermining it. Gertrude Stein did argue persuasively on occasion for her innovative practices, but in so doing she gave her career a symmetry and certitude that it never possessed. The greater part of Gertrude Stein's writing was improvisational. She used her composition books as catch-alls in which she recorded the day's activities, confessed her uncertainties, celebrated her moments of contentment, tried out new techniques, and assessed the quality of her experimentation. For long periods, even though she made no progress, she labored on, awaiting inspiration. The monotony of these thousands of pages of disconnected trivia must be acknowledged if the inventory is to be complete.

Acknowledged, but not in the present instance used as a weapon against her. Gertrude Stein is often accused of a self-indulgent abuse of language, and yet she regarded her primary stylistic goal as accuracy of verbal expression. "I do thoroughly reasonably chuck out what has hitherto hindered office of origin" ("In One," *BTV*, 177). Trained in psychology and in medicine, she eventually threw over traditional formal discipline (or, some would say, ceased to profess fealty to it) in order to create a record of a modern consciousness in words. I believe Allegra Stewart is correct when she concludes that "the total volume of Stein's work belongs to the phenomenology of mind rather than to literature . . ." (*Gertrude Stein and the Present*, 66). Clouds of association, fragmentary statements, covert references, and the arbitrary distortion of grammatical form: these constituted Gertrude Stein's representation of her consciousness in its actual state of existence. At its most complex, her prose is an outpouring of verbal responses to her experience mixed with fantasies generated by the primary experiences and with words stimulated by the appearance or sound of other words already on the page or still in her head.

Biographical detail is sometimes useful in following the lines of association through these tangles. After annotating a volume of Gertrude Stein's writing, Virgil Thomson distinguished three degrees of apprehensibility in it. Some of her pieces were "easy to understand." Others made sense if one were "acquainted with the regions they describe or with their author's domestic life." Still others though, Thomson found "genuinely hermetic" (*BTV*, v). In effect, "hermetic" means that the compositions so designated either treated subjects unfamiliar to Thomson, or were handled in such a way that he could not recognize them. After the public range of Gertrude Stein's references, which included the Arc de Triomphe and Picasso, there was a more restricted circle composed of Mildred Aldrich, Constance Fletcher, Etta and Claribel Cone, and Kate Buss, while still more private were those experiences shared with Alice Toklas. Up to this point, glosses can be helpful, if not conclusive, in plotting the landscape of Gertrude Stein's imagination. But the final pool of references lay within Gertrude Stein's head, and it is material drawn from it or transformed by immersion in it that is most likely to be designated "hermetic," and perhaps to remain so.

When I originally undertook a systematic reading of Gertrude Stein, it was in the expectation of learning how to decipher even the most resistant of her works. That particularly naïve assumption has long since been dispelled. Still, the surest way to begin understanding this unruly mélange is to familiarize oneself with its actual features. In doing so, one can already detect the recurrence of certain words, emotional states, stylistic mannerisms, and general topics. The commencement of Gertrude Stein's interest in saints, for example, can be determined with some precision. Similarly, her reliance upon overt syntactical patterning occurs during a fairly well-defined period of her career. And, it can be demonstrated that much of her writing concerns two persons, who are often at odds: "I bought you a book about knitting./ Yes sir./ Repeat it./ I repeat it. I am deeply grateful to you./ Yes sir./ Little joke in the worst of taste" ("I Often Think About Another," *PL*, 33). Although the assumption that the personal details everywhere recorded in Gertrude Stein's work are accurate reflections of the reality of her life may be open to question, their verbal presence is not. So here, my principal concern has been to trace the continuities and changes actually present in her writing.

☙. "Why cannot you speak in pieces and say no matter."
("Why Cannot You Speak In Pieces")

PART ONE

~. "Once upon a time I met myself and ran."
                    (*The World Is Round*)

1

ᐓ. "Now she is a good example of a sentence without words."

("More Grammar Genia Berman")

During 1894, her second year at Radcliffe College, Gertrude Stein floundered into an approximation of verbal adequacy. The themes she submitted to the Harvard composition course, English 22, show that her problems were manifold.* They affected her spelling, her syntax, her tone, and her logic, and she was never entirely cured of them. She was pleased to call winter "the hoary tyrant," to counsel letting one's mind "wander idly as it listeth," and to cry out against the necessity of preparing a daily theme, "Avaunt thou valeful spectre!" (145, 139, 115). Her reading echoed through her prose, although she was likely to do damage even to trite quotations as in "He is a man take him for all in all," and "In very truth, what fools these mortals be" (147, 133). She sought to dignify her exposition by mounting stilts: "Our hunting zeal had not yet entirely abated" (135). A bluff heartiness entered her descriptions at times, as when her brother emerges from a fall into a pond, "a most forlorn and dripping laddie" (134). She was given to emotional effusions, especially when in the presence of a romantic day, night, landscape, painting, or opera. At such moments she reflected the manner of Edgar Allan Poe, another Baltimore writer: "the villons in the marshes groan and creak" and "weird and fantastic in the mystic light of the moon" (144, 139). She attempted to employ what she was learning at college: "I love to dwell on that word sleep . . . with its somnolent sl and p" (140). Amidst this cultural debris were mechanical errors of the grossest sort:

* These college themes have been printed in Rosalind Miller's *Gertrude Stein: Form and Intelligibility* (New York, 1949). Hereafter page references for quotations from this book will be cited parenthetically in the text.

The eternal feminine is nice to be sure but its painfully illogical. (115)
Her record is there she cannot escape it . . . (121)
She struggle with herself all that night . . . (126)
We poor plebe look on in envy . . . (147)
. . . you only laughed at him and never thought of disprising him. (129)

Leo Stein, Gertrude's brother, confirmed that her expository problems were long-standing, "Gertrude was in her pre-'cubist' days a barbarian in her use of language." She "couldn't write plain English effectively," and "never could use words with precision and force." Leo believed the key to his sister's problems was that she was "basically stupid" (*Journey*, 141, 136, 134, 149).

Before Gertrude Stein entertained serious literary pretensions, others besides her brother and college instructors had complained about her prose. In 1897, Leon Solomons, her friend and collaborator in the Harvard Psychological Laboratory, scolded her for the way she had reported one experiment: "you ought to be ashamed of yourself for the careless manner in which you have written it up" (Gallup, *Flowers*, 15). Still later, in 1902, a professor at Johns Hopkins made a courteously indirect suggestion about one of her descriptions of a brain tract: "I think, too, that when all is brought together, you might go over it once with special reference to the literary form" (Gallup, *Flowers*, 24).

These early demurrers to Gertrude Stein's prose multiplied over the years. When she first submitted her work to publishers, it was rejected with irony, consternation, and contempt. When she contracted a vanity press to publish *Three Lives*, the publisher first supposed that someone for whom English was a foreign language had written the book (*ABT*, 84). Disabused of that illusion, he could then only hope that at least some of the stylistic curiosities were ascribable to faulty typing (Gallup, *Flowers*, 42). From the very beginning, Gertrude Stein distressed her readers.

But minimal assistance had been forthcoming from William Vaughn Moody who had corrected her themes at Harvard. For the most part his comments were perfunctory: "Interesting." "Shows discernment." "Perspicacious." "Makes a point." "Has humor—Some misuses" (121, 122, 127, 132, 114). At least one conference between Moody and his student seems to have ended emotionally, for after it Gertrude Stein wrote a paragraph entitled "Woman." Utilizing the perspective of a man, she described a woman who when reasoned with "immediately gets hysterical and thinks she is calm" (115). Moody responded with that wry tone that permeated Harvard in the nineties. "Point of view," he commented, "nobly remote" (115).

The excitability that marked her conference with Moody was in part responsible for the literary problems Gertrude Stein suffered. When Moody analyzed her output at the end of the year, he took particular note of the "considerable emotional intensity" of her writing (155). She characterized herself that year as "this vehement individual" and described her behavior in the Psychological Laboratory as "emitting fiendish yells, and explosive laughter, [standing] in belligerent attitudes . . . and anon applauding violently" (121). This aggressive exuberance, which teetered on the edge of hysteria, agitated her college themes. The only stylistic means she could find to express her emotion were either an archaic and sentimental diction or the surface objectivity of the scientist. When she tried to compose in her own idiom, or when her imagination became thoroughly engaged in her subject matter, her prose began to buck and sputter. It was not stupidity that caused her miserable prose, but a lack of experience in using the conventions by which people channeled the tumult of their inner life. Later she diagnosed her complaint accurately. "It had not form in her yet, feeling in her, there was really then no way for her to tell any one anything about her feeling" (*MOA*, 413). In the absence of an adequate controlling form, she permitted her feelings to spill messily onto the pages of her college themes.

Her childhood had not been conducive to order. She was last-born in a physically peripatetic and psychologically unsettled family. Her very existence struck her as having been threatened before it began. Her parents had set a limit of five children for their family. Only after two of the Stein children had died in infancy were Leo and then Gertrude conceived. The knowledge never stopped troubling her. "If any one is the youngest of seven children and likes it he does not care to hear about birth control because supposing he had not been born" ("The Superstitions of Fred Anneday, Annday, Anday," *Nassau Lit,* XCIV [December 1935], 6). After she and Leo learned of their near miss, they never mentioned it. It made them "feel funny," she said (*EA*, 134; see also 115, and *MOA*, 743).

It seemed to Gertrude Stein that in childhood everyone looked after her. Being the youngest minimized her familial responsibilities, which gave her a good deal of time for herself (*EA*, 70). It also established in her an imperious indifference to the humdrum details of daily life. The management of practical matters which she initially left to members of her family, later became Alice Toklas's concern. Routine she regarded as "nothing," observing that "I always am managed by somebody because naturally there is nothing to manage" (*EA*, 123–24).

Until she was seven, her family was frequently on the move. She was born on 3 February 1874, in Allegheny, Pennsylvania, a town now absorbed by Pittsburgh. A family quarrel and her father's restlessness sent them to Austria the following spring. After several years residing in Vienna, with the father, Daniel Stein, often absent on business trips and the children in the hands of a governess and a tutor, they moved to Passy, France. By 1879 they had returned to America and the maternal home-ground of Baltimore. Not long after, the last major uprooting of Gertrude Stein's childhood took place in 1880 as the family moved to Oakland, California.

Here Gertrude Stein's conscious life began. Although she later wrote about that early European experience and its possible effects upon her, it was in Oakland that "I really did begin to remember" (*WIHS*, 6). So too, in *The Making of Americans,* a large portion of which chronicles the Stein family, Martha Hersland, who generally represents Gertrude Stein, is born "in the hotel where Mr. and Mrs. Hersland were living when they first came to Gossols" (427).*

Memory was a matter of perpetual interest to Gertrude Stein, for it participated in the formation of one's identity. She realized, though, how easily a false memory could be created. "How can you tell what with photographs and hearing whether you remember seeing . . ." (*EA*, 231). To judge by her mother's diary, Gertrude Stein's early years contained nothing out of the ordinary. She had a canary named "Dick" and she had the measles. She sprained her foot, suffered a case of poison oak, took drawing lessons with Leo, and was given castor oil and birthday parties (Amelia Stein Diary, *passim*).

The Steins lived on the eastern edge of Oakland on a ten-acre plot of land atop a rise. Although after four years they moved to a smaller house closer in, many of Gertrude Stein's memories are of this outdoor setting with orchards and meadows. One of her Radcliffe themes seri-

* Although aware of the dangers of using fiction to interpret an author's life, since Gertrude Stein was an avowedly autobiographical writer, I am not disposed to let theory arbitrarily close off relevant material. Gertrude Stein speaks in her own voice in *The Making of Americans* as well as assigning her experience to the figure of Martha Hersland. The fictional material I use is either duplicated in biographical accounts (as in the present instance), or is a plausible extension of already established conditions.

ously commemorates "The Birth of A Legend." The legend refers to a twenty-mile walk she and Leo made as children through the country-side. Although the account itself is not very convincing, her desire to anchor herself in history is evident: "Thus will we figure in the future folk-lore of California" (*RAD*, 136).

Gertrude Stein drew upon her childhood environment for her initial conception of herself. Both at Radcliffe and in her first novel, *Things As They Are,* she insisted upon the western American as a type distinct from those brought up in the South and in New England. The natural details in the legendary walk are emphatically western, with references to the *madrone,* the *manzanita,* and "the lordly red-wood" (*RAD*, 134). At college she normally regarded herself as a westerner, for that implied "freedom, imagination and unconventionality" (*RAD*, 115). The role of the lazy, sensuous Southerner had some attractions for her, but she had little sympathy for the rigid, cold New Englander. Crude as these stereotypes were, they were the start of her psychological classifications.

More often though, Gertrude Stein saw things in twos—in pairs and opposites. Her Oakland childhood encouraged this. Daniel Stein travelled daily across the bay to San Francisco, while his family remained in a rural suburb. As vice-president of the Union Street municipal railway system, he could provide his family with governesses, music lessons, custom-made dresses, and all the comforts of a bourgeois existence. Yet most of their neighbors lived in a condition of easy poverty. *The Making of Americans* returns again and again to the contrasts of city and country, of rich and poor.

During the Oakland period, Gertrude Stein's mother slowly succumbed to cancer and died when Gertrude was fourteen. She had never exerted an important influence upon the children, "was never important to her children excepting to begin them" (*MOA*, 254). The children in *The Making of Americans* resent one of their governesses because, by encouraging the mother's sense of her self-importance at a time when her husband was neglecting her, this governess gradually came to "own" their mother (254). Gertrude Stein then compactly summarized the poignant decline and disappearance of this psychological cipher:

> Later in her living she was weakening inside her, she was scared then, her children were big around her and outside her, trouble was coming then, the country house living was ending and often then Mr. Hersland forgot her as being and later then she died away from them and they soon, all of them then, lost remembering her among them. (*MOA*, 276)

9

Mothers are often absent from Gertrude Stein's writing. When they do appear, they tend to be pale, ineffectual creatures incapable of controlling their robust and temperamental children. Fathers on the other hand are assigned dominant and antagonistic roles. In Gertrude Stein's fiction the father has several vague occupations, but his fundamental character remains the same. Domineering, suspicious, impatient, and "brutal," he flies into unexpected rages. *The Making of Americans* offers in David Hersland the most extended portrait of the prototypical American man, restless and ever possessed by projects, drawn towards a grandiose future even as he strains to keep up appearances in the present. Bluff and irritated by anything that impedes his progress, swollen with self-importance, frustrated by the failure of his plans to come to fruition, indifferent to his family except when it affords him an opportunity to display his largesse or his authority, he is, in short, the inevitable mate for a withdrawn and vaguely discontented wife.

The frequency, passion and extent of Gertrude Stein's treatment of her father in her writings all indicate his ineradicable primacy in her imagination. She saw in herself his short-lived enthusiasms and his inability to push his ambitious plans through the friction of details. His life seemed a dossier of abandoned rough sketches. "He was too impatient to finish what was not yet begun" (*EA*, 150). Nonetheless, she found this selfish and overbearing man "in some ways a splendid kind of person" (*MOA*, 48). He desired to educate and toughen his children into independence and she believed he had succeeded. When his children reached young adulthood, they "loved the freedom . . . that their father had in his queer way won for them" (*MOA*, 52). If Leo and Gertrude were the actual results of their father's training though, the cost in anxiety can only be regarded as extravagant.

In a Radcliffe theme, Gertrude Stein described her father as "moody, bitter and often tyrannical at home" (111). Leo similarly remembered their father as "stocky, positive, dominant, aggressive" and "exceedingly disputatious" (*Journey*, 187). The children found his blustering authoritarianism especially trying when it was directed towards them. Although he often forgot his own edicts, his vacillation brought as much uneasiness as it did relief (*Journey*, 188). Gertrude recalled that to please him, the children were dragooned into playing card games with him. After a few minutes he would drop out, saying impatiently, "Here you just finish it up I haven't time to go on playing." Understandably, this capriciousness annoyed the children who were then obliged to

10

finish "a game none of them would have thought of beginning" (*MOA*, 129).

Gertrude Stein's animosity was in part aroused because "whenever I had anything the matter with me," her father would reproach her, reminding her that she "had been born a perfect baby" (*WIHS*, 3). Later she would lump all fathers together as dictators, noting the presence of "father Mussolini and father Hitler and father Roosevelt and father Stalin and father Lewis and father Blum and father Franco." Her social views in the thirties merely extended her personal feelings of the eighties. "There is too much fathering going on just now and there is no doubt about it fathers are depressing" (*EA*, 133).

After his wife's death in 1888, Daniel Stein withdrew what little attention he had given the household, whereupon the family disintegrated. The children, adolescent and already independent because of their mother's protracted invalidism and their father's neglect, grew openly rebellious towards their father. In angry family scenes they made known their feelings about his character and his treatment of them. Three years after his wife's demise, Daniel Stein was found dead one morning by Leo. That was the end of the man whom Gertrude Stein found "depressing." Her primary objection to him, it would seem, was that he represented false authority to her, a power lacking genuine substance and irresponsibly exercised.

Still, in spite of certain exasperations, Gertrude Stein did have a reasonably comfortable childhood with the kind of security she once described as "coming home before it is dark in the evening after playing" (*WIHS*, 19). Leo Stein, who was her elder by less than two years, deserves much of the credit for it.

Every available account, including their own, private and public, indicates that Gertrude and Leo were genuinely close friends. They did not regard either Bertha or Simon, the two children just above them on the family ladder, as bright enough to make intimate relations possible. While they did like and respect the eldest brother, Michael, he was too old to share their interests until they were adults. When Daniel Stein died, "Mike" became their legal guardian and in that capacity played the paternal role of benevolent bread winner for her, while Leo assumed the role of cultural mentor.

During their childhood, where Leo went, Gertrude went, what he did, she did. Leo took drawing lessons and so did she. Leo attended Harvard,

Gertrude went to Radcliffe. Leo went to Johns Hopkins for graduate work and Gertrude followed. Leo abandoned his studies and moved to Europe; Gertrude did the same. Their lives, after having been very close in Oakland, ran parallel throughout young adulthood until they rejoined in Paris. One sentence in a letter from a college friend regarding Gertrude's prospective summer vacation with Leo indicates the temper of their relationship. "How happy for you to be with a brother of whom you are so fond and proud" (Gallup, *Flowers,* 8). Leo took the place of a father towards whom Gertrude had been indifferent when not resentful.

She and Leo "spent all the money we had on books" (*EA,* 146). As was inevitable, their tastes diverged and they lived separate imaginative lives (*EA,* 71). In spite of her voracity as a reader, Gertrude Stein remained remarkably free of literary influence in her writing, barren even. Lists of her reading are singularly unhelpful in understanding her development. It only tempts critical ingenuity to learn that as a girl she read extensively in Jules Verne (*EA,* 146). One author who did affect her strongly however was George Eliot, a successful and emancipated woman of letters, plain of feature and moral in tone. When Gertrude Stein arrived at Radcliffe, she was still "under the influence of George Eliot" (*EA,* 153).

Although Gertrude Stein had a poor memory for poetry, one of George Eliot's lines stayed with her: "May I join the choir invisible of those immortal dead who live again" (*EA,* 116).* Significantly, the line concerns survival after death. The fear of death, or, "not so much of death as of dissolution" haunted Gertrude Stein's "dark and dreadful days of adolescence" (*WIHS,* 14). Reminiscing, Alice Toklas remarked that Gertrude Stein's "youthful memories . . . were ones entirely of living in the library and the growing pains of adolescence which really affected her so much." Miss Toklas added that she had been shocked by Gertrude Stein's account of "those bad years." "I'd never heard of anything like that. I said so. I said, 'How horrible.' She said, 'Didn't you have that period too?' I said, 'Not I,' and she said, looking at me, 'Lucky you' " (Duncan, 38).

Late in life Gertrude Stein distinguished the "legendary" existence of the child from the "medieval" and "pioneering" life of the adolescent. A child lives an archetypal life, she argued, because everything that happens seems inevitable to the child. With adolescence, however,

* The poem, "O may I join the choir invisible," appears in *Jubal and Other Poems* (1874).

12

when an awareness of the possibility of choice arises, then conflict develops. As she put it, "When a baby eats and vomits it is not war. But when fourteen eats and vomits then it is war" (*WIHS*, 25). She designated adolescence as "medieval" to indicate its rigidly structured yet insecure condition. It was a time when one's crops, family, and life might all be swept away in a moment. "Nothing is clear and nothing is sure and nothing is safe and nothing is come and nothing is gone. But it all might be" (*WIHS*, 27).

Gertrude Stein regarded her type of personality as characteristically suffering from "really anxious being." People such as herself "almost always have fear in them . . . they feel their pulses to see if they are living . . ." (*MOA*, 202). That persistent insecurity was the cause of her anxiety she hardly recognized, but she did understand the extent of her own timorousness. There is a passage that was dropped from *The Autobiography of Alice B. Toklas,* which says of Gertrude Stein: "She also was afraid of cats. As Gertrude Stein says of herself she is a person who is afraid of everything and as I may add she is absolutely courageous" (ABT ms., vol. 5, YCAL).*

The threat of non-existence was her principal fear, but in young womanhood male aggression was very much on her mind. In this same cancelled passage she tells "a very characteristic story" that took place "in Baltimore one dark night." While walking "in a lonely spot" with some relatives, "somebody came at them from behind the trees, Gertrude Stein quite simply told her little aunts to go on and turned to face the man. It turned out not to have any serious consequences. As she always says anything can scare her but anything."

That Gertrude Stein should have been timid may at first seem improbable. If so, it is because fearfulness does not accord with the image created of her in the thirties when she made her lecture tour of the United States. In general, descriptions and photographs of Gertrude Stein have emphasized a self-satisfied, imperturbable woman. And yet the dozens of photographs of her held by Yale University leave the impression of a predominantly vulnerable woman—sometimes faintly alarmed with a small, apprehensive smile on her lips, sometimes haunted. Rarely does she photograph as forceful and masculine. But she was one who habitually faced down her fears. "Some are frightened and then they do the thing that frightens them" (*MOA*, 714). The hearty, self-assured woman on the American lecture platform had been

* The cancelled passage would have appeared on p. 88 between "rescuing her." and "The family remained."

13

obliged on the night of her first lecture to seek medical assistance for a constricted throat (*EA*, 177). She invariably whistled her way through the dark of her life. In her letters she constantly solicited praise and reassurance from her friends, especially from Carl Van Vechten who was the most generous in providing it. When she referred to her work in correspondence, she countered her own doubts by insisting that the project she was engaged in was awfully good, was the best thing she had ever done, was sure to please the recipient.

Sometimes Gertrude Stein managed to laugh away her apprehensions. Upon meeting her, people were invariably impressed first by her size, then as she grew animated, by her laughter. It was described as "contagious," "enchanting," "hearty," and "boisterous." "She had," remembered one friend, "the easiest, most engaging and infectious laugh I have ever heard" (Imbs, 118). Yet photographs of her smiling are rare.

The vulnerable young Steins shielded themselves with ironic wit. One of Gertrude Stein's college themes, "A Conference," illustrates her ability to absorb potentially infuriating experience and to recast it in the form of an amused irony. The theme describes a professor searching for something in her writing to compliment her on. He settles on the phrase, "twittering birds," saying that they always do remind one of springtime. Then he realizes that the paper concerns autumn, and must readjust his compliment—"Yes birds do twitter in autumn too not so much perhaps." The girl then meekly points out that she was trying to describe mid-summer. Undaunted, the professor shifts his ground one more time. "Mid-summer, why yes, yes of course birds always twitter in mid-summer" (116). The theme demonstrates that Gertrude Stein herself had an objective perspective on the problems that her writing caused and could divert potentially self-destructive feelings into laughter.

Gertrude Stein has the not altogether deserved reputation of being a comic writer. It is true that upon occasion she could display a formidable wit and that inventive stage productions have emphasized and even created the gaiety in her work. Meanwhile, the popular conception of her is as an amiable fraud and eccentric. All of this obscures the fact that the major portion of her writing is unflaggingly earnest when it is not downright desperate. In the main, the literary act served Gertrude Stein by externalizing psychological dilemmas that laughter could not dissolve.

When her experience could not be expressed and was too painful to endure, the passion that sometimes vented itself in laughter, burst out in anger. Displays of temper were a part of the Stein character that "we all are cursed with" (*RAD*, 111). In *The Making of Americans* she describes the autobiographical figure of young Martha Hersland being left behind by the older children. Indignant at being abandoned, she warns that she will throw the umbrella she carries into the mud. When the other children do not respond, she carries out her threat (388). At the time though she thought this stiff-necked response was indecisive evidence for determining her fundamental character. No one then, including Gertrude Stein "could be very certain of the kind of being Martha Hersland had in her" (389).

Such incidents of neglect and frustration were rare in her young life. But with adolescence, her path was more frequently blocked by her father's arbitrary rules. Furthermore, she was obliged to steer through the gales of romantic feelings with little or no assistance. Her mother was ill. She was not only contemptuous of her sister Bertha's stupidity, but also, quite frankly did not like her. She seems to have had no close school chum. Once familiar with the conditions of the young Gertrude Stein's life, it comes as no surprise to read her description of a "very intelligent active bright well-read fairly well experienced young woman"—no bad portrait of the artist—who believed that the menstrual period—"what happens every month to all women"—only troubled women belonging to her church (*MOA*, 495). Whether autobiographical or not, the story indicates her familiarity with the problems faced by a nineteenth-century American girl maturing, as it were, in isolation.

The crescendo of Gertrude Stein's erotic tumult occurred at college, but her fictional reminiscences contain several references to childhood sexual experimentation and menace. In fact, the majority of the specific incidents in Gertrude Stein's early writing are sexual in nature. Even that defiant act of throwing her umbrella in the mud said, If you will not take care of me, I shall do something bad. I shall throw my protection into the dirt.

Martha Hersland is propositioned by a little boy to engage "a little in loving, in things they should not be doing." The situation fails to reach a culmination, not, as Gertrude Stein carefully explains, because she resisted, but because of her nervousness, passivity, and uncertain comprehension of what he desired (*MOA*, 412–13, 416). A similar uncertainty about growing sexuality permeates the account of Martha playing hide-and-go-seek with the neighborhood boys on summer evenings in the Hersland orchard. These games anger her elder brother, who threatens to inform their father unless Martha enters the house. No specific transgression is alleged. Neither child quite knows why it is wrong for a girl to "be playing hide and go seek . . . in the evening" with the boys, but "sometimes then they stayed a long time in the orchard" (*MOA*, 533-4).

When Mrs. Hersland (Mrs. Stein) begins to succumb to a long illness, Martha is going out evenings with the neighboring young people, who are of a lower social class. But Martha "was of the daily feeling . . . of them more than she was . . . of her family living and feeling" (420). Occasionally her father notices that she is not home studying. Angered, he forbids her going out and scolds her brother because "he did not take better care of his sister" (421).* Again, her actual behavior with the neighbors is not specified. The suspicions exist in the paternal imagination. This latter-day Polonius, who reads rebellion and potential disgrace to the family into his daughter's drifting away from the house, reappears in "Melanctha," the main story in *Three Lives*. In both cases, the young women have ineffectual mothers and assert their independence from their fathers in a vaguely sexual way. The core situation of a roving girl and a jealous father is fixed in Gertrude Stein's mind and appears repeatedly in her early writing. "Well," she wrote late in life, "feudal days were the days of fathers" (*EA*, 139).

The sexual transgressions intimated in *The Making of Americans* appear to have been imaginary. Whatever the uncoiling power of erotic feeling within her heroine, she was denied the opportunity to yield to temptation. There is something unfathomably pathetic about her laconic admission, "She was then not really very interesting to any one. She might have been a little interesting a couple of evenings to Harry Brenner but she never really was interesting to him" (*MOA*, 422). There spoke a girl with romantic aspirations, for in addition to sensual gratification, romance brings an expansion of self-confidence. Yet she, through innocence, physical plainness, and bad luck could count her possibilities for fulfillment on the finger of one hand. At college, some of her needs would be met in the intellectual comradeship of student

* One of the psychological inconsistencies of *MOA* is that, even though the Gertrude Stein figure is said to be the eldest child, in situations such as this and the one involving the umbrella, she is clearly a younger child for whom others are assumed to be responsible. That Gertrude Stein chose to make herself the eldest child was probably a protective gesture to obscure the autobiographical resemblances a little. But given her indifference towards Simon and Bertha, it is not difficult to see why they were flatly eliminated from the book.

life; others in different ways. In her youth though, sex was all unfulfilled promise and threat.

The Making of Americans contains one curious exception. It is an anecdote that is included to demonstrate that sometimes people repeat an action over and over throughout their lives. Gertrude Stein recounts the story of a nameless young woman, living away from home. She is bombarded by letters from her father. They tell her "she should not do things that were wrong" for "that would disgrace him." Finally, in exasperation, she retaliates with her own letter. In it she tells him that he hasn't the right to lecture her, since it was he who had started her doing these unspecified "things" that might disgrace them, telling her that he did them with her "so that when she was older she could take care of herself with those who wished to make her do things that were wicked things" (488–89).

This cloudy incident is not offered as evidence of actual incest in Gertrude Stein's youth. But imaginatively, it could be nothing else. No other wickedness is conceivable—the father teaching the daughter to lie, to swear, to cheat—that fits the circumstances as well as a sexual encounter. Upon receiving his daughter's letter, the father read it, threw it into the fire, and told his wife, "Edith she is killing me." And he is "a paralytic always after" (489).* *The Making of Americans* frequently illustrates its psychological analyses with such bizarre and suggestive anecdotes. Gertrude Stein's imagination long writhed in convolutions of desire and repulsion, seductiveness and flight. A suspicious and authoritarian father loomed over the turmoil.

After one more ambiguous encounter, Martha Hersland crosses the continent to start a new life at college. The pivotal experience is obscurely sexual and again involves an umbrella. Gertrude Stein says that Martha Hersland had no "distinct feeling" about the scene which "gave a motion to her" but that it represented "an awakening into realler feeling" (426, 424). As she is on her way to a singing lesson, Martha sees a man strike a woman with an umbrella. The woman appears to be either propositioning him as a prostitute or pleading with him as might a wife. Gertrude Stein says only that the woman's face was red "partly in anger and partly in asking." It is a distinction she does not choose to elaborate. The motive for the man's assault is that he wants "her to leave him alone then in a public street where people were passing."

* Gertrude Stein's New York uncle, a widower and entering his dotage, invited his young niece into his bed to keep him warm. She refused, but refers to the occasion on the page following the incest anecdote (*MOA*, 490; see Katz, 187).

17

Whatever the circumstances, for Martha Hersland this scene was "the ending of the living . . . that she had been living. She would go to college, she knew it then and understand everything and know the meaning of the living and the feeling in men and in women" (*MOA*, 424).

In this incident a concentrated moment of aggressiveness and sexuality was externalized for Gertrude Stein. It suggested to her heroine the desirability of studying the human animal. The motivations of people might be understood and since one shared their dark passions, such understanding would hopefully bring the relief of self-knowledge. It is by no means clear that Gertrude Stein herself comprehended this episode beyond the dramatic terms in which she cast it. But this crucial experience was not a moment of exultation in the natural world nor did it involve a sudden philosophic or religious insight. Rather, when Martha Hersland observed the incident, "she came to have a real attacking moment and it lasted to her beginning her university education" (424). In other words, the incident inspired her to action, action perhaps suffused with the sentiments of the feminist movement.

Once Martha Hersland departs from Gossols, her story diverges from that of her creator in most of its details. She goes to a "typical co-educational college of the west, a completely democratic institution," an institution that more nearly resembles the University of California at Berkeley (where Leo was briefly a student) than it does Radcliffe (431). There she acquires a lover who later marries her, then deserts her and finally expires. It is true that the episodes cited up to this point might be equally fictitious. They all take place, however, in a setting identical to Gertrude Stein's in Oakland, and most of them resemble experiences and attitudes which she elsewhere describes as her own.

At the very point that Martha Hersland's story branches off on its own, one can pick up Gertrude Stein in the person of Hortense Sänger. This girl was another of her imagination's avatars, about whom she wrote extensively at Radcliffe. A theme entitled "In the Library" describes Hortense as motherless, accustomed to solitude, and capable of handling heavy responsibilities. She is a girl with an intense and imaginative temperament who spends most of her time in the library. Nonetheless, she finds that books, "her old well-beloved companions began to pall." Sensing the need for "some human sympathy," she is "often" possessed by "wild moods" (*RAD*, 142). Just as she begins to fear for her reason, her father dies. She is then invited by some relatives "to lead an entirely new life in a large family circle" (142).

So with Gertrude Stein. From 1888 when her mother died and she was fourteen, until 1891 when her father died, the children lived an unconstrained existence. They ate at irregular intervals, treated homework casually, slept when they wished. After Daniel Stein's death, the children clustered in San Francisco for a year under their brother Michael's aegis. The following year, 1892, the family broke up, Michael and Simon remaining in San Francisco, Leo going to Harvard, the sisters Gertrude and Bertha moving to Baltimore to live with their mother's sister, Mrs. Fannie Bachrach. In the fall of 1893, Gertrude Stein travelled north to Cambridge, Massachusetts, to commence her formal training in psychology.

2

Morale was high at Harvard University in the nineties among both
faculty members and students. Extraordinary men like Josiah Royce,
William James, and George Santayana were engaged in stimulating
projects, for which they drew upon the assistance of their students
whom they treated as younger colleagues. When, as secretary to the
Philosophy Club, Gertrude Stein invited Royce to present a paper to
them, he offered two, "in case . . . they could be of any service to
your Club, in whose fortunes I always feel a strong interest" (Gallup,
Flowers, 7). As an Easter present, William James's students gave him
an azalea tree (*Flowers,* 9). Without lapsing into egalitarian intimacy,
the faculty and students maintained a considerable familiarity.

The range of Gertrude Stein's undergraduate education was limited.
The only literary course she ever took was French 2, an elementary
reading course from La Fontaine to Balzac. Her grade was C plus. She
did substantially better in her one history course, European History
from 1600 to 1750, receiving an A. Her ultimate intellectual direction
was determined by the freshman course, Philosophy 1, in which George
Herbert Palmer lectured on logic, George Santayana on metaphysics,
and William James on that new branch of philosophy, psychology.*

One of the assigned texts in the course was James's *Psychology: The
Briefer Course.* Attracted by the subject, Gertrude Stein enrolled in
Philosophy 20a, a course of directed experimentation "primarily for
graduates," held in the Psychological Laboratory. She took it five times

---

* Psychology expanded rapidly in the Harvard curriculum. James had brought
Hugo Münsterberg from the University of Freiburg in 1892 to direct the Harvard
Psychological Laboratory. Münsterberg became chairman of the Department of
Philosophy in 1899. By 1912, it had become the Department of Philosophy and
Psychology.

For Gertrude Stein's academic record at Radcliffe, see Appendix A.

over the next three years, receiving two B's in her sophomore year and A's thereafter. She also joined Philosophy 20b, the "Psychological Seminary" taught by William James in her junior year. In the first half of that course, which was devoted to the feelings, she received an A. But in the spring semester, when the class studied consciousness, knowledge, and the relation of the mind to the body, she did less well, earning only a C.

This experience underwent a transformation in *The Autobiography of Alice B. Toklas.* As Gertrude Stein remembered it, she had been attending afternoon and evening performances of the opera during the final examination period, and "had been otherwise engrossed." Faced with William James's examination on a lovely spring day,

> she just could not. Dear Professor James, she wrote at the top of her paper. I am so sorry but really I do not feel a bit like an examination paper in philosophy to-day, and left.
> The next day she had a postal card from William James saying, Dear Miss Stein, I understand perfectly how you feel I often feel like that myself. And underneath it he gave her work the highest mark in the course. (97–98)

Gertrude Stein took a few other philosophy courses in which she did well—metaphysics from Royce, comparative religion, one on "the content of Christian faith," and one on the German philosophical writers, including Fichte, Kant, and Schopenhauer. Otherwise, Gertrude Stein's education at Radcliffe was restricted to elementary courses required for graduation, such as algebra, solid geometry, and physics. She did indifferently in these and received her lowest grade in college, a C minus, in chemistry.

In her upper division years, she began preparing herself for medical school. Both of her teachers in psychology, William James and Hugo Münsterberg, possessed medical degrees in addition to their doctorates in philosophy. Gertrude Stein recalled that James had advised her that if she were to continue as a serious student of psychology, a medical education was obligatory (*ABT*, 98). So she dutifully enrolled in courses in botany and zoology. While she did B work in them, her enthusiasm was reserved for laboratory work in psychology.

Outside the classroom, Gertrude Stein led an active life of bicycle outings, picnics, boat trips, and operas. She was fond of the ironic mode and regarded her generation as superior to common expressions of sentiment. When Madame Melba performed for the college, Gertrude Stein took issue with her for having sung "Home Sweet Home." "She mistook the temper of young America. The tenderly pathetic is only humorous to us" (*RAD*, 138).

Gertrude Stein found the atmosphere in Cambridge to her liking. Her energy, relish for debate, and western casualness all fitted easily into the Harvard ambience. Precisely how she happened to join the graduate students in their experimental work in the Psychological Laboratory is not recorded, but, given the free atmosphere of exchange, presumably anyone with the requisite intelligence and interest was welcome. Gertrude Stein contracted a full-blown case of hero-worship for William James, whose admiring student Leo had also been. One of her college themes pays a disciple's tribute. "Is life worth living?" she begins. "Yes, a thousand times yes when the world still holds such spirits as Prof. James." He was "a strong man willing to fight, to suffer and endure" (*RAD*, 146).

James remained on politely friendly terms with Gertrude Stein for the remainder of his life. His letter acknowledging receipt of *Three Lives* in 1910 diplomatically indicates a tempered enthusiasm for her work. "You know how hard it is for me to read novels. Well, I read 30 or 40 pages, and said 'this is a fine new kind of realism—Gertrude Stein is great! I will go at it carefully when just the right mood comes'" (Gallup, *Flowers,* 50). His colleague, Hugo Münsterberg, who was in charge of the laboratory, was openly pleased with Gertrude Stein as a student. As she completed her sophomore year in 1895, he wrote her, "I thank you above all for that model-work you have done in the laboratory . . . You were to me the ideal student" (*Flowers,* 4). The evidence available indicates that Gertrude Stein was popular with and respected by students and faculty alike.

Her psychological life prospered rather less. She carried her giant with her, and although diverted by this stimulating environment, she remained inwardly in turmoil. The themes she prepared for her sophomore composition course, English 22, provided the occasion for extensive self-exploration. Forty-seven of these have been collected, ranging in length from short paragraphs to full stories, and including descriptions, literary criticism, parodies, and philosophic meditations. In them she held a mirror before her face, and was awarded a C for the effort.*

* A description of this course by Frank Norris, another member of it, appears in *Frank Norris* by Franklin Walker, pp. 93–94. Gertrude Stein additionally took English C, a course in argumentative composition in her junior year. In it, she was obliged to prepare four "Forensics," each one preceded by a brief. Her efforts earned an A minus.

What kind of person was she? She drew a physical portrait of herself as "a girl rather stout, fair, and with a singularly attractive face, attractive largely because puzzling . . . Her nose just escapes being beautiful for at the last moment it drooped . . . Still in spite of these features she is distinctly lovable" (*RAD*, 123).

Yes, but who would love her? Much of her exasperation with Cambridge derived from dissatisfaction with the inhibited New Englanders surrounding her. Worse still, she saw herself as a bookworm, a drudge, a typical "annex girl" with "a very large head," "loaded down with books" and "very dismal" (*RAD*, 120). Her excitability seemed to her both a mark of distinction and a trouble to the spirit. She regarded herself as "the true lover of debate" for "argument is to me as the air I breathe." With admirable perspective she realized that she tried to win arguments not by force of logic alone, but also by "loudness of voice, number of words and violence of manner" (*RAD*, 129–30). On one occasion, having observed a man standing calmly in a mud puddle after having just missed his trolley car, she extolled his self-control. "Be a philosopher, oh my brother, if you would know perfect peace" (*RAD*, 131–2).

At Radcliffe, Gertrude Stein first began to classify people. The effort originated in her discomfort as a foreigner in Cambridge. Her college themes several times dismiss the cold, rigid New England temperament as inferior to the sensuous laziness of the South and the free swaggering West. A reading of Mary Wilkins Freeman's *Pembroke* triggered a diatribe against New England intolerance, lack of sympathy, inflexibility and "supreme egoism" (*RAD*, 119).

Since her mother's family, the Keysers, came from Baltimore, she sometimes identified herself with the gentle warmth of the South. Baltimore represented a relaxed joy in physical well-being she thought might relieve her passionate intensity. "It is disheartening to come back to Cambridge," she wrote, "after a week of the delicious, dreamy south. Baltimore, sunny Baltimore, where no one is in a hurry and the voices of the negroes singing . . . lull you into drowsy reveries." It was "the essence of contentment, quiet dreamy slothful ease in the full sensuous sunshine" (*RAD*, 139).

The human warmth of the South also attracted her. She recalled that when she first came to Cambridge, only the Negro children smiled at her (*RAD*, 148). She gravitated to the region of open friendliness, but then soon abandoned this ersatz identification with Baltimore. As a moralist, she turned away from full identification with the South, which she associated with animal warmth. She wanted to be free, but not immoral. A strong Puritan, she respected casualness, but not laziness. In time, as a route that would take her away from the passions that assailed her, she chose the *via media* of bourgeois life as her ideal.

Meanwhile, she sought relief from her inner torment by dramatizing it in her college prose. Of special significance are those compositions that imaginatively treat a girl who, if not Gertrude Stein in every detail, suffers the burdens then weighing upon her. In the sequence in which these themes were written, she first appears in an exceedingly disturbed first-person confessional. Later, she is viewed with third-person objectivity and provided the name, Miss Hortense Sänger. As the figure was distanced from Gertrude Stein, the revelations grew increasingly lurid.

The first theme she submitted, entitled "In The Red Deeps" caused her reader, William Vaughn Moody, to respond: "An extraordinary composition. One is puzzled to decide whether it is a personal experience, related in exaggerated terms, or a study from an object [sic] stand point of a morbid psychological state" (*RAD*, 109). His reaction is understandable. The theme would startle and probably alarm anyone. Fairly incoherent and pumped up with melodrama, the piece treats sado-masochistic feelings in a girl. The fear of incest appears. Evidently all the inner turmoil Gertrude Stein was then feeling came pouring out when her instructor said, "Write about something that interests you." That was the only cue she required.

In later years, Gertrude Stein referred to "In The Red Deeps" as her "first story" (*EA*, 282). She pointed out that the title came from George Eliot. Gertrude Stein's lifelong sympathy for the English novelist is a complex matter. She must have been respectfully aware of her since at least 1884 when her mother made the following entry in her diary: "card from Sol with invitation to his lecture on George Eliot before the Young mens hebrew association of Baltimore" (Vol. 4).

At college, Gertrude Stein was identifying with Maggie Tulliver, the fictional heroine whom George Eliot in part patterned on herself. The phrase "In the red deeps" is the title of the first chapter of the fifth book of *The Mill on the Floss*. It refers to the place where Maggie goes for secret meetings with a suitor. In the novel, the place has symbolic features of sexual illicitness and danger. It is composed of mounds and hollows and covered with grass, brambles, and sheltering trees. George Eliot tells us that Maggie had held this place with its suggestive name "in very great awe" as a child, for there were "visions of robbers and fierce animals haunting every hollow" (*Mill*, V, 1).

Insofar as it is possible to be precise about impressions, for Gertrude Stein's imagination the red deeps stood for the depths of madness, for nightmarish visions. Her composition says that while reading Shelley's *The Cenci*, the writer saw "before my eyes, shrinking toward the wall . . . the veritable Beatrice in her flowing white robes." This hallucination she calls "truly the most horrid of the deeps" (*RAD*, 109). Fed by the Maggie Tulliver and Beatrice Cenci associations, a tumultuous sexual motif, involving both father and brother, runs convulsively through the theme.

Maggie Tulliver's resemblance to Gertrude Stein centers in her intimate and unusually demanding relationship with her brother Tom. In her youth Gertrude had modelled her behavior after Leo, and the intimacy between the two as well as the tensions that led to their ultimate estrangement were prefigured in George Eliot's novel. Maggie says of Tom that when she was a little girl she loved him better than anyone else in the world, and that, even as an adult, "the tie to my brother is one of the strongest" (*Mill*, V, 5; VI, 10). Her complaint has to do with her brother's hardness, his lack of pity and his abiding egoism. "You have no sense of your own imperfection and your own sins" (V, 5). Moreover, his mind was inflexible. It is "a mind that we can never mould ourselves upon, and yet that we cannot endure to alienate from us" (VII, 1). Leo's brilliant, intransigent self-preoccupation eventually affected Gertrude Stein similarly. As she remarked of him in *The Making of Americans*, "Some love themselves so much immortality can have no meaning for them" (505).

The conclusion of *The Mill on the Floss* was no solution for a representative of "Young America" with its sense of the ludicrous. Brother and sister drown in a flood, "in an embrace never to be parted: living through again in one supreme moment the days when they had clasped their little hands in love, and roamed the daisied fields together" (VII, 5). Nonetheless, Gertrude Stein felt that mixed dependence and resentment for Leo that a prisoner feels towards his guard. In a few more years, she would carefully detach herself from him, first in her writing, then in her actual life.

It was not only because of the brother-sister relationship in *The Mill on the Floss* that Gertrude Stein could easily identify with the book's heroine. The spirited seventeen-year-old Maggie was physically robust, with a "slow resigned sadness" in her glance, for she was a young woman embarked upon a difficult "self-conquest" (V, 1; V, 4). Her sense of moral obligation was as strong as her passionate nature. "Often, when I have been angry and discontented," says Maggie, ". . . it has seemed to me that I could think away all my duty. But no good has ever come of that—it was an evil state of mind" (V, 1).

Precisely those sentiments, tempered by irony, would later constitute the opening position of Adele, another embodiment of Gertrude Stein who appears in her first novel, *Things As They Are*.

Maggie is under siege by her brother and by two suitors. One of these suitors is a deformed, spiritualized figure, the other direct and physically demanding. Each tempts her with his argument and presence. She tries to bring her emotions under control by nights of penitence on the hard floor, but there remained "a sense of uneasiness in looking at her—a sense of opposing elements, of which a fierce collision is imminent" (V, 1).

This was a tension Gertrude Stein could understand. "In The Red Deeps" emphasized the intensity of her feelings, especially of physical sensations. "When I had a hurt I would press it till the agony of the pain thrilled me with an exquisite delight" (*RAD*, 108). Although the trite language diminishes the effectiveness of her account, there is no mistaking the earnestness with which Gertrude Stein was seeking to describe the source of her confusion. Without giving the slightest thought to concealing her revelations in this first theme, she goes on to acknowledge the pleasure she took in reading about the torture of other people. Furthermore, "I would invent others even worse and enjoy inflicting them" (108). But then at the pitch of her sadistic feelings, her disquiet reversed itself. She became apprehensive lest she be obliged to inflict genuine pain. She admits to "a terrible and haunting fear of loss of self-control" (108). In such melodramatic terms did Gertrude Stein attempt to clarify for herself what she had become in the poisonously close atmosphere of her adolescence.

Throughout her life Gertrude Stein puzzled in her writing over the phenomenon of a multiple self. Sometimes identity seemed to her bewilderingly unstable, likely at any moment to fall to pieces. As late as 1943 one of her characters in a play is warned, "You you, one of these days you will split in two, you you." When he does, he tries to fool people by wrapping himself in string—"so nobody can know . . . that I am not one but two" ("Look and Long," *GSFR*, 75, 77). She found it difficult and yet imperative to reconcile the sundered parts. A good portion of her stylistic experimentation can be traced to this effort. The problem was basic. It set itself in this first theme "In The Red Deeps."

Gertrude Stein's sense of herself as a double person was intensified, she said, when she attended a theatrical performance of "Dr. Jekyl and Mr. Hyde" (sic). So distraught did the representation of her own condition make her, she was obliged to leave at the end of the second act. Consumed by the "dreadful possibilities of dark deeds," she beat her head against the wall in an effort to silence her "horrible thoughts." The composition concludes with an apparition, Beatrice Cenci, who, "having just left her father" is gazing upon her. "Enough enough!" cries the youthful author, "I cannot tell you more. I fear it, I fear it still" (RAD, 109).

At one level it is impossible to take this hysterical self-dramatization seriously. Yet it is precisely the dilemma of the young that they feel such threats to their precarious psychological stability with supreme intensity, yet are forced by inexperience to express their feelings in trite and clumsy ways. The emotional content of Gertrude Stein's apprentice writing deserves sympathetic attention, for it is in the process of taming and exorcising her demons that Gertrude Stein's stylistic course was irrevocably set.

Towards the end of December 1894, in a piece entitled "The Great Enigma", Gertrude Stein tried a new description of a "stout," "vehement and fiery" young girl (RAD, 123, 125). This girl has a lover. He is, however, unsatisfactory. "Perfect antipodes," the pair exist in an emotional stalemate. Gertrude Stein's imagination readily seized simple schematic tensions such as could be expressed in pairs and triangles. Sallie, the girl in "The Great Enigma," is impetuous, cruel, and "very thoughtless." At the same time she is "overly conscientious" and "tremendously moral." "She had a glorious ideal of generosity but for the most part was thoroughly selfish" (RAD, 124). Her lover was "imperturble." Peaceful and slow—"completely negative"—his ox-like passivity so maddens her that "she began to think she hated him" (RAD, 124, 125). Primly, Gertrude Stein hints at sexual activity, for even when Sallie thought she might hate her companion, "she allowed him to take liberties with her, such as no one else had even dared to dream of" (RAD, 125). This "ceaseless struggle" between an ignoble love and her inexplicable attraction for him reaches a climax when she falls unconscious, an obviously expedient means of solving the stalemate.

Asked by Moody to revise this theme, Gertrude Stein eliminated the troublesome narrative line and turned what was left into a pair of static character sketches.

Two other stories submitted as assignments concern this troubled young woman. "In the Library" was subtitled "Chapter I." Although the projected book was never completed, its heroine, Hortense Sänger, reappears in a second story, "The Temptation."

"In the Library" expanded a description Gertrude Stein had sketched in a paragraph written earlier for Moody called "An Annex Girl." * An exasperated student with too much reading to do, she desires "one weak happy naive consciousness that thinks higher education is either rot or has never heard of it" (*RAD*, 120). Similarly, Hortense Sänger is a girl possessed by a "wild impatience." She is "dark-skinned in the full sensuous development of budding womanhood," no "impotent child, but a strong vigorous girl." This girl, her blood heated by the sun, mutters, "Books, books, is there no end to it. Nothing but myself to feed my own eager nature. Nothing given me but musty books" (*RAD*, 141). Her discontent has more authenticity than the abstract and inconclusive affair of Sallie, who performed nameless acts with a faceless lover. The only resolution "In the Library" offers is for Hortense to go for a vigorous walk. "I will walk it down. . . . I must escape from myself" (141).

The basic situation of a demanding physical nature which is regularly challenged by both a sceptical intelligence and a moral character is omnipresent in Gertrude Stein's early writing. The Radcliffe themes provide an extraordinary conclusion for these wild moods and passionate longings. Her last composition, "The Temptation," was submitted in May 1895. It dissatisfied Moody sufficiently for him to ask for a revision. He got one, which elicited from him the reaction "unpleasant in the extreme." But he also admitted that it was "not without psychological interest" (*RAD*, 155).

In its first version, "The Temptation" describes Hortense involved in an incident at church, while in the company of some cousins and friends. It results in their all walking home in strained silence. When her relatives finally level their accusations at Hortense, she heatedly denies them, although in fact their attacks only echo her own self-accusations. Before the revision, the reader does not know what offense she has committed. In the rewriting however, Hortense's behavior at the church service is described in greater detail. Impressed as she is by

* Until 1894, Radcliffe College was known as Harvard Annex.

28

the piety of the congregation, she mutters to herself, "I would not be as they." She returns to her inner struggle, trying "to throw off the weight, the intolerable burden of solving for herself the great world-questions" (*RAD*, 154).

At this point a man leans towards her so "heavily" that she feels his touch. Failing to stir, she sanctions his advance. "She loathed herself but still she did not move" (154). Even when her friends notice what is happening, and her aunt gestures at her, she refuses to acknowledge them. Internally though, she berates herself. "Liar and coward, will you continue this, have you no sense of shame?" (155). Only when a cousin actually comes to fetch her can she be drawn away from this shamefully hypnotic encounter of the flesh.

Aside from the incident's clumsy rhetoric, one is struck by the ruthless candor with which the incident is told as well as by Gertrude Stein's awareness of the contradictory impulses that simultaneously claimed her attention. If this hectic young woman often wrote a careless, deformed prose, it was mainly because she was untrained and emotionally distraught. Still, her perceptions were sound and her honesty exemplary. Her eagerness to learn remained unabated too. Even as she was pouring out her misery in these college themes, she was proving herself an especially prococious student in the Harvard Psychological Laboratory.

Gertrude Stein's closest intellectual companion at Harvard was Leon Solomons, a graduate student also from northern California. The idea of an amorous attachment had at least occurred to her. One of her themes, "A Modern Sonnet to His Mistress's Eyebrows," drew its amusement from the incongruity between a lover's attention to his beloved as it had conventionally been expressed in the past and the scientific scrutiny of Solomons in the laboratory—"Noticeable winking of the eye at every beat" (*RAD*, 114). Otherwise their relationship was that of comrades.

Solomons died prematurely in 1900. According to Gertrude Stein's view, this happened because he submitted to a cancer operation from which he was unlikely to recover. Forty-six years later she did the same.* Upon Solomons's death William James wrote Gertrude Stein a comforting letter, which commented upon his "very peculiar and extraordinary character," a mixture of "wild independence with amiability" and "contemptuous intellectuality with breadth of sympathy." "We

---

* See Katz, 189–90. Donald Gallup however says that Solomons died "of an infection contracted in the laboratory" (*Flowers*, 19).

shall never look upon his like," James concluded, "and seldom upon his equal" (Gallup, *Flowers*, 20).

In spite of the intimacy at Harvard between faculty and students, both Arthur Lachman and Leon Solomons complained of the impersonal atmosphere there. Solomons in particular felt exploited by the Psychological Laboratory. He wrote to Gertrude Stein: "To call a piece of research work done by a student who pays for the privilege of working in a particular laboratory a contribution from that laboratory as though the *lab* had *hired* the man to do the work is misleading to say the least." He went on to say that now, in Berkeley, he would no longer be "in shadow behind the Harvard Curtain" (Gallup, *Flowers*, 11).

Gertrude Stein regarded Solomons as "an intimate friend" and felt that he had "left a definite mark on her life" (*EA*, 265; *ABT*, 95). Her friendship with him led to her first publication. She and Solomons were put to work conducting experiments on the automatic responses of human beings. They sought to demonstrate that the "normal" person could perform certain non-instinctive acts when his attention was distracted, just as the hysteric, whose attention was actually impaired, could. Their experiments involved the use of a pencil with which the subject made certain regular movements while he listened to a story being read aloud to him. Their results were published under both their names in an article entitled "Normal Motor Automatism" which appeared in September, 1896 in their discipline's chief professional journal, the *Psychological Review*. Gertrude Stein was just beginning her senior year at Harvard. Two years later, a professor at the University of Iowa remarked of the partnership: "Encouraging beginnings have been made in American laboratories by Solomons and Stein in two researches upon normal motor automatisms . . ." *

At the time of her greatest celebrity, following the publication of

---

* G. T. W. Patrick, "Some Peculiarities of the Secondary Personality," *Psychological Review*, V (November 1898), 557. The pair's first collaborative efforts were reported under Solomons' name alone in the article, "The Saturation of Colors," *PR*, II (January 1896), 50–56. Solomons also published "Discrimination in Cutaneous Sensations," *PR*, IV (May 1897), 246–50; "Automatic Reactions," *PR*, VI (July 1899), 376–94; and, posthumously, "A New Explanation of Weber's Law," *PR*, VII (May 1900), 234–40. In none of these is Gertrude Stein mentioned. She did, however, serve J. B. Hylan as a subject in an experiment on "Fluctuations of the Attention," *PR*, III (January 1896), 56–63. The evidence then indicates that not only was Gertrude Stein an active member of the Psychological Laboratory, but that the areas of experimentation at the height of her involvement—attention, sensation, automatic response—all bore upon her subsequent development.

The Autobiography of Alice B. Toklas, B. F. Skinner resurrected this article and asked the rhetorical question, "Has Gertrude Stein a Secret?" in the *Atlantic Monthly* (January 1934). Skinner took note of the descriptions of automatic writing in the Solomons-Stein article, then compared them with Gertrude Stein's enigmatic prose in *Tender Buttons.* He concluded that during an aberrant period she had indeed depended upon automatic writing to produce the nonsense which passed in some quarters as avant-garde writing.

She replied to Skinner's article in *Everybody's Autobiography.* She did not attempt to argue the theoretical issues with Skinner, even though they were crucial, but said that Solomons, not she, had written the article. "After all I was an undergraduate and not a professional . . ." The ideas were all his, she went on, "all that had been mine were the definitions of the characters of the men and women whom I had seen . . ." (*EA,* 267).

Several bits of evidence suggest that her defense was more than merely an attempt to rescue an embarrassing situation. First, within the article itself, there were several references to "Miss Stein" as the main subject in the experiments. She is differentiated from the "I" reporting the results, that is, Solomons. Secondly, Skinner unaccountably neglected to consider a second article which Gertrude Stein published in the *Psychological Review* of May 1898, entitled "Cultivated Motor Automatism." In it, she reported the results of her single-handed continuation of the experimental line she and Solomons had initiated. Composed much more loosely, this is the article that Solomons criticized for its "careless" expression (Gallup, *Flowers,* 15). After revision, she resubmitted it for his approval. She did not receive it. "I have looked over your article, and rewritten some of the more illegible words, inserted various punctuation marks, things of which you may have heard even though you so obviously disapprove, and altered a couple of sentences . . ." (letter, 27 February 1898, YCAL). Even with Solomons' alterations, the essay still exhibits the awkwardness and lack of organization that Gertrude Stein displayed so lavishly in her college themes. Therefore, internal evidence also supports Gertrude Stein's contention that Solomons, not she, was responsible for the first article.*

---

* In *ABT,* which stimulated Skinner's inquiry, Gertrude Stein called "Cultivated Motor Automatism" "the first writing of hers ever to be printed" (95). The issue of whether *Tender Buttons* is an example of automatic writing is further discussed in Chapter 6.

The impetus for the experiments Gertrude Stein conducted independently came from the fact that in their previous collaboration, she and Solomons had been the sole subjects. She recognized that the results they obtained might have been peculiar to them. For this reason she expanded her sample to nearly one hundred students, about equally divided between men and women. She also revised the experimental activity. Earlier, the subjects had written words while having a book read to them. Gertrude Stein now taught her subjects to make certain rhythmic movements with the pen—"circles, the figure eight, a long curve, or an m-figure" ("Cultivated Motor Automatism," 296). When the subject was distracted, the automatic activity was supposed to display itself in one of these learned movements. Also, rather than reading to the subject from "literature that is easily followed and emotional in character," Gertrude Stein diverted her subjects' attention by a conversation or by encouraging them to daydream ("Normal Motor Automatism," 508). Her claim in *Everybody's Autobiography* that "I had no results there was no automatic writing, there were some circles and sometimes a vague letter but never any word or anything that could be called writing" is either forgetful or disingenuous (266). Those circles and vague letters were precisely what she had taught her subjects to produce. She had not established laboratory conditions that would encourage automatic *writing*.

The complex bases for Gertrude Stein's literary career were only being roughly sketched in at this stage. As she organized her results in the Psychological Laboratory, her main concern was not aesthetic but personal. Nonetheless, she later said that "Cultivated Motor Automatism" already showed "the method of writing to be afterwards developed in Three Lives and Making of Americans" (*ABT*, 96).*

If the experiments described in "Normal Motor Automatism" made Gertrude Stein more conscious of the ways in which words are cued in the mind, her experience in "Cultivated Motor Automatism" stimulated her interest in classifying people. Scientifically, her article is unimpressive. She spends too little time in defining the experiment and in summarizing its results. Most of her article is devoted to making generalizations about basic types of human beings and to the behavioral particulars of individuals. Gertrude Stein imports the judgments of

* Skinner misuses this statement in two ways. He inaccurately applies it to "Normal Motor Automatism" which permits him to quote at will from the examples of automatic writing that appear in it. And he conveniently discusses *Tender Buttons* rather than the two books specifically designated by Gertrude Stein.

New Englanders that originated in her sophomore themes. She refers to their "habit of self-repression, the intense self-consciousness, the morbid fear of 'letting one's self go,' that is so prominent an element in the New England character" (299).

She broke her subjects down into two basic types. Type One were "nervous, high-strung, very imaginative." She found them "easily aroused and intensely interested" (297). Of these, she concluded that the women were likely to be students of literature, the men, of law. Type Two were blonde, pale, phlegmatic with weak powers of attention and concentration. These subjective and probably unverifiable classifications had found their first form in the theme, "The Great Enigma," in which Gertrude Stein contrasted the fiery Sallie and her passive, nameless lover. During the course of the same experimental work, Gertrude Stein also began to distinguish people as "resisters" and "yielders," categories that would be revived for *The Making of Americans*.

It would be misleading though to make a direct connection with Gertrude Stein's experience in the Harvard Psychological Laboratory and her experimental writing of 1910 and after. She made several major shifts in her career before she entered her esoteric phase. And she evolved in surprisingly coherent stages, rather than suddenly seizing upon innovation.

The balance of Gertrude Stein's education at Harvard is rather dim. She seems to have filled her time with extra-curricular activities—reading, attending the opera and the theater, taking walks. In the summer of 1896 she made the first of a series of annual vacation trips to Europe, where she travelled extensively in Leo's company.

The memories of her contemporaries have sometimes given a false impression of Gertrude Stein in these college years. In large part the problem has been caused by the imposition of what she became in adulthood upon her youth. Even those who knew her well were capable of being deceived by their memories. Arthur Lachman, for example, recalled that at Harvard she was "very mannish in appearance" with her hair cut short, a description that any photograph of the period will disprove.*

So too there is a common characterization of Gertrude Stein as a loud, arrogant bohemian—"big and floppy and sandalled and not car-

---

* Just when Gertrude Stein cut her hair is not clear but in a Man Ray photograph dated 1923 it is still long. In "Abel" (1930) she remarked, "Bats are seen but now that the hair is cut there is no fear" (*SIM*, 228). For references to the haircutting, see *WIR*, 138; Sprigge, 150; Brinnin, 287–8.

ing a damn" (Anonymous in Sprigge, "Gertrude Stein's American Years," 50). In photographs though, the young Gertrude Stein's face is invariably open, soft, childish. In group pictures, she is invariably in the background. Her writings show her to have been troubled, apprehensive, and self-hating. Her romanticism is suggested by a letter written by a friend in 1897. "I never knew a woman who knew the warm sun, the hidden stream, the tender green of spring more than you,—and I know a good many women pretty well" (Gallup, *Flowers*, 16). Neither a militant feminist nor a rampant bohemian, Gertrude Stein was a passionate and intelligent young woman still searching for a personal and professional life adequate to her needs.

The Stein family enjoyed a sustained relationship with Johns Hopkins University. After graduating from it in 1886, Michael had gone on for a year's graduate work in biology. Leo was working for his A.B. when Gertrude made up her mind to attend. He received it in 1898, then like his elder brother, continued as a graduate student of biology during the academic year of 1898–9. The presence of congenial relatives in Baltimore enhanced the University's attractiveness. So, in the fall of 1897, Gertrude Stein entered Johns Hopkins University School of Medicine.*

The School of Medicine had only recently opened with a superior faculty headed by William Osler. Although its hospital had started operations in 1889, the teaching program was delayed until 1893, because the Baltimore and Ohio Railroad had stopped paying dividends to its stockholders, among whom was Johns Hopkins University. The funds required for opening the School of Medicine were raised for the most part by four daughters of trustees.† One of them made her contribution conditional upon women's receiving unprejudiced instruction in medicine.

* Gertrude Stein had never passed Radcliffe College's entrance examination in elementary Latin. Having failed the examination in June 1897, she was not awarded her degree, even though she had completed all other requirements. Instead of continuing with her Latin in the summer of 1897, she enrolled in "a course in embryology at Woods Holl" Massachusetts. But the medical school insisted that she pass the Latin examination as a condition of admission. With the help of a tutor, she managed to do so in September. Her undergraduate degree was conferred in 1898. (Information derived from correspondence exchanged among Gertrude Stein [2 letters], Radcliffe College, and the Johns Hopkins School of Medicine between 17 July 1897 and 27 September 1897. These letters are now held by the Office of the Archivist of the Johns Hopkins Medical Institutions in Baltimore, Maryland.)
† Two of these daughters, Carey Thomas and Mary Gwinn, later turned up in *The Making of Americans* as Dean Hannah Charles and Cora Dounor.

As a consequence, the School of Medicine attracted some of the very brightest and most ambitious young women in America. Their presence amused the male medical students who called the woman's dormitory the "Hen House" and bedevilled them with the question, "Are you a doctor or a lady?" During a debate on diabetes, they were obliged to endure the indignity of receiving a bouquet of sweet peas (Bluemel, 72, 44).

In the beginning, Gertrude Stein seems to have been reasonably contented by the study of medicine. Her grades were good and in a letter written near the end of her first year, a friend remarked, "I am very glad to hear that you enjoy your present occupation, and that you revel in bones" (Gallup, *Flowers*, 17). She herself declared in *The Autobiography of Alice B. Toklas* that she liked the first two years well enough because they involved laboratory work. It was "the practice and theory of medicine" undertaken in the last two years that bored her. She continued her studies, she said, because "she has a great deal of inertia and once started keeps going . . ." (101).*

It is always advisable to check the testimony of *The Autobiography of Alice B. Toklas* against other evidence. In this case Gertrude Stein is corroborated. Her grades progressively declined in her third and fourth years of study. In February of her last year (1901), Leo inquired, "What is all this non-medicated rumble that issues from your quarter?" In her slow way, his sister was evidently making known her intention to revolt. Despite Leo's regret that "the first person in the family who had gone so far . . . should go back on it," she did fail to take her medical degree (Gallup, *Flowers*, 22).

Her airy account of the affair was that the major professors, Halstead, Osler, and others had passed her as a matter of form, recognizing "her reputation for original scientific work." But one professor believed she should be taught a lesson, so he refused to pass her (*ABT*, 101).

In fact, Gertrude Stein failed four of her subjects in her final year. The medical school then graded its students on a numerical scale, with 1 being the top grade and 4 or lower regarded as failing. In her fourth year, Gertrude Stein received a 4 in Opthamology and Otology and in Dermatology, and a 5 in Laryngology and Rhinology, and in Obstetrics. She was the only member of her class of fifty-four to receive a grade lower than a 3. Therefore, when her marks were presented to the Ad-

* Gertrude Stein's record at the Johns Hopkins School of Medicine is reproduced in Appendix A.

visory Board of the Medical Faculty, it voted that she not be recommended for a degree.

If any professor were likely to be resistant to Gertrude Stein, it was the chief of obstetrics, John Whitridge Williams. Nicknamed "Bull" for his deep voice and positive manner, he was a firm believer in the virtues of personal responsibility and self-discipline.* Every fourth-year student was expected not only to spend two months on the obstetrical ward, but to deliver nine babies (Bluemel, 46). Gertrude Stein later remembered that "she had to take her turn in the delivering of babies" (*ABT*, 100). The obligatory construction of the verb is worth noting, for it suggests a certain distaste for the job.

Gertrude Stein's decision to leave medical school upset her student comrades as well as the women who had raised money to insure female education. They believed she "had done harm to their sex" (Bluemel, 76). One Radcliffe girl pleaded with her, "But Gertrude Gertrude remember the cause of women, and Gertrude Stein said, you don't know what it is to be bored" (*ABT*, 101).

Ironically, the year after she had enrolled in medical school, Gertrude Stein had consented to speak before a group of Baltimore women on the topic of "The Value of College Education for Women." † In it, she argued that a college education was essential for the modern woman as a means of realigning and purifying her sexual drives. Heretofore civilization had treated woman as a commodity. She was trained to adorn herself and in a genteel way, to sell herself into matrimony. Once embarked upon her domestic and maternal labors though, she was not "worth her keep." Under natural conditions, a woman would not be dominated by the "sex element," for she "is an individual first and a member of a sex only when the time of functional usefulness begins." Higher education teaches women the discipline and self-reliance necessary to exist independent of men. At the same time, Gertrude Stein assured her audience, such an education "does not tend to unsex but to rightly sex women."

Derivative and rambling as the speech is, its earnestness is patent.

---

* See J. Morris Slemons, *John Whitridge Williams.* Another student said that Dr. Williams was the professor who refused to pass her (Sprigge, 40).
† Typescript in the Cone Collection, Baltimore Museum of Art. The copy in YCAL is tentatively dated 1897–8, but since, as Gertrude Stein acknowledges at the outset, the ideas of the speech are based on the book *Women and Economics* by Charlotte Perkins Stetson Gilman, which was published in 1898, the speech cannot have been prepared earlier than that year, unless she saw the book in manuscript.

Not only did Gertrude Stein dismiss contemporary marital arrangements, but she also asserted the greater force and purity of sexuality in the independent woman. She was unmistakably seeking to validate her own condition.

Gertrude Stein's association with Johns Hopkins University did not cease when she dropped out of medical school. She spent the summer after she was to have graduated with Leo in Europe. She returned to Baltimore in the fall and turned her attention to brain research. The nature of this scientific activity has been passed over uncertainly by her biographers. She herself says very little about it, save that her study of the brain tracts appeared in a book.

To attract neurological specialists, Johns Hopkins was then sponsoring the study of serial sections of the human brain. Dr. Lewellys Barker, the School of Medicine's authority on the anatomy of the brain pointed out in 1899 that there had been unprecedented activity in the field during the decade just past. Research had led to "a complete revolution in our ideas concerning the elements of the nervous organs" (*The Nervous System*, 2). In Gertrude Stein's study at Harvard on "motor automatism," she and Solomons had made certain assumptions about the nerve tracks along which motor impulses travelled. It was therefore natural that she should have been attracted to a research job, studying the brain.

Testimony regarding the quality of her work varies. It is certainly the case that throughout Gertrude Stein's life, as industriously as she worked to build her reputation, others worked to tear it down. Leo reported that his sister told him that the women at Johns Hopkins made models of brain tracts to cultivate the good will of their professors— "men wouldn't waste their time on it." He asserted that although later she grew pretentious about her "research" work, at the time it was merely a cynical diversion for her—"purely mechanical work and rather restful" (*Journey*, 148).

Her mentor, Dr. Barker, had greater respect for Gertrude Stein than those who reported that she "messed up" her slides and "mangled" her model of the brain (Sprigge, "Gertrude Stein's American Years," 50; Bluemel, 75). He assigned her to study the nucleus of Darkschewitsch, a bundle of fibers in the medulla oblongata, that pyramid-shaped part of the brain that narrows into the spinal cord. When, in his eleven-hundred page study, *The Nervous System and Its Constituent Neurones*, he reached the nucleus—which he noted presented "peculiarly puzzling" problems—he drew his information from Gertrude Stein and Florence Sabin, "who have especially studied this region" (721).*

As late as 1902, Dr. Barker asked Gertrude Stein, "Are you to continue work on the nervous system? It would seem a pity not to, now that you have gone so far in this line of work and have so good a background" (Gallup, *Flowers*, 24). Those were hardly the words of an eminent medical scholar addressing an incompetent researcher.

Gertrude Stein spent one last desultory winter in Baltimore, working on a model of the brain. But by this time she was selling off her medical books (Gallup, *Flowers*, 23). In spite of the urgings of feminists, of Leo, and of her teachers, she gave up the study of medicine altogether. In the late spring of 1902 she sailed for Italy where she joined Leo. That summer they travelled together to England.

The long background to her literary career was almost completed. She had spent the past decade in intellectual pursuits of undeniable rigor. Her mind had been affected by, if not bent to, the methods of scientific research. At the same time she had continued to read, to attend the opera, and to frequent art galleries. Her summer vacations had introduced her to Europe. She had already shared the company of leading young intellectuals like Bernard Berenson and Bertrand Russell. Now, indifferent to the practice of medicine, and her considerable energies temporarily unemployed, she stood at the edge of a serious literary career.

After some lonely months during which she read systematically in English narrative prose at the British Museum, she made one last, indecisive trip back to America in February 1903, where she took up residence in New York City with several Hopkins friends and started

---

* As an unknown example of her competence in reporting the results of research, Gertrude Stein's description is worth reproducing. "Miss Gertrude Stein, who is now studying a series of saggital sections through this region from the brain of a babe a few weeks old, describes the nucleus of Darkschewitsch as follows: 'The nucleus is more or less conical in shape. It lies dorso-medial from the red nucleus, being about as thick in a dorso-ventral direction as is the dorsal capsule of the red nucleus in which it lies. At this period of medullation the commissura posterior cerebri, considered simply topographically (that is, as a medullate fibre-mass without particular reference to the course of the fibres), appears as a dorso-ventral bundle, solid in the middle, sub-divided dorsally into an anterior (proximal) portion and a posterior (distal) portion, while ventrally it expands in the form of a hollow pyramid, which rests directly upon the nucleus Dark-schewitsch.' As to the bundle of fibres described above as being situated ventral to the nucleus, and passing forward and ventralward, Miss Stein in the brain she is studying can follow the fibres only as far as the fasciculus retroflexus. The fibres most ventrally situated are very complex in arrangement, forming a whirl in the substance of the nucleus ruber" (Barker, 725-6).

two separate projects. In her first, she undertook to describe the New York Steins, in particular, the impetuous and unwise marriage of her cousin, Bird Stein.* The other project was a novel about three women suffering a triangle of love. Meanwhile Leo had taken up residence in Paris. After one more summer holiday with him in North Africa, Spain and Italy, Gertrude Stein moved permanently to Paris. There, at 27 rue de Fleurus, she finished her first full-length work of literature. She called it "Quod Erat Demonstrandum." What had she proved?

* See Katz, chapters 3 and 4. He is certain that a portion of *The Making of Americans* was written before *Things As They Are.*

3

꣼. "I do not wish to imply that there is
any remedy for any defect."
("If You Had Three Husbands")

For as good a book as it is, *Q.E.D.* (or *Things As They Are*, as its
editors entitled it) has had a minimal reputation. During the first thirty
years of its existence it would seem that only Leo Stein knew about it.
Then, according to the story told in *The Autobiography of Alice B.
Toklas*, Gertrude Stein came upon the manuscript accidentally and,
with some hesitation, gave it to Louis Bromfield to read (104). He
thought it "vastly interesting" and mentioned to her the possibility of
having it published, in spite of the "great difficulties" that might present
(Gallup, *Flowers*, 249–50). But when the *Yale Catalogue* of Gertrude
Stein's writing was compiled in 1941, she denied permission to include
the novel (Haas, "Gertrude Stein Talking," 5). Admirers finally printed
it after her death, but in an edition of only five hundred and sixteen
copies. Although the book has since been received with respect by the
few who have read it, it is now out of print and virtually unobtainable.
This is regrettable, for the book is an indispensable link in the development of Gertrude Stein's prose.

The subject of the book was a dangerous one in 1903—three young
women in a passionate stalemate. It was based upon Gertrude Stein's
frustrated romance with May Bookstaver, a Baltimore friend. In writing the book, she drew upon letters she had retained from the long
affair, letters which Alice Toklas claimed to have destroyed in 1932
"in a passion." * Although one may conclude that the book had to be

---

* Katz, 16–17. It is probable that the distractions of this affair were largely
responsible for Gertrude Stein's poor record in her fourth year at medical school.
But the facts are still insufficiently clear to permit a definitive judgment in the
matter.

written, it is doubtful that any reputable publisher of the time would have accepted it.

Her original title for the novel was the classical signature to a geometric proof. It stood for the presence of a fixed relationship among the three female characters, a relationship "proved" by the logic of the novel. At Harvard, Gertrude Stein had counselled resignation before implacable fate. "You must submit sooner or later to be ground in the same mill with your fellows . . . Be still, it is inevitable" (*RAD*, 122). Although she remembered herself as "very full of convictions" in her youth and possessed by a strong missionary impulse that drove her to try to change people and to get them to "change themselves," she also had a strong fatalistic streak (*LIA*, 136). But if one could not alter one's fundamental nature, at least one could learn to understand it.

Things As They Are, the title Alice Toklas and Carl Van Vechten gave to the book, expresses the mingled ambition and resignation of its ending. It is drawn from the next to the last sentence of the book. "Can't she see things as they are," asks the young heroine, "and not as she would make them if she were strong enough as she plainly isn't" (87). The sentence elevates clear vision over all else. Whatever reality is, that must be accepted. Gertrude Stein felt this strongly enough to repeat the sentiment in the early pages of *The Making of Americans:* ". . . now it had come to her, to see, as dying men are said to see, clearly and freely things as they are and not as she wished them to be for her" (33).

The prospect of understanding brought a measure of relief. It might stabilize the life that swirled uncontrollably around her. Yet, mechanistic certainty in human intercourse is as distressing as chaos. The cost paid for understanding in *Things As They Are* was painful and generated only pessimistic conclusions. The three women had no way out of their impasse. Or, virtually no way out. The thinnest fissure of possible escape was visible in the concluding sentence. " 'I am afraid it comes very near being a dead-lock,' she groaned dropping her head on her arms" (88).

Things As They Are continues Gertrude Stein's study of a spirited young woman who tries to deal honestly with feelings that happen to be forbidden by society. The book is no less candid than her naïvely confessional themes submitted at Harvard. Here was Hortense Sänger undergoing a fresh temptation, except that after the passage of ten years, Gertrude Stein had given up melodrama. Humor, compassion, objectivity—these now govern the portrait of her heroine.

Adele is a hearty young woman, given to exclaiming "Great guns!," "Jupiter!" and "Hang it all" (58, 75). Upon taking her leave, she cries, "Adios" (53). She is associated with freedom and easy informality, with the sun and the western starlight. But the very first sentence of *Things As They Are* tells us that she has just undergone "a succession of wearing experiences." A few pages later, she yields herself "to a sense of physical weariness and to the disillusionment of recent failures" (3, 10). As she descends into a vortex of misery, this attractive girl with some medical experience displays a wry, unflinching candor and a calm resolve.

Adele is obliged to endure an assault upon her emotions from a quarter not only unexpected but also socially prohibited. Coming into the orbit of a pair of women, the gravity of her presence rearranges all the lines of force. The woman to whom Adele is attracted is Helen Thomas, an "American version of the English handsome girl" (4). Over the course of the story, Helen's character changes from what seems to be a wise, maternal tenderness into a passively suffering endurance. She is being kept by one Sophie Neathe. Late in the book, when Sophie gives Helen a piece of antique jewelry, Adele exclaims, "Oh it's simply prostitution" (81). Sophie is the decadent rich girl, the aristocrat, "vulgarized and the power weakened . . . unillumined and unmoral" (5). Heavy about the mouth from "the drag of unidealized passion," Sophie possesses crafty power. Insofar as anyone does, it is she who prevails in the end.

The story is told in three parts, each devoted to one person in the triangle. In summary, the plot is as follows. The three women are on shipboard apparently travelling to Europe. With naïve pride Adele expands upon her "almost puritanic horror" of cultivating the physical passions (9). Even at that moment she is being drawn closer to Helen. After an increasingly intense series of embraces, she spends a summer in Tangiers and Spain, reflecting upon the meaning of her experience.

Later, the trio is found back in the United States, Sophie in Baltimore, Helen in New York, and Adele visiting both. Adele and Helen have some random meetings that culminate in a tryst, a winter night's embrace, and declarations of love. But Sophie, her suspicions aroused, informs Adele of her proprietary rights to Helen. This counterattack leads to an estrangement of the lovers, followed by a reconciliation.

The remainder of the story is a psychological study of the maneuverings necessitated by the fixed character of each woman. The resolutions, failures, readjustments, misunderstandings, pressures, quarrels, fresh beginnings, subtle changes, and predictable consistencies in behavior all conclude in an exhausted stalemate.

While remorseless in exposing the self-deception of her chief character, Gertrude Stein manages it without the slightest taint of self-hatred or cynicism. The pompousness of her heroine is even peculiarly winning. Adele characterizes herself as "a hopeless coward. I hate to risk hurting myself or anybody else. All I want to do is to meditate endlessly and think and talk" (31). She compliments Helen on her ability to stab, straight and hard. She herself has "so many compunctions and considerations" that she would merely scarify the victim's surface anatomy, so that "unless he should bleed to death quite by accident, I wouldn't do him any serious injury" (31). This is the portrait of a Henry James innocent, one capable of devastating her more sophisticated acquaintances quite inadvertently. To protect herself from the reality of her being, Adele leads an abstract, verbal existence. She has yet to mature, to have the opportunity to sin and fall. It takes the fires of illicit passion to melt the armor of moral rhetoric she wears at the beginning of the book.

If *Things As They Are* lacks the guilt-laden atmosphere expected in a confessional work, that is a tribute to Gertrude Stein's ironic objectivity. That is not to say, however, that she was not dramatizing issues of passionate concern to her. The book centers on the clash between Adele's principles and her desires. Its ending is no cautionary instance of sentimentality, no lugubrious lament for the loss of high idealism. Nor is it a brutalized celebration of sensation's triumph over ethics. The integrity of the body is accepted on less than elevated aspirations.

At the beginning of the novel, Adele confidently recognizes only two varieties of feeling—"affectionate comradeship" and "physical passion" (9). The latter she rejects with horror. "As for my instincts they have always been opposed to the indulgence of any feeling of passion" (57). Adele therefore defiantly appoints herself champion of the maligned middle class. As presented, Adele's allegiance is partly the exaggerated posturing of a young intellectual. But her role was not an unnatural one for Gertrude Stein, who in spite of her literary practices consistently opted for normality over eccentricity.

When challenged that she does not seem middle-class, Adele happily takes up the gauntlet. "You have a foolish notion that to be middle-class is to be vulgar . . . commonplace . . . low" (6). Although she admits that she is "rejected by the class whose cause I preach," she contends that "the middle-class ideal which demands that people be affectionate, respectable, honest and content, that they avoid excitements and cultivate serenity is the ideal that appeals to me . . ." (8).

A similar young woman had counselled stoic calm when she was at Harvard. Her arguments would reappear in "Melanctha," this time expressed by the young Negro doctor who despairs of his race's predilection for excitement rather than "regular living." In *The Making of Americans* Gertrude Stein speaks directly to the reader in defense of the middle class, for although she knows "one can find no one among you all to belong to it," she insists that it is "always human, vital and worthy" (34).

This strong commitment to bourgeois decency is dramatically challenged in *Things As They Are*. Helen accuses Adele of being a "passionette," a girl who thinks a lot about love, and flirts with it, but lacks the courage to follow out its consequences. "You are so afraid of losing your moral sense that you are not willing to take it through anything more dangerous than a mud-puddle" (12). This attack is not presented as the sophistry of a seducer. Adele acknowledges the possible justice of the accusation. " 'I never wanted to be a hero, but on the other hand,' she added 'I am not anxious to cultivate cowardice. I wonder—' " (13). When Adele finally yields to an embrace "that seemed to scale the very walls of chastity," she does not lapse into self-recrimination (56). She undertakes the affair in full consciousness of what she is doing and remains observant of her reactions throughout its duration. The combination is an unusual one, for her analysis is neither cold-blooded nor emotionally indulgent. The book's expression of feeling is genuine, but maturely controlled. As the passionately confused young woman of the Radcliffe themes joins the scientific observer of Johns Hopkins, the several parts of Gertrude Stein come together in a drama of learning just what things, in fact, are.

Although there is some stylistic awkwardness in *Things As They Are*, it is nothing like her disastrously uneven college work. On the whole, the book has a forceful economy that is not easily imitable. At times the prose displays evidence of a strained rhetoric and there are moments of uncertain and even neglected punctuation as well as idiomatic imbalance. These traits, along with her admirable clarity, are evident in the following passage, which describes the affair near the end of the book.

Their intercourse in these interviews consisted in impersonal talk with long intervals of oppressive silences. "Won't you speak to me"

Adele exclaimed crushed under the weight of one of these periods. "But I cannot think of anything to say," Helen answered gently. (85)

The excellence of *Things As They Are* is that, without forcing a conclusion, it was able to express the subtlety of human behavior within a controlled framework. The story ends neither in triumph nor defeat, but in a painful human stand-off. Gertrude Stein had not scanted the suffering but had reproduced and accepted it. And yet the absolutism of her proof was unsatisfactory. Her vision exceeded her answer. So, changing her terms, she began again. She was now thirty years old and still only an apprentice in her chosen field.

From the fall of 1903 when she completed *Things As They Are* until the spring of 1905 when she began *Three Lives*, Gertrude Stein was still shaken by her wrecked love affair. Recording it had been insufficient therapy. Withdrawn, despairing, and cynical, she worked at two projects during this period. Both would eventually be fitted into *The Making of Americans*. One was the story of the unhappy marriage of her cousin Bird Stein, begun in New York, the other was the so-called "Hodder episode." Both were imaginative alternatives to the stalemate of *Things As They Are.**

"The Hodder episode" originated in a complicated scandal that involved both people and institutions familiar to the Steins. In brief, the episode concerned a married professor who fell in love with a woman who also taught at his college, and who lived with the female dean of the college. The professor and the dean compete for the affections of the woman. In the course of the contest, the professor leaves his bewildered wife. She returns to her father, and after a short time, her husband dies.

The two academic women are new versions of Sophie and Helen in *Things As They Are*. Dean Hannah Charles is the somewhat sinister avatar of Sophie Neathe. Described as one of those "vigorous egotistic sensual natures" with "general unmoral desires . . . and unmoral ways of calling them into realisation," she "in common with many of her generation believed wholly in the essential sameness of sex and . . . had devoted her life to the development of this doctrine" (434, 463,

---

* For an understanding of Gertrude Stein's preliminary drafts of *The Making of Americans* I have relied upon Leon Katz's invaluable dissertation, "The First Making of *The Making of Americans*," which is based upon an analysis of Gertrude Stein's unpublished notebooks, drafts of the novel, and extensive interviews with her contemporaries.

462). Her companion, Cora Dounor, was "possessed of a sort of trans-figured innocence." But she desired "to experience the extreme forms of sensuous life and to make even immoral experiences of her own" (435). "In this shy abstracted learned creature there was a desire for sordid life" (437–8).

With the abused wife, these two women constitute the basic trio dominating Gertrude Stein's imagination: a strong, clever sensualist possessed of power; a handsome girl of refined intelligence who is hypnotized by the flesh; and a naïve, rather plain moralist with deep affectionate needs running below the surface. Now though, the Adele figure was on the sidelines, suffering and baffled. While her husband and the dean carry on their war, she is left in her misery. "It was a long agony, she never became wiser or more indifferent, she struggled on always in the same dazed eager way" (434).

After completing this bleak episode, Gertrude Stein put her projected "family novel" to one side and ruminated on other possibilities. Several titles occurred to her. "The Making of an Author being a History of one woman and many others" was one example. As an alternative, she tried, "The Progress of Jane Sands, being a History . . ." etc. Even in these titles, the conceptual problems on Gertrude Stein's mind are evident. She hesitated between taking herself as representative of all mankind and creating a universal history. And first she saw herself shaped by the forces around her, then as moving purposefully forward, making progress. Behind these titles, the implicit questions were, am I at bottom the same as everyone else, or am I unique? And, am I the inevitable product of many forces, or am I what I make myself?

She fixed on the title *"Three Histories* by Jane Sands." * That title remained on the ensuing manuscript until 1909 when her publisher prevailed upon her to change it to *Three Lives*. He thought her title "much too formal" and moreover, he did not wish to have her book confused with his firm's "real historical publications" (Frederick H. Hitchcock to GS, 9 April 1909, YCAL). Even though she was paying the printing costs of the book and had resisted all other suggested modifications, she inexplicably accepted the revised title.

Flaubert was the source for the original title of *Three Histories*. In a

---

* The name "Sands" had some deep significance for her. At this time she made a list of possible noms de plume. "Jane Sandys, Pauline Manders, Pauline Sandys and Jane Sandys" (Katz, 73). Twenty years later in a personal letter, she rejected "Sands" as being "for some psychological reasons which I have never fathomed" unacceptable "for names for nom de plumes for almost anything and it should always be refused" (letter to Ellen Daniel, 5? June? 1929, YCAL).

series of retrospective meditations, Gertrude Stein developed a spotty history of her evolution as a writer. *The Making of Americans* was usually the starting-point, but occasionally her theorizing reached back to *Three Lives*. To account for it, she invoked the names of Flaubert and Cézanne. For anyone then seriously concerned with literature, the respectful mention of Flaubert was mandatory. He was a tutelary presence, the artist dedicated at once to a remorseless realism and to the aesthetic restoration of his craft. Leo Stein's enthusiasm for Flaubert induced his sister to read him and even to attempt a translation of the *Trois Contes*. Félicité, the servant woman of "Un Coeur Simple," reminded Gertrude Stein of her own Baltimore housekeeper, Lena Lebender. Félicité's parrot even makes an appearance in "The Good Anna." However, "Anna never really loved the parrot and so she gave it to the Drehten girls to keep" (62). Other than giving *Three Lives* its original impetus, Flaubert was of minimal significance for Gertrude Stein. For a time his example caused her to put her personal concerns to one side. Shortly though they returned to the center of her consciousness.

As for Cézanne, she and Leo had begun collecting his paintings late in 1904. Two things about Cézanne's art impressed her: his skillfully crude depiction of elemental subjects; and his attentiveness to all the details of his composition. Until Cézanne, she said years later, a painting was composed around a central idea. All other elements were subordinated to it. But Cézanne "conceived the idea that in composition one thing was as important as another thing." So strongly did this conception strike her, she went on, that she began to write *Three Lives* (Haas, 8).

Cézanne was one of her brother's enthusiasms, about whom he was then articulating his ideas. In one of his long, didactic letters to Mabel Weeks, Leo wrote that Cézanne always displayed "this remorseless intensity, this endless, unending, gripping of the form, the unceasing effort to force it to reveal its absolute self-existing quality of mass." Cézanne approached the canvas as a plane surface on which his art would be realized. The realization would be a made object, not an attempt at representation. Leo also pointed out that the work of the painters in whom he and Gertrude first interested themselves—Monet, Renoir, Degas, and Cézanne—was "all non-dramatic. When figures are composed in a group their relations are merely spatial. At most they are relations of movement concurrent or opposite" (*Journey*, 16).

Gertrude Stein had already intuitively employed such spatial relationships in her Radcliffe themes and in *Things As They Are*. Lacking a narrative imagination, she concentrated on building her characters with substantial psychological detail. Sometimes she sketched her subject in a summary moment—the man calmly standing in the mud puddle after missing his trolley to Cambridge, or Hortense, throwing her books down in the library. Or she placed two contrasting persons in one another's company—Adele with Helen, Helen with Sophie. By changing a person's location, she revealed new facets of his personality. There was an Adele one, an Adele two, an Adele three, according to where and with whom she found herself. Similarly, the progressive accumulation of experience produced an Adele A, an Adele B, and an Adele C.

With her interest in the analysis of character, Gertrude Stein was naturally drawn to the idea of regarding human relations as a composition. Her affinity for Cézanne arose then from sources deeper than the fact that she lived with Leo. Portraiture and composition attracted her long before she listened to her brother's monologues on aesthetic theory.

The pessimism with which *Things As They Are* concluded recurred in the epigraph to *Three Lives:* "So, I'm unhappy and neither I nor life is responsible for it." *

Three Lives centers on Baltimore's poor, mainly German immigrant women and Negroes. In it, whether hard-working or indigent, moral or loose-living, all are quietly victimized by fate. The three central characters die before their time: Anna of exhaustion following a "hard" operation; Lena while having her fourth baby; and Melanctha in a state of consumptive despair. In spite of its frequent cheerfulness, the over-all impression *Three Lives* makes is of decent people beleaguered by busybodies, disagreeable children, and plain bad luck until at last they succumb out of sheer weariness.

Situations familiar to Gertrude Stein arise obsessively over and over in *Three Lives*. There are parental outcries against their children's willfulness. People are abandoned by their friends and lovers. More specifically, the Bridgepoint where the stories are laid is Baltimore. The unsuccessful and sometimes illicit practice of medicine is in the background. Anna keeps house at one point for a physician, and one of her

---

* "Donc je suis un malheureux et ce n'est ni ma faute ni celle de la vie." Ascribed to Jules Laforgue, the quotation sounds as if it came from *Moralités Légendaires*, but I have not been able to locate it.

48

friends is a midwife whose clientele is principally unwed mothers. Anna's employer, Miss Mathilda, is a silhouette of Gertrude Stein herself. A large and knowledgeable woman who enjoys long "tramps" in the country, she is an art patron who in the summer travels "across the ocean" until at last she leaves permanently for a "new country" (15, 21, 22, 17, 64, 76).

"The Good Anna," first of the *Three Lives* to be written, opens on a sentimental note. It describes the scoldings and mutterings of a loyal servant who is clearly intended to be endearing. A good deal of archness is expended on pet dogs too. But gradually Gertrude Stein begins to build a portrait of a conscience-ridden German-Catholic housekeeper who drives herself and those under her remorselessly, at the cost of recurrent headaches. In particular, she enjoys a maternal badgering of the men for whom she works. In time though, her irritable, "strained worn-out" body gives way. Her last words to the author express her enduring affection. "Miss Annie died easy, Miss Mathilda, and sent you her love" (82).

Gertrude Stein experimented with her style in "The Good Anna." Flaubert's example in "Un Coeur Simple" had suggested new ways of presenting a working-class woman. It is worth noting here that, although the prose of "Melanctha" differs from that of "The Good Anna," the reason for the change is not that "Melanctha" concerns Negroes. Racial distinctions cannot account for the change observable in these two sentences:

> "Mrs. Lehntman, I don't see what business it is for you to take another baby for your own, when you can't do right by Julia and Willie you got here already" (43, Anna speaking).

> "I don't see Melanctha why you should talk like you would kill yourself just because you're blue" (87, Rose, a black girl, speaking).

The important stylistic innovations of "Melanctha" have nothing to do with the Negro, even though some readers have suggested that the story's notable attenuation is due to Gertrude Stein's trying to express the slow, languid life of the Negro. Rather, Gertrude Stein's style evolved as she composed *Three Lives*. In the beginning, with "The Good Anna," she found an entrance to a style of her own through a faintly foreign idiom appropriate to her immigrant heroine. Her own stylistic infelicities were absorbed into the discordant language of the immigrant working-class.

It was easy to blacken all the Drehtens, their poverty, the husband's drinking, the four big sons carrying on and always lazy, the awkward, ugly daughters dressing up with Anna's help and trying to look so fine, and the poor, weak, hard-working sickly mother, so easy to degrade with large dosings of contemptuous pity. (50)

At times the narrative voice addresses the reader directly, as if the story were being told by a reflective neighbor—"You see that Anna led an arduous and troubled life" (13). But it is impossible to assign a single, consistent identity to this voice that will satisfactorily account for its sound. Many odd and discordant phrases turn up in it, some the result of trying to render reality, some the result of forcing the prose surface. One old German woman's English is marked by "the roughness on her tongue of buzzing s's" (17). A rebuke is delivered "to his own good" instead of "for" (37). Such faintly off-kilter usage is common in "The Good Anna." "Then they did the operation" (82). The foreign idiom is audible in "Doctor got married now very soon" (57).

In addition to immigrant speech, there is also the self-conscious college graduate—"a dog that's old . . . is like a dreary, deathless Struldbrug, the dreary dragger on of death through life" (74). And the sophisticated experimenter—"Her half brother never left her out of his festive raisined bread giving progresses" (79). And the philosopher—"In friendship, power always has its downward curve" (54).

The writing preserved Gertrude Stein's several moods. This early in her career she made no attempt to unify the style in revision. Rather she accepted the vagaries of her sensibility. The result was undeniably peculiar. The mixture of patches of normal prose, awkward locutions, cultivated eccentricities, and reflections of servant mentality produced a crazy quilt of a style.

In great part, the irresolution of her prose was caused by the self-education to which she was submitting in the very act of composition. Her vision was lucid enough, but she lacked the means to express it adequately. Sooner than lose her perception of the tangle of life through the pruning of revision, she accepted the mess of her prose. Honesty was her ethic; art, her education; improvisation, her method. As an energetic, clever, fervent, and haphazardly educated young woman, she was gambling that she could turn her very handicaps to creative ends.

Although it was placed last in the book, "The Gentle Lena" was the second written and the shortest of the *Three Lives*. It describes a simple creature who desires only the kindness of others. She is manipulated, notably by an aunt who makes a marriage match for her. Two very fine scenes follow. One concerns Lena, who after having been left at the altar and scolded for it, cries in a street-car on her way home. The other describes her fiancé, who is cajoled by his father to return from New York where he fled to avoid the marriage and to fulfill his obligations. Had Gertrude Stein been willing to cultivate her talent for sympathetic realism, she might have become a superior novelist as that term is customarily understood. But she was far more interested in the inner workings of the mind than in the observable behavior of others. Epistemology consumed her, so that she concentrated upon her own sensibility and its relationship to the world around her.

After Lena and her fiancé marry, they have a reasonably contented relationship, until she dies in childbirth. "When the baby was come out at last, it was like its mother lifeless. While it was coming, Lena had grown very pale and sicker. When it was all over Lena had died too, and nobody knew just how it had happened to her" (279).

No one—Dreiser, Willa Cather, Steinbeck—has written any better in that vein about mild, put-upon people than Gertrude Stein did in "The Gentle Lena." *

But the working-class milieu did not centrally engage Gertrude Stein. She had happened into it through the suggestive examples of Flaubert and Cézanne. But she was more interested in style as a carrier of knowledge than she was in investigating the lives of common people. Therefore, excellent as the story is, the emphasis here will be upon its stylistic distinctiveness.

"The Gentle Lena" possesses a more consistent voice than does "The Good Anna." The prose surface is much less patchy. In part this is because she wrote several very long paragraphs of monologue and of indirect discourse. She was drawn to those slowly revolving speeches in which a person takes a few basic concepts which he then states and restates with slight variations.

> . . . and your mama trying so hard, just so you could be comfortable Herman to be married, and then you act so stubborn Herman. You like all young people Herman, you think only about yourself, and what you are just wanting, and your mama she is thinking only what is good for you to have, for you in the future. (264)

Although such speeches sound authentic, what counted for Gertrude Stein in them was not their mimetic success, but the revelation they provided of human psychology. Such revolving discourse (the speech

* Its original title was "Maggie" (Katz, 71, n. 2). Stephen Crane's *Maggie*, published privately in 1893, was not generally circulated until 1896.

continues in the same vein for another fifteen lines) represented her initial venture into what she would later call the "prolonged present." By this she meant the stretching-out of discourse, pulling it until at last it became the "continuous present," that circular, infinitely slow movement, like taffy in the making, always there, always complete. Stylized extensions of the monologue just quoted dominated her writing around 1910. For example:

> Sound coming out of her comes out of her and is expressing sound coming out of her. Expressing sound coming out of her is something sound coming out of her is doing. Sound coming out of her is something. Sound is coming out of her. (*TWO*, 9)

While the differences between this passage and the one from "The Gentle Lena" are striking, it is clear that the source of its circularity is human speech. Stripping away the narrative line and depersonalizing the references was a job that Gertrude Stein had yet to do, but her stylistic revolution was underway.

Reference to "Melanctha," the longest of the *Three Lives,* is the grudging tribute most critics pay to the endurance of Gertrude Stein's reputation. They regard it not as a curiosity like *Tender Buttons,* nor trivial like the autobiographies of the thirties. It appears to be a work of social naturalism, and better still, it treats the Negro not only sympathetically, but as if he were white.

These are mistaken assessments of "Melanctha." They misrepresent Gertrude Stein's achievement, for "Melanctha" was only an early way-station on her road to artistic maturity. Furthermore, in spite of the general appreciation of her skill at rendering the "primitive mentality," Gertrude Stein's treatment of the Negro is both condescending and false. The principals of the story are not black at all, but only new, revised versions of the characters Gertrude Stein had described in *Things As They Are.* As for the background of "Melanctha," it swarms with clichés about the happy, promiscuous, razor-fighting, church-going darky.*

* Haldeen Braddy's article, "The Primitive in Gertrude Stein's 'Melanctha'" is a representative assessment of the story. Braddy is sometimes a shrewd reader, but his sociological views are less than satisfactory, as when he comments: "As a study of primal natures, 'Melanctha' is almost wholly preoccupied with the subject of sex, perhaps an inevitable concern for simple people with little else to think about" (360). Even were this a tenable human proposition, it would be contradicted by the fact that Melanctha was sufficiently educated to serve as a substitute teacher, and her main affair was carried on with a bourgeois physician.

Equally strange, sensible critics have accepted verbatim Gertrude Stein's claim in *The Autobiography of Alice B. Toklas* that, because she was posing for Picasso at the time she wrote "Melanctha," she wove into the story those "poignant incidents" that she observed as she walked down the hill from Montmartre to Montparnasse (60). It is impossible to imagine what incidents she had in mind, especially since the story has very little action, but rather progresses slowly through a series of psychological encounters.

In fact, "Melanctha" picks up the situation Gertrude Stein had treated in *Things As They Are,* and which she had left there in a stalemate. The frustrated trio is reduced to two persons in a standoff. This permitted Gertrude Stein to show in greater schematic detail how people in love are inevitably attracted to one another, then equally inevitably, separated. Calm seeks passion, conventionality seeks liberation, while conversely turmoil seeks peace and looseness yearns for control. But having located their opposites, these forces are then repelled. Calm finds tumult too unsettling and tumult cannot abide the monotony of calm.

Provided names, the forces are Jeff Campbell, a Negro physician who while attending a sick woman, falls in love with that woman's daughter, Melanctha. Their earlier names were Adele and Helen, and previous to that at Radcliffe, Gertrude Stein had presented the antithetical pair of Sally, the "fiery and impetuous" girl, and her irritatingly passive and nameless lover. The discovery of these "perfect antipodes" first took place in Gertrude Stein's imagination, was then played out in some form in her actual life, then re-entered her imagination for a retrospective analysis. Ideas that she first conceived in the Psychological Laboratory about the essential nature of human beings were fusing, deep in her consciousness. In "Cultivated Motor Automatism," Gertrude Stein had divided her subjects into two types, the first nervous and easily aroused, the second anemic and phlegmatic. She held persistently to this basic duality throughout her early career as she moved towards an ambitious study of men and women. At the same time she was fashioning a style capable of embodying her understanding of how people presented themselves to her consciousness. The one problem was inseparable from the other.

Sophie, the third member of the *Things As They Are* triangle, still exists in the person of the selfish Rose with whom Melanctha lives for a time. But her pragmatic hardness never centrally engages Gertrude Stein's attention. The duller aspects of Adele are now represented by Jeff. Like her, he objects to people who do things simply for the sake of experience. In his case, such people are the bulk of his race. Like Adele too, he defends the virtues of middle-class prudence. Unlike her though, he is priggish rather than independent. His compunctions seem skittish and shallow rather than morally anguished. Furthermore, Jeff lacks the good humor and wry self-knowledge that Adele possesses. Although he suffers as she did, he does so blindly, without wisdom.

The compelling fascination of the story centers in its heroine, "Darkflower." Whether black or not, she is the mysterious woman of deep feeling and irregular behavior rising in all her complexity out of the blonde pallor of America. Melanctha elaborates the contradictory depths of Helen Thomas and in the process, her character expands to absorb into itself the character of Gertrude Stein. Jeff's impoverishment is the result. He yields the positive aspects of Adele to enrich Melanctha. She is moody, but tender, frightened but brave, maternal yet sexually desirable, aggressive yet masochistic. As had Helen, she once overheard her mother and father express their disappointment in her rebellious existence. They remembered their other children—now dead—as quieter, more obedient. Like their creator, Helen and Melanctha both have impatient, suspicious fathers and sweet-appearing, vague mothers. Both fictional girls suffer broken arms in a display of reckless courage, an injury that infuriates their respective fathers. In Melanctha's case, the violence of her father's reaction and the context of precocious exploration in which the broken arm occurs, suggest the conclusion that the arm's fracture is a surrogate for initial sexual experience.* Finally, after the strain of a protracted and indecisive romance, both Helen and Melanctha exhibit increasing passivity. But whereas Helen was obliged to hold up her angle of the deterministic triangle of *Things As They Are*, Melanctha lapses into a decline that ends in death.

"Melanctha" then gathers together Gertrude Stein's main preoccupations: the rejected child, the sexual torment of the impetuous girl, the proddings of conscience, ill-fated relationships, and ultimately, abandonment.

A subject newly raised by the story concerns the distortions of memory. One of the issues over which Jeff and Melanctha quarrel is that she cannot "remember right." The accusation is verified early in the story. When recounting an incident, Melanctha is said to "leave out big pieces," although not deliberately (100). This creates a disparity

---

* I have discussed this point at greater length in "Melanctha," *American Literature*, XXXIII (November 1961), 350–59.

between what she claimed to have done and what she actually did. Yet this flaw is ultimately provided a serious and eloquent defense.

Gertrude Stein's argument on behalf of one kind of "remembering" occurs during a protracted dispute between Jeff and Melanctha. He again accuses her of living only for the moment. Her life lacks the continuity that a systematic and accurate memory can provide. "When you ain't just that moment quick with feeling, then you certainly ain't ever got anything more there to keep you" (180–81). Melanctha's challenge to this interpretation is that "You don't remember nothing till you get home with your thinking everything all over." Rather than displaying appropriate spontaneous reactions, he behaves cruelly and clumsily, which in retrospect he regrets. "You go home Jeff Campbell, and you begin with your thinking, and then it certainly is very easy for you to be good and forgiving." Melanctha speaks on behalf of immediacy. Her name for it is "remembering right." For her, the human way to live is "to remember right just when it happens to you, so you have a right kind of feeling. . . . real feeling every moment when its [sic] needed" (181).

Gertrude Stein poured a reserve of conviction into this defense of behavior which is intuitively sanctioned rather than the result of post-mortem rectitude. Throughout her career the antinomian warred with the scientist. Her conflict originated in her dissatisfaction with any ethic then available to her. She was too puritanic to accept unrestrained hedonism, and yet circumstance was denying her the expression of her considerable passions in conventional ways. She tried to solve her dilemma by understanding it. After the narratives of *Three Lives,* she turned to increasingly detailed analyses of character. But, finding herself perpetually frustrated in her attempts to provide a full, satisfactory description of any one or any thing, she eventually found herself driven to rely upon her own subjective response, expressed in whatever words emerged at the moment of concentration. As in Melanctha's defense here, she came to justify spontaneous composition as living in the present at the front edge of time. It seemed to her superior to living in historical memory, feeding on the aftermath of an existence of which one was never more than partially aware.

In "Melanctha," Gertrude Stein had not yet quite chosen sides. As she had in *Things As They Are,* she presented the debate between a morality of constraint and loyalty to primal feeling, without openly judging the ultimate validity of either position. Jeff's reflective mind attempting to analyze his experience in order to construct a code of behavior is presented almost as sympathetically as Melanctha's breakneck emotional existence the purity of which is derived from the directness of its response to life. "Melanctha" therefore emphasizes the doubleness of human nature. Its protagonists are antithetical, and Melanctha's own duality is remarked upon by Jeff. She seemed two different girls to him: one, whom he would never trust, has "a laugh then so hard, it just rattles;" the other, whom he worships, possesses "a real sweetness, that is more wonderful than a pure flower" (138).

The final point to make about "Melanctha" is that it is by far the most stylistically experimental of the *Three Lives*. Not just eccentric, or careless, or inept, but openly experimental. It is the mental processes imputed to the people the story describes that shape its prose. The story contains a large number of sexual euphemisms. Melanctha's puberty is referred to as "her beginning as a woman" (103). Men respond to her nubile presence with crude double entendres. "Hullo, sis, do you want to sit on my engine." "Do you want to come and see him cookin." "Hi there, you yaller girl, come here and we'll take you sailin." "Do you think you would make a nice jelly?" (98, 101, 102). Her first major trauma of breaking her arm follows her responding to a dare to mount to "a high place." "Come up here where I can hold you . . . when you get here I'll hold you tight, don't you be scared Sis" (102). Melanctha's subsequent relationship with Jane Harden has sexual overtones too. She "wanders" with this woman of "much experience" who teaches her "wisdom" and makes her feel "the power of her affection" (103–5).

These examples could be multiplied. Euphemisms and other kinds of verbal substitution eventually became an important feature of Gertrude Stein's style. Although in time she would provide this activity with an aesthetic rationale, it began as a form of evasiveness. It is true that such euphemisms in part reflected the verbally puritanic milieu about which she was writing in *Three Lives*. But it was also personally useful for Gertrude Stein, since it permitted the broaching of taboo subjects. It may give some perspective to recall that Theodore Dreiser, writing at exactly the same time as Gertrude Stein, was obliged to endure obloquy, censorship and prosecution for what were considerably more genteel and conventionally moralistic statements made in *Sister Carrie* and in *The Genius*.

In "The Good Anna," the narrator observed that a doctor "got into trouble doing things that were not right to do" (64). The context suggests this is an example of society's indirection in referring to an abortionist. But the construction of the reference intrigued Gertrude Stein. It provided a means of making a statement without exposing herself. Rather than say, "Leo hurt my feelings by ridiculing my writing," she could say, "Leo did to me what he shouldn't have done." By selecting general nouns and verbs, and replacing nouns with pronouns that lacked distinct referents and if possible, gender—"one" and "some"—she moved steadily towards abstraction. In miniature, her evolution looked this way:

> Martha was really not telling any one very much in her young living the feeling she had in her about anything . . . (*MOA*, 413)

> Two knowing each other all their living might tell each other sometime what each one of them thought the other one had been . . . (*MOA*, 746)

> He was not in any way one of the two of them. He was one. He was the one who was the one who was the one. (*TWO*, 99)

These sentences seek to stabilize a chaotic world by progressively elevating particular cases of isolation and estrangement to more general categories. Stated at a sufficiently high level of abstraction, individual problems appear to become universal dicta. Gertrude Stein's slow apprehension of this encouraged in her the ambition of preparing a history of all mankind, by which she did not mean a chronological narrative, but a perpetually valid description.

The prose of "Melanctha" reflected not only the euphemistic nature of popular speech, but also its erratic and repetitive qualities. Statements in it are rough-hewn and approximate. "Jem Richards made Melanctha Herbert come fast with him. He never gave her any time with waiting" (218). Meaning leaps gaps, indifferent to normal transitions. "Jem Richards, that swell man who owned all those fine horses and was so game, nothing ever scared him, was engaged to be married to her, and that was the ring he gave her" (219). Identical ideas are reiterated in succeeding paragraphs with only the slightest variation. "Melanctha's joy made her foolish . . ," "Melanctha's love for Jem had made her foolish . . ," "She was mad and foolish in the joy she had there" (219).

While such examples are still tied to the story, it is not difficult to see how they could easily lead to a preoccupation with the prose surface itself, at the expense of the imagined reality she was attempting to create. The dialogues of "Melanctha" might more properly be called duets. The voices sing across one another, following an independent melody, yet influenced by one another's music. One long interchange begins:

> Jeff what makes you act so funny to me. Jeff you certainly now are jealous to me. Sure Jeff, now I don't see ever why you be so foolish to look so to me.

He answers:

> Don't you ever think I can be jealous of anybody ever Melanctha, you hear me. It's just, you certainly don't ever understand me. It's just this way with me always now Melanctha. (176)

In time, Gertrude Stein minimized the colloquial awkwardness and emphasized the patterning. She abandoned any pretense of imitating different people. Rather, all her prose emerged from a single sensibility. This did not mean that the results were invariably unified, for they were not. But it did mean that the stylistic variants emanated from the directing intelligence alone.

Gertrude Stein had some success in trying to render other people in her early work. But she had more compelling problems to solve in her own life than could be handled by polishing the techniques of verisimilitude, were she capable of it. The technical possibilities she had glimpsed in the mottled prose surface of *Three Lives* tantalized her. Her next work was a major and decisive effort at liberation.

4

꙳. "Describe it continuingly and not as a forethought."
("Studies In Conversation")

Gertrude Stein always regarded *The Making of Americans* as her major accomplishment, and so it is and so it isn't. Physically, it is her largest and most sustained literary effort. Containing five hundred and fifty thousand words the printing of which required nine hundred and twenty-five generous pages, it took her almost nine years to complete. Appropriately enough, she referred to it during its composition as "the long book." *

Until it was in print and her reputation established, Gertrude Stein was defensive about this huge child of hers. Alice Toklas and she painstakingly read proof on it, so that although she realized that many people would judge its eccentricities to be the fault of the French compositors, "they are not it is quite as I worked at it and even when I tried to change it . . . I always found myself forced back into its incorrectness" (letter to Sherwood Anderson, quoted in Gallup, "The Making of *MOA*," 68). On the other hand, she had written Carl Van Vechten the year before, "it is rather funny and youthful, there are moments when I think I should prune it out . . ." (Sprigge, 137).

As it happened, until *The Making of Americans* was republished in 1966, readers were likely to encounter it only in an abridged version. Published in 1934, after the success of *The Autobiography of Alice B. Toklas*, the abridgement is apt to rouse false impressions about the original, even though the author herself reduced it in anticipation of a French translation of the book. In 1933 she wrote Lindley Hubbell, "the way the whole has been cut I did it three years ago is I think alright" (letter, 2 June 1933, YCAL). Elsewhere she said that a pub-

* Gallup, "The Making of *The Making of Americans*," 55. Gertrude Stein said the writing took "almost three years" (*LIA*, 135). But see Katz (36, 247), who dates it from spring 1903 to October 1911.

lisher requested her to compress the book to about four hundred pages, which she did. "She spent part of a summer over it and . . . thought it alright" (*ABT*, 306).*

She does not seem to have done any rewriting for the abridgement. A crude expediency guided the reduction process, which was done by paragraphs. Since no amount of abridgement could turn *The Making of Americans* into an entertainment, the whole record of Gertrude Stein's expressive evolution is preferable to the cut version. Even so hostile a reader of Gertrude Stein as Katherine Anne Porter once remarked that while, as with *Ulysses,* reading *The Making of Americans* was a permanent occupation, "to shorten it would be to mutilate its vitals, and it is a very necessary book" (*The Days Before,* 36).

Long as it is, *The Making of Americans* virtually lacks formal resting places. In its full printed form, this massive book was divided into five parts only, with no chapters. The first part was left untitled; the next three were named after their ostensible subjects—"Martha Hersland," "Alfred Hersland and Julia Dehning," and "David Hersland;" the last, "History of a Family's Progress," repeated the book's subtitle.†

It is no play on words to say that *The Making of Americans* is a very American book. It is an improvised work of no identifiable genre in which the creator learned by doing. It is full of momentary wonders and botched long-range schemes, lyrical outbursts and anguished confessions. Precisely those characteristics distinguished *The Making of Americans* from the two twentieth-century masterpieces with which Gertrude Stein chose to compare it, *Ulysses* and *Remembrance of Things Past* (*LIA,* 184). The urbane control of the European writer was not available to her. She stumbled and groped, not so much toward statements worth making, but toward a way of making them. Gertrude Stein began her literary career with such deficiencies that

---

* On the other hand, her publisher Alfred Harcourt refers to "the version cut by [Bernard] Faÿ. He seems to me to have done an amazingly skillful job" (letter to W. A. Bradley, 9 October 1933, YCAL). Chances are that Harcourt mistook one of the translators for its editor. Gertrude Stein permitted the abridged version to be published in English in order to get some version of the book before the public. This decision turned out to be a mistake, for three days after signing the contract, Bennett Cerf asked her permission to publish the complete version as a Modern Library Giant (Gallup, "The Making of *MOA*," 74).

† In the abridged version, the first part was divided into three sections entitled "The Dehnings and the Herslands," "The Hersland Parents," and "Mrs. Hersland and the Hersland Children." In the complete version there are untitled breaks on pp. 3, 4, 33, 150, 382, 598, and 821.

60

passion alone carried her forward, and only candor could redeem her. Even after she began to control some useful techniques of writing in *Three Lives*, she abandoned them and in an act of breathtaking temerity, plunged back into the turbulence of her mind.

Nonetheless, it is impossible to overestimate the importance of *The Making of Americans* as a psychologically liberating work for Gertrude Stein. During the period of its composition, she established herself permanently in Europe, she met and formed a liaison with Alice Toklas, she freed herself from Leo, and in the book she temporarily exorcised certain personal problems, particularly concerning her father. She made a strong bid at taking a psychological inventory of mankind, and she opened up stylistic possibilities that she would never exhaust, and which would win her the glory she ardently desired.

If it is regarded as a novel rather than as a psychological and stylistic daybook, *The Making of Americans* is a disaster. Its form is uneven, its focus erratic and uncertain. It gives the impression of someone learning how to drive. Periodically there are smooth stretches, but these are interrupted by bumps, lurches, wild wrenchings of the wheel, and sudden brakings. All the while the driver can be heard muttering reminders and encouragements to herself, imprecations, and cries of alarm.

Gertrude Stein frequently injected herself directly into *The Making of Americans* to talk about her feelings and her plans so that she appears in it both in fictional guise and as the author. "This is now then some description of my learning. Then there will be a beginning again of Martha Hersland and her being and living" (308). Her remarks range emotionally from confessions of melancholy to declarations of eventual success.

At the outset, she entered the book to discuss a character with the reader with all the boldness of a Victorian novelist. "And so those who read much in story books surely now can tell what to expect of her, and yet, please reader . . . be you well warned . . . from the vain-glory of being sudden in your judgment of her" (15). Shortly though, her voice grows uncertain. She confesses the isolation she feels. "Truly I never feel it that there ever can be for me any such creature, no it is this scribbled and dirty and lined paper that is really to be to me always my receiver . . ." (33).

Convinced that she was sentenced to solitary confinement, a third of the way through the book she announces, "I am writing for myself and strangers" (289). The reason, she explains, is that those around her (at this time, essentially Leo) are indifferent to her labors. They have no wish to know what she has learned about people. "No one who knows me can like it," she said of the book (289). Leo did refuse to admit that his heretofore docile sister possessed any talent. Her creative activity was a reproach to his own increasingly evident sterility. In a letter concerning *Three Lives,* Gertrude Stein revealed her distress: "Leo he said there wasn't no art in Lovett's book and then he was bad and wouldn't tell me that there was in mine so I went to bed very miserable . . ." (Brinnin, 99).

The lack of appreciation often depressed her. "I am all unhappy in this writing," she testified at one point, "nervous and driving and unhappy in it" (348). At another juncture, as she analyzed the disintegration of a feminine triangle—"I am really almost despairing, I have really in me a very very melancholy feeling, a very melancholy being, I am really then despairing" (459).

"Disillusionment" summed up several of the sources of her unhappiness. For her, disillusionment consisted in the discovery that "nobody agrees with you." Worse yet, "no one can," for "they can't change." The trauma of this realization she described as "an awful agony." It sometimes caused "some young ones to kill themselves." To illustrate this feeling of alienation, she says that one feels strange when one likes a clock or a colored handkerchief or a particular food which everyone else "of your kind" rejects (484–5).* Their assumption then is that in claiming to like it, one is seeking a cheap individuality, whereas the preference is genuine.

Hostile readers of Gertrude Stein have frequently accused her of egoism, saying that she imposed her maunderings on the public with regal complacency. Yet the anguish of her apprentice years is plain to see. She was not born to serenity. During much of the composition of *The Making of Americans,* she felt herself thoroughly out of phase with her family, her friends, and her times, and she could only appeal to those "strangers" in whose existence she hardly believed. That realization "makes an old man or an old woman of you," she said. This very project was a persistent source of discomfort to her. "You

---

* In this passage Gertrude Stein inserted one of those euphemistic references that can easily be overlooked in the flood of verbiage, and that are sufficiently vague in any case not to compromise her. Nonetheless, such statements get one important source of her feeling out of step with the rest of the world mentioned. "Or you like something that is a dirty thing and no one can really like that thing" (485).

write a book and while you write it you are ashamed for every one must think you are a silly or a crazy one and yet you write it and you are ashamed, you know you will be laughed at or pitied by every one and you have a queer feeling and you are not very certain and you go on writing" (485).

Her persistence was rewarded. Approval finally relieved her isolation. At last "some one says yes to it, to something you are liking or doing or making . . ." (485). And in truth, Gertrude Stein's mood does brighten in the last half of the book, although she still informs us of moments of discouragement and suffering (548, 573). She was working her way out of her confusion by the very act of writing. So, despite "much lonely feeling and much sighing in one" from the "very sombre burden" of authorship, she found it a comforting thing "being a great author inside one" (593). That first overt claim for her artistic stature signified confidence wooed rather than a critical judgment. But at least she was emerging from that state of profound disorientation of the beginning of the book where she had apostrophized her "Brother Singulars," those eccentrics oppressed by American demands for conformity.

In *Things As They Are* she had addressed herself to the sameness of American girls. "They all look alike not because they want to or because they are forced to do it, but simply because they lack individual imagination" (71–72). The sense of her own estrangement became more acute in the following years. America, she thought, could not tolerate the unconventional behavior that is the mark of a true individual.

> It takes time to make queer people. . . . Custom, passion, and a feel for mother earth are needed to breed vital singularity in any man, and alas, how poor we are in all these three.
> Brother Singulars, we are misplaced in a generation that knows not Joseph. We flee before the disapproval of our cousins, the courageous condescension of our friends who gallantly sometimes agree to walk the streets with us, from all them who never any way can understand why such ways and not the others are so dear to us, we fly to the kindly comfort of an older world accustomed to take all manner of strange forms into its bosom . . . (*MOA*, 21)

No other quotation renders so directly the rejection Gertrude Stein felt in the "adolescent world" of America (47). Nor had she yet established herself in France. In one of the innumerable instances where Gertrude Stein attempted to elevate a personal situation into a universal truth, she tried to convince herself that late development was natural for an American. Because of the freedom America affords its citizens to change their vocation as often as they wish, it was common, she claimed, for them to prolong their youth until thirty. (In her case, that would be 1903, when she wrote *Things As They Are* and became a permanent expatriate.) Then at last Americans find "that vocation for which we feel ourselves fit and to which we willingly devote continued labor" (437).

Hard as she was trying to convince herself of her abilities, the conclusion of the section devoted to Martha Hersland suggests how close Gertrude Stein suspected she might be to permanent failure. "It came very nearly being certain that she would not be succeeding in living" (475). She had nothing more to say of Martha, for the issue was still perilously in doubt, even as she put the words to paper.

The announced intention of *The Making of Americans* is to describe the creation of the American people. Gertrude Stein planned to do this by centering upon a representative family, which she would follow from its emigration out of the Old World to the United States, then through its marriages, and family expansions. It would reach down to the fourth generation and across the American continent from Baltimore to Oakland. "The old people in a new world, the new people made out of the old, that is the story that I mean to tell, for that is what really is and what I really know" (3).

Until some three years after she had started it though, Gertrude Stein hardly realized that she was writing a book about Americans, for it was not composed consecutively. The first segment which she had undertaken in 1903 concerned two sisters, both of whom had married badly, although with antithetical results. The one sister, modelled on her New York cousin, Bird Stein, suffered emotional upheavals in her marriage to a philanderer. She would become Julia Dehning in the final version of the book. The other sister was bored by an empty union. Gertrude Stein retained five chapters from this segment, and discarded about the same amount.

She then turned to *Things As They Are*. After completing it, she wrote the previously described "Hodder episode," recounting the contest of a male professor and a female college dean for the affections of a young woman. She put this second, unrelated segment of "the long book" to one side and once more speculated on fresh possibilities. After taking notes and casting trial sentences, she settled down to compose *Three Lives*. She had finished it by early February 1906.

It was between 1906 and 1908 that Gertrude Stein wrote the first sizable draft of *The Making of Americans*. By this time, her conception of the book had expanded in scale. She eliminated the tedious marriage of the second sister from the 1903 version, shifted the setting (which was never of much moment anyway) from New York to Bridgepoint-Baltimore, and then set about providing a European background for the first sister. The book was becoming a "family novel" in two senses. Gertrude Stein reached back to her grandparents to gain a generational perspective. More important, she provided the eastern Bridgepoint Dehnings with western counterparts. They were the Herslands of Gossols, based on the Steins of Oakland. The identity of the man Julia Dehning was to marry now became confused. Once married, he still displayed some of the unprincipled bounderism that Gertrude Stein associated with Bird Stein's first husband. But in his youth, Alfred Hersland plays the role of Michael Stein, Gertrude's respected eldest brother.

Alfred has a sister, Martha, and a brother, David, who are, in effect, Gertrude and Leo Stein, even though the book does not consistently reflect historical fact. More than one character incorporates Gertrude Stein's experience. As a child, Martha Hersland is largely the author. Then, because she had already cast herself in the role of the bewildered wife of Alfred Hodder, she has Martha marry the professor, thus drawing the Hodder episode into the main story. After their marital split, Gertrude Stein temporarily turned into Selina Solomons, an eccentric suffragette, most of whose experiences were dropped in the final draft of the book. When Martha returns to Gossols, it is as Gertrude Stein in that uneasy truce with her father that took place the year before his death and her departure for college. Even though a great deal more text would follow between 1908 and October 1911 when the last chapter was completed, virtually nothing more was to be added to the plot, for Gertrude Stein then turned to extended and increasingly stylized analyses of character.

Gertrude Stein could not settle in her mind what it meant to write a representative history. Were the descendants of German immigrants to stand for the American experience, or did she wish to describe types of people more fundamentally conceived than nationalism would allow? The answer was that she was doing both. "This is now a history of every kind of them of every kind of men and every kind of women who ever were or are or will be living" begins one sentence. But as it winds its way to an end, its universality narrows, ". . . and now this is a history of these two of them, Mabel Linker and Mary Maxworthing" (220).

Furthermore, her interest in chronicling the progress of a family frequently lapsed as she became absorbed in exploring autobiographical incidents. Late in the book, her attention was diverted to problems of perception and of how she might satisfactorily render in words what she perceived. This led her to abandon *The Making of Americans* in order to undertake another ambitious project, *A Long Gay Book*. It too she abandoned part way through. If this seems flighty, none of her work in this period gives that impression. Intellectual alertness and stamina characterize her efforts in these years.

The Making of Americans is most usefully considered then, not as a fictional narrative nor a philosophic tract, but as a drama of self-education. No genre existed that could contain the pressures dammed up inside of Gertrude Stein. Her genius had to make its own unimaginable way. When she changed her mind, had an idea out of sequence, or only partially understood what she wished to say, she put it down then and there, indifferent to sequential continuity or internal consistency. *The Making of Americans* was Gertrude Stein's path to adequate self-expression.

On the surface, the book's two-paragraph prologue makes very little sense. It moved Gertrude Stein back in time, past the Manhattan house on 100th Street where she had begun *Things As They Are*, past her life as a Baltimore householder and medical student, past her work in the Harvard Psychological Laboratory, back to her first undergraduate years in Cambridge when she was secretary of the Radcliffe Philosophy Club and preparing themes for William Vaughn Moody. The first paragraph of the opening is an adaptation of an illustrative anecdote drawn from Aristotle's *Nichomachean Ethics* (Book VII, chapter 6), while the second incorporates an idea she had submitted to Moody in December 1894—"There is nothing we are more intolerant of than our own sins writ large in others" (*RAD*, 120). Her use of these two sources as well as their relevance to the book as a whole is worth considering. Here is the prologue:

> Once an angry man dragged his father along the ground through his own orchard. "Stop!" cried the groaning old man at last, "Stop! I did not drag my father beyond this tree."
> It is hard living down the tempers we are born with. We all begin well, for in our youth there is nothing we are more intolerant of than our own sins writ large in others and we fight them

fiercely in ourselves; but we grow old and we see that these our sins are of all sins the really harmless ones to own, nay that they give a charm to any character, and so our struggle with them dies away. (3)

In joining the two paragraphs Gertrude Stein reconstituted their meaning. Aristotle had introduced the story of the dragged father as part of an essay on incontinence. After concluding a chapter on pathological pleasures, among which he numbered the indulgence in abnormal forms of sexual intercourse, he used the story to illustrate that men accept "natural" behavior more easily than they do the unorthodox. Filial aggressiveness was recognized behavior, although it was expected to be confined within traditional limits.

Gertrude Stein adapted the story to her own purposes, concluding— as she herself had come to realize after long agonizing over her "singularity"—that it was difficult to overcome inherited character. She does not say, as did Aristotle, that it is easier to countenance displays of anger than indulgence in sensuality, particularly sensuality of the "morbid" or "bestial" sort. Rather, she promulgated a fatalistic and even appreciative acceptance of "our own sins." In time, they turn out to be not only "harmless," but charming.

Her statement is applicable only to certain persistent flaws of character. Supposing the struggle were against hypocrisy or alcoholism or self-hatred, it would be unlikely that one should ever decide that such behavior was either harmless or charming. But, applied to Gertrude Stein's own experience, it is possible to imagine what the irregularities of her young life were to which she had finally yielded as inevitable. She hoped to be able to accept the way things were.

Significant as this prologue was personally to Gertrude Stein, its conclusion failed to anticipate the book itself. *The Making of Americans* exhibits the numerous abrasions and injuries caused when mismated people are thrown together by accidents of birth or romantic errors of judgment. What it most emphatically does *not* provide is sunny instances of reconciliation to one's character and an attendant withering away of psychological distress.

The book actually begins by tracing the fortunes of four matriarchs out of whom the generations of new Americans came. These women all share the characteristic of being "strong to bear" many children. Only one, Martha Hersland—the first of three Martha Herslands in the book and presumably Gertrude Stein's paternal grandmother—is described in any detail. They provide another opportunity for Gertrude Stein to mention the demands for fortitude that birth puts upon the female, as well as the dangers which that process entails.

Very shortly, the story moves to Bridgepoint to examine the Dehnings, whose daughter Julia is to marry Alfred Hersland. In the course of this reasonably conventional character study of a young woman, Gertrude Stein translates the specific tastes of Julia into those of modern America. The new generation has "more plunges, douches, showers, ways to get cold water" than had the old. Their rooms are painted in dull colors, "the shade that so completely bodies forth the ethically aesthetic aspiration of the spare American emotion" (31).

Gertrude Stein also unburdens herself of private observations, among them, on bathing, on the passionate temper, and on the American virgin, whom she found "self-satisfied crude domineering." The American girl was, she thought, "a crude virgin and she is safe in her freedom" (15). She also described "that dubious character, the adventuress." Omnipresent, her type was "eternally attractive in its mystery and daring and always able to attach unto itself the most intelligent and honest of its comrades and introduce them to queer vices" (19).

Although there is a central spine of objective description in *The Making of Americans,* the prose pulls away from it in two directions: towards generalizations and towards observations of personal concern to the author. As Gertrude Stein defiantly reminded her reader, the book "is not just an ordinary kind of novel with a plot and conversations to amuse you . . ." (33).

The preceding section of Part One having ended with Julia Dehning's marriage to Alfred Hersland, the next, logically enough, turns to the Hersland family out of which Alfred came. But, because the Herslands were, in effect, her own immediate family, Gertrude Stein rapidly became engrossed in puzzling over the mysteries of character and environment that formed her, so that for the most part, she neglected to consider the specific bearing of the Hersland family upon Alfred and his marriage. Since it was at this juncture that the reckless first husband (Alfred Hersland) of Bird Stein (Julia Dehning) turned into the dutiful Michael Stein (Alfred Hersland), it is doubtful that Gertrude Stein could have reconciled the two characters anyway. As she herself later commented, "In The Making of Americans I wrote about our family. I made it like a novel and I took a piece of one person and mixed it with a piece of another one" (*EA,* 69). Because various people bear the same name, genealogies are difficult to disentangle. There are three Martha Herslands, three David Herslands, and at least two Julia Dehnings.*

Gertrude Stein does offer a well-conceived account of the emigration of the first generation of Herslands from Europe. The father, a butcher, must be prompted incessantly but patiently by his wife—"strong to lead"—to leave the old country (36–42). Following this interlude though, Gertrude Stein returned the story to her parents. The wandering of her attention is notable, continually giving the impression of indecision and a lack of concentration. Phrases like "And now to come back to . . ." and "And then as I was saying" signal her awareness of her digressiveness. Slowly, waveringly, she closed in upon her mother, Mrs. Hersland.

Whereas Gertrude Stein had very pronounced ideas about her father which she could articulate with ease, her mother remained enigmatic to her. Therefore in this part of the novel a family of women named Shilling, a mother and two daughters, fat Sophie and thin Pauline, gradually assumed the center of the stage. The ostensible reason for their appearance is that they first gave to Mrs. Hersland "the feeling of being important to herself inside her" (56). What the Shillings did to produce this feeling is never explained, probably because Gertrude Stein herself could not determine it. And, though fascinated by this family unit, Gertrude Stein could come no closer to fathoming their mystery than she had with her mother. She tried to generalize on the basis of physical size, even though she realized the statistical uncertainties. "One gets the feeling . . . that there are many more millions of them made fatter than there are millions made thinner . . ." Just as she thought she had at last set down a solid truth, she decided that it was only a subjective impression produced because each fat person "fills up so much more space than a thinner. . . ." (82).

This is ludicrous, unless one realizes that Gertrude Stein was attempting to get a fingerhold on the slippery world around her. Then it becomes a sign of her integrity that she was willing to acknowledge the unreliability of even her physical impressions.

Sensing that the Shillings possessed some distinctive importance in her memory, Gertrude Stein circled around them, trying to bring them into focus. After several pages of trying, the best she could manage in

* Gertrude Stein's name for Oakland—Gossols—was apparently inspired by Picasso's having vacationed in Gosols, Spain during the summer of 1906, when Gertrude Stein was starting to work in earnest on the book (Rogers, 66).

her presentation of this group which was fundamentally irrelevant to her narrative was to say that they produced an "important feeling" in her mother; that they had "something queer" about them; and finally, that the fat sister feared the thinner one "because it would hurt more if pins were stuck into her" (78–79).

Gertrude Stein's first attempt to analyze a small group of people failed. She was trying to get at "feelings," "impressions," and "fears" inchoate but crucial in determining her conception of the world. She labored diligently, but often against herself. Having fenced in an area to secure it from the general confusion, she would then knock the fence down again. She indicated that "millions" were made just like the Shillings. If true, that would provide at least one category of people. But then came the exception. Millions were made like the Shillings— except for their queerness. "That makes them different." No sooner has she said this than she destroys what she has created by observing: "Perhaps there was nothing . . . really queer inside them" (81).

However exasperating such backing and filling is, it does represent Gertrude Stein's fidelity to the full dimensions of her mind. She refused to trim off contradictory feelings in order to achieve a smooth result. In time she would deliberately link contradictory statements, as for example: "She was one dancing and she was one not dancing" ("Orta," TWO, 298). Similarly, she experimented with sequences of change. "He had been a thin one, a fat one, a very thin one, a thin enough one, a quite thin one, a not thin one, a fat one, a very fat one" ("A Man," TWO, 235). Such stylized variants developed out of her early attempts to capture the nuances of her subjective apprehension of the world.

Gertrude Stein came to believe that each person revealed his "bottom nature" in his speech, that "slowly every one in continuous repeating to their minutest variation, comes to be clearer to some one" (MOA 284). But she rarely tried to differentiate speakers. As a matter of fact, soon after Three Lives, dialogue virtually disappeared from her prose. She herself became the instrument for revealing a person's "real being." So her father as David Hersland:

> He was strong in fighting he was not so strong in winning, more and more then at the ending of his middle living fighting in him turned into impatient feeling inside him, more and more then fighting in him in his late living broke down into weakness inside him. (143)

That might be Jeff Campbell or Melanctha describing an acquaintance. Gertrude Stein had to make very few adjustments in order to change her already stylized versions of her characters' dialogue into her own. This incrementally repetitive style with its vague and limited vocabulary provided her a personal voice.

But that voice continued to have trouble finding something definite to say. The plot was at a standstill as Gertrude Stein tried to analyze the Hersland Family and its neighbors. At times, she was reduced to making pseudo-statements about classes of people:

> Many servants get to have in them something that is almost a craziness in them, many have a very lonesome feeling in them not a lonesome feeling of themselves inside them just a lonesome feeling that makes queer, sometimes a little crazy women of them. (168–9)

She was aware of the instability of the little knowledge she did possess. "Sometimes I lose it, sometimes I doubt it, it is too clear or too vague or too confused inside me" (308). Thinking back on the experience of writing the book, she recalled that "as often as I thought and had every reason to be certain that I had included everything in my knowledge of any one something else would turn up" (*LIA*, 144). Discouraging as the new perception might be though, she doggedly gave it entrance. True confusion was superior to false order. Lacking confidence in any other truth, she could at least trust the immediate report. "Always more and more I want to know it of each one what certainty means to them, how they come to be certain of anything . . ." (480). "Now I am not really caring any more anyway about this thing . . ." (543). "To-night I came to be certain about one group of them what kind they are . . ." (726). Goals, changes, progress reports; in the absence of any other clarity, these would have to serve.

Triads attracted Gertrude Stein, although not for any conscious symbolic reason. *The Making of Americans* contains many units of three, or if there are more, she accents the threeness as in a certain "family of women, a mother and there were three daughters" (98). The feminine triangle of *Things As They Are* had been followed by *Three Lives*. In *The Making of Americans* there are the three Hersland children (Martha, Alfred, David); the three Dehning children (Julia, George, Hortense); the three Shilling women; the three girls in the family just cited; there are the Richardsons, "this family the father and the two children Eddy and Lilly, all three of them had religion in them"; there are Mrs. Hersland's "three seamstresses" otherwise known as the "three sets of women who did her dress-making," one of whom was "the woman who had the three daughters . . ." (109, 192,

201, 193). The Hersland children have "three governesses." During childhood Alfred Hersland plays with "the Banks boys who lived near him, there were three of them" (531). To stop the disturbing flux of life, Gertrude Stein eagerly seized upon such simple numerical unities.

Her attraction to threes manifested itself in the rhetoric of her prose as well. While considering three girls, she ejected a flurry of triplets, as in this portion of a long sentence describing their mother's relationship to them:

> . . . first they were in (1) Anna then in (2) Cora and then in (3) Bertha and they were (1) never to the mother a history of her, they were (2) never to her a history inside her, there was (3) never in her any connection inside her with a (1) past or (2) present or a (3) future, these changes in the girls with her were (1) like all the objects around her, (2) like the making of dresses to her, (3) like the (1) changing of the eating from the green stuff they brought to her, through the (2) cooking that was natural for her to the (3) eating that came after . . . (101; numerals added)

This experiment in schematization did not last long at this point. Gertrude Stein turned restlessly to yet another family, the Richardsons. They shared a concern for religion—"it was of them like eating and sleeping and washing" (109). But after a brief series of simpleminded distinctions such as that eating and sleeping are not like loving and breathing, she abandoned her attempt to master this family too. She promised that their character would emerge later "in the history of the Hersland children as they come to know it in them" (112). But it never did.

These foraging expeditions into her childhood neighborhood were minimally successful. Confusing to read, they begin abruptly, revolve through a series of mindless declarations, then are as abruptly dropped. Encountering such portentous observations as "washing is very common, almost every one does some washing," and unaware of what came before and after *The Making of Americans,* one might justifiably dismiss these pages with contempt (111). But even though these psychological analyses were unsatisfactory, Gertrude Stein was learning in these pages how to construct a sentence that was adequate to the task of conveying the complexity of her ideas about a given subject.

When she started the book, Gertrude Stein's paragraphs ran a normal ten to fifteen lines, with one-sentence paragraphs occasionally interspersed. But as she began to add minute variations to her character descriptions, her core paragraphs expanded. By page sixty, the norm was up to twenty-five lines in length and after page one hundred, paragraphs of fifty lines were not uncommon. These giant paragraphs continued through the rest of the book. Their words winding like thread up and down a spindle, their effect is soporific.

Sometimes the paragraph was one protracted sentence, although this was not typical of Gertrude Stein's practice (62, 120). Rather, her mind tended to move in spasmodic units. These were conceptually distinct, but because of a lack of punctuation, they were artificially forced together. "Some just go ahead with the vacant being lying there in them they go ahead and it gives to such of them a being like an anxious feeling but it is not fear in such of them it is only the vacant being in them . . ." (202).

Such long, rambling compound sentences were one means of pulling together the disarray of her consciousness. Another means, more regularly used, was the diagrammatic sentence, such as the following:

> Men in their living have many things inside them they have in them, each one of them has it in him, his own way of feeling himself important inside in him, they have in them all of them their own way of beginning, their own way of ending, their own way of working, their own way of having loving inside them and loving come out from them, their own way of having anger inside them and letting their anger come out from inside them, their own way of eating, their own way of drinking, their own way of sleeping, their own way of doctoring. (150)

The Making of Americans contains thousands of similarly constructed sentences. Yet, if Gertrude Stein depended upon the stylized patterning of her sentences, so thoroughly did she vary those patterns that she undermined the very stability they were meant to provide. The reasons for her extensive variations are not clear. Their source may be neglect, or caprice; or the variants may be vestiges of her stylistic deficiencies. A direct line of awkwardness runs from the Radcliffe themes through the imitations of the foreign-born in *Three Lives* down to *The Making of Americans*. Still, if the coherence of diagrammatic composition answered Gertrude Stein's appetite for certainty, her irregularities may be regarded as her acknowledgement of the mysterious complications of the world.

In any case, Gertrude Stein did use patterned sentences extensively from 1906 to 1912. She would, for example, mention the different ways in which a person might feel important. Then she would point out that the feeling of importance could assist in conquering loneliness in a person. That led to an outline of the different ways in which one might feel lonesome—all of this interlocked and unmistakably diagrammed (156–7). At times, she alternated positives and negatives. Some are certain, some are not certain, some know, some do not know, and so on. Another common tactic she used was to locate a person in relation to a particular condition. "Some smell something" begins one paragraph. "Some smell a good many things." The paragraph develops and complicates the act of smelling until at last it reaches the subject of the particular section in which it occurs. Of him, she concludes, "David Hersland was in a way not such a one" (850).

At such moments Gertrude Stein came close to parodying herself, for this earnest inventorying encouraged foolish results. "He was then in the beginning of the middle part of his middle living" (252). That says no more than that a man was about forty. At this time there is virtually no humor in Gertrude Stein's prose. Later, when she gained self-confidence, her playfulness manifested itself in just such verbal drollery. "We understand that you undertake to overthrow our undertaking" ("An Elucidation," *P&P*, 253).

In addition to schematizing her sentences in search of precision, Gertrude Stein reduced her vocabulary. She remarked in *The Making of Americans* that she preferred to use a restricted vocabulary, for that permitted her to explore the nuances of a few words fully. "I like it when I am feeling many ways of using one word in writing" (539). Some words appeared momentarily then vanished forever. Others turned up again and again. Throughout the book tension is felt between those words that convey wholeness and assurance and those that express tentativeness. "Completely" and "certainly" must fight off the threatened encroachments of "almost" and "in a way." Gertrude Stein's quest for demonstrable and final truth was perpetually undermined by her awareness of exceptions until she found a way to incorporate them into her writing.

As Gertrude Stein approached the end of this section of Part One of *The Making of Americans,* she realized that one of the problems she had in understanding her father was that he, like all people, only gradually established his basic character. This led her to several propositions about identity:

1. Although "there are many millions of them," human beings do fall into a finite number of categories or "kinds."

2. Each man has a different amount of his kind in him, "and

74

this makes a different being of each one of the many millions of that kind of them . . ."

3. Each man also has mixed in him portions of other "kinds" of being.

4. Despite this exceedingly complicated mixture, each person has some strong attribute, "the bottom in them the kind of being in them the kind of being in them that makes them."

5. "Bottom nature" manifests itself through repeated actions.

6. If one is sufficiently observant, "Slowly, more and more, one gets to know them as the repeating comes out in them" (136–9).

Until Gertrude Stein could establish how many "kinds" of people there were, and then furnish a verifiable technique for identifying them, these propositions lacked objective validity. They were really no more than expressions of hope. As such, these articles of faith were of practical use in improving her morale. They took into account the extraordinary diversity of human character, while at the same time formalizing Gertrude Stein's confidence that she might yet be able to order the world.

The last section of Part One of *The Making of Americans* moves with greater assurance through new theories, analyses of others, and self-exploration. In it, Gertrude Stein was able to apply the propositions she had painfully developed.

The section opens with a review and elaboration of the term "bottom nature." It rapidly bifurcates into the categories of "dependent independent" and "independent dependent." Gertrude Stein reached those polarities through meditation upon her mother who, although basically a withdrawn and passive woman, also had a touch of pride. Like her, Gertrude Stein concluded, "many . . . are very dependent all through their living but a little in them is an independent feeling . . ." (165). The opposite classification followed inevitably.

One of the chief identifying characteristics of these groups was that the first fight by resisting, the second by attacking. Antithetical classifications had an overwhelming allure for Gertrude Stein. As late as 1945 in *Wars I Have Seen*, she said that William James impressed upon her that there is a will to live but also a will to destroy "and the two like everything are in opposition" (64). She habitually fell back upon crude opposites, then with her sensibility tormented by qualifications and exceptions, she would begin to elaborate the polar positions until once more she was swimming for her life in a welter of disconnection.

In *The Making of Americans*, "bottom nature" soon changes into "bottom being" and "their own kind of being," then opens out to resemble a theory of humors. In some people, being is "stronger in some parts than in other parts," and "some have it in them drier, wetter, stronger, weaker . . ." (361).

It would be ill-advised to try to reconcile all of the references Gertrude Stein makes to a person's basic character. Later in the book the reader is exposed to preposterous refinements of her characterology. "This one . . . was of the dependent independent resisting murkily engulfing kind of them but . . . this was rather gently and a little drily in him . . ." (551). She specifies types of attacking, among them "sensitive attacking, and trembling attacking, and quivering attacking, and obstinate attacking, and rushing attacking . . ." (605). Such a list can only come to an arbitrary end.

At times she realized that her ambition had exceeded her grasp. "I can never really be knowing all the ways there are of feeling living . . ." (625). Not only did she find it troublesome to know where some persons fit in, but "it is hard to describe what I mean by the names I give to them" (192). Sometimes, she said, "it gets all mixed up to me," whereupon "all of a sudden I lose the meaning out of all of them . . ." (335). The sheer volume of sensation threatened to engulf her. "Sometimes there are so many ways of seeing each one that I must stop looking" (337). Confused, baffled, despairing, even she was driven to conclude that her work was all "only an arbitrary choosing . . ." (341).

Moods such as these were transitory. But each time they came to wreck her tranquillity, they dramatized the dilemma of working with tools insufficient for the job at hand.

As Gertrude Stein worked with her description of the Hersland family, she soon centered upon the friendship of one of her mother's seamstresses with another woman. They are partners in a dressmaking business. Three things about their relationship fascinate Gertrude Stein: their affection for one another; a premarital pregnancy; and the temperamental balance of their partnership.

Mary Maxworthing is the older by five years, the more cheerful, and the better businesswoman (214–15). Mabel Linker is the superior seamstress, who needs someone "to keep her going, to start her, to arrange for her, to hold her down when flightiness seized her" (209,

216). Mary idolizes Mabel. "She liked to write down when she was sitting idling, 'Mabel is an angel, angel Mabel,' and this showed her feeling" (214). A few pages later, Gertrude Stein wrote, "As I was saying . . . she would write when she sat idling, 'angel Mabel, Mabel is an angel,' and this showed her feeling" (229). I do not know whether the discrepancy in the quotation should be attributed to error, to capriciousness, or to deliberate contrivance. The same thing happens in the famous umbrella anecdote too. There, the clinching cry of the angry child is reported in three different versions: "I have throwed the umbrella in the mud," "I did throw the umbrella in the mud," and "I have thrown the umbrella in the mud" (388, 394, 407).

Whether deliberately intended or not, these examples illustrate the nature of memory, which is perfectly capable of holding several versions of the same incident. And since the "actual" statement is nowhere as important as its reality in the mind, Gertrude Stein provided one version that is grammatically incorrect in the manner of a child, one which is emphatic (I *did* throw . . .), and one which is a calm announcement of the action. Does the accuracy of a recording matter? Of effective importance is what we remember. A particular occasion may evolve in time from a proud one to one of faint embarrassment (as some childhood feat which in adulthood seems mere posturing); or a memory may sink into oblivion, disappearing altogether, or leaving only an arm sticking out; or a memory may answer wearing different guises, depending on how we call it out. All of these possibilities are suggested by Gertrude Stein's practice.

Gertrude Stein's writing easily arouses this kind of speculation. If being stimulated into reconsidering one's modes of existence is regarded as valuable, then her work is justified, even though in many instances she neglected to examine the implications of her examples herself.

When Mary Maxworthing unexpectedly finds herself pregnant, Gertrude Stein resolutely ignores the male responsibilities. Mary simply "had something happen to her that surprised every one who knew her" (211). She angers her young physician by denying she knows what is the matter with her. He responds sharply, "You'd better get him to marry you" (212). In her two-page visit to the doctor, suddenly out of the haze of repetition and ruminative murmuring, a realistic incident comes into focus. Mabel cares for Mary throughout her pregnancy, which terminates unsuccessfully. As was the rule when

Gertrude Stein referred to sexual details, the references to the foetus are all slightly twisted. Mary "had a baby in her," then "at six months the baby passed out of her. She almost died when this happened to her" (219).

What should be said of this intimate history? First, it is notable in its length. Although it is of minimal relevancy to an understanding of the Hersland family, over thirty pages are devoted to it. Second, the underlying subject is the affectionate relationship of two women who are individual and independent, yet complementary to one another. Third, a pregnancy is fatal to the child and very nearly so for the mother.

At one point in her description of Mary Maxworthing, Gertrude Stein displays a significant insensitivity to what her terminology was making her say. "She had not a very large bottom in her to her, she had a little sensitive bottom in her . . ." (215). But she was skating along the edge of repressed material. However euphemistic Gertrude Stein was about sexual experience, it maintained its centrality in her work. For example, she described the seventeen-year-old Julia Dehning going horseback riding regularly with a middle-aged man. "Then too Jameson grew gradually less comradely, more intimate, and gross." Such incidents, Gertrude Stein concluded, "are common in the lives of all young women" (20). Here, her meaning is reasonably clear. But at other moments, she revealed even more, although she was operating on intuition alone. Consider the metaphorical origin of the following description of the "attacking" nature. "It can be slimy, gelatinous, gluey, white opaquy kind of thing and it can be white and vibrant, and clear and heated and this is all not very clear to me . . ." (349).

We are observing the following phenomenon: Gertrude Stein commenced writing in a state of manifest tumult. As she uncovered her personal feelings she tried to extrapolate them into universal statements. In time she would give over this attempt and assent to a record of the subjective life as the true one. At the present point, we find her somewhere near halfway in this process.

One sign of her incipient reconciliation to her private vision came when she confessed that she preferred to write about women. "It is clearer . . . I know it better, a little, not very much better" (205). Although hedged with qualification, the admission is an important one for she did prefer to see through the subjective prism of her own consciousness.

The idea that repetition could be revelatory slowly took hold of

Gertrude Stein. Discovery of a person's bottom nature required prolonged observation of his behavior. In time, certain traits manifested themselves over and over. "Slowly every one in continuous repeating, to their minutest variation, comes to be clearer to some one" (284). She was understandably enthusiastic about the idea of repetition as the key to character, for unlike the inert concept of "bottom nature," it allowed for movement and change. And yet, the movement was not random; it fell into patterns. "Repeating is a wonderful thing," she cried (284).

At its most intense, repetition produced a rhythmic sensation in Gertrude Stein. She referred to its "louder beating" and to the "steady pound of repeating" (305, 246). For a time she reproduced this pulsation in her writing. Rather than report her conclusions about a person's character, she attempted to get the very process of discovery down on paper. At one point she gave an open example of how she concentrated on a person. "This one then is not an easy one to be describing. I will begin a little slowly now to be thinking and then I will do a very little writing. To commence now with my thinking. I am thinking now of this one" (568). The following paragraph then actually began her characterization of the person as she conceived her. "This one is of the resisting kind in men and women, might have been of the engulfing kind of them, was not at all of the engulfing kind of them was only a resisting one, had a feeling of being an engulfing kind of them which made this one have very much emotion of dominating with stern action" (568). The idea of repetition temporarily restored her spirits. It made it seem possible again that "sometime there surely will be an ordered history of every one" (284).

What she still did not recognize was that her commitment to writing a narrative rather than a description, and to description of the past rather than to immediate description complicated her attempt to be all-inclusive. But it would be several years before she realized this and began to record her immediate impressions. Her attempts to cram everything in made her prose ponderous and wearing to read. Still, the advances she had made were impressive and generally comprehensible. She had progressed from the concept of "bottom nature" which she had reached at the end of the second section, through the independent-dependent categories, on to the paradox of variation within repetition. Through all this she experimented with the stylistic consequences of her theories. And on top of it all, she was purging her psyche of old ghosts.

Gertrude Stein began the second major part of *The Making of Americans,* entitled "Martha Hersland," by reducing her immediate goals to more modest proportions. "This is now a little of what I love and how I write it. Later there will be much more of it" (289). She still offered plentiful assurances that "sometime" a complete history would be prepared. The insecure condition of her morale forbade enunciation of certain failure. But the problems she had encountered in trying to characterize anyone adequately had made her more cautious. Although she noted resemblances everywhere, she still found a fixed and final identification of a person, "a completed understanding," hard to come by (291). Composed as they are of a mixture of "many kinds," people could be "baffling" for a long time. It required persistent listening to pick out the repeated "most delicate graduation" and "gentlest flavor" of them (292–3). The bottom nature, she now decided, does not often "do very loud repeating." Keeping alert for it could be an arduous and tiresome task. "Listening to repeating is often irritating, listening to repeating can be dulling" (302). "Sometimes," she said, "I get a little tired of it, usually I am always ready to do it, always I love it" (304). Her persistence brought about moments when comprehension of a person's character enlarged in her until it was unendurable. "Sometimes I am filled up so full with that one that I must tell it then to every one . . ." (325).

The pages summarized here are tiresome in the extreme. But in one long and clearly organized paragraph Gertrude Stein outlined the psychological process of discovery. These were the stages as she now understood them:

1. One notes that some action of a person—a way he has of listening, the sound of his laughter—resembles that of another.

2. Such resemblances accumulate until their number becomes more confused than helpful.

3. Slowly, however, the resemblances fall into "an ordered system." This may be very different from what one had at first anticipated.

4. But patience and a resolve never to eliminate any evidence was finally rewarded with the satisfying sensation of having comprehended the whole of a person.

She grasped this formula gratefully, for writing the book made her "nervous" and "unhappy." She even had moments when she felt that her conceptions were only a "fabrication" (348, 362).

The second section of Part Two covers ground already discussed as part of Gertrude Stein's biography. In it, we learn that Martha was of very little interest to her father or anyone else in her childhood; that she was urged into sex play by a neighbor boy, but that, being nervous, cautious, and confused, the result was not very successful and the little boy forgot about her; that she annoyed her father considerably by resisting him; that she feared her governess, Madeline Wyman; that she also irritated her father by being a poor housekeeper, cook, and dressmaker; that her father was suspicious of her going out evenings with friends; that she still was not of much interest to anyone, except maybe a couple of evenings with Harry Brenner, although not really; and that having seen a man hit a red-faced woman with an umbrella, she decided to go to college, was tutored, and left (408–26).

So summarized, it is clear what the main emphases are in these autobiographical portions: the tension between her father and herself; the indifference of the world to her; and the hypnotic puzzle of sex.

At the point that Martha Hersland left for college, Gertrude Stein awkwardly spliced her story to the previously written Hodder episode. At college, she falls in love with and subsequently marries Phillip Redfern, the fictional version of the professor who wins the college dean's friend away from her.

Elizabeth Sprigge has identified Phillip Redfern as Leon Solomons, Gertrude Stein's old chum and collaborator at Harvard (42). This identification is a plausible one for the material immediately preceding and following the adulterous episode, that is, the material Gertrude Stein had to invent to bridge the Martha Hersland material and the Hodder story. Martha and Phillip Redfern were "students in the same studies in the same class" at college (432). They have no romantic exchanges. The one scene with sexual overtones describes Redfern's surprise when Martha permits another boy to rest his head in her lap. The following day, Redfern inquires of her, "Was it alright for Davidson to do so yesterday. I almost believed it was my duty to knock him off" (433). They have no courtship. Suddenly in the narrative the marriage is announced as being of two years' duration already (433).

Their marital incompatibility is ascribed to her inadequacy to his needs. Her mind was too narrow, her manner too insistent and lacking in grace for him (433–4). After their separation, although they never lived together again, "always she was expecting it to begin again . . . and always she was studying and striving and travelling and working. And then he was dead and then she knew they would not live together again" (470).

Solomons had left Harvard in 1896 for the University of California at Berkeley. In the fall of 1897 he returned to Cambridge where he took his doctorate and began teaching in the fall of 1898 at the University of Wisconsin. In 1900, Solomons died.

Redfern too dies young (471). Other than this fact though, Gertrude Stein fails to specify the details of his experience. We do not know what attraction Cora Dounor had for him, nor what degree of intimacy they shared. We are not told when the Redferns separated, nor what caused his death. In one contradictory paragraph summarizing the rest of his life, he seems to have lived a long time, but surely because here she was thinking of Alfred Hodder. "For the rest of his days he was a literary man and sometimes a politician. . . . It was interesting to many . . . to see him go up again and again . . . only to meet with certain defeat" (445). The whole is fragmentary and dreamlike, because Gertrude Stein was trying to fuse two incompatible characters, Solomons and Hodder.

She could not avoid swerving into her own problems. During her discussion of Redfern she launched into a description of the "fateful twenty-ninth year." It was a time when "all the forces that have been engaged through the years of childhood, adolescence and youth in confused and sometimes angry combat range themselves in ordered ranks . . ." (436–7). Until then "one plunges here and there with energy and misdirection during the . . . making of a personality" (437). Gertrude Stein's twenty-ninth year came in 1903, the year she wrote *Things As They Are* and permanently expatriated herself. For Redfern it was the year that he separated from his wife and quit teaching. Gertrude Stein could identify fully with the aspirations of Hodder-Redfern. "He longed for a more vital human life than to be an instructor of youth, his theme was humanity, his desire was to be in the great world and of it . . . he preferred the criticism of life in fiction to the analysis of the mind in philosophy" (437).

The confused progress of the Martha Hersland section is attributable to several causes, each of which is central to Gertrude Stein's character. She was not an inventive writer, so was obliged to depend upon material furnished by experience. (She identified herself at several points in the book with the dependent independent party [595, 301].) Although capable of strong emotion, she correctly regarded herself as more passive and inert than active. "I am fairly slow in action and in feeling . . ." (573). It being almost impossible for her to generate original ideas, she depended on circumstance for inspiration. At the same time she imposed her own preoccupations such as the importance of the twenty-ninth year, upon her fictional characters. Consequently, in "Martha Hersland," this most autobiographical of sections, Gertrude Stein completely lost sight of her original intention of producing a history of the formation of Americans. Her imagination was in the grip of compellingly personal details.

Part Three, titularly devoted to "Alfred and Julia Hersland" actually discusses them very little. When it does, their characters are used as an excuse to introduce contemporary matters, people Gertrude Stein had met, the way she felt. She had already exhausted what she knew of Alfred and Julia's marriage in the first part of the book. Furthermore, her prolonged experience in Paris with the rich variability of human character had made her dissatisfied with her earlier attempts to freeze behavior into rigid categories. Her characterizations now grew looser, opening out into catalogues, although these still depended a good deal upon pedestrian antitheses such as "being a nice one" and "being not a nice one." She also relied upon various qualifications, as in this shrewd distinction between "being failing for a reason" and "being just failing." Sometimes her distinctions represented nothing more than specified idiosyncracies—"being one tired of ocean bathing before they have really been in more than twice in a season" (625; see also 644).

As she embarked upon her portrait of Alfred Hersland she realized that she was "not completely full up with him" (513). Therefore she was obliged to wait. Shortly came an announcement of success. "It is all filling in me now to over flowing" (514). It was not, however. Some thirty pages later, she prepared once more to discuss Alfred Hersland's being, but then held off again. "I am not yet quite full up with the being in him" (541). Indistinctly she was beginning to realize the disintegration of her hopes for a universal characterology. For a time she had felt she possessed people as wholes. Now "mostly every one now in me is in pieces inside me" (519).

While awaiting the gestation of Alfred Hersland, she decided to talk about six men who were of his "kind," but manifested it differently (523–5). Later, as a means of maintaining the illusion of controlled analysis, she took some character trait associated with Alfred Hersland like vanity or inquisitiveness, then elaborated on all the different ways she could remember that different people exhibited that same trait (556–61).

These tortured writhings are irritating to endure. But they constituted part of what Gertrude Stein had to experience in order to reach full subjectivity in her writing. She was moving away from history and memory into the present. "There were to-night eight of them . . ." (679). "I was seeing one to-day who reminded me very much of another one" (607). Alfred Hersland was not even invoked to justify these last associations. The relationship of people in her mind was sufficient excuse for discussing them. She recognized a new need in her for a social life that would provide her material. Now that she had exhausted the past, conversation appealed to her as it never had before. "I am needing something . . . to give me enough stimulation to keep me completely going on . . ." (662).

Personal observations proliferate in "Alfred and Julia Hersland." Gertrude Stein keeps the reader regularly informed on the state of her being. Many of her reports are gloomy. "I am just now altogether a discouraged one" (548). The problem was usually her inability to capture anyone completely, let alone everyone. Yet, at the cost of suffering, she seemed to be getting some perspective on her project. She knew she had been wrong at times (573). She realized that "I have not been very interesting in explaining being in men and women" (541). Her goal was not necessarily attractive to everyone. "I can understand that knowing there are kinds in men and women would not be a comfort to every one" (581).

In spite of her expressed discouragement, this section has a tone of unprecedented equanimity. Its source was very probably Alice Toklas, who had learned to type in order that she might transcribe Gertrude Stein's manuscripts. At some point she caught up with her friend's production of *The Making of Americans*. Henceforth, she was copying the previous day's work. "Doing the typing of *The Making of Americans* was a very happy time for me. Gertrude talked over her work of the day, which I typed the following morning" (*WIR*, 54).*

This meant that Gertrude Stein at long last possessed the unknown reader whom she had addressed early in the book. Furthermore, she was now speaking almost directly to someone in her writing. That person was not an anonymous secretary but an affectionate companion. Therefore, when Gertrude Stein wrote that she was discouraged but would continue, that declaration had an immediate and concerned audience.

She was at the point of offering her personal impression as the most

* The rue de Fleurus household, which was composed of Leo and Gertrude Stein plus Alice Toklas, is discussed in Chapter 5, pp. 110–114.

faithful measure of truth. The book would then be more accurately entitled *The Making of An American*. If all Americans grow in the perilously uncertain way she had, then make one truly enough and you have made them all. She tells two anecdotes in succession that are clearly personal and rather eccentric experiences. Each is given general applicability by designating the subject as an anonymous "one."

The first concerns a person who has more milk delivered than he needs. But he reasons that if he falls ill, then he will need the extra milk, when it would be too late to order it. "In a kind of a way," writes Gertrude Stein, trying to elevate this irrational behavior, "this is very common, not about milk left, but about a way of feeling in living and a way of acting" (543). Typically, she does not argue the legitimacy of her assertion, but merely states it.

The second anecdote is also described as "very common." It concerns "one quite young one" who loves "another one" who is a brunette. But seeing a picture of "a blond one," he muses, "I could love that one." The other objects, "you just said you could only love a dark one." "Yes that is true but I think I could love that one" is the humanly inconsistent answer (543).

Gertrude Stein was losing the need to fit the life she observed into comprehensive schemes. Soon she would offer only what she wanted to. In her 1911 portrait of Mabel Dodge, for example, she wrote: "A bottle that has all the time to stand open is not so clearly shown when there is green color there" (*P&P*, 99). The phrasing is eccentric and the reference is not certain. Perhaps a bottle left open had accumulated a green mold within it which made it hard to see when it stood against a green background. In a sentence like this Gertrude Stein recorded her private ruminations, making only partial efforts to explain what roused them or caused their associative connections. The subjectivity had originated in her occasional addresses to the reader. These expanded into reports on her inner condition and her feelings about a particular person. By degrees she turned inward.

Part Three concludes with the announcement that not only is she finished with Alfred and Julia Hersland, but really that she is through describing people as she had previously done. This was the end "of telling about being having been . . ." (719). That was her farewell to the past.

With the fourth part, "David Hersland," the original plot concerning the Herslands, which had already receded into the background, totally disappears. David Hersland is presented in a vacuum, his only acquaintances being anonymous "somes" and "ones." The subject of Part Four is his character and death.

There is a familiar but perplexing story told in *The Autobiography of Alice B. Toklas* and repeated elsewhere *(ABT, 138; WIR, 55)*. As her friend Janet Flanner told it, "one day when she was writing *The Making of Americans,* she suddenly killed off the hero. She went to tell a friend and said, 'I've killed him.' 'My God, why?' 'I know all about him,' she answered, 'and about them and about everybody in that story.' " ("Introduction," *TWO,* xiii).

The identity of the book's hero is not immediately apparent. Only three central male figures die in it—the two David Herslands, father and son, and Phillip Redfern. None dies a specific death. No cause is given for any of their deaths, and those of the elder Hersland and of Redfern are mentioned incidentally. Mr. Hersland could be regarded as a "hero" only ironically. As for Redfern, although he might be regarded as a flawed hero, he dies too soon for Gertrude Stein to be proclaiming that she possessed knowledge about everyone in the story. David Hersland is the most satisfactory candidate. But, in what sense did Gertrude Stein kill him, and why?

Although David Hersland too has been identified with Leon Solomons, aside from his early death, the resemblance is not compelling (Brinnin, 95). The bulk of the evidence points to the person who represented the final psychological obstacle Gertrude Stein had to overcome, namely her brother Leo.

David Hersland is the younger son, conceived after two older children have died. Leo's self-centered, articulate presence appears in this man who believes in special diets, clear thinking, beautiful women, and revealing precisely what he thinks (899, 732, 791). He frequently advises Martha, and even though she is ostensibly older than he in the book, "certainly she very often listened very much to him" (773, 873, 774). Like Leo, at the time Gertrude Stein was writing this part of the book, David Hersland falls in love. He was "telling it to her . . . and in a way it was not interesting to her . . ." (871). And Leo, who had become "more and more impressed by the supreme importance of nutrition and sexuality in the determination of human personality" did make Gertrude privy to his feelings about Nina Auzias, whom he would finally marry in 1921 *(Journey,* 36, 23, 85).

The self-sufficiency of Leo's egotism made his severe deafness seem to his sister only a physical manifestation of a long-standing psychical

86

condition. It appears in her observation that David Hersland "in a way" had no need for anyone to listen to him (788). He was one of those who "love themselves so much immortality can have no meaning for them . . ." (505). So, Gertrude Stein effectively killed him in her book.

The "David Hersland" part opens on an enigmatic note. Gertrude Stein says that she asks some people how they would feel if they were to discover "they had been born illegitimate." She is particularly interested in their feelings if they learned they had "low" blood in them (723). Thereupon a bland sentence ensues. "David Hersland was the younger son of Mr. David Hersland and Mrs. Hersland." Her imputation is in itself a form of assassination.

Before she turns to David himself though, she offers several long and contorted paragraphs, the first of which says that she is not certain that she can trust what she says when she is in love. This seems to be a cautious disclaimer before she imaginatively disposes of Leo for the sake of Alice. She also remarks that "some one said of some one who was a dead one" that "he does not know he is a dead one" (724). Shortly, it turns out that David Hersland "was dead before he came to the middle of his middle living" (725). When Leo left the rue de Fleurus permanently in 1911, he was thirty-nine.

Death has several significances in *The Making of Americans*. It contributes to Gertrude Stein's central fear of the blankness of existence: her realization that once she never existed, that she might never have existed had it not been for the death of the two Stein children preceding her, and that she might be snuffed out permanently at any moment. The anguish of that potential obliteration never left her. For "some" children, she said, the idea was "completely terrifying" (796).

Still, as a small girl Martha Hersland had sometimes wished she were dead. The paradox was that her desire for the peace of death was because it would alleviate suffering, but that suffering was caused by a fear of death. Gertrude Stein indicated the continuity of her dread by the phrase "then now." She noted that people often say, had I died when I was a baby, "I would not then now have to think of being frightened by dying . . ." (399). With adulthood comes the realization of death's finality. "Dead is dead. To be dead is to be really dead . . . and that is the end of them" (498). Although Gertrude Stein granted the possibility that death might be illusory, most of her comments come down hard on the side of its certainty and its permanence.

In the case of David Hersland, the meaning of death is somewhat confused because Gertrude Stein has multiple intentions for it. In her preliminary notes David Hersland was a man haunted by morbidity—"constantly surrounded by thought of death—puts it away from him—then endeavors to embrace it . . . to conquer it, almost, never quite" (Katz, 180, n. 3). Gertrude Stein never actually prepared his death scene, but her notes for it read: ". . . he decides on cancer . . . ultimately kills himself, through operation like Leon's" (Katz, 190). At this point she was evidently thinking of Leon Solomons as a model for David Hersland. In fact, according to Katz, in an early draft, David Hersland even has a "desultory" affair with "Pauline Sandys"—that is, with a girl bearing one of Gertrude Stein's pseudonyms (189).

However, in the finished version of the David Hersland story, death takes on a rather different meaning. It represents David's failure to grow. He becomes intellectually fixed, a condition to which Gertrude Stein referred in *Two* as not hearing, as psychic deafness. In this respect David Hersland is plainly Leo Stein.

Gertrude Stein had sometimes feared an analogous stultification in herself. At one point in the book, she confessed herself miserable because she was pretty certain that she would end by failing. That would make her "more nearly a completely dead one" (609). Death in this aspect then was a form of psychological blockage. But the balance was tipping in her direction. She no longer felt isolated, for she was now regularly receiving groups of people. Leo was absent more frequently on extended trips, so that his sister found herself the independent mistress of their salon. Consequently, "some who are young men and young women are listening to me now very often" (727). She deliberately contrasted them with the people who "listened" to David Hersland. She in the present tense; he in the past.

Although alive when young, David Hersland became "one being existing" as opposed to "being living" (831, 801). Gertrude Stein made existence alone equivalent to death when she observed that "certainly David Hersland was dying, certainly David Hersland was commencing being existing" (840). In her covert and imprecise way, she said that one (she) came very close to telling one (Leo) that he "will certainly never be doing the thing that one is needing to be one going on being living" (824). "Being living" was the full functioning of the human being rather than the dessicated operation of the intellect alone. In its ideal form it involved "clear thinking and complete emotion and adequate expression and absolute conviction" (779).

Even Gertrude Stein sometimes grew restless with her evasiveness. "I mean, I mean and that is not what I mean . . . I mean something . . . not any one is . . . certain of that thing . . . I mean, I mean, I know what I mean" (782). The toils of discretion could be irksome.

The section on "David Hersland" concludes with a return to his death and people's reactions to it. Even though he was now dead, "some were not certain there was any difference in anything . . ." (904). Gertrude Stein was singing her peculiar elegy as much for *The Making of Americans* as for David Hersland. She had almost reached the end of the book. How did she know? Her explanation after the fact was an admirable example of rationalization. "I decided that since it could be done what was the use of doing it" (*EA*, 266). The opposite was closer to the truth. Since it could not be done, why continue? By this time, *The Making of Americans* was a thoroughly ruined enterprise, which is not to say a useless one. It had been invaluable as a proving-ground for Gertrude Stein, a kind of psychological daybook and laboratory of style. Preserved on its pages was the raw material that generated the propositions rising out of it: "How can anything be different from what it is" (672).

Her alternate explanation of why she ended the book was more candid. "Anyway you always have to stop doing something sometime" (*EA*, 266). There was a time for ending, and she sensed she had reached it. So she tried to convince herself of it by announcing it. "Some one has done something. It is a completed thing, a quite complete thing. It has a beginning, a middle and an end. It is all done" (860).

The fifth and last part of *The Making of Americans* is a brief epilogue entitled "History of a Family's progress." It is a crescendo of repetitive abstractions without a single name or personal reference. "Somes" and "anys" dominate paragraphs that are close-packed with declarative sentences. Some are certain, some know, some believe. Anyone can become old, can become dead. There are many different kinds of people in this world, and they can be listed and described. There are families, some of whose members are living, some dead. "Family living is being existing" (920). The whole complex exists in the mind of the one who remembers family living accurately, for it sums up human existence. Gertrude Stein strained to finish what she had started, to provide an American family that would represent the American experience. But now it was contained in a single mind. And yet, Gertrude Stein's awareness of the limitations of her knowledge persisted to the end. The last clause of the book makes a modest claim. "Some can remember something of some such thing" (925).

Gertrude Stein had begun the first extended draft of *The Making of Americans* with the stated ambition of writing an epic work on the formation of the American character. But she soon found herself unwilling and indeed unable to carry out her plan. Her chronicle of typical families yielded to a theory of universal character types which then turned into a covert analysis of her own life and present situation. After the crude polarities with which she sought to categorize human character had been qualified to the point of parody, she turned her attention to creating a style that could contain the jungle of contradictions her sensibility perceived. Expending prodigious amounts of energy, she thrashed erratically towards innovation.

5

The Making of Americans is a great sow of a work surrounded by sucklings. Having familiarized ourselves with the gross contours of the parent body, it is now time to consider its progeny. They represent fresh stylistic possibilities conceived by Gertrude Stein as she composed the mother work. After their creation, she rejected some and developed some further; still others she later synthesized into new combinations.

The first full draft of *The Making of Americans* had been undertaken in 1906. It occupied Gertrude Stein's attention exclusively until 1908, at which time she began writing portraits. The following year she started *A Long Gay Book,* which in 1910 was succeeded by *Many Many Women* and *Two.* Between 1911 and 1912 she summed up many of the techniques she had developed in half a dozen years of experimentation in a long, radical piece entitled *G.M.P.* And by 1912 she had added the still-life to her repertoire, in the series published as *Tender Buttons.*

The early portraits very much resemble the characterizations found in *The Making of Americans,* but with the important difference that they are not connected to the family history. Portraiture was the means by which Gertrude Stein broke away from the tyranny of the narrative form which demanded of her what she could not furnish, a story. The portrait permitted her to do what she preferred, to concentrate upon the individual character. At the same time, it absolved her of the need to relate her observations to a larger system of classification.

A few of her early portraits considered large groups of people, such as the Italian nation. Others presented the relationships of small groups of people. A sizable number were portraits of single individuals. Her dominant movement was towards the particular.

"Italians" concerns all the people of that country. Virtually unique

91

in this, it draws upon Gertrude Stein's personal observations, for she had visited Italy regularly from 1896 until 1912. When she wrote it, she still believed in representative types. "If one knew any of them one knew all of them" (*G&P*, 46). She characterized Italians with the same confidence in stereotypes as she had the Negroes, Germans, and New Englanders. For her they were all small, dark, harsh, sweet, quick people with long fingernails who stared at you. Her best observation was that because of their perpetual optimism, Italians were always looking forward to something happening. Hence, "they are ones waiting quickly" (*G&P*, 46).

Her two other large group portraits are "Bon Marché Weather" and "Flirting at the Bon Marché." The first evokes the panorama of customers in the Parisian department store as they discuss the weather and their purchases. The second, which has nothing overtly to do with flirting, considers the tedium of some people's lives, which they hope to alter by shopping. The result is predictable. "In some some changing, in some not very much changing" (*TWO*, 355).*

For these early portraits, Gertrude Stein more commonly chose to describe small groupings. Such pieces were truly exercises, skeletal in structure, mechanical in execution. People were squared off against one another according to their dominant qualities. Then she ran through a variety of minimally changing permutations. For example, "Four Protégés" is a diagrammatic description of four men who were expected to succeed, but did not. For such portraits, her basic technique was to introduce the group, then treat each member in turn. So here, the first protégé was beautifully strong but no one wanted that; the second didn't work to be strong and was dead; the third was strong and working, but still didn't succeed in living; and the fourth didn't work, was beautifully strong, and remained dissatisfied and unsuccessful.

Other portraits of the period like "Four Dishonest Ones," "A Kind

---

* Janet Flanner gives a brief account of the genesis of these and other early portraits in her introduction to *Two*. Unfortunately, her information, while interesting and very likely authoritative, has little or nothing to do with the portraits as they appear in print.

It is also worth noting that the *Yale Catalogue* lists the two Bon Marché portraits at the end of the period 1908–12. If they were composed in 1912, then it becomes of more than casual significance that Picasso completed a painting-collage in the spring of 1913, entitled "Au Bon Marché." It is reproduced as plate number 24 in Gertrude Stein's *Picasso*. Coincidence, shared interest, influence, or collaboration?

of Women," "Men," "Five or Six Men," and "A Family of Perhaps Three" all deal schematically with people knotted in family relationships, intimate friendships, and professional aspirations, especially concerning the arts. These persons are compared in their relative success or failure at achieving identity or "being." Gertrude Stein was obsessed with the various ways in which a person may fail to mature. Her favorite summary phrases were "succeeding" and "being living."

Mechanical as the basic form of these group portraits was, they still contained some mysteries. Just as there is no evidence of flirting in "Flirting at the Bon Marché," so there is no indication of dishonesty in "Four Dishonest Ones." "Five or Six Men" is accurately titled, for a series of men is ticked off over its course. But while it is possible to determine that she had shifted from one man to another, it is far from clear where the precise divisions occur. There are indeed five—possibly six—men described. When "A Family of Perhaps Three" finally settles down, it treats two sisters, but it opens with a disconcerting blur. "When they were younger there may have been three of them sisters, and a mother. When they were younger there may have been three of them one a brother, and a mother. When they were younger there were certainly two of them, sisters, and a mother" (G&P, 331).

The uncertainty in that portrait may emanate from any of several sources. It may be caused by the narrator's lack of information about the background of the sisters. It may be employed to disguise the subject of the portrait. It may be a deliberate challenge to the reader's complacency. More likely, all of these causes are involved. At any rate, the unexpected was typical in Gertrude Stein's writing and turned up in the smallest details. For example, the punctuation is accurate in the phrase quoted a moment ago—"there may have been three of them sisters . . ." Yet, a moment later, she punctuated an analogous phrase conventionally—"two of them, sisters . . ."

The first of the single portraits was "Ada" according to Gertrude Stein, although the *Yale Catalogue* shows it as the eleventh in a group of twenty-five written between 1908 and 1912.* "Ada" is a portrait of Alice Toklas. Its style is distinctly mixed. By and large it is written

---

* "Ada" is dated "the winter of 1908–9" by Janet Flanner (*TWO*, x). Katz dates it December 1910 (144). Its genesis is described in *ABT*, 139. It is one of Gertrude Stein's works the manuscript of which is largely in Alice Toklas's hand. See Chapter 11, p. 210–211 for a discussion of that fact's significance.

with the factual solidity of early parts of *The Making of Americans,* but it also contains some incremental repetition. Numerous details about Ada's brother and father are offered, and later the portrait explains that Ada has been telling "some one" these stories for a long time. At bottom though, the portrait is a love poem, describing the idyllic relationship existing between Ada and "the some one who was loving" her (*G&P*, 16).

As Gertrude Stein depersonalized her prose, the "ones" and "somes" proliferated bewilderingly. But for a time, "some one" seemed to refer to the author. There is no doubt about it in "Ada," and the ascription clarifies a more problematic piece, "Rue de Rennes." A much more complicated piece of prose than "Ada," what it comes down to is that "some one" is "frightened" by "something." That something is "a way of living," of "being living." Some consider it "dreary," some "dirty," some "pleasant," some "important," and so on. For "some one" though, it simply remains "frightening." And although no one else seems able to believe that it is frightening, "some one" keeps on "telling it again and again" (*TWO*, 349–50).

"Some one" also plays a major role in "Harriet Fear." This portrait describes a woman who was "afraid in being living." The name "Fear" is generic therefore, and stands for the character's main emotion. "Some one" who was normally fearful, ceased being afraid when she saw Harriet's fright. Eventually Harriet—"this one"—learns to do something which "some one" is also studying. This causes "some one" to hate and despise Harriet, although she never tells her so (*TWO*, 343–6).

"Harriet Fear" is a curious piece. Although contorted in its presentation and equivocal in its references—afraid of *what?* learning to do *what?*—it creates a feverish atmosphere of gossip, as when girls tell tales, but obscure their references with ellipticality. Concealment of private matters was one of the uses to which Gertrude Stein put her style. By sufficiently abstracting the material, she could include intimate details of her friends's lives in her writing without compromising herself or them.

Aside from "Ada," two other portraits, "Miss Furr and Miss Skeene" and "Storyette H. M." are unusually accessible because both are dominated by a narrative line. They are also both atypical.

"Miss Furr and Miss Skeene" is favored by commentators on Gertrude Stein because it successfully adapts her stylistic peculiarities to conventional ends. The story's elliptical references and ironic repetitions were imitated by Ernest Hemingway in several of his early stories, notably "Mr. and Mrs. Elliot." But Gertrude Stein herself turned away from such easy success. It did not represent the road she wished to travel, but was an incidental byway. And although her subsequent efforts were considerably drearier than "Miss Furr and Miss Skeene," they were also more principled. "If it can be done why do it"? she asked later (*LIA*, 157). Her prose was not meant to transport the freight of packaged emotion back and forth over established routes. It was exploratory, and that meant stumbles, long journeys in false directions, backtracking, and often, meager rations.

Still, the subtlety of "Miss Furr and Miss Skeene" had best be indicated to remind the scoffers of what Gertrude Stein could do when she wished to. The piece is a brief, lucid account of two women possessed of good voices. They meet while training to be singers, whereupon they live and are "gay" together. Eventually, Georgine Skeene goes to visit her mother and apparently never returns. But Helen Furr goes on being gay. "She was quite regularly gay. She told many then the way of being gay, she taught very many then little ways they could use in being gay. She was living very well, she was gay then, she went on living then, she was regular in being gay, she always was living very well and was gay very well and was telling about little ways one could be learning to use in being gay, and later was telling them quite often, telling them again and again" (*G&P*, 22).

In its repetitions, this last paragraph resembles any of a thousand Gertrude Stein produced. Here though, rather than emanating from the author, they seem to reflect Miss Furr's state of being. The abandoned Miss Furr is the weaker of the two women. Her voice is not quite so good as Miss Skeene's, and she has a family she does not care to visit. When Miss Skeene leaves her, she launches an insistent gaiety, keeping it up, even giving lessons on it. "Gay," which always had a faintly mocking edge to it, at the end turns ragged and hysterical as Miss Furr tries to endure her rejection, making this a pathetic portrait rather than, as both Elizabeth Sprigge and Carl Van Vechten have found it, a "charming" one (87; and *SW*, 562).

Still, the model for Miss Furr wrote a letter to Gertrude Stein in 1933, at which time she and Miss Skeene were living together. "Miss Furr still likes gay things," she said, "& being gay & wanting everybody & everything else to be gay" (Gallup, *Flowers*, 269). This suggests that either Gertrude Stein invented the abandonment or that there had been a reconciliation. Further, what I read as an ironic edge to "gay" was evidently not felt by Miss Furr herself.*

"Storyette H. M." is a title very much in the Gertrude Stein manner. As it happens, "H. M." refers to Henri Matisse (who is also the "M." in *G.M.P.*), but for the unprivileged reader, it could as well concern Hugo Münsterberg or anyone else. (See Katz, 124, for a notebook entry on this piece.) Gertrude Stein habitually played fast and loose with identifications. In another portrait written at this time entitled "Purrmann," the subject is referred to as "Carman" throughout, with no explanation why.

"Storyette" is a witty, one-paragraph account of a husband "going away to have a good time" (*P&P*, 40). The reiterated yet varied phrases of the conclusion mark a husband's pressing to gain his wife's approval of plans that make him—but not her—"glowing." So, "the one that was going was saying then, I am content, you are not content, I am content, you are not content, I am content, you are content, you are content, I am content" (*P&P*, 40). Such distillations of human psychology were rare for Gertrude Stein. Having found in the repetition of key words like "gay" and "content" a legitimate, if limited, technique of expression, Gertrude Stein proved indifferent to capitalizing on it.

The rest of the early portraits, like "Roche," "Julia Marlowe," and "Russell" are of minimal interest, because in them Gertrude Stein tried to eliminate as many specifics as possible in order to create a uniform prose surface. For example, in "Orta, Or One Dancing," she used a single distinctive feature as the motif for the portrait.† Orta Davray was "one believing in dancing having meaning" (*TWO*, 289). Dancing becomes the symbol of her life. "She was one being one. She was one having been that one. She was one going on being that one" (*TWO*, 287). Her unity is achieved by devotion to a single art. In particular, "she was then resembling some one, one who was not dancing, one who was writing . . ." (297). The repetitiveness of "Orta" suggests the intensity of her single-mindedness.

* There is one other possibility. "Gay" has long been slang for homosexual. Perhaps everyone understood precisely what was meant. The sketch certainly has sexual overtones of a particularly cynical sort throughout. Miss Furr made one more uninformative appearance in *A Long Gay Book*: "Miss Furr was one, she had come to be that one, she was keeping being that one" (*GMP*, 42).
† Alternate titles for this were "Orta Davray," "Alma Davray," and "Isadora Dora Do." The last suggests that the portrait had some connection with Isadora Duncan —whom the Steins knew well.

"Being living" reached the level of abstraction at which these early portraits aimed. Variant uses of it turned the surface of her prose flat and neutral.

> Some knowing this one were quite certain that this one was one not being living . . . ("Elise Surville," *TWO*, 318)

> This one was all his living being living and this was quite a satisfaction to quite a number who were living then. ("Hessel," *TWO*, 348)

> One might be one being more wonderful than ever in being one being living. ("Chalfin," *TWO*, 341)

The latter part of *The Making of Americans* also centered around words like "being," "living," and "remembering." Their value to Gertrude Stein was that they were sufficiently general for her to state something "true" without being obliged to attach the usual kinds of qualification required to describe the activity of individual people. For example, "family living," the phrase dominating the last section of the book, contained within itself a whole complex of social experience. But once she had conceived the phrase, Gertrude Stein no longer felt the need to enumerate all the contradictions and variations she perceived in the family. She was as grateful for words with "many meanings, many ways of being used," as she was for the discovery that "different ways of emphasising can make very different meanings in a phrase or sentence" (*MOA*, 539).

The multiplication of verbal nouns is particularly noteworthy. Gertrude Stein had early utilized the progressive form of the verb to extend the action. "As I said" became "As I was saying." But subject and verb were still separated by grammatical convention, even when present participles were placed in apposition to a subject. "She pursued her way expounding philosophy, imbibing beauty, desiring life" (*MOA*, 437). The action hung from the subject like a handbag.

Gertrude Stein's escape from this was the gerund, which at once represents an entity and a continuous action. Unity and movement were fused in what for a time became her favorite word-form. Her shift from narratives to portraits has its equivalent in her replacement of a noun and verb with a gerund. "Thinking," "owning," "ending," "finding," "feeling," "marrying," "beginning," "succeeding," "resisting," "believing," "forgetting," "asking," "loving"—these became the basic components of the abstract style of *The Making of Americans*.

Gertrude Stein created several unreadable styles, of which this was the first. Built from a simplified, abstract and repeated vocabulary, and utilizing participles, gerunds and impersonal pronouns moving with maddening deliberateness through diagrammatic sentences, its worst excesses were limited to half a dozen years in her career. This style suffers from what she designated as "insistence." Her next step was in the opposite direction, towards the discontinuities of the impressionable mind. In other words, sometimes Gertrude Stein's prose was irritating because it communicated too little too clearly, but at others it said too much too obscurely. Here is one extreme:

> Some in any family living are older ones than any other one. Some in any family living are younger ones than any other one. Some in any family living are not so old and not so young as any other one in family living. (*MOA*, 922)

Here is the other:

> A window has another spelling, it has "f" all together, it lacks no more then and this is rain, this may even be something else, at any rate there is no dedication in splendor. (*TB, SW*, 507)

Along with the portraits, Gertrude Stein also undertook an ambitious second work which she called *A Long Gay Book*. Her purpose in it was to regain a lost paradise, namely the integrity of self, lost in the process of becoming self-conscious. The first sentence of *A Long Gay Book* reads: "When they are very little just only a baby you can never tell which one is to be a lady" (*GMP*, 13). The condition of being a "lady" is never explicitly defined, but from what follows it becomes clear that it means the state of unity in an adult.

According to Gertrude Stein in *A Long Gay Book*, the human being begins as a "helpless" baby with "no conscious feeling" (13). Then at some point in their lives, people suddenly perceive that time has changed them. This historical perspective can cause a destructive self-consciousness. In some it creates "an uncertain curious kind of feeling." It demolishes their inner unity ("makes it all a broken world for them that they have inside them.") Along with that unity, their confidence in a personal immortality disappears (it "kills for them the everlasting feeling") (13). The significance of this description of the establishment of psychological insecurity is unmistakable. The instability of a self perceived as changing in time was to remain Gertrude Stein's main theme throughout her life.

A Long Gay Book, however, includes responses other than her own.

If some persons feel this insecurity, others presumably do not, but remain unaware of the threat to their existence. With some disdain, Gertrude Stein also notes that those who are weak, tender, and have little pride, remember the passivity of infancy with pleasure. But those whom that thought repels must "win for themselves a new everlasting feeling" (13). The commonest solution was also the crudest. "They make a baby to make for themselves a new beginning . . ." (13).

Gertrude Stein proposed to achieve her ladyhood by some means other than the organic. She was soon making the familiar assertions that the world contained many kinds of people, of whom this book would provide a description. But despite her desire to chart every type of human character, she still did not know how to manage. In trying to plan her best course of action, she embarked upon the book itself.

With a new book, Gertrude Stein freed herself from her earlier terminology. "Bottom nature" started as "fundamental nature," then yielded its central position in her scheme. She had discovered in *The Making of Americans* how long it took her to determine the bottom nature of a person. This was because it did not exist in a pure state, but was mixed with portions of other bottom natures. In *A Long Gay Book* she decided to call that mixture "a flavor" and to use it as her determining principle. In some, she now believed, "the flavor in them is . . . more real to them than the fundamental nature in them . . ." (16–17). While reluctant to give up the reassurance of objective classification, Gertrude Stein was moving steadily towards the pre-eminence of subjective assertion.

A Long Gay Book then would treat "pairs of people and their relation . . ." (17). She compiled a list of subjects, which kept swinging back to the true north of herself:

> Ollie, Paul; Paul, Fernande; Larr and me, Jane and me, Hattie and Ollie, Margaret and Phillip . . . everybody I know, Murdock and Elise, Larr and Elise, Larr and Marie . . . everybody I can think of ever, narrative after narrative of pairs of people . . . everybody Michael and us and Victor Herbert, Farmert and us, Bessie Hessel and me. (17)

Further down on the same page though, she was planning in terms of groups of people rather than pairs—"the Pauline group and . . . the Pauline quality in Ollie." As she continued to record her ideas, old names and old themes emerged, chaotic in their sequence, but true to Gertrude Stein's mind.

> And then one can go through whole groups of women to Jane
> Sands and her relation to men . . . Then one can take a fresh
> start and begin with Fanny and Helen and run through servants
> and adolescents to Lucy . . . Then going completely in to the
> flavor question how persons have the flavor they do . . . (17–18)

Hopeless, it would seem. Jane Sands, Gertrude Stein's nom de plume for *Three Lives,* was back. Servants and adolescents she had already considered at length in *The Making of Americans.* Even her efforts to plan ahead only reflected the subjects obsessing her at the time. Her plan to "take a fresh start" was only a variant of "beginning again," of never finishing anything except by running down, of new hopes perpetually succeeded by darkening confusion. "There can be lists and diagrams," she wrote, "some diagrams and many lists. There can be lists and diagrams. There can be lists" (23). Lists survived, for they were merely sequential, whereas diagrams required plausible inter-connections.

As soon as she had finished recording the jumble of her plans, Gertrude Stein shifted into that monotonous, generalized, and repetitive style we have just examined. In it, she defended randomness. "Meaning something is something. Meaning something and telling that thing is something" (26). She was beginning to put her faith in sheer activity. "Any one being started in doing something is going on completely doing that thing . . ." (18). The product was undeniably real. "Anything is something" (21). Even abortive efforts are significant. "Not coming to anything is something" (21).

When purged of these notions, she then constructed a series of paragraphs, each of which was cued by a surname. Some, but by no means all, were names that she had included in her original outline. Her characteristic procedure for this part of *A Long Gay Book* was first to provide a generalized paragraph, then follow it with descriptions of how various people act in light of the main subject. The first, for example, concerns listening. We learn that "Some one, Sloan, listened and was hearing something," that "Hobart did not expect anything in . . . listening," and that "Watts looked in listening" (28–29). As she proceeded she became increasingly vague and repetitive.

> Lamson is one. He is one. He is that one. He is one going on
> being that one. He is that one going on being one. In going on
> being one he is being that one. He is that one. (49)

100

While Gertrude Stein justified such seemingly mindless sequences with the statement, "Anything put down is something," there is more to them than that (48). If her basic problem was an inability to order the welter of her perceptions, then here she manages a provisional solution. It was a very conservative and cautious one, to be sure, but by keeping to elementary and generalized statements such as these, she found it possible to make statements she could regard as true. Furthermore, like her contemporaries and friends, the cubists, she was emphasizing the elements of her medium.

For example, "one" has a different role to play in each of these three sentences: "Lamson is one. He is one. He is that one." In the first instance, "one" is outweighed by the specificity of "Lamson." In the second, "one" stands as an equal with "he." In the third, the weight of the sentence slides towards the predicate, although "one" is now over-shadowed by its qualifier, "that." These permutations cannot be dismissed as inconsequential. Everything, no matter how minute, makes its effect.

About halfway through *A Long Gay Book*, two new patterns took over. One of them went: In doing such and such, one is such and such.

> In knowing that he was living he was knowing that he was feeling. (54)

> In trying to be telling something that one can come to be saying something . . . (59)

This was Gertrude Stein's way of trying to complicate her statement without losing control of its accuracy. One condition of being is overlaid upon another. The procedure was prudent, hewing close to the line of certainties. The statements were connected according to the requirements of grammar. Gertrude Stein felt exempt from concern for what preceded or followed. "In completing everything beginning and ending has no meaning and why should beginning and ending have meaning if everything is something" (56).

The evidence furnished by *A Long Gay Book* permits one to see the direction in which Gertrude Stein's ideas were heading. It included her tentative plans, which were attempted on the fly, as it were, with all deficiencies left uncorrected. Although the actual performance only remotely resembled the original outline, this in itself accurately represented the operation of the human mind. While it was possible to revise rough drafts until they were smooth and consistent, the final results would only be one version of the truth. They no more reflected actual experience than do the trained movements of the acrobat or juggler.

The other sentence form Gertrude Stein commonly used in the middle portion of *A Long Gay Book* went, "If such and such, then such and such." Gertrude Stein departed from the self-evident with the greatest reluctance. "John is happy" then became, "If John is happy, then John is happy." Complications were introduced by inventing variations of what remained basically the same statement. "If he were seeing clear if Gibbons were seeing clearly he would clearly see that he was describing what he was seeing" (70). Yet she insisted that it was impossible to repeat, even when using exactly the same words, for as William James had observed, one's mind is never static. "When the identical fact recurs, we must think of it in a fresh manner, see it under a somewhat different angle, apprehend it in different relations from those in which it last appeared" (*Psychology*, 156).

It is true that Gertrude Stein proved the point at excessive length. Still, things must play themselves out in their own way. Whatever one may think of the shambles of her early work, it is clear that she produced it for compelling personal reasons. It is difficult to conceive of anyone putting down on paper the thousands of words that she did between 1906 and 1912, unless he were sentenced to it. Gertrude Stein was tunneling her way out of prison, a spoonful at a time.

No distinct line of demarcation separates the two main parts of *A Long Gay Book*. The prose changes gradually like colors on the spectrum, and the characteristic style of the first part is never altogether purged from the second. The two styles are distinct, however. Compare:

> Not enough can be enough and being enough quite enough is enough and being enough enough is enough and being enough it is that. (74)

> Wet weather, wet pen, a black old tiger skin, a shut in shout and a negro coin and the best behind and the sun to shine. (114)

The first example illustrates Gertrude Stein's propensity for stating the obvious in various ways. The second declares nothing but merely chants seemingly random items, most of which are somewhat ambiguous in themselves. The diction is now enlivened.

This second style, which culminates in *Tender Buttons*, we have not encountered before. In it, a series of items possessing irregular but pronounced relationships of sound are frequently listed. These items may also display uncommon formal connections, as in the last sentence quoted where both "weather" and "pen" are qualified as "wet"; where the tiger skin and the coin share a color; and where the word "shut" does literally appear in the word "shout."

At base, this new style is incongruous and discontinuous. Odd adjectives are attached to nouns—"a fairy turtle," "a real red intoxication" (114). Verbs, often in the imperative mood, make inexplicable demands upon nouns—"bake the little stay away," "please tell the artichoke to underestimate valor," "argue the earnest cake" (104–5, 111). Word-play is common—"four sses are not singular," "Coo cow, coo coo coo" (108, 115). Motifs can be discerned running through paragraphs, even though the sentences themselves remain puzzling. "Candy is lively. The kindness of smelling. That last scent is lingering. If the precious thing is ripe it has been washed. Smelling is not patient. It is reduced and remembered" (107).

After the Lenten self-denial of Gertrude Stein's first portrait style, this is positively sybaritic in its colorfulness and giddy indifference to the proprieties. Whereas the earlier style was doggedly rational, this is explosively subjective. A guiding intelligence is still visible, but Gertrude Stein has liberated her verbal imagination.

In *A Long Gay Book* this new style emerges gradually. Initially, an instance of synesthesia appears on the horizon, a cloud no larger than a fist. "A tiny violent noise is a yellow happy thing" (82). The energy of that sentence is surprising in the monotonously grey atmosphere. Then more specific nouns and more colors appear, soon filling the stage.

Gertrude Stein habitually educated herself before the reader's eyes. Here, not long after the description of a tiny violent noise as yellow and happy, she suddenly remarks, "Singing is everything" (87). The idea had entered her mind that lyricism contained a fuller measure of truth than could ever be encircled by making endless, laboriously deliberate statements. Shortly, she adds that, although not worrying or suffering, she was fatigued and "not satisfied with everything. She said she did not care to repeat what she had said." Then, a moment later—"Now I have it. Now I see. This is the way. Not that way. The other way is not the way" (87).

The date of the stylistic change was quite probably some time in the spring or summer of 1912. In part this date is based on Gertrude Stein's indication that *A Long Gay Book* was written over a period of three years, 1909–12, and on the fact that the new style appears in the last quarter of the book. This portion of the book also contains a rare reference to bull-fighting—"the hardest way to kill the whole bull that is charging in and running" (89). It was in 1912 that Gertrude Stein and Alice Toklas made their first trip together to Spain. The trip seems to have relieved Gertrude Stein's intellectual inhibitions. She gained confidence in her lyric abilities, and now saw that she could justify her efforts not solely on the grounds that they were demonstrably true, but because they were demonstrably beautiful. "Beauty is the thing to see when beauty is there" (100). Sheer exultation in the wonder of things overtook her. The grim psychologist who had planned a long analytic book yielded to the poet. "I sing and I sing and the tunes I sing are what are tunes if they come and I sing. I sing I sing" (107). Later, in *Lectures in America,* she explained that *A Long Gay Book* changed because "I myself was becoming livelier just then. One does you know . . . this being livelier inside me kept increasing . . . // I was really very lively" (150–51). She finished *A Long Gay Book,* or rather broke it off, on a positive note. "All I say is begin" (115).

In *The Making of Americans,* Gertrude Stein said that she preferred to write about women (205). Yielding to this preference, she veered off to a consideration of *Many Many Women.** Seventy-nine pages in length, *Many Many Women* is of unparalleled opacity. It employs no proper names, only the pronouns "one," "some," "she," and "they." In the style of the early portraits it presents a series of females who marry, study, suffer. It is an accomplishment of some magnitude to be able to say even that much. The book's prose is a desert—much sand, each grain distinct and the dune-paragraphs of different shapes, the sun shining, and occasionally an oasis. Still, a desert. "She was that one one completely mentioning everything and mentioning it again and again and always then completing that thing completing mentioning everything. She was then that one completing again and again and again mentioning everything. She was that one" (*GMP,* 132–3).

Many Many Women is a formal rarity in that Gertrude Stein

---

* The *Yale Catalogue* dates *Many Many Women* 1910, the year after *A Long Gay Book* was begun. But in both *The Autobiography of Alice B. Toklas* and *Lectures in America,* Gertrude Stein says she started it at the same time as *A Long Gay Book,* and that both were interrupted by portrait writing (*ABT,* 139; *LIA,* 148).

sustained its subject and style over so long a stretch. On the other hand, there is no apparent development in *Many Many Women*, nor any particular reason that it should stop when it does, even though it does conclude with a long, lyrical chant, which goes in part: "Any one and any one, one and one and two, and one and one and one, and one and many, and one and some, and one and any one, and any one and any one . . ." (197–8).

It has a significant beginning though. Before Gertrude Stein commences with the portrait of those who are "believing in loving and marrying and having children" she describes a person who is simply one. One *what* we are never told. The first sentences merely read: "Any one is one having been that one. Any one is such a one" (119). A short history then follows of this person. When the revolving sentences are analyzed, these details are disclosed. The woman both remembers and forgets "that thing." The identity of the thing is ambiguous. "She is forgetting anything and she is remembering that thing, she is remembering that she is forgetting anything" (119). The woman is next described kissing. Shortly though, it is revealed that she is lonesome. "Being lonesome," however, "was not coming to be anything" (121). Feeling the sterility of a life without love, she worries—"was always worrying"—and she pays for things, pays for very many things (122). Next "she was feeding something," "something" being defined as "being one knowing something." And soon "she was loving some one and some one was loving her then" (123). On that idyllic note, the opening sketch concludes.

The terms of this sketch are general enough that it need not be autobiographical. It might, in fact, describe Alice Toklas, for in the first notebook devoted to this project, she wrote "How women are lived and what they are," followed by a list of names drawn from her actual circle of friends, and headed by "Alice." By this time, she and Alice had known one another for several years, and Alice had recently joined the ménage at 27 rue de Fleurus. And as the portrait of "Ada" reveals, a new, rich element had entered Gertrude Stein's life in Alice's person. "Certainly this one was loving this Ada then" (*G&P*, 16).

Towards the end of *The Making of Americans*—that is, some time after "Ada" was composed—Gertrude Stein announced that she had become reconciled to the nature of her affections. Many people, she observed, have prejudices about how love shall be expressed. "Some say alright all but one way of loving, another says alright all but another way of loving . . ." She herself had learned tolerance. "I like loving. I like mostly all the ways any one can have of having loving feeling in them. Slowly it has come to be in me that any way of being a loving one is interesting and not unpleasant to me" (606).

Some years ago, after reading *Things As They Are*, Edmund Wilson speculated that the vagueness of Gertrude Stein's prose was in part attributable "to a need imposed by the problem of writing about relationships between women of a kind that the standards of that era would not have allowed her to describe more explicitly" (*Shores*, 581). However, when the first volume of Gertrude Stein's unpublished writings appeared after her death, Wilson reconsidered. Inasmuch as this prose was vague too, he now thought that "I may have exaggerated . . . the Lesbian aspect of Gertrude Stein's obscurity" (*Shores*, 586).

Both of Wilson's opinions seem to me to have been correct. Lesbian sentiments contributed to Gertrude Stein's stylistic impenetrability, although Wilson did initially exaggerate their importance as an influence. While the problem of expressing her feelings without irrevocably compromising herself was far from being the exclusive determinant of Gertrude Stein's stylistic evolution, the obscurity of her several styles did serve to protect her. At one point in *The Making of Americans*, she remarked that some day she would tell the full story of a rather ugly woman, and that when she did, "this one will not know then it is this one. That is the very nice thing in this writing" (567).

Her principal device for obfuscation at this point in her career was the indefinite reference. But she also substituted names freely throughout her career. "Let us regret Sylvia. / I dare not use another name" ("Coal and Wood," *PL*, 5). It was typical for her to confess her private uses of the language. "No one sees the connection between Lily and Louise, but I do" ("Sitwell Edith Sitwell," *P&P*, 92). (The same line appears in "Or More (or War)," *UK*, 137. Both pieces were written in 1925.) Such substitutions permitted her to treat intimate topics while minimizing her vulnerability.

In connection with this function of obscurity, it is worth mentioning that until around 1930, many of Gertrude Stein's compositions have the flavor of the inside joke. Probably Alice Toklas alone knew the meaning of most of the oblique references. There is something at once cozy and malicious about their shared secrets. Like a pair of schoolgirls giggling in a corner, they assert their superiority by covert ridicule of others. A few of these jokes Gertrude Stein later revealed in *The Autobiography of Alice B. Toklas*. They could be funny, as when T. S. Eliot reluctantly solicited a contribution from Gertrude Stein for the *Criterion*, because his patron, Lady Rothmere, desired it. But, he warned, it must be your very latest. Gertrude Stein thereupon wrote a portrait which she entitled with that day's date, "The Fifteenth of November" (246–8).

During the period between 1910 and 1912, the curtain of style served Gertrude Stein in one other important personal way. It enabled her to discuss her relations with Leo, without overtly revealing how she felt about them. In a long piece, *Two*, subtitled "Gertrude Stein and Her Brother," she described and solved her problem with Leo. The title itself has a dual meaning, for it refers first to brother and sister, then to sister and friend. In effect, the book describes the transformation of the number's meaning.

To understand this last personal crisis in Gertrude Stein's early life, we must remember that she and her brother had begun living together at 27 rue de Fleurus in 1903, Alice Toklas joined them in 1909, and sometime in 1912 or 1913—the evidence is not clear—Leo moved out permanently.*

During the first years of her expatriation, Gertrude had docilely followed Leo wherever he went. She shared his friends, listened to his monologues, and provisionally accepted his taste. Unable to participate actively in the painting revolution, Leo sought to become a major aesthetic theorist. He was more than competent in this role, for he has been described as having been at that time "possibly the most discerning connoisseur and collector of twentieth-century painting in the world." † He was the chief speaker at their regular Saturday night salon, brilliant, voluble, arrogant.

He was positive he was talented, but he could not harness his powers creatively. He tried painting, but the results did not satisfy him. In his frustration, he suffered severe neurotic symptoms that sent him in

---

* Katz says they separated in 1911 (141). Brinnin says 1912 (196). Sprigge says 1913 (84). Gallup says the fall of 1913 (*Flowers*, 86). Alice Toklas said Leo moved to Florence in the spring of 1914 (Duncan, 114). Gertrude Stein says 1914 too (*EA*, 74). The break took place during Gertrude Stein's absence, for she and Leo divided the paintings by correspondence. Alice and she were travelling a good deal in 1912. They spent the spring and summer in Spain. In the fall they were at Mabel Dodge's Villa Curonia in Italy. And in January, 1913, they made an extended trip to England. Whether they stayed at the rue de Fleurus at any time during this period, I have not been able to determine. By May 1913, however, they had returned, for they attended the second performance of Stravinsky's *Le Sacre du Printemps*.

† Alfred H. Barr, Jr., in Aline B. Saarinen, "The Steins in Paris," *The American Scholar*, XXVII (Autumn 1958), 447.

search of cures. He tried Spartan diets, special ways of eating, psychiatry. Nothing could solve his problem of being an intricate engine racing at top speed, but producing nothing. He later felt that "the same neurosis that kept me from painting kept me from writing also" (*Appreciation*, 169).

During this period, Leo could always count on an audience of one in Gertrude. As her older brother, he had a comfortable sense of superiority towards her which manifested itself in condescension and teasing. We have one unusually graphic glimpse of the two bent over the writing desk as Leo completed an undated letter to Mabel Weeks:

> Gertrude says to tell you that her lapis lazuli chain is beautchiful. She says that I'm to say it's beautiful. She says that's not a nice way to act, that I'm to say it. She wants to know whether I don't think it. She says don't be nasty. She repeats that remark four times. She drools some more. (*Journey*, 18)

All through this period Gertrude Stein was writing steadily, but with no encouragement from Leo. She was changing too as she moved into her middle thirties and acquired friends independent of Leo, as she grew familiar with Leo's aesthetic positions and their limits, and as she continued to clarify her own literary ideas. Her determined productivity could hardly have pleased her brother. So, without any dramatically explosive incidents, they grew increasingly distant.

In the meantime, Alice Toklas had arrived in Paris, accompanied by Harriet Levy. After housekeeping in San Francisco several years for her widowed father, she, a single woman and three years Gertrude Stein's junior, had decided to go abroad.

The prevailing impression of Miss Toklas is of a tiny, mustached shrew. But that is because most photographs and accounts of her come from the last forty years of her life. As a young woman she verged on plumpness, and with her glossy black hair, deep eyes, full mouth, and colorful dress, she made an exotic and sensual figure.

Her background strikingly resembled Gertrude Stein's. In appearance, neither was conventionally beautiful, although both were attractive. Both had traveled in Europe as children, then been raised in the San Francisco Bay area. Both had lost their mothers early. Alice Toklas described hers as "a very serious person who had no particularly serious interests" (Duncan, 46). She had received a normal education for a young woman of her day. She had studied the piano, attended the University of Washington for a year, and she especially admired Henry

James. Behind this genteel facade were high spirits that delighted in pranks, and a will of steel. She was a combination of aristocrat and gypsy, of imperious *grande dame* and bohemian. Her account of an incident on an Italian journey is typically spirited and unconventional: "The next morning we went on to Florence. Because of the heat I got rid of my cerise ribbon girdle in the dressing room of the train, throwing it out the window. When I returned to our compartment Harriet said, What a strange coincidence, I just saw your cherry-colored corset pass by the window" (*WIR*, 48).

Those who knew her differed widely in their assessments of her character. Even Gertrude Stein, soon after she had made Alice Toklas's acquaintance, described her as "conscienceless," "sordid," and "without ideals of any kind" (Katz, 235). In her own autobiography, *What Is Remembered*, she is dignified, independent in judgment, tolerant of moral irregularity yet capable of being shocked, ready to render a frank opinion, but charitably discreet as well. Above all, the tartness of her memories stands out. "I sat next to James Branch Cabell who asked me, Is Gertrude Stein serious? Desperately, I replied. That puts a different light on it, he said. For you, I said, not for me" (*WIR*, 150).

As part of her study of human character, Gertrude Stein had for several years begged and even demanded correspondence from her friends so that she might analyze it for evidences of bottom nature. In this way she became acquainted with Alice Toklas long before she ever laid eyes on her. Without Alice Toklas's knowledge, Annette Rosenshine permitted Gertrude Stein to read the letters from her San Francisco friend as they arrived. The two women finally met in September 1907, on Alice Toklas's first day in Paris. That first meeting was in the presence of others. Their second was alone. Alice Toklas was late for the appointment, and although she sent a message ahead, a peculiar scene followed her arrival. Gertrude Stein opened the door wrathfully. "She was now a vengeful goddess and I was afraid. I did not know what had happened or what was going to happen."

"Nor," continued Alice Toklas, "is it possible for me to tell about it now. After she had paced for some time about the long Florentine table made longer by being flanked on either side by two smaller ones, she stood in front of me and said, Now you understand. It is over. It is not too late to go for a walk. You can look at the pictures while I change my clothes" (*WIR*, 23–24).

This same crucial scene is evidently referred to in "Didn't Nelly and Lilly Love You" as part of the reminiscences of their life together.

When they kindly met and were not meeting as it were where
they had representatives when they kindly met they met to be asked
will you come and see me.
She came late I state that she came late and I said what was it
that I said I said I am not accustomed to wait.
We were so wifely. (*AFAM*, 226)

Although the incident obviously constituted a memorable point in the
two women's life together, the significance of Gertrude Stein's imperi-
ousness is still far from clear.

Alice Toklas began making herself useful to Gertrude Stein by reading proof for *Three Lives*. Then, having learned to type for the purpose,
she started to transcribe the enormous manuscript of *The Making of
Americans*. Alice and Harriet Levy summered in Italy near Leo and
Gertrude. Then in 1909, when Harriet Levy decided to return to the
United States, Gertrude invited Alice to move in with her. "You don't
want to go back to the apartment alone, do you, and I said no, and so
it was" (Sprigge, 83–84; see also *WIR*, 61–62).

Henceforth Alice Toklas never relinquished her place in Gertrude
Stein's life. Although she had a mind and a will comparable to Gertrude
Stein's, she never attempted to compete with her. She was unswervingly
loyal and capable of doing anything to assist her companion: typing,
shopping, planning travel schedules, acting as receptionist and cook,
keeping up the correspondence. Her influence on Gertrude Stein's decisions was considerable. Many people courted her favors, and many
more feared her power. No one has been described with more malicious
relish than she.

Some of Gertrude Stein's other women friends reacted with varying
degrees of resentment to Alice Toklas's appropriation of the role of
factotum. Etta Cone, who had typed *Three Lives* for Gertrude Stein,
was obliged by ill health to yield her secretarial labors. In a 1907 letter
she asked, "Has my successor done her duty by my place what she
usurped . . . ?" Her tone was jocular but plaintive. "I am sometimes
envious" (Pollack, 91). Annette Rosenshine, who had known Alice
Toklas well in San Francisco, and had preceded her to Paris, became
an early subject for Gertrude Stein's intensive psychological analysis.
She remembered Alice had long sought a cause "worthy of her talents;
now she could concentrate her efficiency and her cleverness both in fur-
thering Gertrude's literary career, as well as catering to any indulgence
that the spoiled child craved. In part, friendships with both Harriet

Levy and me had shown her need to pull strings, but we, her San Francisco puppets, had been too inconsequential" ("Life's Not A Paragraph," 83). Mabel Dodge suggested that Alice Toklas had carefully insinuated herself into the Stein household, then dislodged Leo. She reported that at the time Leo had been perturbed to see Alice "making herself indispensable," while Gertrude grew increasingly "helpless and foolish from it and less and less inclined to do anything herself . . . he had seen trees strangled by vines in the same way" (*European Experiences*, 327).

But Gertrude Stein had never been more than selectively independent. From childhood on, she had always left the practical responsibilities to others. Leo had been the head of the rue de Fleurus household. Now, he, the surrogate father, had to be replaced. Alice Toklas would take over the problems of daily routine. Pablo Picasso would furnish Gertrude Stein aesthetic stimulation, although not as a superior or competitor, but as a friend and equal. Through him she could keep in touch with avant-garde activity, without being bludgeoned by his opinions, as she had been by Leo's.

Alice Toklas did not sunder brother and sister. As a matter of fact, the break-up suited all three parties. On Leo's side, he disagreed with Picasso's movement into cubism. After severely lecturing the painter and finding him adamant, he simply turned his back on him. He was equally contemptuous of what Gertrude was doing. "I can't abide her stuff and think it abominable" (*Journey*, 52). The Spanish painter and Leo's literary sister were inalterably associated in his mind as two willful children. "Both he and Gertrude are using their intellects, which they ain't got, to do what would need the finest critical tact, which they ain't got neither," he told Mabel Weeks in 1913, "and they are in my belief turning out the most Godalmighty rubbish that is to be found" (*Journey*, 53). Years later, after insisting that Picasso was being childish in claiming that noses should not be modelled but drawn as triangles, Leo once more linked him with his sister: "When once you know that a nose is not a nose is not a nose you can go on to discover what all the other things are not . . ." (*Appreciation*, 183).

Leo's splenetic rationalism is amusing. So was his exasperation when these two intellectual infants proceeded to achieve international celebrity. He continued to insist upon their superficiality, their clumsiness, and their childishness, especially in comparison to his own superior gifts. After *The Autobiography of Alice B. Toklas* came out, he wrote a friend: "Gertrude and I are just the contrary. She's basically stupid and I'm basically intelligent" (*Journey*, 149).* But alas, Leo still had not been able to harness that intelligence, due to "the upsetting, complicating and stultifying effects of a terrific neurosis . . ." (*Journey*, 149). By the time of their split, Leo realized, "There is practically nothing . . . we don't either disagree about, or at least regard with different sympathies" (*Journey*, 52).

Gertrude Stein, on her side, now had a close companion in Alice Toklas, one who could manage practical affairs, protect her from loneliness, and love her. Moreover, after the publication of *Three Lives* in 1909, she had begun to achieve some recognition in the world of letters. The book was reviewed respectfully and publishers wrote her letters of inquiry. Then in 1912 Mabel Dodge bound and distributed three hundred copies of Gertrude Stein's verbal portrait of her. That same year, Gertrude Stein made her first appearance in a periodical when Alfred Stieglitz printed "Matisse" and "Picasso" in his *Camera Work*. Early in 1913 she returned to England where the publisher John Lane made her a regular guest at his salon. Meanwhile the Armory Show had opened in New York, giving the American public its first exposure to modern art. Brancusi, Duchamps, Picasso, Leger, Matisse, and Kandinsky were all represented. A special issue of *Arts and Decoration* which was distributed at the exhibition reprinted the "Portrait of Mabel Dodge" along with Mabel Dodge's essay on Gertrude Stein, "Speculations, or Post-Impressionism in Prose." The attendant publicity delighted Gertrude Stein. "I am as proud as punch," she wrote. *"Hurrah for gloire"* (Brinnin, 186).

Now, given a loyal companion, public recognition, and Leo's contempt for her efforts, the time had come for Gertrude Stein to free herself from his inhibiting presence. The stages by which she achieved her liberation appear in the aforementioned piece entitled *Two: Gertrude Stein and Her Brother*.

Two analyzes the Stein household situation. The notes Gertrude Stein jotted on the endpapers of her notebook indicate that persons other than Leo and herself were to be treated in the book, notably their sister-in-law Sarah (Sally) Stein. But although specific references are sometimes

---

* In *Everybody's Autobiography*, Gertrude Stein made a contrary assessment. "It was I who was the genius, there was no reason for it but I was, and he was not . . ." (77).

uncertain, the essential conflict between brother and sister is visible enough. *Two* is a portrait of the artist as a young woman, couched in her favorite form of pairs and opposites. It shows her learning about herself in Leo's company, then slowly drawing away from him toward Alice, while he disappears into egotistic self-absorption. At its center are two literal facts: that Leo and Gertrude shared a life, and that Leo was growing increasingly deaf. The book diagrams the shifting significance of the number two, and of various expressions of sound.

The number two represents brother and sister, unified but separate, and imperceptibly pulling apart. Eventually it also stands for the two women friends. "There were two, she and she was there . . ." (*TWO*, 135). Twoness at once suggests separateness and unity. "One" has an equally complex meaning. It stands for the growing isolation of Leo, indifferent to anyone else's existence, save as an audience for his ideas. This inevitably destroyed the family unit. "If one is one and one is not one of the two then one is one . . ." (100). But oneness also represents the unification of Gertrude Stein's psyche, the concentration of her talents through work, and her achievement of self-confidence and maturity. Whereas "in being one he was not loving," she "was succeeding. She was preparing" (47, 57). "She was the peculiar center that was the heart of the nucleus . . ." (108).

The condition of being one or two found a dynamic counterpart in "sound." Leo "was one coming to be one not hearing" (34). This was the case both literally and psychologically. "The one is one hearing himself . . . the other one is one hearing some one . . . They are not alike" (2). As Gertrude Stein began to emit sound, Leo became ironically incapable of hearing it. For her, that sound was a sign of individuality—"the sound coming out of her was . . . that she was one" (15). This sound then represented her ideas, whether expressed in conversation or more importantly in her writing, to which she turned in face of Leo's contempt for her pretensions as an independent thinker.

Gertrude Stein outlined the stages of how she felt about self-expression in *Two*. It was not only reassuring and stimulating; at times it was "terrifying as something that would be coming" (11). "That sound was sounding the meaning of something" (15). It was "feeling being existing" (11). She was aware of the change underway in herself. The sound was "using strength as if strength were existing," but as yet, "she was not a strong one" (19). Still, through the expression of her ideas, "she is giving to anyone the impression that she is one," that she does have a unified personality (20). As she continued she realized the need in herself to keep expressing herself. She was "needing sound sounding," and moreover, "being one compelling listening" (27, 26).

Leo later said that although a feud had been imputed between them, "we never quarreled except for a momentary spat. We simply differed and went our own ways" (*Journey*, 298). *Two* dramatizes the isolation of their separate egos which, by and large, made quarreling impossible. "They were not differing as they were not hearing . . ." (121). In the somewhat easier language of *Everybody's Autobiography*, Gertrude Stein recalled that Leo "continued to believe in what he was saying when he was arguing and I began not to find it interesting" (72). The generational comedy was played out this time between brother and sister, with the debate centered on Gertrude Stein's increasingly obscure writing. As the conclusion of *Two* indicates, she had now cast her lot with values that were not necessarily capable of being rationally communicated. "A belief that has translation is not all there is of exaltation" (142).

Because this position was the basis of her independence, she could not afford to have Leo undermine it. But he insisted that in itself her work meant nothing. "He said it was not it it was I. If I was not there . . . what I did would not be what it was" (*EA*, 76). Leo, that is, thought Gertrude's friends were making a fuss over her work, not for itself, but because of her. "I knew it was not true," she later wrote, "but it destroyed him for me . . ." (*EA*, 77).

So it did. Once very close, the brother and sister met on but one occasion after they separated. Leo made a conciliatory gesture in 1919, writing her that his former antagonism had dissipated and that he really felt "quite amiable" towards her (*Journey*, 77; see also 71 for an earlier overture). But she continued to guard her independence by ignoring the former head of her household. Her literary response was definite: "Brother brother go away and stay" ("Names of Flowers," *BTV*, 217). They never saw one another after 1920. Gertrude Stein had gained her freedom by means of a permanent alliance with Alice Toklas. One was still two.

PART TWO

ᔓ. "What is my another name."
                ("Lifting Belly")

6

꒰. "A book which when you open it attracts attention
by the undoubted denial of photography as an art. . . .
A book in translation about eggs and butter."
("Descriptions of Literature")

Gertrude Stein's first portrait style was austerely mechanistic. Identity
and action were reduced to a few basic terms: he thinks, one fears, they
feel. She advanced by means of tautological variants: one is not two,
one is not three, one is one; two is not one, two is not three, two is two.
These equations were slightly changed by adding or removing qualify-
ing elements, or by varying the tense of the verb.

> He had been exercising . . .
> He had been almost completely exercising . . .
> He had been completely exercising . . .
> He was exercising . . .
> He was exercising . . .
> He could be exercising . . . ("A Man," *TWO,* 238)

Gertrude Stein regarded this early work as "a thing that is growing
in a certain arrangement that is a solid, unexciting, definite, beautiful
enough thing" ("Italians," *G&P,* 51). Whatever her personal uncertainty and confusion, assertions made in this manner were virtually
unassailable. These incantations were defensive gestures. They dwelt
obsessively upon the supreme importance of overcoming fear, of certainty, of knowing, of being, most importantly, of being *something.*
Success consumed Gertrude Stein's mind.

Then, with her alliance with Alice Toklas firm, Leo effectively out of
her life, her celebrity growing, and the aesthetic innovations of the
Parisian avant-garde provoking her imagination, her prose was pro-
pelled out of its dogged monotony.

Artists had always dominated the Stein Saturday evening salon. It
was without doubt this association with painters that first suggested

portraiture to Gertrude Stein. A number of her early subjects—"Frost," "Roche," Purrmann," "Nadelman," "Manguin,"—were painters and sculptors of varying degrees of merit whom she knew at the time. (See *ABT*, 140–41.) They and women sat for her early portraits. Then as the pace of innovation quickened in painting, Gertrude Stein's methods of portraiture underwent extreme revision. The examples of Matisse, Picasso, and Braque utterly transformed her writing.

Her initial portraits of Matisse and Picasso, dated 1909, were in the old style. Matisse was seen suffering as he struggled to be certain that what he was doing was legitimate. After he was certain that "he was a great one," disciples gathered to imitate his discoveries. Then controversy arose as to whether Matisse's art reflected a genuinely creative struggle. Gertrude Stein withheld her own judgment in the portrait, although she did end it on the negative note that some believed he was "not greatly expressing something being struggling" (*P&P*, 16). The chances are that she herself was still undecided. But when Picasso and Matisse went their separate ways, she herself chose the Spaniard while the Michael Steins remained the chief patrons of Matisse.

The 1909 portrait of Picasso was less solemn than the one devoted to Matisse. Gertrude Stein presented him as a working artist with some following, but with neither the reputation for greatness Matisse then possessed, nor a large number of imitators. His work was solid and complete, unlike that of some of the other artists, whom Gertrude Stein regarded as capable of scintillating but insubstantial effects. The distinctive feature of Henry Charles Manguin, for example, was that his work was "pretty" and when he finished it, anyone could see that it was finished (*P&P*, 54–56). "Manguin A Painter" implies that he was a skilled technician, but much less interesting than Picasso, who, in his struggle to create, produced ugly canvases that the viewer might even suspect were incomplete. So Picasso's work was termed not only "lovely," "simple," and "clear," but also "perplexing," "disconcerting," and even "repellant" (*P&P*, 17–20).

In *Picasso*, a brief study she wrote in the late thirties, Gertrude Stein suggested her development was parallel to his. "I was alone at this time in understanding him, perhaps because I was expressing the same thing in literature" (16). She felt they both sought vision beyond factual realism, because "faith in what the eyes were seeing, that is to say the belief in the reality of science, commenced to diminish" (12). Their goal was not the expression of "things remembered," for that would be an artificial "reconstruction from memory" (35, 15). In Gertrude

Stein's retrospective view, she and Picasso sought "to express things seen not as one knows them but as they are when one sees them without remembering having looked at them" (15).

As early as 1911 in the piece *G.M.P.*, she put herself in the company of the two leading modern painters. The title is an off-key abbreviation for *Matisse Picasso and Gertrude Stein.**

Seventy-seven pages in length, it is one of the least commented upon of her compositions, no doubt because it is her soporific work *par excellence*. Still, it begins with colors, and thereafter generally imparts a sense of being about painters. Although the referents are obscure, throughout the first half, a "he" is set off from "they," as if an innovator were being contrasted with a group. "He turned away and said that he had come to stay" (*GMP*, 208). Put less obscurely, this artist set off on an independent course, fully confident of his permanence. *G.M.P.* does not, however, seem to describe a rebel in opposition to conservative members of the academy. "They were contemplating intelligent developing" (205). All agreed that the sterile imitativeness of the contemporary artistic scene was lamentable. "It is a grief to almost any one that all that is being done . . . is what has been done . . ." (201). After the dominance of "he" and "they" throughout the first half, these pronouns fade away and thenceforth make only sporadic appearances. Whether or how Picasso, Matisse, or Gertrude Stein figure in the piece is not clear.

Many years later in an interview, Gertrude Stein said that towards the middle of *G.M.P.* "words began to be for the first time more important than the sentence structure or the paragraphs" (Haas, "Gertrude Stein Talking," 10). It is true that as "he" and "they" disappear, a broader vocabulary enlivens the prose surface which up to that time had been exceptionally bleak. More nouns and verbs, and particularly foods and colors show up. This change had been anticipated earlier, however, through the introduction of grammatically unorthodox sentences, which had never before been her practice.

Her earlier procedure had been to repeat the obvious in a series of minute variations. In these she retained a conventional sentence structure, but fogged over the referents. For example, the first half of *G.M.P.* (like the middle of *A Long Gay Book*), has numerous "if-then" sen-

---

* Both the title page of the volume and *Lectures in America*, 148, confirm the meaning of the initials. It is a minor but I think significant point that in the version using initials—that is to say in the equivocal title—Gertrude Stein put herself first.

tences. They are syntactically sound, however obscure their meaning. "If there was the whole way to go when there was a ticket that was bought then certainly they did not go to stay away" (237). The final breakup of the ice of inhibition began when even her syntax failed to observe the amenities.

He having staying was staying, he being staying of his being staying staying. (207)

He was the pronouncer who was not undertaking the way to have enough listen to every one. (222)

It is true that these examples are only mildly eccentric, and depending how flexible one is in such matters, they can be accommodated to normal discourse. But, as it turned out, they presaged the total melting away of Gertrude Stein's early stylistic practices. So did the scattering of surrealistic phrases. The references to "a in-between gold fisher," "the black cucumber," and "the educated banana" were not then nor ever had been characteristic of Gertrude Stein (259, 254, 258). By the end of *G.M.P.* the style had almost completely changed. Words appeared in incongruous combinations and without a verb. *G.M.P.* began with a description of a number of innovating artists, and before it was over, the book itself had undergone a stylistic revolution.

A contemporary remembered Gertrude Stein saying of the "Portrait of Mabel Dodge at the Villa Curonia" (1911), "Well, Pablo is doing abstract portraits in painting. I am trying to do abstract portraits in *my* medium, *words*" (Ronnebeck, 3). Although as Gertrude Stein had reason to know, memories often shape the past into a coherence it never possessed, in this instance Leo Stein, in a letter written at the time, corroborated the gist of the statement. Mabel Dodge's portrait, he said, "was directly inspired by Picasso's latest form" (*Journey*, 53).

The portrait's subject was a patron of the arts whose career stretched from Gertrude Stein to D. H. Lawrence, from Buffalo to Florence to Taos, through four husbands and an indeterminate number of male and female lovers. Perhaps for this reason Gertrude Stein's alternate title for the portrait was, "Mabel little Mabel with her face against the pane . . ." (YCAL). The first volume of Mabel Dodge Luhan's autobiography is filled with rather endearing Freudian gush, stimulated mainly by girlish homosexual eroticism. On the occasion memorialized in her portrait when she entertained the two companions at the Villa

Curonia, "Gertrude . . . sent me such a strong look over the table that it seemed to cut across the air to me in a band of electrified steel—a smile travelling across on it—powerful—Heavens!" She attributed the cooling of her friendship with Gertrude to Alice Toklas's jealousy (*European Experiences*, 332–3). Before that happened though, she arranged to have her portrait printed and circulated widely—and also prepared, for the 1913 Armory Show, the first critical article to take Gertrude Stein's efforts seriously.

Because of its subject's energetic proselytizing, the "Portrait of Mabel Dodge" elicited numerous responses. Edwin Arlington Robinson inquired mildly, "How do you know that it is a portrait of you, after all?" Logan Pearsall Smith read it to Israel Zangwill. "Zangwill was moved. He said, 'And I always thought she was such a healthy minded young woman, what a terrible blow it must be for her poor dear brother.'" But when Smith persisted in advancing Gertrude Stein's cause, Zangwill burst out angrily—"How can you waste your time reading and rereading a thing like that and all these years you have refused to read Kipling" (Robinson and Smith letters to Mabel Dodge, *Movers and Shakers*, 137, 33–34).

Leo Stein thought the portrait "damned nonsense" and affirmed that although he knew Mable Dodge intimately, the portrait "conveys absolutely nothing to me" (*Journey*, 53). His exasperation with it was so extreme that he was moved to write several parodies of it, one of which begins: "Size is not circumference unless magnitude extends. Purpose defined in limitation projected. It is the darkness whose center is light." He showed this to his sister, but by this time she was sufficiently self-possessed to outflank his attack. "Gertrude and even Alice have the cheek to pretend that they understand this (which I can do in part sometimes) but as Gertrude thought it very nice and I had very sarcastic intentions we evidently didn't understand it the same way" (*Journey*, 49).

There is no intrinsic reason for the celebrity of Mabel Dodge's portrait. It is a transitional piece, composed of a series of elliptical but coherent statements, normally paragraphed. There are the familiar "if-then" sentences, and sentences that begin, "In doing such and such," then finish off, "there is not such and such." Some sentences are organized around a common structure—"it is not sinking to be growing, it is not darkening to be disappearing, it is not aged to be annoying" (*P&P*, 100). The whole is comprehensibly framed. "The days are wonderful and the nights are wonderful and the life is pleasant" Gertrude Stein commences and ends by acknowledging that the whole of experience is never achieved. "There is not all of any visit" (*P&P*, 98, 102).

If anything, the villa is more visible in the portrait than its mistress. Not that this is a specific sketch of the estate, for Mabel Dodge described the house and grounds at length in her memoirs, and her description and the portrait fail to correspond at all. Rather, Gertrude Stein incorporated incidental details of personal relevance. There are references to packing, to the warmth of blankets, to a velvet spread, to the largest chair, to a garden, to a vase.

Unlike the monotonous repetitiveness of her early portraits, this one does constantly stretch and tease the imagination. Some of its observations are concrete—"A plank that was dry was not disturbing the smell of burning" (101). Some are abstract—"The absence is not alternative" (98). Nonetheless, they promise solution. This portrait then is fairly conservative in execution; it is especially so if compared to the riot of language waiting just offstage.

One other portrait written contemporary to that of Mabel Dodge concerned their mutual friend, the novelist Constance Fletcher (who under the pseudonym of George Fleming wrote *Kismet*). The "Portrait of Constance Fletcher" falls into two distinct stylistic halves, making it at once more conservative and more radical than "Mabel Dodge."

The first section is in the early portrait style, cued by such phrases as "family living" and tracing a tiresomely revolving course through simple statements needlessly complicated. "She was thinking and feeling then in being one not losing anything of any such thing as being one being full then" (*G&P*, 158).

The second half of "Constance Fletcher" though goes quite beyond "Mabel Dodge." The break comes with a paragraph that starts: "If they move in the shoe there is everything to do. They do not move in the shoe" (159). Up to that point, Gertrude Stein had provided circling generalizations about a "she," presumably the title figure. But no referent exists for "they"; the action of moving into a shoe is unprecedented (save in Mother Goose); and the line jingles. Gertrude Stein had entered quite another world.

She started talking again about what she was doing. The talk is muffled and indirect, but still audible. At the cost of violating the full effect of her prose, I shall excerpt some of the pertinent phrases.

> There was the writing and the preparation that was pleasing and succeeding and being enterprising. It was not subdued when there

was discussion, it was done where there was the room that was not a dream.

Perfection is not adulteration.

This did not mean more than all. It meant all and the result of the precious and precise way was that there was that preparation and not the disintegration when there was that distinct evolution. (159–60)

These comments assuredly refer to her newly developing means of expression. Paraphrased they testify to the pleasure her writing gave her, and to the pride she took in its boldness. Rather than adulterating expression, this new technique perfected it by being more scrupulously faithful to reality. The results were neither mystical nor transcendent. Nor was her writing proof that her mind was giving way—disintegrating. This style evolved through a series of gradual modifications, each of which sought greater precision.

Encountered by themselves, Gertrude Stein's statements about her seriousness and exactitude are likely to be regarded as playful at best. But for anyone who has followed the development of her prose, the literal truth of what she claimed is not hard to see.

After commenting on her method and its legitimacy, Gertrude Stein then turned to an illustration of it. Her subjects are only dimly visible, save the first, which is an oak tree. It she makes the exemplar of concentrated presence, free of "disguise," of "discussion," of "obligation," of "composition." The tree itself does not change. But when named and placed in a literary context, considerations of meaning other than the tree distort it by obliging it to observe a syntactical order, to serve argument, and to contribute to aesthetic ends.

The latter part of "Constance Fletcher" gave evidence then—admittedly murky—of Gertrude Stein's renewed concern for rendering existence purely in the present. In that critical year of 1911–12, with *The Making of Americans* completed and both *A Long Gay Book* and *G.M.P.* undergoing metamorphoses in midcourse, she found herself at a crucial juncture in her career. Following her first autobiographical fictions, Gertrude Stein had undertaken successively, a universal history, a universal system of characterology, a description of some people, a description of one person. With "David Hersland," near the end of *The Making of Americans* she had reached the portrait.

For her, the portrait had the advantage over the narrative of promising only fidelity to the moment of composition. The portrait did not show action in time, but was an act of immediate perception. Nonethe-

123

less, her results in this genre did not satisfy her. She still could not capture the full complexity of her impression of a person.

Gertrude Stein had tried numerous techniques in her previous efforts to match her conception of a person with a style. She had generalized and reduced her vocabulary in order to make true statements, however simple-minded. She had constructed long, cumulative sentences on the model of This-is-the-house-that-Jack-built to convey the feeling of slowly becoming familiar with a person. She had run through verb tenses, added and withdrawn qualifiers, coupled contradictory assertions, all in an attempt to preserve the vagaries of her mind. Now, after almost a decade of effort, she realized that the existential swarm of her impressions, the messy realities of her mind still resisted translation into communicable form. She therefore concluded that greater fidelity of representation might be achieved if she simply recorded the verbal responses her consciousness made to a particular subject, while minimizing her own manipulation of them.

To assist herself in this experiment, she temporarily gave up portraiture. Human subjects, she later said, distracted her by awakening memories. So she turned to the still life, where "looking was not to mix itself up with remembering" (*LIA*, 189).

For Gertrude Stein, *Tender Buttons* represented her full-scale break out of the prison of conventional form into the colorful realm of the sensitized imagination. But it did not signal an abandonment of control. Her practice was to concentrate upon an object as it existed in her mind. Her imagination was stimulated then not by the object's particular qualities alone, but also by the associations it aroused, by random interruptions of the act of composition, and by the words as they took shape upon the page. So far as Gertrude Stein could determine in her subjective isolation, all of these made up the object's full and authentic existence insofar as it had any reality for her. The object could not be separated from its context. It was entangled in an infinite web of relationships. If illuminated from a single source, fixed in a specific position, and viewed from one perspective only, the object would inevitably be falsely conceived. Gertrude Stein perceived that it was immersed in a continuum of sound, color, and association, which it was her business to reconstitute in writing. The woman who previously had sought to classify everyone by reducing each to a fundamental posture of attacking or resisting now luxuriated in the rich diversity of the inexhaustible present. She compared her accomplish-

124

ment in *Tender Buttons* to Shakespeare's creation of the forest of Arden. He had done it "without mentioning the things that make a forest. You feel it all but he does not name its names" (*LIA*, 236).

Because in *Tender Buttons* Gertrude Stein seemed to veer off into meaninglessness, the book has a certain notoriety. Max Eastman's comment typifies the shallow journalistic contempt it attracted. Eastman referred to the "parlor tricks" of "her silly book, *Tender Buttons*— equivalent in every respect except sincere passion to the ravings of a lunatic . . ." (*Great Companions*, 71, 47). John Malcolm Brinnin called the book a "great and resonant error" and "an eloquent mistake" (137, 138). Even a loyalist like Donald Sutherland was reduced to describing it as "a sort of Wonderland or Luna Park for anyone who is not too busy" (84).*

Despite its difficulties, *Tender Buttons* is Gertrude Stein's most original and cohesive work. One thousand copies of the slender, canary-yellow book were printed in 1914. Just when it was composed and in what order remains uncertain.†

Tender Buttons is unusually resistant to interpretation. As a consequence, critics have too often resorted to isolating small sections of it in order to show either that it is possible to "translate" it, or that it is gibberish. But, like most examples of literary art, the book should be treated as a whole. It builds, explains and illustrates its premises. The first step in fathoming it is to read it through.

Although I do not possess an infallible pass-key to *Tender Buttons*, there is no doubt in my mind that the book will yield its meanings as readers grow more familiar with it. In *The Development of Abstractionism in the Writings of Gertrude Stein*, Michael Hoffman has already described the local stylistic features of the book in considerable detail

---

* Oscar Cargill must be the only critic ever to have complained that *Tender Buttons* was overburdened with apprehensible content. Of the section "A Red Stamp," he concludes, "The trouble with the poem is that the parts have too conscious a reference; the piece has too much meaning" (*Intellectual America*, 295).

† The *Yale Catalogue* dates it 1910–12. But in *ABT* Gertrude Stein recalled that a portion of it "had been written during our first trip into Spain [the summer of 1912] and Food, Rooms etcetera, immediately on our return" (192). If her memory was accurate, *Tender Buttons* could not have been composed earlier than 1912. *ABT* compounds the confusion elsewhere by stating that after the return to Paris, Gertrude Stein "described rooms and objects, which joined with her first experiments done in Spain, made the volume Tender Buttons" (146). Both versions indicate that the third part, "Rooms," was written in Paris, but what was composed in Spain is still unclear. The book contains no recognizably Spanish images to assist in solving the problem. In her memoirs, Alice Toklas skirts the chronological problem by simply not mentioning *Tender Buttons*.

(175–97). He has not gone much beyond that, sensibly resolving not to assert more than he knows. More recently, in *Gertrude Stein and the Present*, Allegra Stewart has argued that *Tender Buttons* is a mandala, "a 'magic circle' or enclosure for the unconscious mind, originating in its maker's unconscious but elaborated with more or less conscious purpose, as an act of self-creation" (72). She regards the book's three sections as representing, (1) the clarity of perception, (2) assimilation and purification, and (3) integration at a transpersonal level. Although Professor Stewart's Jungian interpretations are sometimes more puzzling than *Tender Buttons* itself, it is heartening to discover that one can agree upon the importance of the book's opening section, and upon certain themes running through it. However it be interpreted, the book's tripartite structure is unusually suggestive. "Objects"—what we perceive outside us. "Food"—what we absorb. "Rooms"—what enclose us.

The use of a small group of words was always an identifying feature of Gertrude Stein's prose, even though her verbal palette changed over the years. In the *Three Lives* period, "certainly" was an important word for her. It was later replaced by such central terms as "being," "living," and "succeeding." In the *Tender Buttons* period, numerous expressions of courtesy and endearment began to appear, among them "please" and "thank you." These expanded in the next years into overt expressions of affection and even passion, into "dear," "baby," and "darling."

In *Tender Buttons* specifically, colors predominate, especially versions of red—pink, scarlet, crimson, rose. There are also words of transparency: glass, spectacle, eye glasses, carafe. Images of opening are common: gate, window. There are also ones of closing and obscurity: glaze, dusty, curtain, cover. One cluster of words concerns polishing and its effect: rubbing, shining, glittering. There are numerous receptacles: cups, plates, sacks. And there are images of breakage: crack, separate, shatter. These images of unity and separation, of obscurity and dirt, of clear vision and cleanliness, of blockage and of opening, of containers and of holders are all involved in the thematic development of *Tender Buttons*. Whatever the errors in their interpretation, their presence is undeniable and must be the starting-point for understanding the book.

There are other certainties in the book. It is divided into three parts of approximately the same length, although each differs slightly in the way in which it presents its material. "Objects" is composed of fifty-eight separate sections, each one possessing a title of its own. "Food" begins with a table of contents which is followed by fifty-one sections, each also having a title. "Rooms," the third part, has no separate sections, however, but is only paragraphed. The whole of *Tender Buttons* is a mélange of allusive theoretical statements, partial glimpses of a physical world, and spates of free association. It is all but impossible to transform adequately into normal exposition.

And yet it is founded in the ordinary world. About half the "objects" Gertrude Stein chose for her still lifes were reassuringly commonplace—a box, a plate, a seltzer bottle, a piano, a chair, a new cup and saucer, eye glasses, an umbrella, a handkerchief, shoes, a shawl. One set of objects though is slightly off-key, but still susceptible to explanation without resorting to excessive ingenuity—"A Piece of Coffee," "A Mounted Umbrella," "Careless Water." Other titles are conventionally phrased but uncertain of reference—"Glazed Glitter," "A Frightful Release," "In Between." Finally, a few titles are as eccentric as some of the prose of the book—"A Method of a Cloak," "A Little Called Pauline," "Suppose An Eyes." These come late in the first section. After a radical beginning—"A Carafe, That Is A Blind Glass"—Gertrude Stein normalized her section titles until she reached the last quarter of "Objects." Then they grew increasingly surrealistic, until they culminated in the weird trio of "Peeled Pencil, Choke," "It Was Black, Black Took," and "This Is This Dress, Aider."

Tender Buttons opens with an illustrative description of an opaque breakable container. "A Carafe That Is A Blind Glass" reads:

> A kind in glass and a cousin, a spectacle and nothing strange a single hurt color and an arrangement in a system to pointing. All this and not ordinary, not unordered in not resembling. The difference is spreading (*SW*, 461).

With this beginning, Gertrude Stein at once defends and illustrates her new method of representation. It is a conservative lesson, reasonably available. The carafe is made of a glass tinted grey-green or purple, the color of a bruise, a "hurt color." The carafe is a "kind" of glass container, one not so familiar as a pitcher, which is part of the immediate family of containers, but "a cousin." It is at once something to see and something through which to see, "a spectacle." Unfamiliar as its representation may be, however, it is "nothing strange." Its arrangement is part of a larger system which is not without order itself, even though it does not represent things in an ordinary way. The difference exemplified by this opening still life is "spreading," spreading in the book itself and into the world at large.

Although the meaning of any given sentence in "Objects" may be uncertain, an identifiable set of attitudes runs through it. They are couched in references to dirt, dust, and spots. "Dirt and not copper makes a color darker" (*SW*, 464). Contrasted to the images of dirt are the acts of washing, cleaning, and polishing. "The one way to use custom is to use soap and silk for cleaning" (463). Dirt is not construed as irrevocably bad. Its presence signifies the common condition of things as they are, which civilization, exemplified by soap and silk and literature, seeks to improve. "Book was there," Gertrude Stein writes, "Stop it, stop it, it was a cleaner, a wet cleaner . . ." (476). She is prepared to acknowledge that "certainly glittering is handsome and convincing" (461). But dirt "makes mercy and relaxation and even a strength to spread a table fuller" (464). Very likely Gertrude Stein intended to encourage moral tolerance here as well, an acceptance of doing "dirty" things. Dirt was the measure of existence. When accepted, it could humanize a person and release him from the mania for improvement. "Clean little keep a strange, estrange on it" (491).

By contrast, whiteness becomes the all-color, no-color emblem of purity, abstract perfection and absolute understanding, that great whale that had evaded and maddened Gertrude Stein as she sought to bring herself and the world to order. As she feelingly remarks, "A white hunter is nearly crazy" (475). It is greyness that has the most negative connotations. There are references to the "sick color that is grey" and to "a quite dark grey" that is "monstrously ordinary . . . because there is no red in it" (465, 467). The implication is that grey is monotonously unhealthy, as white by itself is inhuman. White has a place in existence though. The ideal furnished the perspective by which one can perceive the comic disparity between human aspirations and performance. Life should be lived passionately but seen objectively. "Go red go red, laugh white" (475). Gertrude Stein regarded it as shameful to preserve a superficial purity in fear of committing an error. Imperfection has its attractions. "A light white, a disgrace, an ink spot, a rosy charm" (471).

Gertrude Stein had given up trying to express the absolute as represented by whiteness. She chose rather the mess of existence. "A Sound" reads, "Elephant beaten with candy and little pops and chews all bolts and reckless reckless rats, this is this" (474). This is this. Existence, whatever its nature, furnished its own excuse for being. And why not?

"There is no pope" (473). In literature people had become habituated to reading narratives set in the historical past. And yet, "in a change that is remarkable there is no reason to say that there was a time" (471). The time was now, and "any occasion shows the best way" (469). Gertrude Stein confidently proclaimed the intuitive revolution. "The change has come. There is no search" (461). Her method neither drew upon the past nor calculated its effects. "To choose it is ended, it is actual . . ." Moreover, this record of actuality was accomplished "more easily much more easily ordinarily" (468).

Although "Objects" contains many images of cutting, sectioning, and otherwise dividing, Gertrude Stein distinguished the act of deliberate separation from unavoidable breaking or cracking. "A single image is not splendor" (463). When "a piece was left over," that meant the "the rest was mismanaged" (469). The complexity of the whole had to be respected, "nothing breaking the losing of no little piece" (466). Gertrude Stein concentrated upon the unique identity of the object. She offered it without cleaning or polishing it, or reducing it to an abstraction, or isolating it. Trouble, she thought, lay in constriction. "No evil is wide . . ." (491).

Towards the end of "Objects," the mood darkens. There are hints of salutary murders. The section "Peeled Pencil, Choke," reads simply, "Rub her coke" (476). The coke rubbing was evidently accomplished, for the next section is entitled, "It Was Black, Black Took," and it begins, "Black ink best . . ." (476). In what follows, Gertrude Stein rejects notions of service—of social welfare and financial obligations (as she remarks later, "a price is not in language" [484]), of responsibility. "Excellent not a hull house, not a pea soup, no bill no care no precise no past pearl pearl goat" (476).

The final section of "Objects," "This Is This Dress, Aider," begins on a melodramatic note already present in the title—This is distress, Ada. The section culminates with a killing, followed by a calm, although perhaps it is the calm of obliteration.

> Aider, why aider why whow, whow stop touch, aider whow, aider stop the muncher, muncher munchers.
> A jack in kill her, a jack in, makes a meadowed king, makes a to let. (476)

Someone is calling for assistance for another person—"Aider." That person is threatened by "the muncher," who is possibly the "pearl pearl goat" of the preceding section. Assistance is delayed by questioning.

129

Why aid her? Who? How? ("whow"). She is killed by a "jack." The consequence is a king in a meadow and an empty place to rent. Although sexual experience may form the metaphorical base for this bizarre conclusion, one may also take it to be a dramatization of the death of conventional literary practice. A monarch has been overthrown and rusticated or buried, and although the actual deposition was alarming, it has made room for something new.

The second part of *Tender Buttons* provides nourishment. Like "Objects," "Food" possesses a basic coherence. Among its fifty-one items are "Breakfast," "Lunch," and "Dinner" in that order. Each meal is surrounded by food appropriate to it, lunch being the main meal of the day. The food is simple and for the most part American. Considering Miss Toklas's reputation as an exotic cook, it is even rather dowdy—roast beef, potatoes, sausages, asparagus, chicken, cranberries, butter, rhubarb, salad, cocoa, milk, and oranges. The only odd items are "Single," "End of Summer," "Way Lay Vegetable," "Chain-Boats," and "Orange In." The sections of "Food" do not quite correspond to its table of contents. The title in the table of contents is often expanded or varied in the text, and some announced titles never appear at all.

While the points of reference in "Food" are standard items on the menu, the themes first introduced in "Objects" are continued. Gertrude Stein again argues the case for presenting the whole impression as it is received. "Considering the circumstances there is no occasion for a reduction . . ." (478). Her way is "melting and not minding." Such permissiveness produces "an outrage which is simultaneous" and "principal" (482). The philosophy behind it is one of serene acceptance. "Claiming nothing . . . this makes a harmony . . ." (480).

The major images are now of ingestion and absorption: there is a meal in mutton; students chew something; if there is a sudden change, it brings nausea (482–3). Gertrude Stein realizes that "the whole thing is not understood," but "this is not strange considering that there is no education . . ." (478). Near the end of *The Making of Americans* she had dismissed teachers outright, for "when I asked something they did not answer that question. . . ." Having endured answers all around the question, she became "certain that they cannot explain anything anything I ask them" (768). Now in *Tender Buttons* she had become the teacher nourishing her students with precepts embedded in examples. Recognizing that there would be resistance and confusion

130

caused by her unfamiliar methods, she resolved to "lecture, lecture and repeat instruction" (483).

Again and again she explained her new mode of expression:

A sentence of a vagueness that is violence is authority and a mission and stumbling and also certainly also a prison. (481)

This innovative writing of hers was obscure, and it did violence to ordinary expectations. But it also had the authority of reality. She did not overlook the dangers of her style. Missionary she might be, but she knew she could lose her balance, and that in its way, her work imprisoned her.

Tender Buttons was a book of impossible ambition. Tension is felt throughout it between the need for fresh expression, and the realization that the moment any word was put down, meaning had been restricted. Gertrude Stein felt her most successful moments were those that employed indirection. "A bent way that is a way to declare that the best is altogether . . ." Indirection she valued for itself. It reached no conclusion—"a bent way shows no result" (484). Towards the end of "Food," the incidence of puns heightened, for, "what language can instruct any fellow" (483). A "mussed ash" is discoverable, as are "in specs," "be where," "pea cooler," "bay labored," and "egg stir" (490, 493, 494, 495). These puns lead up to a bold aesthetic statement that sums up the themes the book has been developing—"real is, real is only, only excreate, only excreate a no since" (496). Gertrude Stein rarely made serious statements by means of such Joycean word-play, which here says that reality is the creative excretion of the moment, which may be regarded as non-sense.

"Food" then deals with obtaining, cooking, serving, slicing, eating, and digesting the outside world, of transforming it without destroying its integrity. The culinary mystery is the aesthetic one: that the whole can be sectioned and prepared, but never lost. In one sentence Gertrude Stein tried to unify space, time, color and odor. "Cut the whole space into twenty-four spaces and then and then is there a yellow color there is but it is smelled, it is then put where it is and nothing stolen" (487). Nothing must be lost in cooking. "Take no separation leniently," she counsels (485).

As had happened in "Objects," in the latter part of "Food" the offerings become extremely elusive. Gertrude Stein invents vocabulary, violates grammar, and makes extraordinary verbal juxtapositions. And yet the book's themes persist. "A type oh oh new new not no not knealer knealer of old show beef-steak, neither neither" (495). The more her writing was accepted without straining after its meaning, the more absolutely complete it became—"rest in white widening" (493). This whiteness was not achieved by traditional laundering of reality. "Washing is old" (492). Careful preparation of reality brought minimal results. "What is bay labored what is all be section, what is no much" (495). Gertrude Stein's "Food" was offered as nourishment of intrinsic value, "a bestow reed, a reed to be." It promised no more than that. "Read her with her for less" (497).

The third and last part of *Tender Buttons,* "Rooms," is paragraphed but not otherwise divided. As Gertrude Stein observes, "the whole section is one season" (509). Its topics are climate, the seasons, and the organization of interiors.

The last section of "Food" was entitled "A Centre In A Table." Gertrude Stein had already defined a table as "a whole steadiness" (474). "Rooms" picks up the idea of order expressed by a table and by a center. It starts, "Act so that there is no use in a centre" (498). A center presumes that everything in a composition radiates out from a main point. But Gertrude Stein did not believe that consciousness perceived in that way. Custom, she said, was "in the centre" (483). There in the very conception of a centre was the false reality. She asserted the need for shock and change, for establishing a coherence that was something more than a rest home for the aged.

> Anything that is decent, anything that is present, a calm and a cook and more singularly still a shelter, all these show the need of clamor. What is the custom, the custom is in the centre. (483)

Therefore: "Act so that there is no use in a centre." The preferable condition is when "a wideness makes an active center" (508). Rather than existing at a fixed point, the center moves and is everywhere and nowhere. "A wide action is not a width" (498).

In "Rooms" Gertrude Stein continued to defend the legitimacy of describing things without evoking either their names or their attributes. Why should she be so perverse? Because "a window has another spelling," because "this cloud does change with the movements of the moon" (507). Change was the fundamental principle in nature. Nothing was fixed, nothing isolated. "The name is changed because . . . in every space there is a hint of more . . ." (504–5).

132

In this connection it is impossible to overlook Gertrude Stein's former mentor, William James. She had studied his *Psychology* while at Radcliffe, and although I know of no evidence that she continued to read him after she left America, she did send him a copy of her newly published *Three Lives* in 1909, the same year that Leo was characterizing James as "a wonder" who "goes directly to my most innards" (*Journey*, 20). So his name was still in the air at the rue de Fleurus.

In *Psychology*, James had emphasized the selectivity of the human mind. In order to function, the mind is obliged to pick out and organize specific details from the possibly infinite extension of the not-me. As an illustration, James pointed out that "the real form of the circle is deemed to be the sensation it gives when the line of vision is perpendicular to its centre," just as "the real sound of the cannon is the sensation it makes when the ear is close by" (171–2). But the reality of the circle and of the cannon fire is much more varied and complex than such expedient selectivity can possibly suggest. Each person has heard numerous cannons from varying distances and under differing circumstances. The sum of those impressions, mixed with other related impressions, constitutes the sound of cannon fire for us. Yet, at the surface where people normally operate, a single word is assigned to the phenomenon, which, society agrees, will represent it. This is a practical compromise. The danger lay in mistaking the social compromise for the actuality.

This was especially the case, James pointed out, with objects of daily use such as paper, ink, butter, an overcoat. We grow habituated to them and their stereotyped functions until "we end by believing that to conceive of them in those ways is to conceive of them in the only true way." But, James insisted, the stereotypes are not real. They do not provide us with true ways of conceiving objects—"they are only more frequently serviceable ways to us" (357–8).

Nothing in James's universe had a separate, distinct existence. For all practical purposes, the universe exists in the conscious mind. James therefore sought to determine the nature of consciousness. It "does not appear to itself chopped up in bits . . . it is nothing jointed: it flows" (159). In trying to describe the consciousness, James compared the definite images in the mind to boulders in a stream, each of which "is steeped and dyed in the free water that flows round it" (165). James was seeking to impress upon his audience that substantives were only the most prominent part of the consciousness. "It is, the reader will see, the reinstatement of the vague and inarticulate to its proper place in our mental life which I am so anxious to press on the attention" (165). The vague and inarticulate were the sense of relations, "near and remote" that flowed around and splashed over the substantive image (165–6).

These dynamic aspects of consciousness also required statement. "The great blunder to which all schools are liable," James argued, is the failure to register "the transitive parts of thought's stream" (162). In other words, nouns dominate conception in all fields of human expression. That J. A. M. Whistler's painting, "Arrangement in Grey and Black," the title of which suggests merely color relationships, should yield in the popular mind to "Whistler's Mother" testifies to the enduring, but psychologically false, pre-eminence of substantives.

Although no longer directly under William James's guidance, Gertrude Stein could encounter variants of his ideas in the Parisian world of art, and in the philosophy of Henri Bergson, whose lectures she may have attended in Paris in 1908.* Bergson complained that psychology proceeded by analysis, as Gertrude Stein had early in her career. "It resolves the self . . . into sensations, feelings, ideas, etc. which it studies separately." In consequence, "an external and schematic representation" was substituted for "the real and internal organization of the thing" (*An Introduction to Metaphysics*, 31–32). This "reduces the object to elements already known," or in Gertrude Stein's terms, one's impressions of an object were distorted by bending them to the rigid demands of grammar (24). Bergson further insisted, as had James, that "reality is mobility. Not *things* made, but things in the making, not self-maintaining *states*, but only changing states, exist" (49).

By the time she composed *Tender Buttons*, Gertrude Stein had come to similar beliefs. Focussing on a single target brought inevitable loss, or mechanical results, as she knew from the experience of trying to capture a single personality with the long, diagrammatic sentences of *The Making of Americans*. Now she abandoned the notion of centrality. "Nothing aiming is a flower" (508). Her resolute acceptance of her principles resulted in her most coherently irrational book. Since she no longer sought analytic order, she characterized "A Time To Eat" as "a pleasant simple habitual and tyrannical and authorised and educated and resumed and articulate separation" (472). She wanted none of it, but rather stew, anytime.

The blind carafe with which *Tender Buttons* opened had been de-

* Allegra Stewart, "The Quality of Gertrude Stein's Creativity," 498, n. 46.

scribed as "All this and not ordering, not unordered in not resembling." The last sentence of the book picks up the collective phrase, "all this" to summarize and conclude what the description of the carafe had started.

> The care with which there is incredible justice and likeness, all this makes a magnificent asparagus, and also a fountain. (509)

With this final statement Gertrude Stein proclaimed the quality and power of *Tender Buttons*. In it, she attested the care with which she had worked to assemble the collection of still lifes. They were accurate, although she realized that that contention strained belief. As a whole, the book was food and water. And what had begun with a container of limited capacity ended in a flowing source.*

The degree of intelligent artfulness displayed in *Tender Buttons* makes it impossible to answer B. F. Skinner's question, "Has Gertrude Stein A Secret," affirmatively. Skinner proposed in his article that *Tender Buttons* was an example of automatic writing. (See also Chapter 2, pp. 30–32.) However, in drawing a parallel between Gertrude Stein's laboratory work at Harvard, and *Tender Buttons*, which was written almost twenty years later, Skinner chose to neglect her prolonged and arduous development as a writer.

Although Gertrude Stein diplomatically told the editor of the *Atlantic Monthly* where Skinner's article appeared, that she thought him a "pretty good" psychologist "when he is not too serious," she firmly denied his thesis (letter to Ellery Sedgwick, February 1934, YCAL). Over the years though, her denials took various, inconsistent forms. Logical exposition was not her forte. She explained to Sedgwick, "No it is not so automatic as he thinks. If there is any secret it is the other way to. I think I achieve by xtra consciousness, xcess . . ." (YCAL). However, the first report, "Normal Motor Automatism," had noted that "the ability to write stuff that sounds all right, without consciousness, was fairly well demonstrated by the experiments" (506).

Before Skinner made consciousness an issue, Gertrude Stein had felt free to locate her creative efforts apart from it. In 1932 she scornfully countered the charge of being imprecise and mystically fuzzy. "I take things in and they come out that way independent of conscious process. All this foolishness about my writing being mystic or impressionistic is so stupid. Every word I write has the same passionate exactness of

---

* I am indebted to Allegra Stewart for this last perception. See *Gertrude Stein and The Present*, 132.

meaning that it is supposed to have. Everything I write means exactly what it says" ("Biography," preceding "Grant Or Rutherford B. Hays," *Americans Abroad*, 418).

That argument was no longer tenable after Skinner's article. By 1937 when she reached the subject of automatic writing in *Everybody's Autobiography*, she had conceived a new, bland defense. First, Leon Solomons, not she, had prepared the article. As his junior, she went along with his conclusions, even though she did not believe them. Although automatic writing was conceivable to her under abnormal conditions like hypnotic states, she was positive that neither she nor Solomons wrote automatically. "We always knew what we were doing" (267). In at least one interview given during her American tour of 1934–5, she had declared flatly that the Harvard experiments had led her to conclude of automatic writing "that there is no such thing" (Baltimore *Sun*, 24 December 1934).

As for how she actually did compose *Tender Buttons*, she hardly deigned to indicate. "One must realise what there is inside in one and then in some way it comes into words and the more exactly the words fit the emotion the more beautiful the words . . ." (*EA*, 267).

In spite of all this defensive dust-throwing, Gertrude Stein could legitimately insist that her method of composing *Tender Buttons* differed from her activity as a participant in the 1895 Harvard experiments. At Harvard, the subject's attention was diverted by a second person so that the act of writing would take place with as little participation of the consciousness as possible. Eventually, it is true, Gertrude Stein "found it sufficient distraction often simply to read what her arm wrote, but following three or four words behind her pencil" ("Normal Motor Automatism," 506). So at Harvard her attention had no stable focus, only the inadvertent and changing influence of carrying on a conversation or listening to a book being read, or reading what her pencil produced.

But, as best one can determine, in composing *Tender Buttons* Gertrude Stein sought to reproduce her verbal responses to selected objects with the imposition of as little formal organization upon the words evoked as possible. She fixed her attention, therefore, on a particular object, then recorded the words that it stimulated in her mind. If anything, rather than being distracted, her attention was preternaturally focussed; and on a single, stable object. Although the results she achieved may not differ appreciably from those produced in automatic writing, the psychological distinction is a fundamental one.

136

7

♫. "Please do it. Gertrude doesn't like to be
frightened."

("No")

Tender Buttons had been an audacious undertaking. In it, Gertrude
Stein had successfully managed to advance the case for reporting the
full and subjective verbal response to an object, while at the same time
demonstrating what she meant. Until the coming of the war, the pieces
she wrote subsequent to *Tender Buttons* resembled its individual sections. Generally brief and difficult to decipher, they were marked by a
vocabulary of containers, colors, food, and light.

As she approached her fortieth birthday, Gertrude Stein had thousands of pages of unpublished manuscript. The neglect periodically depressed her—"about every three months I get sad. . . . where oh where
is the man to publish me" (Sprigge, 110). Early in 1913 she traveled to
England, hoping to attract the publisher John Lane to her cause.
Turned down once more, all she could do was join "resignation with
neglect" and maintain her "strength of purpose." She recognized the
peculiarity of her work but affirmed its value. She offered "celebrations
and bursts and specks and a kind of thing that has no particular name
but is useful . . ." ("England," *G&P*, 93–94).

Meanwhile she experimented fitfully, with no particular end in mind
other than novelty. A good deal of incidental word-play showed up,
such as references to a "bycicle," "vagrant wellies," "estranged speats,"
and "a couple of condies" ("Old and Old," *O&P*, 222, 225, 228). The
same piece idly turns the phrase "the rest is popular" into "the rest is
pole teller" and "the rest is pope and wheeler" (229). She invented
numerous puns like "archie texture" and "leet ill" ("In," *BTV*, 46, 45).
"Millionaires" was transformed into "meal one airs," "Sunday" into
"sunny," and "Wednesday" became "weeding day" ("Meal One,"
BTV, 147; "Finished One," *BTV*, 171).

In this pre-war period, Gertrude Stein's portraits also assumed the new style of *Tender Buttons*, although, unless the Yale chronology is in error, she was liable to fall back upon older techniques. In 1913, for example, she offered the likenesses of three friends in three distinct styles.

"A Portrait of One, Harry Phelan Gibb" begins:

> Some one in knowing everything is knowing that some one is something. (*G&P*, 201)

That abstract and repetitive style gave way to a more variegated surface in her portrait of "Braque." Discussing the art, theories, and problems of the sober craftsman, she very nearly made conventional sense throughout.

> Brack, Brack is the one who put up the hooks and held the things up and ate his dinner. He is the one who did more. He used his time and felt more much more and came before when he came after. (*G&P*, 145).

The more extreme syntactic dislocations and private language of *Tender Buttons* is visible in her portrait of "Guillaume Apollinaire," which reads in full:

> Give known or pin ware.
> Fancy teeth, gas strips.
> Elbow elect, sour stout pore, pore caesar, pour state at.
> Leave eye lessons I. Leave I. Lessons. I. Leave I lessons, I.
> (*P&P*, 26) *

The vocabulary of *Tender Buttons* also dominated three of Gertrude Stein's most celebrated portraits, "Susie Asado," "Preciosilla," and "Sacred Emily." Carl Van Vechten has suggested that the first two were inspired by "the same flamenco dancer," presumably the Argentina, with whom both Alice and Gertrude were very much taken (*SW*, 548). However, Preciosilla was the stage name of a singer in Madrid, whom Alice describes in *What Is Remembered* (71). The Stein Collection at Yale possesses a tinted picture postcard of her.

"Sacred Emily" contains the first appearance of Gertrude Stein's famous sentence, "Rose is a rose is a rose is a rose" (*G&P*, 187). A conservative version of the sentence's structure had appeared in *A Long Gay Book*—"A day that is a day is a day" (*GMP*, 37). It is worth

---

* Michael Hoffman has analyzed the system of sound associations in this portrait in *Abstractionism*, 173–4.

noting that in its original form "Rose" is a given name and not a flower. This was the version Gertrude Stein adopted for her monogram. The first instance I am aware of in which "rose" is preceded by the indefinite article occurs in 1922 in "Objects Lie on a Table." There Gertrude Stein asks, "Do we suppose that all she knows is that a rose is a rose is a rose is a rose" (*O&P*, 110). The acerb and imperial tone may be ascribed to the fact that she is addressing a somewhat bumptious apprentice. In the very next piece written, "As Fine As Melanctha," she observed serenely, "Civilization begins with a rose. A rose is a rose is a rose is a rose" (*AFAM*, 262).*

In 1912 Gertrude Stein made one other notable technical advance. The innovation occurred in "Monsieur Vollard Et Cezanne," a piece concerning the Parisian art dealer whose portrait Picasso had completed in 1910. For the first time in her career, Gertrude Stein placed single words, phrases and sentences in vertical columns.

> This is truth.
> Trust.
> Thrust to be.
> Actually.
> Reveal. (*P&P*, 37)

The consequence was that her word-play was emphasized as had never been possible when it was crowded into a paragraph. The possibilities struck her as attractive. As she finished the piece (which contains the edginess of a lovers' quarrel), she signalled her awareness of the novelty. "Yes I have gotten a new form" (39).

Subsequently, her writing, which was already utilizing the discontinuities of the *Tender Buttons* style, often accentuated her words by surrounding them with white space. At the same time, she pushed their format as far as she could:

> Was.
> Was. Cream.
> Pear----ery.
> Cut----ery
> Slice ear-------ie
> A creamerie. ("In," *BTV*, 44)

---

* There are four roses in the basic sentence, but variants appeared as "presently I will establish rows and rows of roses" ("Didn't Nelly and Lilly Love You," *AFAM*, 242). Also see, "A rose tree may be may be a rose tree may be a rosy rose tree if watered" ("A Diary," *A&B*, 205). Once GS referred to ABT's putting the device on their chinaware: "Indeed a rose is a rose makes a pretty plate" ("A French Rooster," *SIM*, 213).

The formal resemblance of such an arrangement to dialogue did not escape Gertrude Stein. The title "Scenes. Actions and Dispositions of Relations and Positions" already indicated that plays were on her mind. This piece moved directly out of the concerns of *Tender Buttons*. The dramatic world was latent in a collection of still lifes. But in transforming the external world into art, she insisted that it was essential to respect actual placement. "To have that position and . . . to show the way which is not changed as a pleasant greeting and that recognition is all there is of all reunion" (*G&P*, 99–100). No artistic synthesis was justifiable other than the artist's primary encounter with his subject. That encounter "does not copy relation," nor does it produce a "realistic" representation, but "it does have that movement" (100).

In her opaque way, Gertrude Stein seems to have been arguing the case for serial composition, for placing "one by the side of another." That was what "disposition" meant to her—the repositioning that takes place when things are translated into words. "Any language cannot be foreign" (114). The translation will be understood intuitively as valid. "If there is a faithful action then belief is certain . . ." (98).

"Scenes," like *Tender Buttons*, argued for the scrupulous retention of everything. "That which is useful is the thing that is individual . . ." and "to keep on is to use what there is . . ." (97). Composition must start with the world as given, for it is sanctified. "Blessed are the patient particulars" (106). Fidelity to the ensemble of particulars will necessarily produce a response. "So the whole thing means this that if there is a continual use of it all there can be and there is the expression of that emotion" (106). Any limitation of the full experience is self-defeating, or, as she declares at the end of "Scenes": "There is no use in no more" (121).

As she first conceived it, the dramatic experience for Gertrude Stein was something resembling a mental pageant. *Tender Buttons* had attempted to render the existence of various objects without ever naming them. Now she turned to people in "What Happened A Five Act Play," which she later designated as her first play (*LIA*, 118). Her intention in it was, "without telling what happened . . . to make a play the essence of what happened" (*LIA*, 119). Inasmuch as the filtering agent was her mind, her "plays" predictably resembled her still lifes and portraits composed in the *Tender Buttons* manner.

The only theatrical characteristics to "What Happened" are its title, which announces that it is a play, and its division into five acts. Otherwise, the writing utilizes Gertrude Stein's familiar techniques, such as

140

the question which is given a sybilline answer. "A birthday, what is a birthday, a birthday is a speech . . ." (*G&P*, 208). Or she employed the more recent violent syntactical and semantic dislocations of "A tiger a rapt and surrounded overcoat securely arranged with spots . . ." (205).

Nor are the pieces written in the following years and designated "plays" notably different from the still lifes. But Gertrude Stein did turn gradually to the human voice, for recording it promised a modicum of order. "What a system in voices," she exulted, "what a system in voices" ("Pink Melon Joy," *G&P*, 356). She admitted that "I cannot tell a consecutive story," and that "I often talk about nothing" ("How Could They Marry Her," *Envoy*, IV [January, 1951], 66; "He Said It," *G&P*, 270). But she did arrange speech in short bursts, broken occasionally by meditations. The dialogue was often an inner one carried on between Gertrude Stein and herself. The drama was minimal.

I like plays.
To write
Yes that way. ("A Very Good House," *PL*, 28)

If the drama was minimal, so at times was her inspiration. At such moments, working for the sake of work, she incorporated her purposelessness into her composition. The whole of "One or Two. I've Finished" reads:

There
Why
There
Why
There
Able
Idle (*BTV*, 179–80)

Suddenly, the reign of vacuity was interrupted by the First World War. Gertrude and Alice had traveled to London in July 1914. They were staying as weekend house guests with the Alfred North Whiteheads when the war actually began. Since travel was uncertain, the two women remained in the country with the Whiteheads until mid-October, when they made their way back to Paris. For the next five years, Gertrude and Alice were to be on the move, first fleeing the war, then assisting in the alleviation of the misery it caused. Not until May 1919 were they again securely settled at the rue de Fleurus.

The impact of the war on Gertrude Stein's writing was profound. The alterations in her environment affected her prose. It was in this period that her prose began to absorb heard speech seriously. "Crete" was the first of several pieces that seem to be running dialogues, somewhat disconnected and a little out of focus, but much more normally expressed than the sentiments of *Tender Buttons*. "Crete" starts, "Is Miss Clapp at Newnham now. She has been about ten days in bed. Oh I am so sorry" (*BTV*, 172). This familiar discourse is occasionally derailed, sometimes arbitrarily. "She said something and I did not put it down. I put down Donald" (*BTV*, 172). But the norm is regularly re-established. Here as elsewhere, it is impossible to determine whether the dialogue is between Gertrude Stein and another, or between Gertrude Stein and herself. Long portions seem to be verbalized inner monologues, broken by external exchanges. The inclusion of a good deal of recognizable but slightly disconnected speech gave Gertrude Stein's pieces an aura of eccentric chatter. Other examples of such dottiness are "In One" and "Gentle Julia." All were reportedly written during the 1914 trip to England.

It is probable that Guillaume Apollinaire was in part responsible for this change. He had been experimenting with a "Cubist" prose in which disconnected passages were juxtaposed. He also created a few "poèmes-conversations" in which he would record his meditations upon a subject, interspersing them with snatches of speech he had overheard, but which were otherwise unrelated to his train of thought.* Apollinaire also eliminated punctuation from his collection of poems, *Alcools* (1913). Since Gertrude Stein knew Apollinaire personally and adopted all of these mannerisms between 1912 and 1914, which is precisely the period when Apollinaire was experimenting with them, it is reasonable to infer his influence.

Judging by internal evidence, the first piece written after war was declared was "Painted Lace." It describes how the war reached Gertrude Stein. References to the Czar, to "this ever rising tide of national enthusiasm," to killing, retreats, fights, and "thousands of skilled stirrups" come sifting through various domestic concerns (*PL*, 1–3).

"Painted Lace" also displayed an irritability—"Oh shut up"—that would recur regularly in the years to follow. "A New Happiness," for example, was evidently written after the two women returned to Paris, for it mentions Beffa, their male Parisian concierge, the month of January, and Belgium. Although the piece started out as a paragraph, it soon evolved into vertical one-word statements mixed with informal reflections. "Blame was thrown upon the queen. / Not yet. / Is your

* For an example, see "Lundi rue Christine" in *Calligrammes*.

father living yet. / Not yet. / But her friends were truly sincere. / Adversity. / Near. / Belgium" (*PL*, 152). A good deal of anxiety and pleading occurs near the beginning of "A New Happiness." It apparently originated in a proposal to leave Paris, and culminates in a gratified outburst. "We won't go to England. Oh blessed baby . . . Oh cherished joy. That's what you are. . . . Oh you cherub" (*PL*, 155). But even after this particular crisis is surmounted, a number of intimations are heard of a prevailing domestic upheaval. Friends were leaving, there were problems retaining servants, and coal was hard to find.

The shock of the war, which had inconvenienced, frightened, and dislocated her, changed her prose. Events intruded implacably upon the trivial, time-killing word-play that had characterized the year 1913. Normal speech and an increasing number of personal details entered Gertrude Stein's writing. Names of friends, recognizable objects, domestic quarrels and tender reconciliations constituted the bulk of her subject matter.

Nonetheless, Gertrude Stein continued to write short pieces in which she followed associations wherever they might lead: "be low . . . below . . . bed low . . . bid low . . ." ("Tubene," *BTV*, 179). She also invented new ways to distort normal practice. "Bird Jet" offered phrases concluded by a period, then followed by a word starting with a small letter. "Eight eggs. acting" (*BTV*, 179).

The longest such piece was called "One Sentence." It is not one sentence, but runs to over thirty pages of mostly one-line statements, interspersed with a kind of surrealistic vaudeville. The continuity of the whole may be cued by the early sentence, "An elderly couple talking much much or much talking too much to much" (*AFAM*, 73). Its subject may be a family or perhaps a fixed circle of friends. At any rate, considerations of an Isabella dominate the middle portion, of a Fanny, the last. Many of the statements are critical judgments. "Isabella's neck did not look well" (82). "She is a polite silly woman" (77).

Gertrude Stein and Alice Toklas fled Paris for Spain in March 1915, then settled in Mallorca. Encouraged by the French victory at Verdun, which halted the German advance, they returned to the rue de Fleurus in the spring of 1916. This adventure seeps into her prose frequently. Although "One Sentence" is assigned to 1914 by the *Yale Catalogue* it almost surely dates from 1915, for it contains the remark, "The accounts from Paris are not pleasant," as well as mention of Palma

(*AFAM*, 90). Also, the writing composed during the period the two women spent on the Mediterranean is often preoccupied with the physical attributes and behavior of women. "One Sentence" initiates this subject. If not written in Mallorca, then it was probably done in Barcelona, where the two companions went first.

"One Sentence" furnishes a sophisticated model of the new style Gertrude Stein had been cultivating since *Tender Buttons*. It was a composite of statements made by a single speaker. The procedure was for a declaration to be made, followed by associative elaborations if they arose spontaneously. If not, a new declaration was made. The effect is one of banal queerness. Here is a representative sequence:

> They refused not to be dirty.
> I believe she is crazy.
> He was as he often is extremely disagreeable.
> The others I do not know.
> What a disagreeable old woman and a safe. She sees combinations.
> That is false. (*AFAM*, 75)

Occasionally the remarks are bizarre. In some instances playfulness produced the unexpected as in "He is drinking glasses," or "I certainly took a fan for him" (79, 98). At other times the situations contrived are exceedingly incongruous. "There is a needle in her leg." "They killed and salted some kangaroos" (78, 99). However strange the statements though, they generally retain an informal familiarity. As she remarks, "It's wonderful how it always comes out. / Conversational" ("Johnny Grey," *G&P*, 168).

"One Sentence" contains numerous personal references. The names used may be unfamiliar, but as Gertrude Stein explained elsewhere, "I make a new name, and yet every name is the same . . ." ("Saints and Singing," *O&P*, 73). So, although she might be reproducing the voice or correspondence of an acquaintance, it is difficult not to take these details as reflecting Gertrude Stein's life at this time when one reads, "I have very bad headaches and I don't like to commit to paper that which makes me very unhappy" or "Fanny and I are alone the weather is fine and hot. / We read aloud to each other in the evening" (*AFAM*, 105).

During her Mallorcan exile, the volume of Gertrude Stein's technical and aesthetic remarks notably diminished. When she did refer to her compositions, it was likely to be in the context of urgent personal relations. At one point in "This One Is Serious," her energies ran down before the reader's eyes. She had opened the piece with some para-

graphs of monologue, then shifted to one-line sentences. Near the end
she roused herself into a wearied acknowledgement of the change:

> When I finish this I will begin again.
> I keep on saying this one is serious.
> I am so tired.
> And sleepy.
> And I started the other way. (*PL*, 23)

She was absorbed in the complexities of her domestic life. "Now I
change the subject, I will change to a description of our leisure" ("No,"
AFAM, 37). Alice Toklas evidently continued to serve as copyist for
Gertrude Stein, but had strong opinions about some of her companion's
methods. "Don't you understand trying to stammer. / No indeed I do
not" ("I Like It To Be a Play," *G&P*, 288). Gertrude Stein tried to
pacify her. "I should have told you that . . . on top there's a space
. . . That meant a space and you see you didn't leave it. . . . You
won't get angry" ("No," *AFAM*, 39).

She also made some unguarded comments about her work. "I have
little chickens. / That doesn't mean anything" ("Pink Melon Joy,"
G&P, 361). It is not clear whether that criticism is self-generated, or
records the opinion of her sceptical intimate. Once that voice gives a
peremptory command.

> This must not be put in a book.
> Why not.
> Because it mustn't.
> Yes sir. ("Bonne Annee," *G&P*, 302–3)

Sometimes the censorship she acknowledges is absolute. "I have been
so careful. / I will not say what I feel" ("All Sunday," *A&B*, 118). "I
do not wish to write down what I hear" ("Decorations," *BTV*, 186).
Sometimes she acknowledges a substitution in terms. "I am sadly tormented with flies, I do not mean flies" ("All Sunday," *A&B*, 109).
Similarly: "We eat our breakfast and smoke a cigar. That is not so
because we call it by another name" ("Bonne Annee," *G&P*, 302). The
monitors appear to be both the disapproval of Alice, and her own reluctance to speak directly of certain subjects.

Alice Toklas entered these Mallorcan pieces rather frequently under
her given name. Once, in "Do Let Us Go Away," her surname was
included: "Miss Alice Toklas wishes Roberts to kindly send her by
registered mail—under separate cover—I Ivory soap—and a good
face soap that Roberts can recommend" (*G&P*, 225).

Other references indicate that Alice served as a source of information and advice. ". . . she asks have we ever heard of a poet named Willis. / Alice has. I have not. She says he belonged to a group. Like Thoreau" ("He Said It," *G&P*, 273). She is called upon to discuss a meaning. "Explain looking. Explain looking again. Alice explain looking again." And in the same play, "Not Sightly," the narrator asks, "Alice why do I say blow noses. Alice I hear you" (*G&P*, 290, 294). Such social and domestic interplay remains particularly strong in this period away from Paris.

Moreover, it carried directly into the boudoir. Perfectly homely details emerge in the midst of comments of uncertain significance. "I'd like to go back. Cook knows everybody. I am going to put grease on my face do you mind." So far so good, but the next sentence is "A continuance roundness makes a shimmer." Others follow, equally oblique, such as "Shawls have hair. Bicycles are skylarks and a silk night has stars . . ." Then the commonplace question and answer reappears. "What are you doing my precious. Taking grease off my face my love" ("All Sunday," *A&B*, 100).

This intimacy extends to washing hair, to the need for woolen stockings against the cold, and to wondering why "stockings come down in hot weather" ("No," *AFAM*, 38; "All Sunday," *A&B*, 104, 126). And it goes beyond the women's physical life into their emotions. Even as Alice Toklas is directly mentioned, so is Gertrude Stein herself, or at least Gertrude. Not only does the "I" in "Farragut or A Husband's Recompense" say "I am now going to begin telling everything," and "I was naughty," and "I am going to be happy in winter," and "I don't like rain," and "Some day we will be rich. You'll see. . . . and then we will spend money and buy everything a dog a Ford letter paper, furs, a hat, kinds of purses"; she also notes "I was born at eight o'clock" which is precisely when Gertrude Stein was born (*UK*, 9, 8, 10, 12, 15, 9). "Please do it," she implores in another piece. "Gertrude doesn't like to be frightened" ("No," *AFAM*, 51).

The two companions carry on an active social life, make plans, debate alternatives, pass judgments on people they have met. Gertrude Stein was often discontented, which led to expressions of pique and even actual quarrels. "I want to be good and happy and cheerful and not blameworthy or peevish," she declared, but again and again admits, "I have been foolish excitable and irritable" ("No," *AFAM*, 60, 54). She seems not only to have been excitable, but a shouter, and "just at first there was a dispute." The explosion was followed by contrition. "What is shouting. / It is a disease" ("Farragut," *UK*, 9). This explosiveness was but a single manifestation of her frustration. "I am often angry. Sometimes I cry. Not from anger. I only cry from heat and other things. I love to be right. It is so necessary" ("This One Is Serious," *PL*, 20).

Against these uncorsetted displays came the other's icy firmness. "I don't care to hear your opinion," she will say, or, "You have answered me defiantly," an accusation that was instantly denied—"I have not" ("Henry and I," *PL*, 274; "He Said It," *G&P*, 268). Sometimes the note is one of curt dismissal:

Oh do not annoy me. ("If you had three husbands," *G&P*, 390)

Let me alone. ("Independent Embroidery," *PL*, 82)

Do not speak to me. ("Miss Cruttwell," *AFAM*, 181)

Exacerbated as they were by the tensions of war-time, the most trivial occurrence could set things off, such as merely turning the pages of a book:

Don't turn the leaves.
Because they make a noise
Yes.
Do not say so to me.
Is it very necessary.
We were so tired.
To-day. ("This One Is Serious," *PL*, 22)

Domestic concord was achieved through open acquiescence to a militant, even sadistic tone.

I give you this.
Yes.
You give me this.
Yes.
Yes sir.
Why do I say yes sir. Because it pleases you.
("Bonne Annee," *G&P*, 302)

That same voice of command addresses that same yielding voice here: "If you want to be respectable address me as sir. / I am very fond of yes sir" ("Mexico," *G&P*, 317). The full measure of the dominance appears in this paragraph:

You will give me orders will you not. You will tell me what you prefer. You will ask for what you want . . . I see what you wish, you need to have instant obedience and you shall have it. I will never question. Your lightest wish shall be my law. ("Water Pipe," *larus*, I [February 1927], 6)

As is often the case, it is difficult here to make out just who the speaker is. A dialogue that is proceeding normally will suddenly veer out of control, the "I" and the "You" seemingly changing places. At times this happens because Gertrude Stein fused separate episodes without warning. While reproducing a colloquy with Alice in the present, suddenly she would flash back to an exchange heard earlier in the evening at a dinner party. On other occasions, what seems an external dialogue is probably a debate between separate parts of her personality.

Sometimes Gertrude Stein used false names, just as she created code words for certain censorable material. "What is my another name," asked this woman who had long projected facets of herself into fictional guises ("Lifting Belly," *BTV*, 66). The problem was doubly complicated because the code was not consistently observed. But she occasionally permitted a glimpse of her arbitrary methods: "Let us give this name Jenny excellent here. Do not mistake which Jenny. No I will not" ("All Sunday," *A&B*, 122).

The heavy concentration of authoritarian demands—"address me as sir"—in the writing of the Mallorcan year may have nothing to do with Gertrude Stein's actual life. Still, it is probably significant that most of the pieces in this general period were published, like *Things As They Are,* posthumously. In part this delay may be ascribed to their length. The most revealing, like "Possessive Case," "No," "Pink Melon Joy," "A Sonatina Followed By Another," and "Lifting Belly"—are in general also the longest. But discretion would also argue withholding them from publication.

The imperious demands for respectful address were matched by numerous instances of impassioned pleading. Their core is sometimes "please forgive me," sometimes "Please me please me," but always "please" and always "me" ("Miss Cruttwell," *AFAM*, 177; "This One Is Serious," *PL*, 20). Everywhere come these cries for understanding, for remembrance, for support, for love, for forgiveness. "Believe me. Believe in me," cries the desperate voice. "I do," responds the cool one ("I Like It to Be a Play," *G&P*, 288). The refrain is so insistent that once Gertrude Stein merely put down, "Please baby please etcetera" ("Possessive Case," *AFAM*, 112).

These vulnerable outbursts modulated readily into the need for affection. "Neglect me and believe me and caress me" ("Mexico," *G&P*, 305). "You dear you are so sweet to me" ("He Said It," *G&P*, 270). Gertrude Stein understood clearly that, "To accomplish wishes one needs one's lover" ("Woodrow Wilson," *UK*, 111).

There seem to have been temporary flurries of infidelity. That at least is the suggestion of many of these pieces, as in the titles "I Often Think About Another," and "If You Had Three Husbands." The opening lines of "No" are a stuttering version of a military marching chant: "Left, left, you had a good wife but you left." The disorientation manifest in her version suggests the effect of the situation:

Left.
Left.
Pretty.
I
had
pretty
a
good
pretty (*AFAM*, 35.)

Some of the affection expressed was chastely infantile. "B is for birthday baby and blessed. / S is for sweetie sweetie and sweetie. / Y is for you and us is for me and we are as happy as happy can be" ("Farragut or a Husband's Recompense," *UK*, 12).* When the tone flames up—"Jenny kiss me kiss me Jenny—I'll let you kiss me sticky"—the effect is disconcerting ("Universe or Hand-Reading," *PL*, 268–9). Reading Gertrude Stein in this period is rather like listening to an interminable tape recording made secretly in a household. Amid domestic details, local gossip, references to failed ambition, to sewing, to writing, recriminations, apologies, and expressions of remorse come passages of intimate eroticism, sometimes quite overt in meaning. Physical passion had been virtually absent from Gertrude Stein's work since *The Making of Americans*, or at least sufficiently disguised to be invisible. Now though, as she entered her forties, the demon of noon capered openly through her writing.

The key erotic work of this period is "Lifting Belly," a fifty-page love lyric, composed mostly of one-line tributes to "lifting belly." These are often followed by a cool and even sardonic response. Virgil Thomson has described it as concerning "the domestic affections," and so it is, luridly so ("Lifting Belly," *BTV*, 64).

Names again shift bewilderingly, although certain ones have a steady relevance. "Baby" is a frequent term of endearment, universally ap-

* The "Farragut" of the title seems to be a jocular reference to Gertrude Stein as the admiral of the boat by which the two women crossed from the mainland of Spain to Mallorca. So, in the last sentence of the piece, the husband, Farragut, and the writer are the same person. "A husband's recompense is to have his wife so Farragut finishes." (18)

plied. "Baby is so good to baby" ("Lifting Belly," *BTV*, 85). External evidence attests that "Pussy" is Alice Toklas, as in "Pussy how pretty you are" ("Lifting Belly," *BTV*, 78). Alice is also addressed in "Little Alice B. is the wife for me. . . . she can be born along by a husband strong who has not his hair shorn" ("A Sonatina," *BTV*, 12). Other names of uncertain application appear in "Daisy dine / You are mine," and "Call me Helen" ("No," *AFAM*, 59; "Lifting Belly," *BTV*, 90). But it does not require much ingenuity to decide who "fattuski" and "Mount Fatty" are ("Lifting Belly," *BTV*, 86, 97).

As the quotations already offered indicate, Gertrude Stein thought of her relationship with Alice Toklas in heterosexual terms. "She is my sweetheart," she announces, and at other moments she exclaims, "Darling wifie is so good," and "Little hubbie is good." The request "Please be the man" is answered directly, "I am the man" ("Lifting Belly," *BTV*, 92, 110, 110, 112).

"Lifting Belly" then sings of "stretches and stretches of happiness" (*BTV*, 87). The title phrase designates both a person and an act. "Lifting belly is so strong. I love cherish idolise adore and worship you" (*BTV*, 80). "Lifting belly is kind and good and beautiful" (75). "Lifting belly is alright. / Is it a name. / Yes it's a name" (68). But lifting belly is also "a permanent caress" and "an occupation I enjoy" (98, 96). "Lifting belly high. / That is what I adore always more and more" (91). "I can go on with lifting belly forever" (100). The ambiguity permitted the fusion of the loved one and the act of love. "I am fondest of all of lifting belly" (79).

This "bathing bathing in bliss" came at a time of considerable insecurity in Gertrude Stein's life (*BTV*, 86). Cut off from her Parisian circle of friends, she depended even more upon the support and company of Alice Toklas. The "dance of the emotions" assumed a prominence impossible to overlook ("One Sentence," *AFAM*, 97). Gertrude Stein continued to experiment, but her aesthetic advances were overshadowed by autobiographical details. She had been reading about Henry the Eighth. Her dog chased goats and so was obliged to wear a muzzle. Their house needed whitewashing, for the wood fires had smoked its walls. The winter wind and rain displeased them. She chafed under the uncertainty. "I don't know how it is going to turn out" ("We Have Eaten Heartily and We Were Alarmed," *PL*, 42).

When the two women returned to France and became involved in the war effort, this outburst of love poetry ceased, but it flowered anew in the early twenties, beginning with "A Sonatina Followed By Another.

150

Dedicated By Request to D. D." * Written during a vacation in Vence, the piece is quite clear, and kittenishly erotic. Gertrude Stein accurately characterized it as a "honeymoon" ("Mildred's Thoughts," *The American Caravan,* 656). She still often referred to the relationship she enjoyed with Alice as a marriage, using the conventional designations of husband and wife for them. "She was born in California and he was born in Allegheny, Pennsylvania" ("Didn't Nelly and Lilly Love You," *AFAM,* 223). She offers one little tableau of Alice embroidering and herself writing: ". . . she with a sheet of linen and he with a sheet of paper . . ." ("A Lyrical Opera," *O&P,* 57). The marital identities are often unmistakable. "I am a husband who is very good I have a character that covers me like a hood and must be understood which it is by my wife whom I love with all my life" ("Didn't Nelly and Lilly Love You," *AFAM,* 245).

In this second set of love poems, the endearments of "honey," "baby," and "pussy" continued to be used. One diary-like entry in "A Sonatina" reads: "Pussy said that I was to wake her in an hour and a half if it didn't rain. It is still raining what should I do" (*BTV,* 6). Alice is also referred to as the "jew." "I love my little jew. . . . I care for her hair and there for the rest of her too my little jew" ("A Sonatina," *BTV,* 31).

Much of the sensuality during the Mallorcan period was expressed in terms of food. "Lifting belly is to jelly." "I am very well satisfied with meat" (*BTV,* 80, 86). "It does make a nice cake" ("No," *AFAM,* 43). "What is a melon. A little round. / Who is a little round. Baby" ("A Lesson For Baby," *BTV,* 197). The main course in this erotic menu was made overt in, "Tiny dish of delicious which / Is my wife and all. / And a perfect ball" ("The Present," *BTV,* 212).

This culinary enthusiasm was continued in the twenties, but added to it was the word "cow." "I marvel at my baby. I marvel at her beauty. . . . I marvel at her generosity. I marvel at her cow" ("Coal and Wood," *PL,* 4). Gertrude Stein further reveals that "All of us worship a cow. How. By introducing and producing and extension" ("A Sonatina," *BTV,* 31). The "cow" is associated with food, with wetness, and with an emergence, which on one occasion is not unlike birth.

A fig an apple and some grapes makes a cow. How. The Caesars know how. Now. ("A Sonatina," *BTV,* 20)

* Alice Toklas declared there was no "D. D.," that the initials were only a Steinian fantasy (*BTV,* 3).

There was a little apple eat.
By a little baby that is wet.
Wet from kisses.
There was a good big cow came out.
Out of a little baby which is called stout.
Stout with kisses. ("The King or Something," *G&P*, 124–5)

And little trinkets is most moist when little cow comes out head foist. ("Nest of Dishes," *PL*, 101)

I bless the cow. It is formed, it is pressed, it is large it is crowded. It is out. Cow come out. Cow come out and shout. ("A Sonatina," *BTV*, 9)

Cows are very nice. They are between legs. ("All Sunday," *A&B*, 101)

The other main term in this network of erotic symbolism is "Caesar" or "Caesars." They appear repeatedly as custodians and masters of ceremonies for the cow.

Have Caesars a duty. Yes their duty is to a cow. Will they do their duty by the cow. Yes now and with pleasure. ("A Sonatina," *BTV*, 10)

Break of day, break of day, what do the big Caesars say. They say One Two Three Cow. ("Nest of Dishes," *PL*, 107)

Once a description was offered. "Caesars are round a little longer than wide but not oval. They are picturesque and useful" (*Two Poems*, n. p.). The Caesars and the cow are sometimes rhapsodized in concert:

Do you remember that a pump can pump other things that water. . . . Yes tenderness grows and it grows where it grows. And do you like it. Yes you do. And does it fill a cow full of filling. Yes. And where does it come out of. It comes out of the way of the Caesars. ("A Sonatina," *BTV*, 26)

The Cow.
Yes Caesars.
The Cow.
Oh you blessed blessed planner and dispenser and joy.
My joy.
The Cow. ("The King or Something," *G&P*, 127)

The references to "cow" and to "Caesar" appear in some half a dozen pieces written over a period of at least four years, but they make the most sense as parts of the body, physical acts, and character traits in "A Sonatina." Even as she approached her fifties, Gertrude Stein's need to record her passions remained unquenchable.

152

"Birth and Marriage" Gertrude Stein designated as "a continuation of a sonatina followed by another," by which she meant that it was a love poem (*A&B*, 198). This long, cheerful piece concerns a "he" and a "she" who are born, then married. "She" was born on April 30 and was one of two children in a family, after having for a long time been the only daughter (184). Both details apply specifically to Alice Toklas. The male marriage partner is one of seven children, which Gertrude Stein was, counting the two dead children she and Leo replaced.

"A Third," written the following year, concerns an interloper who at least temporarily disrupted the union. "To change two to two and a third" (*AFAM*, 335). The piece attempts to exorcise an indiscretion, during which "she prefers Bourbons to Jews, wives to weddings and it happens that it happens and not as well as finished" (340). Temporarily, "A third is always first." But who might that third be? "That is for you to find out my fat wife" (340). Late in the text, the name "Gertrude" is used, whereupon the following observation is made: "This is the first time to have mentioned mentioned mentioned repeat mentioned" (347).

"A Third" attests that "Apples and figs burn. / They burn" (350). Eventually though, the erring party comes round. "When she heard of three she preferred two. When she heard of me she preferred me" (351). If there is any crucial moment, it comes when the narrator finally asserted herself rather than passively yielding. "One day I said to her I like it like that . . . She likes it like that . . . This is the way they enjoyed everything. . . . She needs me" (354). The Steinian tone is never vindictive. Her conciliatory nature was summed up in a sentence which was first used in 1921, variants of which turned up throughout the rest of her prose. "How do you do I forgive you everything and there is nothing to forgive" ("Reread Another," *O&P*, 124). The crisis successfully weathered, the conclusion is a happy one: ". . . when she settles settles and sits then . . . it succeeds" (*AFAM*, 357). With that psychological storm over, the narrator can turn to "now an entirely different matter. Our mind can linger on the subject of cows and fishes in abundance" (356).

By the middle twenties, references to cows still turn up occasionally, but no longer in an erotic context. The bovine associations now appear to refer to her literary productivity. "On my return once more as a cow . . . I intended to settle down to it" ("Equally So," *AFAM*, 270). Placid, ruminative, regularly productive: these were the attributes of the cow and of the writer for whom Alice Toklas, like Milton's daughters, served as milkmaid. In her earlier stormy moments, Gertrude Stein had indicated that tranquillity at home was essential. "This is in building. Now now now have a cow have a cow. / Concentrate" she enjoined herself, for "in this way preparations may be undertaken." But her meditations were interrupted by a really malevolent irritability. "Sit and sit smell and smell. Go to hell go to hell" ("Subject-Cases," *AFAM*, 4).*

The dislocation of life in Mallorca was relieved in the summer of 1916, when the two women decided it was safe to return to Paris.†

Old friends like Maud Cruttwell and Claribel Cone reappeared at once in Gertrude Stein's prose, as did figures of the Parisian world of art and music like Erik Satie ("I Can Feel the Beauty," *PL*, 85). With the title "Marry Nettie" Gertrude Stein played upon the name of the leader of the Futurists, Filippo Marinetti, although she made no other reference to him in the portrait. She did pray in it, "May the gods of Moses and of Mars help the allies" (*PL*, 46).

The war was unescapable. The two women therefore decided to assist the American Fund for French Wounded. They arranged to have a Ford motor car shipped over from America, which they then had converted into a truck. On 18 March 1917 they set off to open a supply depot in Perpignan, so their involvement preceded America's entry into the war, which took place on April 6 (GS letter 18 March, 1917 to Henry McBride, YCAL).

Gertrude Stein's direct involvement in the war reduced the passionate egocentricity of the Mallorcan year. She and Alice were charged with establishing depots and then delivering supplies to hospitals. During the actual war, their assignments were all in the southern regions of France, well away from the actual fighting. As Alice Toklas remembered it, when they were given a choice of where to serve, social considerations determined her choice. "I said Perpignan because we knew some people there" (*WIR*, 95). The two women showed no disposition

---

* Unless it is misdated, "A Lyrical Opera Made By Two To Be Sung" regresses almost a decade in style and subject matter. Apparently written in 1928, it is a series of outcries of domestic passion, such as those epitomized by "Lifting Belly." The "cow" reappears as a sensual word, and the air is filled with coy endearments directed to little wifie, sweetie, darling, and the like. (See *O&P*, 49–60.)

† Here, the *Yale Catalogue* does not accurately reflect the situation, for most—perhaps all—the pieces shown as written in 1916 are Mallorcan pieces, even though Gertrude Stein had left the island in the spring of that year. Moreover, most of the pieces attributed to 1917—there are only twelve in all—were probably written in Paris in the latter part of 1916, to judge by their contents.

to be in the center of the conflict, but neither were they tempted to return to the United States. When the second World War broke out, they again retreated into provincial France. As Gertrude Stein noted, "Kicking is relegated to the Midi. . . . Disturbances are confined to the North" ("Kicking," *BTV*, 213).

Neither in the pieces composed at the time, nor in her reminiscences did Gertrude Stein give much evidence that the war impressed her. A few references derive from her service. The Ford truck appears, the Red Cross is mentioned, the formulaic phrase for military commendation, "exceptional conduct," becomes one of her titles (*BTV*, 183, 198, 207). But the violence of the war and its aftermath of sick and wounded men fails to penetrate her prose. Gertrude Stein habitually turned away from physical suffering, although with the perspective of time, she found it possible to take a wry view of one death. In *The Autobiography of Alice B. Toklas* she tells of an American soldier mortally injured in a fall from a train. "He did not believe that the little french trains could go fast," she observed, "but they did, fast enough to kill him" (227).

The pieces Gertrude Stein wrote in 1918 were very brief, bits of her consciousness possessed of virtually no formal unity. "Call It a Table," for example, reads in its entirety:

Do not dispute me.
Oh no.
Do you call it a table. (*BTV*, 183)

For some reason "can" was the key word, as in "Can You Behave Better" and "Can You Sit in A Tree" (*BTV*, 207, 209). Otherwise, these were no more than the mechanical gestures of a writer keeping her hand in, while her attention was elsewhere. At best she experimented with phrasing. She played literary divisions off against the natural rhythms of oral statement. In "A Patriotic Leading," she distributed the dialogue in separate "verses," but that term was no more than a variant of "pages" or "acts." The limits of "Verse III" were defined by one voice making a statement, then a second seeking clarification, and finally the first confirming it. "We are worthy of everything that happens. / You mean weddings. / Naturally I mean weddings." But "Verse V" and "Verse VI" exchange a question and its answer. "Do you think we believe it," asks Verse V. "It is that or bust," responds Verse VI (*UK*, 81).

The one exception to the general triviality of the pieces written during war-time service is a piece entitled "The Work." It is the first example of Gertrude Stein actually explaining prose she had written in her more obscure moments. On these grounds alone it merits some attention.*

"The Work" is about a third shorter than "Work Again" because it eliminates a large section of material that concerns private feelings and circumstances. It concentrates upon hospital experience, for the revision was specifically undertaken for the audience of the *Bulletin* published by the American Fund for French Wounded. In it, Gertrude Stein supplemented her elliptical statements with commentaries, each prefaced by the phrase, "By this we mean . . ." or by a variant like "This meant that . . ." "This refers to . . ." and "This is apropos of . . ." The result cannot be offered as a model of lucidity; still, it is considerably clearer than the original. Furthermore, the specific glosses show the kind of abbreviation that took place when Gertrude Stein strung together her associations.

For example, one sequence of phrases in "Work Again" reads: "Then then. / All the leaves. / All the hotels. / All the boils" (*G&P*, 393). In "The Work," its revised version, an explanation follows "All the leaves." "This means that as we went South there were leaves" (*BTV*, 191). For a reader unfamiliar with Gertrude Stein's recent history, even that concession was minimal. We can deduce that as the women drove south from Paris in March 1917, they were impressed by the leaves beginning to bud on the trees. Following "All the hotels," she elaborates: "Of course there were hotels and many of them were most sympathetic." She then goes on to tell a rambling anecdote about a landlady. The phrase "All the boils" is dropped, perhaps as being too personal to merit further explanation. A later sentence, "The wind blows," is supplemented by the remark, "Naturally we think about the wind because this country of Rousillon is the windiest corner in

* "The Work" also exhibits the bibliographical problems that compound the difficulties of understanding Gertrude Stein. "The Work" is a revision of another piece called "Work Again." But "Work Again" does not appear as such in the *Yale Catalogue*. Rather, one is referred to items 185, 186, and 187. However, only one of these, number 185, "Barrels," can be identified in "Work Again." They all precede "The Work," which is item 202.

There is more. In December 1917, Gertrude Stein published in the old *Life* magazine, a piece entitled "Relief Work in France." According to the story she tells, *Life* was then publishing parodies of her work by Kenneth Roberts, so she wrote the editor proposing that he publish a sample of the original, since she was funnier than her parodists (*ABT*, 210). When *Life* accepted, she played a joke of her own. "Relief Work in France" cannibalizes at least four other pieces: "Tourty" and "Work Again" both subsequently published in *Geography and Plays;* "The Work" and "Wood" which appeared posthumously in *Bee Time Vine*.

France" (*G&P*, 394; *BTV*, 192). "They ask have we a stocking" generates a full paragraph:

> This is apropos of the colonials. We see a great many. They fight so bravely and as they have many of them no people they are so grateful we like them so much. And they have such pleasant ways of speaking to each other. We get to talk to them. (*BTV*, 191)

The commentary is disconnected and impressionistic. The original, unexplained statement stimulates more interest than does the glossed version, for there the imagination is at least free. Since there is no evidence that these glosses of her ambiguous prose were intended to be satirical, the glimpses they afford into the mind of Gertrude Stein during the period of her obscurity are not propitious. The mind that so expresses itself is not only commonplace, but compared to the Radcliffe student, actually regressive.

As this example shows, Gertrude Stein had moved closer to normal usage. The meaning of "All the leaves. / All the hotels. / All the boils" was unclear only because the referents were insufficiently elaborated. Fantasy and verbal play were not eliminated, for her work always contained remnants of old habits as well as trials of new possibilities. It may be useful to review some representative sentences of the past, which serve to recapitulate Gertrude Stein's career through the first World War:

> Melanctha Herbert always loved too hard and much too often. She was always full of mystery and subtle movements and denials and vague distrusts and complicated disillusions. (Ca. 1904, *Three Lives*, 89.)

> As I was saying pairing of friends and pairing in loving is always a repeating of the coming together of the kinds of them and this is not just general repeating but very detailed repeating, wonderfully alike the pairs are then in character and looks and loving and living. (Ca. 1908, *MOA*, 221.)

> In being an honest one, in telling what she was telling, she was needing being one an honest one in being a good one in being one being telling what she was telling. (Ca. 1910, *MMW*, 156.)

> Wet crossing and a likeness, any likeness, a likeness has blisters, it has that and teeth, it has the staggering blindly and a little green, any little green is ordinary. (Ca. 1912, *TB*, 486.)

> Buy that.
> I don't.
> Have to.

Why.
Because it's mine.
        (Ca. 1915, "No," *AFAM*, 67.)

We have no worries.
What can you think of a bone.
It is useless to think.
        (Ca. 1918, "Work Again," *G&P*, 399.)

As her war service came to an end in 1919, Gertrude Stein's spirits visibly lifted. "In the midst of our happiness we were very pleased," she wrote, ending "Accents in Alsace" (*G&P*, 415). This piece which was subtitled "A Reasonable Tragedy" drew together a number of variegated units which she distinguished with subtitles and impish designations like "Scene," "Another Act," "February XIV," and "Act 425." Laid in Alsace, it begins with an awkward account of a boy who deserts the German cause and joins the French foreign legion, which causes his family to be harassed.* Mixed with this story were numerous personal endearments, as well as such casual observations as, "We like the road between Cernay and the railroad" (*G&P*, 412).

The most notable stylistic feature though is the intermittent rhymed gaiety of the piece. Gertrude Stein used couplets, triplets, and even quatrains. "In the daylight / And the night / Baby winks and holds me tight" (*G&P*, 410). And she imitated the Alsatian accent, England becoming "Eggland," "What," "Wha," and "Petite," "Petide" (*G&P*, 411, 409, 409).

The same enthusiasm for doggerel appeared in "Prim Roses," a series of emphatic statements about victory. Simple declarations were enhanced by childish rhymes. "Patience and wishes. / Wishes with fishes. They knew the day. / We will sway and pay" (*BTV*, 212). The assertive mood of this period sometimes became positively hearty. "Old dogs. / Old dogs are we. / Old dogs / Old dogs merrily / We see. / Hurrah. / Sunday" (*BTV*, 213). That is the whole of "Old Dogs."

"Tourty or Tourtebattre," subtitled "A Story of the Great War," proceeds in a different direction. Like "Accents in Alsace" it draws upon the history of a stranger rather than personal experience. But "Accents in Alsace" devoted only its opening lines to the soldier and his family, whereas Tourtebattre's story runs through the whole of his piece. It is unique in this, and in the fact that it is the last composition devoted to war-time matters. Tourtebattre was a wounded Frenchman known in a hospital by "us." His name may have some semantic rele-

* There is a paragraph on this family in *WIR*, 103.

158

vance. Literally it means "fool to beat" which, generously construed, summarizes the sketch. He had suffered some difficulty with his wife; she may have deserted him. And although "they" gave him colored beads which he worked into picture frames, they too avoided him in their private lives. "Tourty" is a rather sad, wry story about an amiable man, universally rejected.

After a prologue summarizing Tourty's relationship to "us," there are four sections, each entitled "Reflections." These reflections are carried on with the assistance of a second voice. The implications of Tourty's situation are ruminated upon as the story advances. The effect is that of reminiscence carried on by friends, with the attendant correction of detail. The narrative is interrupted by realistic exchanges:

> Can you think why Marguerite did not wish Jenny Picard to remain longer.
> Because she stole.
> Not really.
> Yes indeed. Little things.
> This will never do. (*G&P*, 404)

There is also sharp criticism in the digressions. To the question, "What did he ask for" comes the response, "Why I don't know," followed by:

> Why don't you know.
> I don't call that making literature at all.
> What has he asked for.
> I call literature telling a story as it happens. (*G&P*, 403)

"Telling a story as it happens" was precisely what Gertrude Stein was trying to do. The story of Tourty was being filled in and brought up to date before the reader's eyes. Rather than first quiz her companion about details and then tell the story, Gertrude Stein tried to do both simultaneously. "Facts of life make literature" (*G&P*, 403).

"Tourty" is a freak of nature in Gertrude Stein's garden. She did not follow up the technical possibilities provided by its form. Indeed, for her they were distinctly conservative possibilities. Still, in its "recollections" of a soldier, "Tourty" did signal the end of the war in her writing. Observing the international negotiations following the armistice, Gertrude Stein asked herself, "What is this." Then she answered in the only way then possible. "You can't say it's war" ("Scenes From the Door," *UK*, 78).

8

ה. "A cook does not mean that there is cooking."

(*G.M.P.*)

Upon her return to Paris, Gertrude Stein turned temporarily to second-hand sources for her subject matter. Politics, particularly the kind generated by the peace conferences, briefly entered her writing as it had never done before. "Who can neglect the papers," she asked in "The Psychology of Nations or What Are You Looking At" (*G&P*, 417).

Alfred North Whitehead's daughter, Jessie, had come to Paris with the Peace Commission (*ABT*, 180, 233). Judging by the frequency with which Gertrude Stein mentioned her name in connection with remarks about the disposition of countries, it appears that the involvement of a personal friend stimulated Gertrude Stein's interest in diplomatic negotiations. During 1920, the League of Nations, Poland, South Africa, and General Smuts all entered her prose, as did President Wilson and Zionism. Wilson's first name was invariably linked in her mind with the subject of wood, which was just then the principal fuel and not easy to obtain.

Great Britain having accepted a mandate over Palestine in 1920, the Jewish issue was very much in the news and on at least one occasion touched Gertrude Stein directly. "The Reverie of the Zionist" was evidently inspired by a challenge flung at her. Her response was defensive. "Can we believe that all Jews are these" (i.e., Zionists). Her conclusion was, "Judaism should be a question of religion." For that reason, "I don't want to go to Zion" (*PL*, 94).

Gertrude Stein had never been a practicing Jew. However, even though Gertrude Stein neither observed Old Testament laws and customs, nor believed in a personal God, as a young woman she had felt an emotional tie to Judaism. During her junior year at Radcliffe

160

in a twenty-five page essay prepared for her "Forensics" course, she defended the proposition that "The Modern Jew who has given up the faith of his fathers can reasonably and consistently believe in isolation." By "isolation," she meant "no intermarriage with an alien." She argued that Judaism was a "race-feeling" which ought to be perpetuated as a "brotherhood devoted to noble aims and great deeds" (Typed copy, YCAL).*

By the time she was working on *The Making of Americans*, Gertrude Stein had already become ambivalent about her Jewishness. In successive revisions, the qualification "Jewish" became, first, "German," and then "middle-class" (Katz, 207). Thereafter, her references to Judaism were infrequent. Mostly they identified Alice Toklas, "my little jew," or were of no more consequence than the pun, "May June and Jew lie . . ." ("A Sonatina," *BTV*, 31; "A Lyrical Opera Made By Two," *O&P*, 53).

International politics proved to be a brief enthusiasm for Gertrude Stein. But the idea of formal theatricals continued to occupy her after the war. "I do not care to see plays. I like to write plays" ("Coal and Wood," *PL*, 6). Her efforts to date had been haphazard and amateurish. Although most of her pieces through 1920 which she identified as plays did contain numerous spoken lines, dramatic form was otherwise absent. She never would attempt a traditional dramatic arc of emotion. Meanwhile, lacking the cumulative force of a plot, her plays needed some formal structure which she had not yet found. Essentially, "play" meant to her the liberation of her fancy.

She did enjoy the dialectic of conversation, and turned her attention to dialogue again. "Once more I think about conversations" ("A Circular Play," *LO&P*, 145). Further, "I love conversation . . . I like it to come easily . . ." ("What Is This," *UK*, 78–79). Rather than string a series of variants together, she distributed them to separate voices, usually two. Verbal exchanges permitted her to amplify her meaning in separate lines, as well as to raise objections to herself. At the same time, the confusion caused by contradictions was reduced.

Because his correspondence was published in 1920, Henry James turns up on two occasions. "We are all agreed that we like the letters of Henry James," she remarks ("A Circular Play," *LO&P*, 143). More characteristically eccentric is her reference to "Henry James Winner"

* Although the fervent idealism of the essay is altogether consistent with Gertrude Stein's undergraduate views, its fluency and orderliness are quite unlike anything else she wrote at that time. My conclusion is that someone assisted her with it.

followed by "Howells hold all" ("Scenery," *BTV*, 218). Howells had died that year. Alice Toklas tells us in her own memoirs that when Gertrude Stein and T. S. Eliot met in 1922, the poet asked, "Can you tell me, Miss Stein, what authority you have for so frequently using the split infinitive? Henry James, said Gertrude" (*WIR*, 115).

References to saints occurred sporadically too, and Gertrude Stein reminded herself, "Develop Spanish. / Thoughts. / Thoughts. / Thoughts. / Thoughts" (*BTV*, 217). She tried her hand at a movie scenario, which permitted her to write a telegraphic prose. "Back tomorrow. Called up by chief secret service. Goes to see him" ("A Movie," *O&P*, 396). The climax was a slapstick chase—"two american crooks with motor cycles on which they try to escape over the top of the Pont du Gard, great stunt, they are finally captured" (397). The scenario concludes with a mock-heroic procession under the Arc de Triomphe with William Cook "waving the american flag Old Glory and the tricolor" (397, no period).

So, in the immediate post-war period Gertrude Stein found herself as uncommitted as she had been just before the war. Her work displayed a good deal of variety, was alert and lively, but it lacked urgency and direction. By this time, too, the Dadaists and Surrealists were more than matching her enigmatic prose. Although their compositional techniques differed, these writers produced bizarre verbal surfaces that exemplified their interest in the relationship of consciousness to language. This flowering of the irrational in literature was at once an opportunity and a threat for Gertrude Stein. Practically speaking, it offered her greater opportunities for publication. Through 1917, only eight of her submissions had been accepted by periodicals, but from the end of the war through 1925, she had twenty-three pieces and two books published. On the other hand, with these new and prodigiously bright competitors, Gertrude Stein felt obliged to clarify her aesthetic ideas. Her attention focused again on the use of language.

Her observations are scattered through her compositions of this period. She began by affirming her preference for her native tongue. "I like to speak english I like to write english" ("Coal and Wood," *PL*, 6). She soon refined that preference. The war having activated her patriotism, she made the first of what would be many declarations of her nation's literary superiority. "Americans can write better English. Americans can express the language" ("Woodrow Wilson," *UK*, 108).

Her words continued to pass through dizzying metamorphoses, often carried out with Alice Toklas in mind. "Whimsies consist in pleasing a wife in instantaneous reference" ("A Circular Play," *LO&P*, 148). So thoroughly permeated with her companion's presence was she that when a dialogue ensued, the second party might be Alice, or merely Alice's sceptical voice in Gertrude Stein's mind. "Do I sound like Alice," she asked. If so, the reason was that "when I am accustomed to them their voices sound in my ears" ("A Circular Play," *LO&P*, 150). She regarded herself as one with Alice. "God bless me which is you" ("Lend A Hand," *UK*, 206). On one occasion she furnished an explicit example of consultation over a code word. "I said what word would best suit the expression of my appreciation. And she suggested, exquisite. I said I considered daisy more decorative and she and I said we will say that. I'll say it" ("Didn't Nelly and Lilly Love You," *AFAM*, 240–41).

She now affirmed her disjunctive arbitrariness. "I have come to increasing isolated reflections," she noted, "by very simply asserting that . . . they easily come and that it is necessary that they come at all" ("Didn't Nelly and Lilly Love You," *AFAM*, 241). She was prepared to insist that what is, no matter what it is, must be what it is. She demonstrated her mental processes. How might a merry-go-round which is picking up speed be described as a "rapidly growing waterfall"? She provided the linkage. "I can remember the word cascade and the word carrousel. For merry-go-round" ("Didn't Nelly and Lilly Love You," *AFAM*, 241).

Gertrude Stein had long played with such verbal permutations as "I am a complement to you. You compliment me" ("Saints and Singing," *O&P*, 77). Now, however, she started to think explicitly about the meanings beyond homonyms and cognates. "Standard," she mused, "has two meanings it can be a banner or an estimate" ("Didn't Nelly and Lilly Love You," *AFAM*, 236). Similarly, "To an American an Indian means a red-skin not an inhabitant of the Indies, east or west" (Ibid. 247). Ambiguity was built into the language. "Words are shocks," she said, and so they were for her ("Woodrow Wilson," *UK*, 111). Striking her sensibility, they immediately sprayed into new combinations. "St. Cloud and you," she begins one passage, the rhyme indicating that the French pronunciation was wanted. Then she crosses over to the English—"Saint Cloud and loud" ("Photograph," *LO&P*, 152).

During these post-war years Gertrude Stein also meditated upon the resemblances of words as an influence upon their production. One piece starts, "First poise," then pauses to reflect, "Poison is nearly here." Later, cued by the word "rabbit," she asks, "How do you eat hair." When this brings the admonishment, "Spell correctly," she then proceeds to demonstrate how relative spelling is. "Heynse. Irish. / Heinz. German. / Heins. Swiss. / Heines Austrian and / Haines Australian" ("Capture Splinters," *BTV*, 218–19).

Such verbal relationships stirred her sense of humor. "A knee is necessary for kneeling" is only a variant of the discovery that "poise" nearly contains "poison" ("Singing To a Musician," *P&P*, 235). In "Jokes for Jessie," she observed: "In England they call them drawing rooms. / The English cannot draw" (*BTV*, 222). Elsewhere, "The sea is water colour" ("B. B.," *P&P*, 163).

Just as Gertrude Stein began to cultivate the humorous possibilities of her prose, she seems to have felt a whiff of mortality. It was her forty-eighth year. Elizabeth Sprigge is the only one of her biographers to mention that Gertrude Stein underwent a "minor operation" after the war, but even without this clue, there is evidence that she suffered some medical problem severe enough to require hospitalization (128).*
In a short piece entitled, "I Feel a Really Anxious Moment Coming," she noted, "I have an entirely new bed-room" (*PL*, 236). The unfamiliar surroundings seem to have been especially trying. "We find an operation to be exceedingly difficult if there is an absence of the accustomed . . ." ("As Fine As Melanctha," *AFAM*, 262). There are also references to radium and to the X-ray, to resting, to being on "the road to restoration," and finally, the exultant cry, "Baby is all well baby is all well baby is all well all day and all night too" ("Saints and Singing," *O&P*, 77; "As Fine As Melanctha," *AFAM*, 263, 264; "Mildred's Thoughts," *The American Caravan*, 660). The nature of the illness is never specified, although it may have involved some sort of oral surgery. Once she advises, "Do not neglect a tooth . . . do not neglect positive poison . . ." ("Didn't Nelly and Lilly Love You," *AFAM*, 246).

References to nuns began to accumulate at this time too, suggesting that Gertrude Stein was in a Catholic hospital, attended by nursing sisters. If so, she was involved with Catholicism for the first time in

* In a letter to Harry Phelan Gibb, 23 December 1921, Gertrude Stein remarked, "I was laid up more or less for a month . . ." (YCAL). She did not elaborate, and I have been unable to locate any other reference to an illness, in her correspondence, or elsewhere.

her life. It may have stimulated her already existing interest in saints. "The origin of mentioning saints singing were nuns praying" ("Saints and Singing," *O&P*, 86). Someone impressed Gertrude Stein by observing that her writing was blessed with innocence and beauty. She remarked of saints, "I am said to resemble them." The characteristic she shared with them she identified as uninhibited responsiveness. "I feel saints feel readily" ("Talks to Saints," *PL*, 111, 109).*

Circumstances other than the challenge of the Dadaists and Surrealists encouraged Gertrude Stein to analyze her achievement in the early twenties. As she was making no particular progress, the time was ripe for a review of her career. Another motivation was the discovery of the young Ernest Hemingway at her door, come, at the instigation of Sherwood Anderson, to learn the art of writing. Still another was her decision to publish a representative selection of her work. These stimuli turned Gertrude Stein to self-explication, an activity she carried on industriously for the rest of her life.

Hemingway arrived in Paris in December of 1921 and met Gertrude Stein in March of 1922. Someone very like him turned up almost immediately in an important piece written in that year, "Objects Lie On A Table" (*O&P*, 105–11). Its air is distinctly didactic, that of a master enlightening the apprentice. The initial stimulus seems to have been that Gertrude Stein had learned that nuns enjoyed her writing, probably *Tender Buttons,* whose first section was "Objects." "Nuns ask for them for recreation." She is questioned, "Have you meant to have fun and funny things. Do you like to see funny things for fun" (105). The pleasure the nuns took in her work stimulated Gertrude Stein. She began to explain how she composed. "Objects lie on a table. / We live beside them and look at them and then they are on the table then" (105). Later she elaborated, "Objects on the table . . . mean to us an arrangement" (106).

When the apprentice arrives, she instructs him too. Their colloquy contains an exchange on the achievement of authenticity:

> And he says I am very willing but I have had to invent something to fill in and I say to him you had better really have it and he said I am not able to get it and I say to him I am sorry I have not one to lend you . . . and he replied, I do not doubt that you will be of great assistance to me and as for the result that is still in question. (*O&P*, 108)

* Juan Gris may have stimulated her interest too. She had recently revived their friendship, and in 1922, he did a painting called "La Religieuse" of a nun standing with a halo around her head, See D-H. Kahnweiler, *Juan Gris,* plate 27.

The pupil was not always as attentive as might be wished in the presence of an established figure. "When visiting they had said to him, listen while we are talking" (109). Gertrude Stein's short portrait of Hemingway, written the following year, 1923, emphasizes the conventionality of his courtesy as well as his desire to learn from the two women. "How do you do and good-bye. Good-bye and how do you do. Well and how do you do" ("He and They, Hemingway," *P&P*, 193). These formal politenesses were coupled with a barely concealed arrogance that assumed that Gertrude Stein, although a leader now, was "nearly finished." It was evidently Hemingway's ambition to furnish what the ladies could not offer—a "memorial of the failure of civilization to cope with . . . extreme savagedom" (193).

In time, the apprentice was asked to practice rendering objects, apparently without naming them. "Imitate a cheese if you please. We are very well pleased with gold coin and ribbons. . . . We were not pleased with the imitation of the lamb" (*O&P*, 110). The teacher prided herself upon her perceptiveness. "I have a special taste in feeling. . . . I readily recognise the object that has the most perfect quality of imitation" (110). Furthermore, she would not suffer herself to be regarded as a fool. "Do we suppose that all she knows is that a rose is a rose is a rose is a rose" (110).

Like "The Work," "Objects Lie On A Table" was one of the growing number of compositions in which Gertrude Stein attempted to illuminate her past work. "Made A Mile Away" (written in 1924) provided a "Description of all the pictures that have attracted some attention" (*transition*, VIII [November 1927], 155). That the attention was Gertrude Stein's was verified in her 1934 lecture, "Pictures," which glossed this piece composed a decade earlier. The elliptical manner in which she expressed herself in the twenties was demonstrated as she expanded her original reaction. Of El Greco she had said, "Longer so much longer and so much" (156). In "Pictures," she explained that she liked El Greco's paintings because "every thing in them was so long" (*LIA*, 73). Her first, oblique reference to Courbet was, "You see Courbet and it is so resembling." This was expanded to, "Courbet really did use the colors that nature looked like to anybody . . ." ("Made A Mile Away," *transition*, 157; *LIA*, 74). The reader further discovered in the lecture what could not have been determined before: the subjective meaning of references to "Juan and Juanita." Gertrude Stein explained that there was a painting by Jean Charles Cazin "called Juan

166

and Juanita or *at least that is what I called it to myself* because at that time I was reading a story that had these two names, I think actually it was called something biblical." (*LIA,* 68. Italics added.)

With the desire to explain her work growing in her, Gertrude Stein made a direct attempt in "An Elucidation" (1923), which she later termed "her first effort to state her problems of expression . . ." (*ABT,* 256). However, "An Elucidation" failed to provide the enlightenment promised by its title. Gertrude Stein did try to supply examples of how her mind functioned when she wrote, but after a reasonably clear beginning, she disappeared into a fog of private associations, remarking as she departed, "We may fancy what we please." After all, "preparation is not everything" (*P&P,* 249).

One of her examples showed that she arbitrarily accepted the word "halve" but rejected its homophone, "have" (246). Similarly, she revealed that "Madrigal" and "Mardigras" were related in her mind, but that they failed to stimulate her imagination, other than that each one began with the letter "m." For this reason, each reminded her of "Em which is a name for Emma" (247). Analogous examples traced the eccentric paths followed by the verbal particles in the cloud chamber of her mind. But the revelation was minimal, and even the very desirable prospect of being published by the *Atlantic Monthly* could not tempt her to change or abridge the essay. On her behalf Alice Toklas wrote the magazine's editor: "In Elucidation there are examples of various forms of expression, each one being given as concentratedly as possible. For this reason it would be impossible to cut it and also because the variety of examples selected are needed to make a whole" (Gallup, "Gertrude Stein and the *Atlantic*," *Yale University Library Gazette,* XXVIII (Jan. 1954) 116).

After "Elucidation," "Composition As Explanation" was Gertrude Stein's next attempt to formulate her literary theories.* She centered

---

* A portion of "Composition As Explanation" is included in *A Novel of Thank You.* More specifically, the long second and brief third paragraphs of the lecture appear on pp. 131-2 of *A Novel* with only minor changes. The "Composition" material appears a little beyond midpoint of the book. Gertrude Stein had been invited in the early spring of 1926 to address the Literary Society at Cambridge University, and actually delivered the lecture in May of that year. She had started *A Novel* in the summer of 1925. (See *ABT,* 276, and *A Novel,* ix, for dating.)

The relevant section in *A Novel* is preceded by "She gave an address. / Tenderness" (131). In the manuscript (vol. 14 of *A Novel,* YCAL) there is a marginal note in Gertrude Stein's hand—"Put in." What follows, up to the end of that chapter ("time-sense." on p. 132) is copied from "Composition As Explanation."

In the line on p. 132 beginning "To come back to the fact . . . " "fact" should the argument of this lecture on a straightforward proposition: namely, that generations are "all alike"; only the relationships of their components change (*SW*, 513). Such change means that each generation perceives a new order, a variant patterning, or, in terms of her lecture, a different composition. Nothing changes then except what is seen, the composition. And that "depends on how everybody is doing everything" (516). Composition is determined by the manner in which life is being conducted at any given moment. Everything derives from that notion. Gertrude Stein argues for the inevitability of compositional change and for the artists who accurately embody those changes.

In addition she was making her bid for immortality. The true "creator of the new composition in the arts" she said, "is an outlaw until he is a classic" (514). The audience lags several generations behind the creative person, then "almost without a pause," they discover that what formerly irritated them is now a classic. "The rapidity of the change is always startling" (515).

With the help of these ideas, Gertrude Stein found it possible to undertake a reasonably coherent review of her own career. Starting with "Melanctha," she outlined her efforts to escape chronological narrative, to move from the "prolonged present" to the "continuous present." As she was "groping for a continuous present" in the "enormously long thing" that *The Making of Americans* had become, she also sought it "within a very small thing." It was, Gertrude Stein told her audience, at the point that she was doing portraits, that her aesthetic problem clarified in her mind, "became more definite" (519). Meanwhile, the war intervened, which speeded up public recognition of the new, contemporary world. Now, Gertrude Stein confided that she was concerned with "equilibration" and "distribution," terms that she failed to clarify and never used again. The variety and aimlessness of her work since the war demonstrates that she had long since lost her theoretical bearings.

"Composition As Explanation" was not a satisfactory aesthetic statement, for its argument was too abbreviated and unclear. Still, it was a signpost that indicated Gertrude Stein was reviewing her position and trying to state where she was and how she got there. To do this, she employed the very manner she had developed, though with

read "part" as it does in the *Dial* printing of "Composition As Explanation," in the Hogarth Press edition, and in the *Selected Writings*. In manuscript the word can easily be mistaken for "fact," but three pages later in the manuscript appears the phrase, "part of a house." There, the word "part" is identical to the word which has been misread as "fact" (vol. 42, *A Novel*, YCAL).

less obscurity. She was ever attracted to private mystifications on the one hand and to public enlightenment on the other. The reassurances of fame, however, were gradually drawing her back to comprehensibility.

After the anxiety displayed early in 1922, Gertrude Stein's prose abruptly turned tedious and mechanical again for a short time. She reverted to dreary paragraphs of counting and to ticking off mindless grammatical variants like "You know and I know, I know and you know . . ." ("Jo Davidson," *P&P,* 197).

There is a plausible explanation for this brief spell of reaction. Gertrude Stein was preparing a collection of her past work, that was published in December of 1922 as *Geography and Plays.* Its fifty-three selections reached as far back as 1908–9 to portraits like "Italians" and "Ada," and as far forward as 1920 to "The Psychology of Nations." * Significantly, her last composition for 1921 was entitled "Reread Another," which was precisely what she was obliged to do—reread her own past work. In the course of this review, she was temporarily affected by stylistic techniques that she had long ago abandoned. It would be hard to exaggerate the extent of Gertrude Stein's suggestibility. She responded remarkably to stimuli.

With the publication of *Geography and Plays* (which she subsidized), Gertrude Stein hoped to consolidate her position as a serious artist. "Every day will be Sunday by and by," she commented at the time. "And now we dream of ribbons and skies. / We will win prizes" ("Sonnets That Please," *BTV,* 221). But her dreams were premature.

For her first retrospective exhibition, Gertrude Stein chose to show only about one out of every four pieces then available. The title under which she gathered them is not literally accurate. Sixteen pieces are designated as plays or as some theatrical equivalent such as "curtain raiser." But while there are pieces on "France" and "England," the word "Geography" would have to be liberally construed to cover the remaining pieces. In fact, the organization of *Geography and Plays* created additional barriers to the understanding of Gertrude Stein's career. She was a writer who pre-eminently evolved in time. Themes, techniques, words were approached, expanded, explored, then

* Three more such collections appeared in her lifetime: *Useful Knowledge,* 1928; *Operas and Plays,* 1932; and *Portraits and Prayers,* 1934. *Last Operas and Plays* appeared in 1949, three years after her death, and the eight posthumous volumes in the Yale series also collected pieces composed at quite different times.

169

diminished in importance until they finally disappeared. She however thought of herself as an exemplar of presentness, as an artist superior to the insecurities of change. So she deliberately mixed the items in her collections. Only with *Operas and Plays* in 1932 did she supply the dates of composition for individual pieces. Even then she did not arrange them in chronological order. The chronology of *Geography and Plays* is approximate. The whole ends on what was becoming an obsessive line for her: "When this you see remember me" ("The Psychology of Nations," *G&P,* 419).

The experience of reviewing her career through 1920 and planning this volume enhanced Gertrude Stein's sense of her own importance. She began to think of herself as someone with a history. She no longer needed to live resolutely in the present, for now she possessed a substantial body of achievement to look back upon.

In the summer of 1922, when Gertrude Stein judged the manuscript of *Geography and Plays* to be in order, she and Alice departed for a vacation in St. Rémy in the south of France. They stayed there until the following March, while she produced bucolic work with religious overtones. Bees, sheep, water, and trees all entered her daily writing.

This fact bears upon the 1923 portrait, "Cezanne." Because it concerns a famous painter, it has attracted rather more attention than most of Gertrude Stein's portraits.*
Its last lines read:

> Bees in a garden make a speciality of honey and so does honey. Honey and prayer. Honey and there. There where the grass can grow nearly four times yearly. (*P&P,* 11).

To understand these lines, one would normally seek to establish a relationship between the images they evoke and the painter or his art. Applied to Cézanne, bees, honey, and grass might be regarded as suggesting his industry, his nourishing qualities, and his perennial freshness. In fact, however, these words do not seem to have been evoked primarily by the idea of Cézanne. They and other words in this portrait like "Caesar," "prayer," and "water" were simply being used regularly by Gertrude Stein at this time. These words, strongly associated in her mind with the area around St. Rémy in southern

* It is analyzed in McMillan, 94–106. McMillan's dissertation contains useful discussions of cubist and Futurist aesthetic theories in relation to Gertrude Stein's practice. He is especially good in his comparison of multiple perspective in painting and multiple points of view in Gertrude Stein (120–32).

170

France, emerged to form his portrait. Perhaps the arrangement of the words was influenced by the thought of Cézanne, but the associative process took place in Gertrude Stein's mind, which accepted the material present there at the moment she was writing.

During the St. Rémy period, quartets were temporarily favored by Gertrude Stein. "A Village Are You Ready Yet Not Yet" records the discussion of four villages. "Capital Capitals" somewhat better known because Virgil Thomson set it to music, offered the conversation of the four capitals of Provence: Aix, Arles, Avignon, and Les Baux.

The most substantial of these quartets was "Lend A Hand or Four Religions." It has four unspecified religions as speakers. Each elaborates upon pastoral subjects: a woman kneeling, water flowing, a shepherd and his flocks. The title of the piece came from Gertrude Stein's childhood, when she belonged to a society that encouraged children to assist adults in doing chores (*EA*, 86). Just as saints entered her imagination, Gertrude Stein was also thinking about the lost directness of childhood. It was at this time that she started to introduce nursery rhymes into her writing. "Star light star bright I wish I may I wish I might have the wish I wish to-night. And I have not told you what it was" ("Lend A Hand," *UK*, 206).

Opera, the lyric extension of the drama, was also seeping into her consciousness. In 1922 she noted, "There is really an interest in words and music of an opera" ("Lily Life," *PL*, 132). Singing had the attraction of requiring no defense; it was its own excuse for being.

When the two women finally returned to Paris from St. Rémy, "The reason we gave for leaving was that the climate was unpleasing" ("Praises," *PL*, 124). Alice Toklas offered a more dramatic account of the rigors of the mistral which drove them north. "Suddenly I found myself crying. Gertrude said, What is the matter? The weather, I said, can we go back to Paris? She said, Tomorrow" (*WIR*, 121). Immediately thereafter, Gertrude Stein, who thrived in the country, made some disspirited attempts at composition—group portraits, lists, precepts—but she was clearly working to be working. So purposeless was her activity that even the popular boxer, Battling Siki, crossed her pages ("A List," *O&P*, 90).

Meanwhile various persons, among them Jane Heap and Carl Van Vechten, were trying to get Gertrude Stein's early work published. Ernest Hemingway managed to get Ford Madox Ford to agree to serialize *The Making of Americans* in the *transatlantic review*, although Ford barely understood what a commitment he had made. Reflections of all these efforts are visible in "Subject-Cases: The Background of a Detective Story." Although it is a long, repetitive piece, often stuck fast on the shoals of sound association, underneath it is autobiographical, even confessional. In particular it indicates that before one or more manuscripts were submitted for perusal, certain steps had been taken to conceal some of the references in the narrative. "This is to be antedated. Confederate, to confederate" (*AFAM*, 6). "It can be seen to have been done in collaboration, collaboration and collusion . . ." (11). One of the works in question is specified. "You took, the long gay book. Along. Thank you very much" (22).

The various negotiations involving *The Making of Americans*—attempts to get it published in America in 1923, its partial serialization in the *transatlantic review* in 1924, and finally its publication in France in 1925—all kept the style and subject matter of that lengthy book in the forefront of Gertrude Stein's mind. As had happened during the preparation of *Geography and Plays*, preoccupation with the book notably affected her creative efforts. Her pieces lengthened, often running to twenty-five and thirty pages. She discussed American topics by means of the mechanistic dualities of *The Making of Americans* in such pieces as "Wherein the South Differs from the North" and "The Difference Between the Inhabitants of France and the Inhabitants of the United States of America." Several pieces such as "Birth and Marriage" and "A Comedy Like That" have as their subjects, families—their members and their histories.

Gertrude Stein also found that she had something to say that required length. It was to be "a narrative of why she wanted to keep her" and "of why any one entered on the period of unreliability" ("Elected Again," *PL*, 48). "A Third" had already discussed the temporary intrusion of a third party into the Stein-Toklas relationship. It had been written against a background of a "fat wife," of reading and of page numbers, all suggesting the arduous sessions of proofreading the two women engaged in for *The Making of Americans* (*AFAM*, 340). In 1925 then, Gertrude Stein undertook her "history of what we heard when we said it" ("Elected Again," *PL*, 49). It was two hundred and thirty-seven pages long and named *A Novel of Thank You*. Carl Van Vechten characterized the book as "one of her most hermetic," and accurately commented that, despite its imposing length, it has been virtually ignored (*NOTY*, ix).

Gertrude Stein herself summarized its contents. "The central theme of the novel is that they were glad to see each other" (72). While the details of the book are indeed formidably difficult to comprehend, its main movement is not. It records a temporary imbalance in a relationship, followed by a return to equilibrium. Responsibility for the affair is evidently the narrator's. "What did I do for her. I arranged that she had a friend and that that friend would show to advantage" (16–17). The stages of the unhappy episode are, in the beginning, "How many more than two are there" (3). Toward the middle, "Come and kiss me when you want to . . ." (106). At the end, ". . . let us hope that she will not regret . . . having decided to give up Lucy . . ." (235).

A Novel of Thank You was the first work of substantial length that Gertrude Stein had written since the days of *The Making of Americans, A Long Gay Book,* and *Many Many Women,* a novelty that she acknowledged early in the book. "What is a surprise. A continued story is a surprise. This is a continued story . . ." (13). After having sustained her narrative, she remarked, "Having come to this point in the novel it has come to seem quite as easily done as before . . ." (144). She was pleased, because the novel was clearly the successful genre at this time: "A novel makes a man" (30).

Formally, *A Novel of Thank You* presented a series of short, diary-like chapters, erratically numbered. "Daily daily every day what did they say" reads the whole of chapter 192 (165). Scattered throughout the book are numerous disconnected observations on the novel form, including mention of Victor Hugo and Tolstoi (188, 203). For, "who can think about a novel. I can" (113). Gertrude Stein asked herself if a novel could be changed into an adventure story, and what the implications were if she made it "historical" (112, 116). A novel, she decided, "can tell everything that is true." It "tells it as it was" (134, 151). Her own effort she regarded as both specific and universal. It was "historic" but also "makes it be theirs too" (198, 217). The book was quintessential, "a novel of thank you and not about it" (185).

Given Gertrude Stein's impressionability and the fact that she was living in Paris, it is not out of the question to suppose that the self-conscious involution of the book, with its blending of diary and observations on the literary art, was influenced by Gide's *Les Faux-Monnayeurs,* which had begun appearing serially in the *Nouvelle Revue Française* in March 1925. There is no evidence however, that she ever read Gide, although she had met him around 1912 at Mabel Dodge's Villa Curonia. "It was a rather dull evening," she remembered (*ABT,* 161). Later she noted that Bernard Faÿ once said to her that "the three people of first rate importance that he had met in his life were Picasso, Gertrude Stein and Andre Gide . . ." Her response was brisk; she countenanced no rivals. "That is quite right but why include Gide" (*ABT*, 302).*

The following year, 1926, Gertrude Stein wrote "A Little Novel." It concerns some fourteen people, probably summer visitors, who "have been known to come again" (*NOTY*, 261). It possesses one distinctive oddity. It breaks off in mid-sentence and concludes without terminal punctuation. The last sentence reads: "And they" (*NOTY*, 262). Insignificant in itself, the title indicates Gertrude Stein's continuing concern about the literary form that follows characters through an action.

The novel was obliged to compete with what was by this time a fixed principle for Gertrude Stein—that an account of events arranged in a linear sequence of causality was no longer appropriate in the modern world. The sovereign of the present was Random. The contemporary world could be truly unified only by the subjective consciousness. In "Natural Phenomena" she took up the argument of "Composition As Explanation" again, reiterating that "everybody always is the same." The only difference consists not in their appearance, but in the world they see—"what they look at not what they look like" (*PL*, 220). Nonetheless, Gertrude Stein felt obliged to come to terms with the dominant literary genre of her day. This she did by redefinition. To her, the novel was a combination of presence and pleasure, "an arrangement of their being there and never having been more glad than before . . ." ("Edith Sitwell and Her Brothers," *PL*, 298).

Her preoccupation with plot extended from 1925 to 1927. It is to be found centrally in a series of meditations, "Regular Regularly In Narrative," which later formed part of her book, *How To Write* (1931). In it, she reflected on how narrative differs from conversation, description, and other verbal modes. Journalism she dismissed altogether. "There is no use at all in describing the Hall Stevens murder nor any disaster . . ." (*HTW*, 226). Narrative too, she concluded, was not pleasing to her. It dealt, after all, with others. "There is this difference between narrative and portrait," she wrote, "a narrative

* Wylie Sypher devotes his chapter, "The Cubist Novel," in *From Rococo to Cubism* to placing *Les Faux-Monnayeurs* in a perspective that includes both Gertrude Stein and the Cubist painters.

Gide's journals make no reference to Gertrude Stein or Mabel Dodge. There is a scornful reference to Leo Stein though. Gide remarks that Leo likes the work of a certain artist "because it can be grasped without effort" (*The Journals of André Gide*, tr. Justin O'Brien [New York, 1955], I, 237).

makes anybody be at home and a portrait makes anybody remember me" (*HTW*, 228). Her theoretical objection to narrative was that it imposed an artificial order upon experience. Subjectively though, she found that she became "impatient when anybody tells a story this means a story of others" ("A Diary," *A&B*, 201). Her attitude toward narrative blended her consummate self-engrossment with her perception of the revelatory uses of synchronic prose.

Having asked herself therefore, "Why does a narrative replace a diary," she answered firmly, "Because it does not" ("A Diary," *A&B*, 201). Shortly after writing "A Little Novel" she turned to "A Diary" in which she simply recorded the visits of friends, the menu her cook prepared, and some quite direct comments about her career. "Wrote a great many sketches. / She asked me not to introduce surprises nor leavings nor annoyances and I did not but it seems so. She also asked me if I would not like to receive for them a great deal of money" (*A&B*, 203).

Ultimately, she rejected the idea of "a daily diary." It threatened to impinge upon her creative work, supposing that is what "the other" refers to in this concluding statement: "There will not be a daily diary . . . in order not to have it be as important as the other . . ." (*A&B*, 218). Meanwhile, as she debated the meaning, function, and problems of narrative, she paused to record, prophetically, "Preparing for opera" ("Regular Regularly," *HTW*, 250).

9

ฐ. "Saints are made in France."
("Coal and Wood")

Four Saints In Three Acts occupies a more important position in Gertrude Stein's canon than its intrinsic worth can justify. The reputation of the piece is maintained by external considerations: Virgil Thomson's musical score; the publicity surrounding the original staging of the opera in 1934 and its revival in 1952; the use of a black cast; and journalistic popularization of the phrase, "pigeons on the grass alas." Were the libretto known in a different form it is unthinkable that it could ever have achieved its present celebrity.

In 1927, having already set several of her shorter pieces to music, Virgil Thomson commissioned Gertrude Stein to prepare an opera libretto for him. The genesis of the subject finally chosen is unclear. Thomson claimed credit for the theme—"it was the artist's working life, which is to say, the life we both were living" (*Virgil Thomson*, 90). His statement of the theme is sufficiently general and the text sufficiently ambiguous for the two to accord. Thomson said that they arrived at a subject only after some negotiation. Gertrude Stein inclined toward American history, but after Thomson vetoed George Washington, "we gave up history and chose saints, sharing a certain reserve toward medieval ones and Italian ones on the grounds that both had been overdone in the last century. Eventually our saints turned out to be Baroque and Spanish . . ." (*Thomson*, 91). Gertrude Stein's memoirs simplified the decision. She had always liked two saints "better than any others," namely Theresa of Avila and Ignatius of Loyola, so she selected them, and set to work in the spring of 1927 (*ABT*, 281). However, Thomson cites a letter from her in March 1927, in which she says she has "begun Beginning of Studies for an opera to be sung," and that in her opinion the opera should concern "late eighteenth-century or early nineteenth-century saints" (*Thomson*, 91).

176

This last testimony is particularly significant, for it explains the uncertainty of purpose evident through much of *Four Saints*. The conditions under which it was initiated were unparalleled in Gertrude Stein's career. Both the form and the subject matter were at least partially imposed upon her. Her habitual method of composition was to follow whim, but in this instance plans had to be made in consultation with another person. The collaboration with Thomson helped to coax Gertrude Stein out of her cave of mystery.

Since the early twenties, Gertrude Stein had evinced some interest in saints. She had also given some thought to the operatic form. It seemed appropriate for her, a lyric composition in which sound and feeling took precedence over sense and plot. (She later referred to *Four Saints* as "a play" which "made a landscape" [*LIA*, 131].) The formal demands of the genre were far from imperative for her. The setting in which she proposed to place her saints was consonant with her mood in that period. "Make it pastoral," she wrote Thomson. "In hills and gardens. All four and then additions. We must invent them" (*Thomson*, 91).

But, Gertrude Stein's powers of invention being weak, four saints do not play central roles. Who, in fact, the second pair of saints is is not altogether certain. The longest study of the text to date concludes that "St. Chavez is the third saint, and St. Settlement probably the fourth," without indicating the grounds for this opinion (Garvin, 9). Saint Plan has more than twice as many lines as Saint Settlement.* Whatever the case, as might have been guessed, the opera is about Saint Theresa.†

That both saints were Spanish must in part be regarded as a tribute to Alice Toklas. When the two women first visited Spain together, Alice insisted, "I must stay in Avila forever" (*ABT*, 141). Furthermore, in notes Gertrude Stein kept when writing *The Making of Americans*, she referred to her new friend as "St. Therese" (Katz, 277). Gertrude Stein's own feeling was that "Avila was alright," but "she needed Paris." They remained there happily for ten days, since "Saint Theresa was a heroine of Gertrude Stein's youth" (*ABT*, 142).

---

* Saint Plan appears to be literally named, while—given the Stein-Toklas interest in cooking—Saint Settlement very likely refers to the famous *Settlement Cook Book*.
† In the printed version of *Four Saints* Gertrude Stein used the form "Saint Therese." The correct French would be Thérèse. In *ABT*, she referred to her as "Saint Theresa" (142), while in Thomson's abridged version of the libretto, she is "Saint Teresa."

That the young Gertrude Stein did admire Saint Theresa is credible. As with George Eliot's Maggie Tulliver, a certain resemblance obtains. Furthermore, George Eliot had begun *Middlemarch* by eulogizing Saint Theresa, whose "passionate ideal nature" later reappeared in other women (like Gertrude Stein), who "tried to shape their thought and deed in noble agreement," even though "to common eyes their struggle seemed mere inconsistency and formlessness" ("Prelude"). Theresa was a passionate, witty, individualistic young woman whose mother died when she was thirteen and whose father exhibited a stern moral probity. She read chivalric romances, had adventures with an elder brother, and learned adolescent "evil" from a somewhat older female cousin. In addition to these biographical resemblances, there are stylistic ones of unusual closeness. Theresa's diction has been described as natural, artless, and unaffected; the outstanding syntactical features of her prose were the use of the apostrophe, repetition, and alliteration; she was liable to confuse her reader by her ellipses; and she was fond of illogical interpolations and digressions.*

Even with a genuine interest in St. Theresa, Gertrude Stein experienced considerable difficulty in reaching her. The libretto opens with a brief statement of her plans. She was going to "prepare for saints." Her mechanism for preparation would be narrative—"In narrative prepare for saints" (*O&P*, 11). At first, she found herself with nothing to say about her subject. "Saint saint a saint. / Forgotten saint." Recognizing her barrenness, she turned to a more congenial and familiar topic: "What happened to-day, a narrative" (11). For the next four pages, Gertrude Stein discussed matters in her domestic life, occasionally reverting to thoughts of how to manage a presentation of Saint Theresa. So not only does the listener learn that "we had intended if it were a pleasant day to go to the country," but also he is told "Imagine four benches separately" (11, 12). She tried to reassure herself that she could manage this act of creation. "Easily saints. / Very well saints. / Have saints" (13). She insisted upon the necessity of carrying it through. "Four saints at a time have to have to have to have to" (13). And as she worked at "a narrative to plan an opera," she felt mounting apprehension. "Come panic come" (14).

* These observations are drawn from "Saint Teresa's Style: A Tentative Appraisal," chapter 3 of *Saint Teresa of Jesus* by E. A. Peers. The only evidence I possess that Gertrude Stein was actually familiar with the prose of St. Theresa occurs in an interview given during her visit to New York in 1934. She said that she had "read the meditations of St. Therese whose mysticism was 'real and practical'" (New York *Times,* 17 November 1934, 13).

In short, the early portion of the libretto includes Gertrude Stein's planning sessions as well as the feelings that the project engendered in her. No matter what the occasion, the essence of the refrain, "When this you see remember me," echoes through her writing.*

In his "Sound and Sense in *Four Saints In Three Acts*," Harry Garvin vaults over this introductory material to the point specified as the beginning of Act One. Garvin's essay suffers the curse of most Stein studies: his translations and interpretations of Gertrude Stein's lines are arbitrary and neglect to indicate how much problematic material has been omitted between the passages chosen for discussion. But Garvin is a sympathetic reader. He sees the theme of *Four Saints* as "the different ways in which two saints achieve a spiritual life" (6). The polarities occur in Ignatius, the "mystic and disciplinarian," and Theresa, the "believer in kindness and charity" (9). Garvin's urge to clarify the text and provide it a coherent movement is understandable but excessive. When, for example, he is faced with the phrase "must be theirs first," he arbitrarily bifurcates the Catholic Church, so that the pronominal adjective "theirs" will fit the following interpretation: "Theresa realizes that she must first of all give herself completely to the Church and to its discipline" (3).

In her preliminary ruminations, Gertrude Stein had decided to "begin suddenly not with sisters" (12). When she finally opened the first act, she did indeed give no consideration to the saint's childhood or family, but presented her heroine dramatically: "Saint Therese in a storm at Avila . . ." Saint Ignatius? He still was "not there" (15). Having provided a dramatic context, she summoned Saint Theresa— "Come one come one." But—"No saint to remember." Shortly she decided "Repeat First Act," whereupon the scene changed. These lines suggest that Gertrude Stein was trying to grasp the essence of her historical figure, but finding the task troublesome. A letter to Thomson confirms as much. "I think I have got St. Thérèse onto the stage, it has been an awful struggle and I think I can keep her on and gradually by the second act get St. Ignatius on and then they will be both on together . . ." (*Thomson*, 92).

Although eccentric, the course of the composition is internally coherent. St. Theresa is introduced in a context replete with her known affinity for water imagery—rain, snow, a river. This passionate woman is uncertain about her commitment to the holy life—"if to stay to

* The phrase appears whole or in part on pp. 13, 42, 45, and 47 of *Four Saints*.

cry." The introductory material then serves as a miniature portrait of the saint. Her balance of common sense and compassion is memorably embodied in the famous question and answer that concludes the first part of Act One. "If it were possible to kill five thousand chinamen by pressing a button would it be done. / Saint Therese not interested" (16).*

Harry Garvin is correct when he suggests that the thematic phrase "very nearly half inside and half outside" indicates Theresa's ambivalence. It goes beyond the specific problem of her taking holy vows though; it was a fundamental aspect of her personality. The actual Theresa's attractiveness derived from the way her worldliness fused with an impassioned faith in God. Her gaiety and piety produced tensions that were not reconcilable on earth. "Who settles a private life," asks Gertrude Stein's Theresa, five times over (16–17).

Preoccupied with Saint Theresa, Gertrude Stein made only a gesture at bringing Ignatius on stage. "Introducing Saint Ignatius." Then, failing to elicit any response in herself, she remarked, "Left to be" and returned to her preferred topic: "Saint Therese seated seated . . ." (17). The unhappy fact though was that, for all her fondness for Theresa, Gertrude Stein lacked information about her. Invariably her habit previously had been to write about her immediate activities and state of mind, or, if she selected a subject other than herself, it was someone whose personality was currently making an impression upon her. Writing about a historical figure without doing research was causing her difficulties; the signs of her ignorance were manifold.

She was therefore obliged to fall back on quite distant associations. "Saint Therese could be photographed having been dressed like a lady and then they taking out her head changed it to a nun and a nun a saint and a saint so" (17). In *Lectures in America*, she explained this otherwise mystifying sentence. Gertrude Stein had long contemplated the window display of a shop on the Boulevard Raspail in which the transformation of a girl into a nun was pictorially symbolized. Over the course of four or five photographs, the girl's face remained the same, but her clothing changed until at last she appeared in the full

---

* The lines came from Gertrude Stein's own experience. In *Everybody's Autobiography*, she recalled Hutchins Hapgood presenting her with an ethical puzzle. "Would I if I could by pushing a button would I kill five thousand Chinamen if I could save my brother from anything. Well I was very fond of my brother and I could completely imagine his suffering and I replied that five thousand Chinamen were something I could not imagine and so it was not interesting" (89–90).

180

regalia of a nun (130). This display represented Saint Theresa's experience for Gertrude Stein.

During the course of the first act, as Gertrude Stein meditated aimlessly on her heroine, the following question emerged. "Could a negro be . . . with a beard . . ." The answer was, "Never have . . . seen a negro there and with it so" (18). In spite of this remark, Gertrude Stein did not conceive of *Four Saints* with a Negro cast. That was Virgil Thomson's inspiration. "I had chosen them purely for beauty of voice, clarity of enunciation, and fine carriage" he later remembered. (Liner notes, RCA Victor Red Seal *Four Saints in Three Acts*, LM2756, 1964.) *Newsweek's* review of the production suggests that his plan miscarried. "The diction left a good deal to be desired," remarked the reviewer, complaining of the incomprehensibility of the text, quite apart from the problems caused by Gertrude Stein herself (17 February 1934, 38). Initially, Gertrude Stein objected to Thomson's plan. "I still do not like the idea of showing the Negro bodies . . . It is too much what modernistic writers refer to as 'futuristic.' I cannot see its relevance to my treatment of my theme." However, she gave Thomson a free hand—"it is for you to make a success of the production" (letter, in Hoover, 81). At one point Thomson even intended to paint the Negroes white (Virgil Thomson to W. A. Bradley, 6 May 1933, YCAL).

Thomson added a compère and commère to the script, and divided Saint Theresa's part between two singers. "Saint Therese" became the more euphonius "St. Teresa." After first scoring the text exactly as he received it, Thomson made some cuts "to facilitate staging" (Liner notes). Both photographs of the production and Maurice Grosser's scenario indicate that the production owed not a little to the atmosphere of Marc Connelly's *The Green Pastures,* produced in 1930. Also Hall Johnson's choral play, *Run Little Chillun,* seems to have made its effect, since Carl Van Vechten reported that at its intermission, Virgil Thomson exclaimed that he would have *Four Saints* sung by Negroes ("A Few Notes About Four Saints in Three Acts," *Four Saints in Three Acts* [New York, 1934], 7).

With her imagination stalled so far as Theresa was concerned, Gertrude Stein was reduced to verbal play. Homonyms: "Add sum. Add some." Rhymes: "With seas. / With knees. / With keys. With pleases." Assonance: "In clouded. / Included." And she asked, "Is there a difference between a sound a hiss a kiss a as well" (20). All this random activity signified a mind virtually devoid of response to its set task. "Virgil Virgil Virgil virgin virgin" she doodled (21). When enough such verbiage had accumulated, she felt ready for some aggressive recapitulation. "Saint Therese has begun to be in act one" (23). By this time it was the spring of 1927, to judge by the remark, "It never snows in Easter" (23).

Now pressed by the need to introduce Ignatius, Gertrude Stein reluctantly yielded her preliminary consideration of Theresa. Once she had declared the saint to be fully present on stage—"Saint Therese meant to be complete completely"—then her duty was plain. "This meant Saint Ignatius Act II" (24).

The choice of Saint Ignatius of Loyola as the second principal is not easily accounted for. He was Spanish, to be sure, and as a male, he balanced Theresa. Like her he too was a sixteenth-century figure and the founder of a holy order. He had studied in Paris from 1528 to 1535. Beyond that, his attractions for Gertrude Stein are uncertain.* Gertrude Stein said that she associated Ignatius with "a rather large porcelain group" displayed in another Parisian shop window. It portrayed "a young soldier giving alms to a beggar and taking off his helmet and armour and leaving them in the charge of another" (*LIA*, 130). Through this display, (which probably represented St. Martin of Tours), Ignatius became "actual" for her, although as she confessed, "not as actual as Saint Therese in the photographs but still actual and so the Four Saints got written" (131). Ignatius never came alive for her even to the degree that Theresa did, but in spite of this obstacle, the work was completed.

"Act II" begins then on a note of wan hope. "Saint Ignatius was very well known." As the founder of the Society of Jesus, he indubitably was, but not especially to Gertrude Stein. "Scene II / Would it do if there was a Scene II," she inquired, then continued with a series of phrases, each of which demonstrates how little Gertrude Stein had to say of Ignatius.

> Saint Ignatius and more.
> Saint Ignatius with as well.
> Saint Ignatius need not be feared. (25)

* Kathleen Hoover found the answer easily. "Loyola was a natural choice. Gertrude Stein had grown up in San Francisco, where there is an impressive church dedicated to him, and had from early youth been familiar with the Ignatian literature" (Hoover, 63). Unless the phrase is broadly construed, Gertrude Stein did not grow up in San Francisco. She lived there only in 1891–2. Still, Gertrude Stein herself nurtured the myth, telling an audience that "As a child in San Francisco . . . she spent much time in the Church of St. Ignatius and later she read his confessions" (New York *Times*, 17 November 1934, 13).

Having reassured herself with the concluding statement, she then pondered whether "Saint Ignatius might be very well adapted to plans and a distance." Following a little work in that direction, she considered making some direct contact with Ignatius's work. "Saint Ignatius might be read." But the magnetism of Theresa proved irresistible. In a moment we hear, "To be interested in Saint Therese fortunately" (25). And after reflecting that after all, "There are many saints," she momentarily even entertained the possibility of relegating Ignatius to a subsidiary position. "Saints four saints. . . . / Saint Ignatius might be five" (25, 26). With that Theresa moves center stage once more, and Ignatius returns to the wings while Gertrude Stein does a little research. "Saint Ignatius Loyola. A saint to be met by and by . . . continue reading . . ." (28). With that, the stage fills with saints, men and women sanctified in the main by the playwright: Saint Settlement, Saint Parmenter, Saint Lys, Saint Plan—"any and all saints" (29). Shortly, Gertrude Stein took a sounding. "How much of it is finished" (30). The inquiry was made in various ways, but the only answer is the phrase "once in a while" repeated twenty-six times (30–31). Her yearning to be done with the uncongenial commission is evident.

Two-thirds of the way through *Four Saints*, Ignatius finally comes to life. Gertrude Stein's solution of the dilemma of her being unresponsive to him was to accept the best illusion she could provide—"It is easy to resemble it most." Full portrayal she left up to the actors—"and leave it to them with individuality." Saint Ignatius therefore appears "In seems;" that is, not truly actualized but represented (36).

This solution sparks the famous "pigeons on the grass alas" aria. Insofar as the lyric has an interpretable meaning, it is anti-supernatural and pro-humanist. The contrasted images are of the pigeons on the grass who can cry, and the magpie in the sky who cannot. What little has been written about this celebrated passage has regarded it as a mystic vision of Saint Ignatius, which in some unexplained way fuses pigeon and magpie into the Holy Ghost.* Although the opera's staging has encouraged that interpretation, it is not easy to extract from the text itself. The one line susceptible to this reading is: "He had heard of a third and he asked about it it was a magpie in the sky" (36). Assuming that "he" is Ignatius, it is possible to read Trinitarian significance into this line. But the cues are minimal for this reading.

* See Maurice Grosser's scenario in *Four Saints in Three Acts* [New York, 1948]; Virgil Thomson's RCA Victor Red Seal liner notes; and Garvin, 4–5.)

Rather, the elements in this configuration suggest earthbound souls contrasted with a distant and unattractive deity. In Gertrude Stein's formulation whiteness, gentleness, and compassion are attributed to a grounded creature who may or may not still be capable of flying. The magpie, occupying divinity's traditional place in the sky is black, raucous, and thieving. Even the setting for the pigeons is equivocal. The grass is described as "shorter longer yellow." The whole passage opens on a note of lamentation—"Pigeons on the grass alas"—and sustains the frustration of this existence—"the magpie in the sky on the sky and to try and to try alas on the grass . . ." But it moves toward a prayerful conclusion in which improvement is at least conceivable. "They might be very well very well very well . . ." The passage ends with an incantation to light and purity, each significantly personified as female. "Let Lucy Lily Lily Lucy Lucy let Lucy Lucy . . ." (36). In the text the passage is not attributed to any particular character. Therefore it is not unreasonable to regard it as an authorial statement stimulated by the religious context of the saints.

The gathering of the saints suggests universal holiness. For Gertrude Stein, in moments of concentrated attention, all was sanctified. No response was too trivial to be excluded, so long as it was true, which to her, since *Tender Buttons,* had meant detached from memory and from artifice. *Four Saints* evolves into a statement on behalf of accepting the present life. It attempts to consolidate the visible world in grace, "never to return to distinctions" (37).

For this reason, Gertrude Stein regarded Ignatius in his public role as General of the Society of Jesus, dedicated to the propagation of the faith, to martial discipline and spiritual calisthenics as the lesser saint. "There is a difference between Barcelona and Avila," she remarks (39). Barcelona was where Ignatius undertook his clerical education and attracted his first disciples. Ignatius sought a faraway and perhaps unattainable goal. Certainly it was an unnecessary one. "He asked for a distant magpie as if that made a difference" (37). The opera counsels moderation. Improvement should be attempted, but failings accepted too. The intermingling of endeavor and tolerance appears when Saint Pellen says: "There is every reason why industriously there should be resolution and intermittence and furnishing of their delight" (39). Saint Pilar likewise comprehends the wisdom of passivity. "Floating and adding makes smiles" (40). Such statements repudiate strict Ignatian discipline, or at least propose its modification.

It is the mystic, visionary, loving side of Ignatius which the libretto encourages and validates. In addition to being a military leader, Ignatius was a humble man who could be possessed by God. "Once in a while and where and where around in a sound. . . . Around differing from anointed now" (42). To be anointed was to submit to a ritual signifying a transcendental truth. The authorial voice however was speaking of "ordinary pigeons and trees" (42). Those committed to the phenomenal world do not ask "If they were not pigeons what were they" (36). Ordinary pigeons and trees: they constituted the Emersonian fidelity to the things of this world, the voluntary assumption of one's place at the feet of the low and the common. Not that this was an egotistical isolation. The authorial voice had observed that "It is very easy to love alone. Too much too much" (39). The challenge was to share reverential joy in the common. "In face of might make milk sung" is Saint Theresa's counsel, "sung face to face . . ." (42). The guiding voice underlines the utility of singing milk. "Many might be comfortabler. This is very well known now. When this you see remember me" (42).

Gertrude Stein went on to dismiss theological disputation (always supposing the magpie to be the posited deity). Clerics spend their time locating God and debating whether he is one or three. "Having arranged magpies so only one showed and also having arranged magpies so that more than one showed" (43). Although such time-consuming activities had traditionally been valued, this late in civilization's day, Gertrude Stein firmly declined to participate. "A great deal of the afternoon is used by this as an advantage. It is meritorious that we do not care to share" (43).

Here in the latter part of the play Gertrude Stein had finally broken through to a theme that she consciously perceived and deeply felt. She rejected formal religion in favor of uncomplicated awe and union. Sanctity was in the eye of the beholder. "Saints and see all out but me" (46). She, the author, was the repository of vision and the projector of impressions. As she remarked elsewhere, "How can a language alter. It does not it is an altar" ("Woodrow Wilson," UK, 108). Yet the vision must be shared. "When this you see you are all to me." In union there was purity. "Wedded and weeded" (45).

Following this triumphant cresting of Gertrude Stein's ideas, signs of an end begin to accumulate. "Let us come to this brink." The cast, all creatures of her imagination, now draw together. "The sisters and saints assembling and re-enacting why they went away to stay" (46). Following the instruction, "Let all act as if they went away," the saints start to do so, "one at a time" and "laterally." This is art without history. Immediacy lacks the vertical dimension. Elements occur side by side, "one at a time," as the mind focuses on them. Being resumes the importance it had for Gertrude Stein in the first decade of the century. "They have to be," she insists. "They have to be to see." Vision depends upon existence, and communication upon vision. "To see to say." How? Sideways, obliquely, slant. "Laterally they may" (47).

The final scene of the fourth act assembles for review the motive forces of this opera: a maker, one who cares, a planner, and a disciplinarian. Saint Theresa is the presiding and efficient force, "Who makes who makes it do." The agent of solicitous concern is Saint Chavez, "Who does and who does care." The functions of the second pair of saints are less directly stated. "Who may be what is it when it is instead," Gertrude Stein inquires. The answer is Saint Plan. A plan is important and can answer the question, "What is it?" (In the present case, the answer is given in the subtitle—"An Opera to be Sung.") But the actual creation will inevitably differ from its conception. The actualization of the plan is "when it is instead." Lastly, Saint Ignatius's role is "who makes it be what they had as porcelain." Literally, the porcelain refers to Gertrude Stein's memory of that statuary group in the Parisian shop window. More generally, it stands in her mind for artifice, for craft. Theresa gives the creation life and movement, the ability to "do." Ignatius, in his capacity as orderer and disciplinarian, provides the artful form.

As the commander, Ignatius also arranges the ending. "Saint Ignatius and left and right laterally to be lined." The statement invites the director to spread his cast across the stage for the curtain. All that remains to be said is a reminder that to saints all are saints. The numbers four and five are merely arbitrary conveniences. Then comes the concluding statement, simple, confident, solidly existential. "Last Act. / Which is a fact" (47).

This reading runs counter to the scenario of the original production as well as to the few opinions thus far printed about *Four Saints*. In their understandable desire to make the piece playable, Virgil Thomson and others responsible for its staging parceled out the very long sections of authorial commentary to characters invented for precisely that function, a commère, compère, and a Chorus. These liberties have obscured the dominant role played by the narrative voice in the text.

While many speeches are attributable to specific characters, the bulk of the text is unattributed and therefore assignable only to the creator herself.

Approximate figures will give an idea of how the lines are distributed. There are some 915 speeches in the text. Of these, 111 are given to Saint Theresa, 59 to Saint Ignatius, 49 to Saint Chavez, and 20 to Saint Plan. Numerically, *they* are the four saints, a presumption verified by the conclusion where they assume central positions. Minor saints speak some 77 other lines. In all 316 lines are assigned to specific characters. This means that almost two-thirds of the text is composed of authorial statement and commentary.*

Four Saints in Three Acts is an improvised piece that struggles along uncertainly, then suddenly picks up and sails confidently through to a positive conclusion. Virgil Thomson had encouraged Gertrude Stein to compose an opera libretto, but once committed to the project, she was baffled by it. Therefore, her text began with declarations of purpose, expressions of concern and trepidation, followed by exhortations and several tentative solutions. Saint Theresa, with whom Gertrude Stein found it easy to identify, gradually absorbed the energies of the text. Although briefly admitted, Ignatius was ignored as uninspiring. Not until late in the composition did Gertrude Stein permit him entry and then only that she might repudiate his intellectualism and institutional bias. By this time Gertrude Stein was fully possessed of her theme—acceptance of the world as given. The invocation of a supernatural agency she found unnecessary. The complexities of things as they were furnished sufficient wonderment and mystery.

Other Spaniards, less holy than Theresa and Ignatius, "cruel and pleasurable" men, were also on Gertrude Stein's mind in 1927 ("Two Spaniards," *PL*, 309). The piece "Relieve" describes a certain "Paul" who is married to a Russian and has a son who dresses as a cowboy —most assuredly Pablo Picasso, his wife Olga Kolkhova, and their son Paulo (*P&P*, 308; see also Brinnin, 308).

Juan Gris died that same year, only forty years old. His death

* A "speech" was identified as any verbal unit marked by paragraphing. It might run from two words—"Up hill" (12) to twelve lines— "All Saints. Any and all Saints." etc. etc. (29). A speech was attributed to a character when a period followed the name, thusly: "Saint Ignatius. Meant and met" (15). Otherwise— "Saint Therese something like that" (14) it was not. On some eighteen occasions Gertrude Stein provided a name with a period following but no speech. "Saint Anne. / Saint Answers. Saints when" (32). There are, by my count, 36 saints with singing or speaking roles.

inspired Gertrude Stein's elegy, "The Life of Juan Gris. The Life and Death of Juan Gris." She had begun to purchase painting from Gris late in 1913 or early in 1914. They subsequently quarreled and remained estranged until 1920. From their reconciliation in that year until he died seven years later, they were reasonably close. Quite aside from the financial assistance Gertrude Stein provided him, Gris evidently respected her judgment. In 1924 he asked her to permit him to read his lecture "On the Possibilities of Painting" to her before he delivered it publicly. Later in the same year he encouraged her to assess his work. "No one will write better about my painting than yourself" (Letters 116 and 199 in *Letters of Juan Gris*, tr. Douglas Cooper, London, 1956). She characterized the lament she wrote for him as "the most moving thing" she had ever written (*ABT*, 260). It may have been so for her; no one today is likely to value it as an important elegy. Its one interesting feature is that its exposition, especially at the beginning, is unusually forthright. The first twenty lines offer direct biographical detail that is unprecedented in Gertrude Stein's work of the past decade. "Juan Gris was one of the younger children of a well-to-do merchant of Madrid. The earliest picture he has of himself is at about five years of age dressed in a little lace dress standing beside his mother who was very sweet and pleasantly maternal-looking" (*P&P*, 48). With the composition of *The Autobiography of Alice B. Toklas* five years off, this brief spate of communication represents the tentative movements of a long sequestered creature preparing to emerge.

After a time, the piece does waver. Tempted by "one" and "any," Gertrude Stein indulged herself in some stale verbal permutations. "Juan Gris was a brother and a comrade to every one being one as no one ever had been one" (49). Still, on the whole she summarizes Gris's career succinctly and sensibly, paying him measured tribute. She concludes with an overt assertion of Gris's respect for her. She points out that in his last years, despite the efforts of his dealer, D.-H. Kahnweiler, people were still not buying Gris's paintings. "And he smiled so gently and said I was everything" (50). Gertrude Stein's need to record what was a legitimate friendship but then to underline her own importance in it is at once painful and revealing. Gris had assumed unusual importance for her. She was not close to Picasso, Braque, or Matisse at this time, so that following the death of the only major artist she was then sponsoring, she seems to have been driven to end her elegy with his tribute to her.

Another short piece entitled "An Advantage" and written almost at the same time probably concerns Gris too. "It is about him. He is twenty-six years old having been seventeen. He will be dead when he is forty-one . . ." (*PL*, 304). The significance of the ages is, first, that Gertrude Stein believed Gris arrived in Paris when he was seventeen, although he was actually eighteen or nineteen, for born in 1887, he came to Paris in 1906. When he was twenty-six Gertrude Stein bought her first painting from him. As for dying at forty-one, she may have mistaken his age, or was prophesying a longer life for him than he actually had. In any case, "An Advantage" contains numerous statements about Gris, such as, "He was a man who thought twice before he was disagreeable" (*PL*, 306).

Gertrude Stein's central concerns in the twenties—the pastoral landscape of the region around her summer residence in the eastern mid-region of France, not far from Lake Geneva, the sanctity of the good-natured vision, and the literary form of the narrative—all coalesced in "A Novel of Romantic beauty and nature and which Looks Like an Engraving," the main title of which was *Lucy Church Amiably.** Critical judgments of the book are sparse. Those offered invariably reproduce or expand Gertrude Stein's own characterization of the book. Donald Sutherland has called it both her "most important novel" (with the exception of *Mrs. Reynolds*) and "the purest and best pastoral romance" of the twentieth century (*Gertrude Stein*, 138, 143).

Lucy Church Amiably does possess the external characteristics of a novel. Its chapters are organized in units of fifteen to twenty-five pages. The paragraphing and sentences are of modest and varied proportions, however puzzling their content. The chapters are even sequentially numbered. Toward the last though, the chapters shorten, and the forty-eighth is only a single sentence. As often happened with her privately generated projects, Gertrude Stein started off enthusiastically,

---

* 240 pages in length, *LCA* was the first volume in an ambitious project Gertrude Stein conceived for publishing all her unprinted work. Although now possessed of reasonably reliable evidence that she was a serious writer, she remained frustrated in her attempts to get the enormous backlog of her work into print. Therefore, she took the decisive step of selling Picasso's "Girl with a Fan" to Mrs. Averell Harriman in order to launch, with Alice Toklas as editor, what she called the "Plain Edition" (Gallup, *Flowers*, 246). Other titles published under that imprint were *Before The Flowers of Friendship Faded Friendship Faded* (1931), *How To Write* (1931), *Operas and Plays* (1932), and *Matisse Picasso and Gertrude Stein* (1933). Gertrude Stein's goal of being published in full was posthumously realized (with a few exceptions) in the eight-volume Yale edition, which was subsidized by her estate.

then lost momentum, until at last she was obliged to rely upon sheer eccentricity to carry her to a point that she could designate as the end.

As a physical production the book disappointed the two women. Miss Toklas remembered it as "badly printed." Worse still, it "would not stay closed and its back broke" (*WIR*, 136). The volume does have an unusually high incidence of typographical errors. Beyond these mechanical irritations, Gertrude Stein was not altogether satisfied with the work itself. She did not specify wherein she found it wanting, but she did recall later that after starting to summer in Bilignin, she had come to feel that "landscape was the thing." For this reason, "I had tried to write it down in *Lucy Church Amiably* and I did but I wanted it even more really . . ." (*LIA*, 122).

The book is essentially a long, lyric diary, begun in May, lackadaisical as a vacation, and little more than what she herself called it, "a landscape . . . in which there are some people" ("Advertisment," *LCA*, 7). She correctly observed that "Lucy Church made mountains out of mole hills" (84). Her prose is rarely less banal than that example. The book is a leisurely summer book. "If she sits and rests it is very much a very great pleasure to observe her. / 2.30, 3.30, 4.30, 5.30, 6.30, 7.30, 8.30" (66). With just such monotonous geniality does time pass in this book. The quality of the discourse is equally casual and muted. "Conversation can be how do you do. / How do you do. / How do you do" (46). When Gertrude Stein rises to sustained comprehensibility, the information communicated is of little moment. "Lucy Church prefers . . . a temperate climate where snow does not stay upon the ground where the mountains are poetical the rivers wide and rapidly flowing the meadows green . . ." (111).

The burden of the book is composed of local reference. The plants, natural features of the area, and celebrities associated with it are mentioned throughout. Thyme, mint, box, fuchsias, and sweet peas appear. Above all, the hunting and identification of mushrooms is dwelt on. The region around Belley has been described by its most eminent son and former mayor, the gourmet Brillat-Savarin. It is "a charming countryside where one finds high mountains, hills, rivers, clear streams, waterfalls, chasms—a true English garden of a hundred leagues square" (*The Physiology of Taste*, xliii). The streams and cascades figure centrally in *Lucy Church Amiably*. They even inspire its remarkable epigraph: "And with a nod she turned her head toward the falling water. Amiably."

Belley and its tiny suburb, Bilignin, as well as the more distant cities of Bourg, Chambery, and Grenoble are all mentioned, indicating Gertrude Stein's pleasure in touring the region. Local celebrities from Madame Recamier to brigands are also mentioned. Among the most prominent are the poet Lamartine, who was educated in Belley, the painter Joseph-Léon Bonnat, and the dramatic poet, Paul Claudel who had a chateau in nearby Béon. Alice Toklas noted in her cookbook that while the cuisine of the Hotel Pernollet in Belley where the two women stayed until they acquired a house had been enthusiastically recommended, it turned out to be flatly "poor." She hinted that the reason was that the cook "preferred reading Lamartine in a corner to doing his work in the kitchen" (100–102).

Two unhistorical names appear regularly, Simon Therese and John Mary. Some details are provided about them. Simon Therese was the youngest of ten children, for example, and John Mary had a brother James Mary. It is striking that the names are composed of a masculine and a feminine element. Inasmuch as many of the remarks about them concern marital and familial relationships, it is conceivable that Gertrude Stein was drawing upon two specific French couples for her commentary, a Jean married to a Marie, and a Simon married to a Thérése. But it is difficult to make out just what is happening, for their stories are not coherently presented in the book. Disguises, transformations, and renamings are the central pre-occupation.

Lucy Church in particular has at least a dual identity throughout the book—that of a building and of a woman. After reiterating the warning not to expect any regular coherence in any of Gertrude Stein's works, one may say that both church and woman represent the spirit of the place.

The building was a specific church located in the nearby hamlet of Lucey. Its peculiarly bulbous steeple led Gertrude Stein to observe that "the steeple is a pagoda and there is no reason for it and it looks like something else" ("Advertisement," *LCA*, 7). (There is a photograph of the church in Sprigge.) The steeple was supposedly Russian, brought back to France by a soldier after the Napoleonic campaign. If so, it was a remarkable trophy to carry on the retreat.

Most of the references apply to the woman. "Lucy Church said that she found it unpleasant to have marble under her hand" (83). The woman generally resembles Gertrude Stein at her best, relaxed and on vacation. "Lucy Church was amiable and very much resuscitated" (51). The notion of herself as a church accorded with the religious orientation of Gertrude Stein's recent thought. Holiness she regarded as conferred by one's state of mind. "Lucy Church maybe any one" (132). And in fact Alice Church, Madeline Church, Jessie Church, and other Churches appear in the book as well, presumably when they possess an amiability comparable to that of the presiding deity (61, 120). Sad to say, a few other Lucy Churches confuse the central reference, among them a married woman with two small daughters (239). But Gertrude Stein never lost sight of her main subject. "Who knew how many Lucy's have been called Lucy Church," she asked, and her answer was simple and inevitable. "I do" (224).

"Alice Babette" is mentioned once, as are the problems of house-hunting (150). Lucy Church, we learn, rented a valuable house, but could not immediately take possession of it because a naval lieutenant was still living in it (130–31). A similar episode occurred in the lives of the two women, who after spending six summers at the Hotel Pernollet in Belley, leased a house in Bilignin, a cluster of dwellings a mile from Belley.*

Over the course of the book Gertrude Stein underwent a change of attitude toward pseudonyms. Early on, criticism of her practice brought upon the offenders her ultimate punishment—annihilation through refusing to acknowledge the malefactors' existence.

> They said they were sorry but they were afraid she was not intelligent enough to disguise herself.
> What happened to them.
> They were not mentioned again . . . (*LCA* 52)

But eventually Gertrude Stein came round. "It is better to name it naturally than to have it changed from Jack to Jaqueline or from Henry to Henrietta" (240). Candor, that peculiarly American virtue, here known as "naming it naturally," was beginning to seem feasible to Gertrude Stein. Her long period of obscurity was coming to an end.

---

* The leasing adventure has been told in various ways in *ABT*, 281–2; in *WIR*, 123–4; in *The Alice B. Toklas Cook Book*, 102; and yet another version appears in Elliot Paul's *Understanding the French* (New York, 1955), 20–22. The passage concerning the house appears in volume 3 of the *LCA* manuscript at Yale, with no evidence that it was inserted later. In the passage the episode seems to have reached its climax. If so, this suggests that the writing of *LCA* extended a good deal beyond 1927, the year assigned for its composition, for the Bilignin house was acquired in 1929. In May of that year, Gertrude Stein wrote Henry McBride from "Billignin," ". . . it is a nice place . . . to decide about a house . . . we don't yet know whether we are spelled with one l or two . . ." Then on 18 November 1929 she wrote him, "We did have a beautiful summer, we got our home and we were so pleased . . ." Finally, in a letter to Ellen Daniel with the assigned date of 1930, Gertrude Stein remarks: "Otherwise what news, Lucy is all done and looks quite pretty . . ." (YCAL).

She was undertaking new subjects: explanations of her work, memories of her friendships with the now famous figures of the European world of art, the delights of rural France. The old manias and devils were disintegrating and blowing away in the sun. Sexual passion, the insecurities of reputation, the tyranny of father and brother were no longer paramount in her writing. Already amiable, Lucy Church was on the verge of becoming comprehensible.

10

⌐. "I do see how infidels talk. They talk with the
language of dishes and daylight."
                              ("Why Are There Whites To Console")

From 1927 on Gertrude Stein turned her thoughts increasingly to the
origins and operation of language. She collected her findings in 1931
under the title of *How to Write*. Its eight parts were written out of
sequence and do not seem to have been conceived originally as an
integral work. *How to Write* is a dense and bewildering book, but
possessed of some familiarity with Gertrude Stein's habits of mind,
one can discern its general purport.

In the first part actually composed, "Finally George A Vocabulary
of Thinking," Gertrude Stein contemplated her numerous acquaintances
all named George. "George is the name of George Lynes George,
George Bracque, George Ullman, George Joinville, George Williams and will with it and George Middleton. This makes it recognizable
as the name George" (*HTW*, 273). The specific range of the Georges
whom she knew contributed to her sense of the name "George." They
filled "George" for her with a unique combination of associations.
"George" assumed the identity it possessed for her, not through any
lexical key, but through the long accretion of personal experience.

"The Georges whom I have known have been pleasant not uninter-
esting," she reflected, but one in particular—"finally one"—turned out
to be "very well estimated" (289). This was probably Georges Hugnet,
the French poet. The French spelling of his name induced this series:
"Georges Allans Pauls Christians and Virgils" (*HTW*, 279). Hugnet
had won Gertrude Stein's gratitude by translating what he himself later
published as "Morceaux Choisis de *La Fabrication des Américains*." *

---

* Gertrude Stein wrote a portrait of Hugnet in 1928, which she later called "the
most completely the thing I wanted to do . . ." (*LIA*, 199). However, when she
read it to American audiences, she used only the last six lines, without informing

This particular George coalesced all the associations the name had for her. "They can be united in resemblance and acquaintance" (289). Despite their common association in her mind, these men each had distinctive features, beginning with their surnames. "Georges have many names . . ." (282). Some might literally be known by another name. "Frank could be called George if one were used to it but one is not" (286). The point of all these observations was that for Gertrude Stein verbal identity—the relationship between the world perceived and the expressive medium—was a dizzying welter of similarities and distinctions. The early part of "Finally George" is filled with twins, pairs, rhymes, and other embodiments of similarity but not identicalness. "What is the difference between repeating and back again (276). The problem was verbal. She emphasized the inadequacy of language to handle the full range of experience in the statement, "Identical twins do not look alike" (274).

Little else can be said with any confidence of "Finally George." Its long, convoluted sentences give the impression of saying something, and yet both the referents and their relationships remain obscure. The subtitle, "A Vocabulary of Thinking," offers a single light. It indicates that Gertrude Stein had turned her attention to the function of words in the operation of thought. And in two other pieces, also written in 1928 and subsequently gathered in *How To Write*, she headed straight into the complex question of how words were generated.

"Arthur A Grammar" opens in the dense, paragraph style of "Finally George," but it soon shifts to a series of unusually intriguing and often apt statements, cued primarily by the word "grammar."

As the accepted linguistic system by which the perceived and intuited world is described, grammar has a useful function. "Grammar is in our power." "Grammar readily begins" (73, 74). But once one has accepted the communality of grammar—"A prize for tractability is grammar . . ."—much is lost (75). Gertrude Stein realized that "there is no resemblance without a grammar" (87). But barely hidden behind that realization was her belief that such resemblance was ultimately illusory. This was an almost impossible conclusion for Gertrude Stein to reach, accept, and articulate. A totally particularistic world threatened a fatal incoherence. In personal terms, it meant no love, no appreciation, no security for Gertrude Stein. She had been seeking to achieve and maintain the proof of union for some twenty-five years, but her hard-

---

them of her abridgement. Like other portraits composed in 1928, "George Hugnet" uses the name "Geronimo" a good deal—for reasons unknown (*P&P*, 66).

headedness persistently challenged the needs of her heart. Put as brutally as possible—"Grammar is useless because there is nothing to say" (62).

Gertrude Stein's scepticism about grammar was roused by its coerciveness. "Grammar will." "Grammar. Obliged" (51, 68). By forcing the original impressions into accepted forms, it perverted them. "Grammar is not grown" (58). Grammar is constructed. "Grammar means that it has to be prepared and cooked . . ." (101). Seeing things directly, she was impressed by their essential uniqueness. If grammar created resemblance, then it must be false. "Literalness is not deceptive it destroys similarity" (70). Unfortunate perhaps, but it could not be helped. That was how things were.

The strongest position Gertrude Stein took in her writing through the twenties was that grammar was probably untrue. It must be, she said, "very long or else unsatisfactory" (91). "Very long" meant infinite, since only in infinity could she systematically account for all the possible relationships existing among words, objects, and the mind. The totality of her writing constituted her own grammar. It demonstrated what things related to what other things at what particular time in her particular life. However impenetrable, the record she furnished was theoretically absolute. Whatever else might be true, it was undeniable that at this time, concentrated on this subject, these particular words emanated from Gertrude Stein in precisely this order. Words, not the rules for their disposition, constituted reality. "The question is," she wrote, "if you have a vocabulary have you any need of grammar . . ." The obvious response was "no." But there was one qualification—"have you any need of grammar except for explanation . . ." (60). Gertrude Stein was willing to come part way to explain what she was up to. Exposition required a more careful observance of grammar than she could justify in her creative work. Otherwise, it was "forget grammar and think about potatoes" (109).

Whoever "Arthur" may be, the combination of his name and "A Grammar" stands for the synthesis of spontaneity and convention. While Gertrude Stein was on the side of organic immediacy in composition, she was willing to admit the occasional usefulness of traditional verbal order. One of her definitions embodies just this point. "Appointed is grammar," she writes. Grammar appoints words to perform certain duties. They gain their power through the authority conferred upon them by the linguistic system in which they operate. She continues: ". . . at and when is description." Something located in a particular time and place is distinct in her mind from grammar.

Responding freely to an external stimulus with words was the activity she called "description." It was unfettered by formal requirements. However, "Arthur a grammar can be both." And she indicated the practical function that grammar can fulfill. "Once in a while may carry. Carry me across" (79). Gertrude Stein did not deny the occasional utility of formal conventions. Her prose was then "partly a grammar," a "grammar of intermittence" (89). Conventions had a pragmatic value for her in making transitions, but they were of secondary importance.

The smaller structure of the sentence also preoccupied Gertrude Stein in 1928. "Sentences" forms a hundred-page segment of *How to Write*. Like "Arthur A. Grammar" it is filled with injunctions to herself to ponder the subject. "What is the sentence." Answers and examples come in abundance. While not appreciably clearer than the other sections of the book, this one does give further evidence of how intensively Gertrude Stein brooded over the forms of prose. Her conclusions often have an aphoristic solidity.

She naturally regarded the sentence with suspicion. It was a compromise at best, a surrender to predictability rather than an acceptance of the perils of audacity. "A sentence is when they have abandoned will they" (*HTW*, 166). But the sentence like the line in drawing, had a potential liberty which the "grammatical" construct of, say, Napoleon on a horse at Iena lacked. The sentence, could, she suspected, be arbitrary and therefore free. "A sentence is when they start." "A sentence is made up of whatever they mean." "A sentence is when they end" (185, 136, 151). Her tone was admonitory. "A sentence must not be bought . . . must not be taught . . ." (174–5).

Gertrude Stein also considered the elements of the sentence. Her loyalty to the noun never wavered. The sheer existence of a noun alarmed people, she thought, by making no concessions. It is not static, but brims with potential. "What is a noun. Refer. What is a noun. A noun does not make an ending and therefor. A noun does not destroy their change. A noun does not lighten which is why they are frightened. A noun with an inelegance makes it plain" (191).

If nouns were people and things, then sentences expressed the possibility of their union. "A sentence is their wedding" (123). Therefore, when Gertrude Stein spoke of the sentence, she was likely to be making symbolic formulations that referred to human relationships as well as to verbal ones. Sometimes a sentence was a verbal fulfillment, evidence of a subtle joining. "A sentence says you know what I

197

mean. Dear do I well I guess I do" (34). If successful, the sentence was the paradoxical combination of absolute self-possession and absolute dedication to another. "A sentence hopes that you are very well and happy. It is very selfish (29). When, before our eyes, Gertrude Stein generates a sentence of which she approves, its significant elements are that two people—"we"—have known another person who was kind. "Think of a sentence. A whole sentence. Who is kind. We have known one who is kind. That is a very good sentence" (30).

The union referred to might also be that of attention and object. Were this fusion accomplished with a concentration comparable to the sanctified focus of love, the sentence would then be sound. Then "a sentence is a duplicate" (35). A little later, in "A Grammarian," Gertrude Stein explored the meaning of "duplicate" further. "I believe in duplicates," she declared. "Think well of this. You cannot repeat a duplicate you can duplicate. You can duplicate a duplicate." With that she admonished herself and her reader, "Now think of the difference of repeat and of duplicate" (110).

The distinction was a fundamental one, unflinching in its avowal of the unique particularity of every thing and every action, yet offering the possibility of relationship. Nothing can become anything else, but certain resemblances can be shared. So put, Gertrude Stein's point is obvious enough, but it bore importantly for her both upon the medium of art and upon human relationships. A sentence is as incapable of repeating any other sentence as it is of repeating experience. But it can duplicate experience by embodying it in another form.

By 1930, she had become aware that "It is very hard to save the sentence" ("Sentences and Paragraphs," *HTW*, 30). "I would use a sentence if I could," she wrote, then puzzled over her malaise. "Why does it not please me to be sitting here." The answer lay in the very sentences she was then creating. "Who likes to hear her hear of them. See how bad that is . . . / It is not very easy to save the sentence" (33). Some of her compositional problems seemed caused by flagging attention. "Remind oneself carefully of every word. / Cannot" ("Basket," *P&P*, 182).

As she worried at the knot, the relationship of the sentence to the paragraph clarified. "Sentences are not natural paragraphs are natural and I am desperately trying to find out why" ("More Grammar For a Sentence," *AFAM*, 371). Her alternate statement of this, which was to remain a key perception for her, was "A Sentence is not emotional a paragraph is" (*HTW*, 23).

Sentences were formal collocations of words, arranged according to rule. They were "not natural"—that is to say, they were not emotional, intuitive constructs—because the rules constricted the original verbal material that rose in the mind. A paragraph, on the other hand, was composed of a set of sentences, which need not be associated according to any grammatical convention. The individual sentence might be compromised by bending it to grammatical necessities, but a group of sentences fell together in a "natural" construct, formally uncoerced. This natural union might yet be achieved then in a paragraph. "A sentence is a hope of a paragraph" ("More Grammar For a Sentence," *AFAM*, 372). Within a year this position could be seen solidifying. "She is my wife. That is what a paragraph is. Always at home. A paragraph hopes for houses. We have a house two houses. My wife and I are at home" ("Pay Me," *PL*, 139).

"Forensics," the last part composed for *How To Write*, also concluded the book. This clear, personal piece, resembles the ones on history, grammar, and sentences in that it mixes her ideas about the announced subject with the associations and interruptions that occur during the act of composition. This was the strongest—most coherent, yet individualized—form of experimental writing she ever conceived. But why forensics? The title was that of her junior year writing class at Radcliffe. She meant by forensics argumentation for the sake of victory rather than truth, the shrewd utilization of emotional appeals, distortion, and simplification wherever necessary to win. "Forensics is eloquence and reduction," she said. "Forensics leads to reputation." But, "Forensics may pale. It often does" (386, 388, 394). So this was her dismissal of rhetorical strategy in composition.

From her beginnings as a writer, Gertrude Stein had found it difficult to construct coherent paragraphs, to sustain a tone, an idiomatic level, or an idea. She therefore consistently defended the virtues of the fragmentary perception, uniquely expressed. Her perennial enemy was formalism and planning before the fact, as the art of forensics required. For her, How to Write was How I Write.

During this period preceding her emergence as a best-selling author, Gertrude Stein lacked any central interest other than her concern for the theoretical foundations of her style. Consequently, her writing continued to depend heavily upon the details of provincial life. Someone was injured by a stick while gardening. Renewing the lease on the Bilignin house caused problems. Basket, her poodle, now began

199

to make frequent appearances in Gertrude Stein's prose. So often in fact, that she once remarked, "A basket if it is mentioned dates it" ("To Kitty or Kate Buss," (*P&P*, 104). Even *How To Write* starts with a French colloquial expression of indignation or surprise directed at a dog. "Qu'est-ce que c'est cette comédie d'un chien" (13). Subsequent references to a *caniche* confirm that this was surely Basket. Some domestic crises also made their mark. "I know who cried about Etta" (18). "I have never been so sorry about anything as I was about Friday" (19). "I was overcome with remorse. It was my fault that my wife did not have a cow. This sentence they cannot use" (*HTW*, 25). In 1928, Gertrude Stein and Alice Toklas were evidently prevailed upon to draw their wills. Gertrude Stein seems to have been shaken by the experience, "very near to tears" ("A Bouquet. Their Wills," *O&P*, 213). In conference with the lawyer, she was struck by the fact that should a couple be killed at the same instant, for legal purposes the man was presumed to have lived the longer, and therefore inherits his wife's portion. It was a law that obviously had paradoxical meaning for this particular household, and that could not fail to re-enforce Gertrude's Stein's sense of the insufficiency of words.

Other than recording impressions from her personal life, Gertrude Stein's literary activity consisted of a series of unsustained gestures in a variety of genres. She prepared a new collection of her writings, she produced a set of formal lyrics, she composed more "plays," she translated a poem from the French, and she created a film scenario.

The second collection of Gertrude Stein's short pieces was entitled *Useful Knowledge* and appeared in 1928. According to the account given in *The Autobiography of Alice B. Toklas*, when Joseph Brewer expressed interest in publishing some of Gertrude Stein's work, she suggested "he should make it all the short things she had written about America . . ." (297; see also 210). As she had done with *Geography and Plays*, Gertrude Stein selected for publication about one out of every four pieces she had available in manuscript. Six of the twenty-one pieces had been composed early enough to have been included in *Geography and Plays*. "Farragut," the oldest piece, dated from 1915 and her Mallorcan sojourn. "Allen Tanner," the most recent, was written in 1926. Although the pieces are not dated in the table of contents nor do they appear in strict chronological order, they *are* generally on American subjects.

Also in 1928 Gertrude Stein tried her hand at formal verse with a charming series of brief lyrics entitled "For-Get-Me-Not." Touched by the Bilignin atmosphere, they sing of poplars, birds, pansies, and country pleasures. The whole is divided into sections, each of which has a subtitle. Each section has twelve stanzas, or in one instance, twice twelve. The stanzas begin as approximate quatrains with occasional rhymes and caesuras that are emphasized by full stops.

> Eighty stretches. From here. To there.
> Here to there corrects everywhere.
> She may be counting. One to four.
> Or she may. Not be counting. Any more. (*SIM*, 231)

The sections are reasonably clear in themselves, and they usually circle back to a recognizable conclusion. However, as is the rule with Gertrude Stein, the form she chose to approximate—in this case, the ballad stanza—slowly began to fray, then deteriorate, until near the end of the series, a "stanza" may be no more than a word or a phrase. Because she could not or would not sustain her original form, she rarely carried her work through to a predictable end. Her defense would be that these strong beginnings and languishing endings accurately reflected her changing attitude toward her subject matter.

The same phenomenon was observable even when Gertrude Stein had another's text to lean upon. George Hugnet finally published his translation of portions of *The Making of Americans* in 1929. Gertrude Stein decided to reciprocate the next year by translating his long, ambitious poem of sexual reveries entitled "Enfances," their efforts to be printed on facing pages. However, before publication, the two quarreled over their billing in the prospectus. Hugnet wrote Gertrude Stein politely, "Those whom I have questioned . . . have all said that your name beside mine would give the impression of a collaboration, when, don't you agree, there is no question of that" (Gallup, *Flowers*, 244). In Gertrude Stein's version, she remembered that the announcements "for our book . . . said it was his book and . . . did not say it was my book" ("Left to Right," *Story*, III [November 1933], 17). The two former friends also failed to reach a commonly acceptable term for Gertrude Stein's contribution. She regarded it as "reflection," he as "free translation" (Gallup, *Flowers*, 245). In her pique, Gertrude Stein managed to get the title changed to "Poem Pritten on the Pfances of Georges Hugnet." Then in her Plain Edition version, "Before The Flowers of Friendship Faded Friendship Faded," she eliminated Hugnet's text altogether.

Although the result of their bickering, this expedient was a wise one for both parties. Gertrude Stein's version suffers badly in the presence of the original which it purports to reflect. She could not be expected to translate a work of any length. The very act ran counter to her habits of work. In this instance, her greatest fidelity was to the first line. "Enfances aux cents coins de ma mémoire" she rendered as "In the one hundred small places of myself my youth" (*Pagany*, II [Winter 1931], 10, 11). After this she freely improvised, retaining for a time only the dominant verb or noun of Hugnet's line. So, "je vous mesure au trajet de la vie" became "to please to take a distance to make a life" (10, 11). Gertrude Stein's liberties were so extreme that, did they not emanate from her, one might reasonably conclude that the translator knew too little French to do the job properly. In time she even abandoned the line equivalence. She expanded and contracted her version at will, until at last giving up all pretense of offering a text related to Hugnet's, she offered variants from her other compositions, such as "I love my love with a v / Because it is like that / I love myself with a b / Because I am beside that / A king" (35). As she observed, "I follow as I can" (13).

The other point worth making about Gertrude Stein's translation is that she carefully censored Hugnet's images of death, sex, nudity, and onanism. For a woman who offered lines of fearsomely coy sexual innuendo, Gertrude Stein remained, even in her middle fifties, prudish, or at least, evasive. She translated "J'aime t'avoir" as "He likes to be with her" (28, 29). More fancifully but no less euphemistically, "Mon sex a respiré / entre leurs mains moites" became "And there is a well inside / In hands untied" (12, 13).

Before The Flowers is not a satisfying composition to read. Its sentiments are as random as those in other of her works, but with the difference that much of the content is imposed by Hugnet's text. Throughout it Gertrude Stein intermittently indicated her restiveness with the project. "Believe me it is not for pleasure I do it" is a remark unrelated to any of Hugnet's sentiments (17). Equally significant, she adapts her favorite catchline to her situation of subservience: "When this you do not hear and do not see believe me" (31). It is ironic that this creative abortion should, with its "Antique Montval" paper and a full page provided for each section, turn out to be the handsomest volume by far in the Plain Edition.

In the "plays" Gertrude Stein wrote in these years, it is rarely clear who the characters are, who is speaking, or indeed if anyone is speaking. Her deliberately undramatic dramas remained a mixture of narrative and of private reactions. The piece "Short Sentences" reached an extreme of literary mannerism. It listed some five to six hundred names, each of which had a phrase or sentence attached to it. Her main stylistic feature of this period was the short, staccato phrase punctuated by the full stop. "It is in union that there is strength. And they divided. And therefor. One of them. Was stronger. Than before. More so" ("Brim Beauvais," *MR*, 287). In addition, she frequently preceded her sentences with an exclamatory "Oh," although that too was only a temporary mannerism.

In 1929, Gertrude Stein composed a scenario entitled "Film Deux Soeurs Qui Ne Sont Pas Soeurs." This was the first piece in French that she had ever published (*Yale Catalogue,* item 65, p. 40). It is entirely lucid, despite a delightfully absurd plot, in the contemporary tradition of silent film comedies, dominated by swift arbitrary action. It features the ladies Stein and Toklas, their poodle and their automobile.

The plot line is as follows: a laundress is discovered looking at a photograph of two white poodles. Two women arrive in an automobile, ask to see the photograph, and admire it. Meanwhile, a beautiful young woman enters their car and commences to weep. They summarily eject her and leave, whereupon the laundress discovers that her photograph is missing. In the next scene, the two women show a second laundress the photograph. Again the young woman arrives and throws herself in their car. The two women return to the car, dropping a little package as they depart. Two days later, the first laundress is approached by the young woman who is carrying a little package. Just then the automobile passes with the two women and a white poodle in it. The poodle has a little package in his mouth. The laundress and her companions see, but do not understand what they see (*O&P*, 399–400).

The scenario features elements of superiority, arbitrary appropriation and rejection, and triumphant mystery. In essence it says we, two sisters who are not sisters, are a team, superior to others. We take what we want, we dismiss whom he wish without apology, and we dominate by our possession of the mystery. The underlying ruthlessness of the plot is disconcerting, but its assertion of strength through union is altogether characteristic of its author.

By the early thirties Gertrude Stein's writing had become peculiarly unrewarding to her. Her imagination was failing, and she seemed incapable of pushing forward. While awaiting inspiration, she held tenaciously to her sense of her own importance. "I am determined to be king," she announced ("Louis XI and Madame Giraud," *O&P*, 346). Despite the apparent random quality of her work, she had standards and could tell when things were going wrong. "Nobody knows what I am trying to do but I do and I know when I succeed" ("More Grammar For a Sentence," *AFAM*, 365). Only when she turned back upon herself and began to explain her past did she revive. This pre-eminently a-historical woman rediscovered her energies in her own history.

She had begun to meditate upon history in the middle of 1930. As had been the case with grammar, her feelings were mixed on the subject. In "History or Messages From History," she created a number of memorable aphorisms about the art of recording the past. The burden of her critique dealt with what history excluded. "Moonlight in the valley is before and after history" (*A&B*, 228). History filtered out the lyricism of life. "In history one does not mention dahlias mushrooms or hortensias" (228). Yet she recognized history's reliance upon particularity. "Human nature is the same that is not history" (232). History attracted her by its existential solidity and perpetual openness. "Intention is not history nor finality finality is not history" (232). In another piece composed almost at the same time, she indicated how history might be improved. "One likes," she observed, "to have history illustrated by one's contemporaries" ("Abel," *SIM*, 226).

As she floated in these creative doldrums, the reality of her reputation began to take possession of her. She had been known and admired before, but something happened around 1931 to inflame her self-importance. She felt herself to be a historic personage. "He did say. It would. Be important. To the biographer" ("Winning His Way," *SIM*, 187). "Winning His Way" is a long and interesting poem concerning both poetry and fame. Characteristically, gender is of no importance in it, for "she is winning her way" also appears in it (*SIM*, 169). At several spots, the Stein-Toklas ménage definitely appears, as in references to Baby, Caesar, and the making of tapestries (160, 178, 186).

The upward movement suggested by the Horatio Algerian title is reflected in a taut summary Gertrude Stein provided of her career. It starts when she was the silent puss-in-the-corner at Leo's soirees. "Now first he had no enemies and no one thought but he could. Surely it is advantageous." Then, having covertly launched her career, she took pleasure in writing, although she remained unrecognized. "Secondly no success. But satisfaction." Her present stage was one of steady production, driving toward immortality. "Thirdly. All or out. Pages.

Pages" (*SIM*, 157). "Winning His Way" describes the self-confidence and discipline that was necessary for her to endure. Her firm conclusion is "This glory. / It is. In no way. An accident" (165).

The agent that confirmed Gertrude Stein's sense of her genuine artistic merit may well have been *Axel's Castle*, Edmund Wilson's study of symbolism published in 1931. Here, in a book by an important intellectual journalist, Gertrude Stein found herself discussed in the company of Proust, Joyce, Yeats, and Eliot. Although Wilson was by no means uncritical of her talents, he nonetheless characterized her as "a literary personality of unmistakable originality and distinction" (253). It is known that she read *Axel's Castle* for she wrote Carl Van Vechten in response to it: "I was not born in Baltimore, and I am not *german*, and I do make poetry which can be read otherwise I was pleased" (Sprigge, 169).

If it was not Wilson's serious review of her career that exhilarated her, it was something similar—perhaps Marcel Brion's warm appreciation, "Le Contrepoint poétique de Gertrude Stein" (1930), in which he compared her poetry to the fugal art of Bach. In 1932 Gertrude Stein wrote longingly: "She hopes that she will be again / Recognized as carefully" ("A Play of Pounds," *LO&P*, 256). As it turned out, she alone could satisfy her own longing for appreciation.

This growing consciousness of herself as an historical figure supplied one motive for Gertrude Stein to undertake a retrospective account of her life, and her creative lassitude encouraged the project. Aside from the actual deadness of her work, there were other signals that her imagination had run down. One piece ends with the flat admission, "I can no longer remember how she says what she says" ("Marguerite Or A Simple Novel of High Life," *MR*, 373). She pondered the very origin of her need to compose:

> The problem resolves itself. Into this.
> Does a poem. Continue. Because of. A Kiss.
> Or because. Of future greatness.
> Or because. There is no cause. Why.
> ("Winning His Way, *SIM*, 164)

This was perceptive self-scrutiny. Why write? For Alice, for glory, or for the sake of writing itself. It is remarkable how long Gertrude Stein was obliged to curry her companion's favor. "If any one is angry with me now I am not angry with them" ("A Little Love of Life," *SIM*, 277). The source of the quarrel was specified later. "She is as always right he is not a genius but a great painter." Then, after a moment comes the conciliatory remark. "Eat your apple darling" (282). Although Alice was rarely heard directly, at times that withering voice still countered the poet's enthusiasm. One incident involved the excitement of unexpectedly seeing an eclipse of the moon.

> And she. May be. Said to be. Not very. Interested.
> And she may be said to be. Not interested.
> ("A Ballad," *SIM*, 265)

Alice Toklas's approval was a powerful stimulus for Gertrude Stein. And Alice, although loyal and protective of her companion's welfare, was an acidly opinionated woman.

All these conditions—heightened fame, a creative slump, and the hope of pleasing Alice—probably generated the composition in 1932 of *The Autobiography of Alice B. Toklas*. After twenty years of enigmatic utterances, Gertrude Stein at last chose to speak in a voice of singular clarity. She was fifty-eight years old.

PART THREE

⌇. "How can anything be different from what it is."
(The Making of Americans)

PART THREE

11

⮞. ". . . and anyway what am I I am an American,
Alice says a civil war general in retirement,
perhaps . . ."

(Letter to H. McBride, 22 May, 1929)

Information about the writing of Gertrude Stein's most famous book
is sparse. By her own report, she composed *The Autobiography of
Alice B. Toklas* swiftly in the fall of 1932, specifically, during October
and the first two weeks of November (*EA*, 9, 40). Alice Toklas remembered that the project was originally suggested by their friend Sir
Robert Abdy who had told Gertrude Stein, "You should write the history of your friends and time" (*WIR*, 160). She did precisely that,
with the odd twist of offering the history in the voice of Alice Toklas.

That voice constitutes the foremost problem of the book. Its ironic
precision was utterly foreign to Gertrude Stein, and therefore it is
natural to wonder if her companion was in any way responsible for
the drastic stylistic metamorphosis.

One possibility is sufficiently heretical that no one has dared advance
it directly; but there have been hints that Alice Toklas composed her
own autobiography. W. G. Rogers, a longtime friend of both women,
reported that "one way to rile Miss Toklas, and one out of many, is to
tell her you suspect her touch in the Stein genius . . ." The more he
knew the two women though, he continued, the more he "wondered
whose light was being hidden under whose bushel" (*When This You
See*, 33). Virgil Thomson remembered that Gertrude Stein would often
begin a story, then lapse into increasing vagueness and begin to repeat
herself until Alice Toklas would interrupt, " 'I'm sorry, Lovey; it wasn't
like that at all.' 'All right, Pussy,' Gertrude would say. 'You tell it.' "
And "Alice's way," Thomson concludes, "was its definitive version"
(*Virgil Thomson*, 177). Thomson did add an important and diplomatic
qualification though. "In every way except actual authorship," he said,

209

the *Autobiography* was "Alice Toklas' book" (176). When asked by an interviewer, "But you must have helped in prompting her at times, I suppose?" Alice responded: "No, the only things I helped her with were the two incidents which she should have mentioned . . . and which she had forgotten really" (Duncan, 85).

The manuscript notebooks of the *Autobiography* at Yale show that Alice Toklas played a somewhat greater role than she was willing to acknowledge in the editing of the book. As Gertrude Stein's typist, she habitually made notations in her friend's manuscripts, usually with a red pencil. For the most part these additions consisted of numbers only, correlating the page of the typescript with the manuscript. Sometimes too, Alice would write a word in her own hand to clarify Gertrude Stein's scrawl. For example, in "The King Or Something," she did this with the words "insulted," "satisfy," "nations," and "neglect." But she also changed a few words in that particular piece. What Gertrude Stein had written as "This is not imagination," Alice Toklas changed to "This is not inauguration" (*G&P*, 122). And the original, "We are not annoyed . . ." was changed to "They are not annoyed . . ." (*G&P*, 130). While the changes are trivial, they are not errors in transcription, but conscious revisions.

The extent to which Alice Toklas participated in Gertrude Stein's compositions can only be settled after thorough study of all the manuscripts held at Yale. Two at least contain sizable portions written in her hand. One is "Ada," the piece that Gertrude Stein designated as her first portrait. She described the occasion of its composition in *The Autobiography of Alice B. Toklas*. Upon completing it, she said, she was very excited and forced Alice, who was its subject, to read it, even though supper was just being served. "I can still see the little tiny pages of the note-book written forward and back," said Alice Toklas. "I began it and I thought she was making fun of me and I protested, she says I protest now about my autobiography. Finally I read it all and was terribly pleased with it. And then we ate our supper" (139–40).

There is no reason to believe that the surviving manuscript notebook is not the original, although it is always possible that it is not. A good deal of the writing is in the hand of its subject, Alice Toklas. "Ada" appears to be a collaborative effort. For example, in the last paragraph, Alice Toklas wrote the first three sentences. At that point, Gertrude Stein picked up. In her segment, the following remark was later cancelled—"every one was meaning certainly meaning that Alice was one being perfect in being loving." Then, the final three sentences, beginning with "Trembling" are again in Alice Toklas's hand.

If this is the original version, it means that Alice Toklas composed the major part of her first, brief autobiography. She had already typed hundreds of pages of Gertrude Stein's work by this time, and was now perhaps being rewarded with the opportunity of trying her own hand at creation. Although her contribution (if it is hers) tends to be more factually direct than Gertrude Stein's, she was clearly an apt mimic. In effect, after Alice sketched her life in a version of Gertrude Stein's style, then Gertrude Stein entered to praise this Ada who had been telling charming stories to "some one." The portrait concludes by affirming their common identity. "Trembling was all living, living was all loving, some one was then the other one" (*G&P*, 16; and YCAL).

Given the special emphasis Gertrude Stein put upon this portrait; given its subject; given its date somewhere around 1909–10; given the manuscript in two hands; and given the conclusion that the two people are one, the evidence is persuasive that this was a collaboration of symbolic significance, sealing the relationship between the two women.

A Novel of Thank You, it may be remembered, was a book-length work of 1925, which gratefully celebrated the return of a strayed partner to the domestic fold. It contains some nine lengthy passages in the hand of Alice Toklas. While it is possible that she was merely taking dictation from Gertrude Stein, it is more reasonable to conclude that she actually participated in creating this account of a reconciliation. As Gertrude Stein specified, the book is "A novel of thank you and not about it" (185). In other words, Gertrude Stein's gratitude was directly manifested, not merely described, by permitting Alice Toklas to share in the composition.*

* The passages in Alice Toklas's hand are as follows:
—37, from "And yet it is very remarkable . . ." through 38, "Everybody can change a name . . ." (There was originally a period after "name," but it was scratched out.) Gertrude Stein picked up with "they can change . . ."
—50, from "Did anybody say it went around . . ." through 52, ". . . when there is a reason for it."
—55, from "Chapter XLV. Who can be shorter . . ." through 56, "Gradually who knows how."
—57, from "When she was . . ." through 58, "They will be cooler."
—62, from "Not looking." through 63, "You can always tell."
—65, from "Three chairs and place . . ." through 65, "Charles or Charlie to make them all the same as one."
—164, from "Control control . . ." through 166, "Once in a while" plus the next "Chapter" but no number.
—181, from "Perhaps it is." through 182, ". . . once in a while they went away."

The physical evidence indicates that *The Autobiography of Alice B. Toklas* was written by Gertrude Stein alone, with few hesitations or changes. There is at Yale, however, a preliminary notebook in which she made several false starts at the book. They are false, that is, if compared to the Alice Toklas who appears in the book. Otherwise, they are altogether characteristic of Gertrude Stein, the writer who found it difficult to maintain a single tone or topic for very long. So, in this early draft, Gertrude Stein soon allows the normally self-possessed voice of Alice Toklas to simper—"I was charming I was delicate I was delicious . . ." At another point, she lapses into repetitive incoherence—"the result I have had that I have what I have and I always have as I always will had to have that which I have."

At some stage of rewriting, these flaws disappeared. Whether other drafts existed and were destroyed is not clear, but it is entirely possible that the present manuscript is a fair copy of the whole. It does, however, contain interpolations and cancellations by Alice Toklas.

The manuscript of *The Autobiography of Alice B. Toklas* contains occasional question marks in red, sometimes referring to illegible handwriting, but elsewhere questioning the accuracy of the information. Sometimes Alice Toklas took emphatic exception. When Gertrude Stein said that she had completed the job of reading proof for *The Making of Americans* by herself, Alice objected—"Never" (275). Regarding Picasso's move to Montrouge, she commented "No," and supplied the correct date, "1915" (173). In neither instance did Gertrude Stein change her version, although she did accept the correction of the cost of Fernande Olivier's perfume (31).

In some places, Alice Toklas cancelled phrases outright. After Gertrude Stein referred to the *Guide de Gourmets,* Alice lined out the remark, "I think it was Hemingway who first told me about these xcellent guide books" (274).* She particularly refused to be on record as enthusiastic about *The Making of Americans.* She cancelled the ital-

---

—185, from "It might be allowed." through 185, ". . . not helping it all the same."

The manuscript of *A Novel* appears in eighty "volumes," which is to say, in eighty French schoolchild's cahiers, each of which runs to about fifteen pages. The passages appear in vols. 12, 17, 18, 19, 20, 55, 56, 64, 67. On the back cover of vol. 19, there is a crude line drawing of two united figures. A similar drawing appears in the manuscript of "Scenes from the door" (YCAL).

* Alice Toklas distinguished her enemies and her favorites very clearly. In an unpublished manscript, "American language and literature," after Gertrude Stein had mentioned Anderson, Hemingway, and Faulkner as representative contemporaries, Alice Toklas added the names of Thornton Wilder and Dashiell "Hammit" (YCAL).

icized phrases in the following two sentences: "Mildred was very fond of Gertrude Stein and took a deep interest in the book's ending *and so did I*. It was over a thousand pages long and I was typewriting it *and I enjoyed every minute of it*" (138).

The present manuscript of *The Autobiography of Alice B. Toklas* does not solve the problem of the abrupt change in Gertrude Stein's habits of writing. The puzzling change, moreover, did not persist. Although its sequel, *Everybody's Autobiography,* is a work of unusual merit, it is much more loosely constructed than *The Autobiography of Alice B. Toklas.* The tart economy of the *Autobiography* can be found in only one other book—Alice Toklas's own memoirs, *What Is Remembered.* The question inevitably arises of who influenced whom.

Alice Toklas seems to have served as some kind of monitor for the *Autobiography.* Her instrumentality may have been no more than her presence in Gertrude Stein's imagination. "Do I sound like Alice," she asked in 1920. "Any voice is resembling. / By this I mean when I am accustomed to them their voices sound in my ears" ("A Circular Play," *LO&P,* 150). Elsewhere she affirmed her aural memory. "In imitating a voice I hear it" ("All Sunday," *A&B,* 94).

Gertrude Stein realized that she was not equipped to exercise the selectivity that a history required. "My memory does not tell me how and what to remember and so what do I do. I remember everything" ("Reread Another," *O&P,* 130). She relied therefore upon the judgment of Alice. "I can be as stupid as I like because my wife is always right" ("Reread Another," *O&P,* 125). The evidence indicates that on at least a few occasions, Gertrude Stein invited Alice Toklas's active participation in the act of creation. Moreover, "Subject-Cases: The Background of a Detective Story" contained references to some sort of collaborative revision of a manuscript (*AFAM,* 6, 8, 11, 20).

That something similar took place in 1932 is suggested by "Stanzas in Meditation." It was written concurrently with *The Autobiography of Alice B. Toklas,* as a Steinian apologia for consenting to produce a popular book. Near the end of the *Autobiography,* its completion was noted. "The last thing that she has finished, Stanzas of Meditation, . . . she considers her real achievement of the commonplace" (276).*
While the "Stanzas" are far from easy to understand, they do suggest

---

* It is still unclear when Gertrude Stein did finish the "Stanzas." Virgil Thomson said that stanza 83, the last one of Part V, was completed in 1935 (*Thomson,* 189). In *EA,* Gertrude Stein refers to the "two hundred . . . I have written . . ." (300). In its printed version the "stanzas" total 164. Part III has two stanzas numbered "II" and two numbered "XVI."

that certain people urged Gertrude Stein to write her memoirs in a straightforward manner, that Alice concurred, and that, with considerable reservations, Gertrude Stein finally agreed to undertake some sort of collaborative effort. Money appears to have been an important motive for her to engage in what she regarded as "a compromise" (*SIM*, 90).

> I had no doubt that it a difference makes
> If there is doubt if money is about
> I also know . . .
> If when they give and take they give in a hurry . . . (105)

Gertrude Stein seems to have worked at the *Autobiography* by day, then turned to the "Stanzas" in the evening. Her nocturnal creation pleased her as the commercial enterprise could not. "It is not easy to turn away from delight in moon-light" (116). But she affirmed her efforts to produce in good faith a work that would give pleasure. "I have tried earnestly to express / Just what I guess will not distress" (99). Upon finishing the manuscript, she immediately informed her agent that it would "very likely be commercially successful" (GS to W. A. Bradley, ?13 November 1932, YCAL).

The "Stanzas" have three main characters—"they," "she," and "I." Their identities are ambiguous, save that "I" is most certainly the author. "She" is probably Alice Toklas, although "she" may also be that portion of Gertrude Stein's personality that consented to engage in this commercial undertaking. Similarly, "they" might be Gertrude Stein as a multiple personality, or Gertrude Stein and Alice Toklas. In one reference we do learn, "They are not a simple people / They the two of them" (132). Elsewhere, the question arises, "will they worry if they lose their dogs" (146). "They" might also be Sir Robert and Lady Diana Abdy, whose curiosity about "Paris as it had been" originally stimulated the writing of the *Autobiography* (*EA*, 300; *WIR*, 160).

The specific identity of "they" is finally less important than "their" characteristics. "They" represent the normal reading public to whom Gertrude Stein had to appeal in the *Autobiography*. "They" were the verbal conservatives who "call a pail a pail" (*SIM*, 14). She was not unfriendly toward them, although she was aware of their courteous scepticism about her oblique methods of composition. "I caught a bird which made a ball," begin the "Stanzas," "And they thought better of it. / . . . they were in a hurry yet / In a kind of a way they meant it best . . ." (3).

214

Having suppressed her scruples, she set out to satisfy the public appetite for entertaining and understandable anecdotes. What seems to have happened then is that she submitted samples of her work to the conventional "they." Her anxiety about their approval is evident.

> They have been here to leave it now
> But how foolish to ask them if they like it
> Most certainly they like it . . .
> But they might easily like something else (*SIM*, 21)

At first her compromised style was apparently accepted. "They like my way it is partly mine . . ." (18). But soon, their interest wanes. "They are very . . . tired with more of this" (20). If Gertrude Stein's narrative style was as mixed as it is in the one preliminary notebook at Yale, the objections are understandable. Resolved to do a successful job, she reminded herself, "it is more than ever necessary / That they should never be surprised . . ." (22).

Early in Part II of the "Stanzas" Gertrude Stein's independence clashed with her wish to give pleasure. "What do I care or how do I know . . . not only what they like but who they like" (29). But in a moment she exclaimed, "Can they like me oh can they like me." The answer she already knew. Therefore, "Let me listen to me and not to them" (30).* But debate between preserving her integrity and ordering her memories in order to satisfy others continued. She was "anxious to please" but also "anxious to mean" (63). She stubbornly adhered to the sufficiency of her work as it was. "Should it be mine as pause it is mine / That should be satisfying" (34). Still, the request for clarity continued to be heard. "Please be plain for this time" (30). After all, "they are just how they are" (31).

Eventually, Gertrude Stein seemed to become reconciled to her compromise. "I say this I change this I change this and this" (66). One can hear her rationalizing her behavior. She was willing "to change it fairly" and to "think well of which is theirs" (68, 69). Her motives for writing in this manner she specified.

> Believe me it is not for pleasure that I do it
> Not only for pleasure for pleasure in it that I do it.
> I feel the necessity to do it
> Partly from need
> Partly from pride
> And partly from ambition. (71)

* The 1936 play, "Listen To Me," specifically concerned the Abdys, suggesting that the phrase was associated with them in her mind.

The first line repeats the sentiment she expressed in translating Hugnet's *Enfances* (*Pagany*, II [Winter 1931], 17). But in spite of such self-justification, she could not conceal her misgivings.

Stanza V

I think very well of my way.

Stanza VI

May be I do but I doubt it. (71)

The subject of all this fretting was finally confirmed halfway through the "Stanzas." "This is her autobiography one of two / But which it is no one . . . can know." The woman to whom "her" refers is Alice Toklas, for "She knew that she could know / That a genius was a genius / . . . She did know three or so / So she says and what she says / No one can deny or try" (77). The three geniuses were specified in the *Autobiography* as Whitehead, Picasso, and Gertrude Stein (6). Her strength is evident. Gertrude Stein's attitude toward her fluctuates. At times she was eager for assistance. "She asked could I be taught . . . / And I said yes oh yes" (80). But elsewhere she felt beaten. "Who is winning why the answer of course is she is" (90). The possibility had arisen that "They could however collaborate" (51). In a tantalizingly clouded statement, Gertrude Stein decided that "perhaps it is as well / Not to belie a change of when they care / They mean I like it if she will do it" (77). If such hints mean that she accepted the editorial guidance of Alice Toklas to ensure the success of the project, then the purport of the following variants of her persistent tag line becomes clear: "she will be me when this you see" and "Not at all by me / When this you see" (78, 82). Expediency prevailed. "To make it do she offers it as a compromise" (90).

Periodically though, Gertrude Stein continued to reveal the distress that her capitulation was causing her. "How I wish I were able to say what I think" (79). She offered a harsh bill of particulars against herself. "I have been thought to not respect myself / To have been sold as wishes / To wonder why and if and will they mind" (134). Her answer to this accusation was a terse couplet: "I wish to say / That it is her day" (134).

Still, she emerged confidently from the "Stanzas." They constituted her fidelity to herself. "Now that I have written it twice / It is not as alike as once" (145). The *Autobiography* was retrospective. In its return to the past, it sacrificed Gertrude Stein's enunciated principles concerning the necessity of spontaneous creation. But this parallel auto-biography redeemed the betrayal. With the immediacy of a diary, it displayed the hard as well as the soft truth about Alice and herself. While affirming that "I do love none but you," it rescued Gertrude Stein's integrity (150). Whatever the motivation for writing the *Autobiography*, Gertrude Stein insisted "I know the difference between two" and "the whole of this last end is to say which of two" (150). She had not sullied herself as an artist. "Everybody knows that I chose." This version proved it. Its candor would secure her welcome "When I come / Because I am coming" (151).

This dual effort, this stubborn, ingenious response to a conflict of will is unique in literature. The irony is that were it not for the attractiveness of the compromised *Autobiography*, about which she worried for such a long period, "Stanzas in Meditation" would never have been read.*

The Autobiography of Alice B. Toklas has been ill-served by its excellence. It yields such immediate pleasure in such an artless manner that, like a child's inadvertent witticism, it is taken for granted. When published, the *Autobiography* rapidly became a best seller, and contemporary reviews testified that it won its reputation legitimately. Edmund Wilson found it "an instructive and most entertaining book" (*Shores of Light*, 575). William Troy declared that "among books of literary reminiscences Miss Stein's is one of the richest, wittiest and most irreverent ever written" (*The Nation*, 6 September 1933, 274).

The sole dissent came from people whom the book had pricked. Eugene and Maria Jolas published a small pamphlet, *Testimony Against Gertrude Stein* (1935), with contributions from Matisse, Braque, André

* Germane to this interpretation of the "Stanzas" (a good portion of which remains inexplicable) is the fact that in September 1934, *Vanity Fair* published "And Now," a collection of Gertrude Stein's thoughts about the success of the *Autobiography*. In the magazine the article was subtitled "And so the time comes when I can tell the story of my life." In the *Yale Catalogue*, however, the subtitle is "Confessions." At one point in this piece, Gertrude Stein proposed to add a few anecdotes that had previously escaped her mind. One of them, curiously enough, described Alice Toklas's being given credit for a work of art she did not create. A painter ineligible to enter a particular competition submitted a canvas under her name. When Picasso was shown the catalogue with Alice Toklas listed as an exhibitor, he was "terribly upset." Nobody, he insisted, "who has never drawn or painted a picture can paint a first picture and send it to any salon and have it accepted, it is not possible." When he learned the truth, Gertrude Stein said, Picasso was very relieved. "It just could not be possible otherwise nothing would have any meaning" (*Vanity Fair*, 65). It is an odd anecdote for Gertrude Stein to have forgotten in the first place, and although she told it once more in *Picasso* (4–5), Miss Toklas chose to ignore it in her own memoirs.

Salmon, and Tristan Tzara. Their rejoinders made some ludicrously inconsequential corrections of fact, impugned Gertrude Stein's knowledge of art and of the French language, and accused her of a sordid prostitution of her art. More than anything, the malicious heat of the document was symptomatic of the sting of Gertrude Stein's wit. Although the charge of factual inaccuracy was occasionally true, it was irrelevant. The book was, to use Leo Stein's term, a "romance" (*Appreciation*, 152). In the *Autobiography*, Gertrude Stein transformed the passionate engagement and stunned misery of her personal life into a just faintly shadowed tale of success.

The sheer artfulness of the *Autobiography* has been overlooked. Critics have acknowledged the book's humor and have plundered it for its aphorisms, then attacked Gertrude Stein for her failure to communicate. B. L. Reid in particular remembered that he had initially been "moved and instructed" by *Three Lives* and "amused and excited" by the *Autobiography*. As he read further, however, he suffered a "gradual disenchantment." His distress ultimately reached such proportions that he was driven to write a book-length "essay in decapitation" (*Art By Subtraction*, vii). Reid's response was ill-conceived. Despite the pleasure he professed to take in the *Autobiography*, Reid did not pause to reflect upon the art by which the book evoked this response, but simply dismissed it is "chitchat" (186). That very dismissal measures Gertrude Stein's achievement. So innocently discursive is the book's style that it is regarded as gossip, pleasant to read but undeserving of serious critical attention. Yet, Cyril Connolly found that the *Autobiography* "stands up to any amount of re-reading." It therefore seemed to him "a model of its kind" (*Previous Convictions*, 283). For one unconvinced of the worth of Gertrude Stein's experimental writing, perhaps the more prudent step then would be to treat it as the necessary preliminary to the durable accomplishment of the *Autobiography*.

Gertrude Stein had vowed to write the *Autobiography* "as simply as Defoe did the autobiography of Robinson Crusoe," and she did (310). Her economical use of detail is exemplified by her characterization of Ezra Pound. "Gertrude Stein liked him but did not find him amusing. She said he was a village explainer, excellent if you were a village, but if you were not, not" (246). At her best, the telling detail was never strained; Gertrude Stein achieved her effects with the commonest of words and gestures. In a three-sentence paragraph she summed up the first autumn salon in Paris at which the new artistic insurgents exhibited. Most of their work was tame rebellion, the one exception being that of Matisse.

> The show had a great deal of freshness and was not alarming. There were a number of attractive pictures but there was one that was not attractive. It infuriated the public, they tried to scratch off the paint. (41)

The early part of the *Autobiography* is crowded with such precise miniatures. A whole human complex is captured in her ironic description of Raymond and Isadora Duncan.

> The Duncan family had been then at the Omar Khayyám stage, they had not yet gone greek. They had after that gone italian renaissance, but now Raymond had gone completely greek and this included a greek girl. Isadora lost interest in him, she found the girl too modern a greek. (53)

Even the book's sixteen photographs were carefully placed in the first edition.* The frontispiece is captioned "Alice B. Toklas at the door." In a dimly lit foreground Gertrude Stein is seated at a table, writing. At the rear standing at a three-quarters open door and facing the camera is Miss Toklas. The photograph symbolizes the book, not only by introducing Miss Toklas through Gertrude Stein's writing, but also by suggesting the two women's respective positions and personalities.

Like a serpent with its tail in its mouth, the book concludes with a photograph of the first page of the manuscript, thus returning the reader to its beginning. Only now, he possesses information withheld until the last sentence of the book—that Gertrude Stein has written Alice Toklas's autobiography for her.†

Even if her autobiography was written by a surrogate, in it Alice Toklas developed a distinctive character. That character differs somewhat from the one who appears in her own memoirs, *What Is Remembered*. There, her impudent, raffish, gypsy wildness is given much greater latitude.

"Before I Came to Paris," the brief opening section of the *Autobiography*, establishes the character of the purported author, and in so

---

* Gertrude Stein originally sent "some twenty photographs" to Harcourt, Brace & Co. (unsigned letter to Allen Lane, 17 February 1933, YCAL). Her agent, W. A. Bradley, referred to "the corrected proofs, with all the illustrations in place" in a letter to Gertrude Stein, 4 May 1933 (YCAL).

† Gertrude Stein originally ended the manuscript as Mark Twain had the *Adventures of Huckleberry Finn*—"Sincerely yours, Alice B. Toklas,"—then cancelled it.

doing, sets the tone of the book.* The sensibility through which the artistic revolution is to be seen is that of a "gently bred" young woman of intelligence, poise, and cool wit (3). The very first information conveyed is that, having been born in San Francisco, she has "always preferred living in a temperate climate but it is difficult, on the continent of Europe or even in America, to find a temperate climate and live in it" (3). Despite its rarity, her ideal is moderation. As a girl she "had some intellectual adventures . . . but very quiet ones" (3).

Alice Toklas appropriately mentions her admiration of Henry James early. More specifically, she invokes her youthful enthusiasm for *The Awkward Age*. Like Nanda Brookenham, Alice Toklas in the *Autobiography* possessed a level-headed innocence when she first entered the European arena. She floats through the swirling currents of intrigue and corruption with her eyes open, and she watches quietly, judges, and in her mild, firm way, succeeds.

Her starting position was that of a moderately contented housekeeper for her father and brother. Her life, she says, "was reasonably full and I enjoyed it but I was not very ardent in it" (4). The San Francisco earthquake literally shook her out of this placidly dull existence. The disaster brought the Michael Steins back to assess the damage to the family holdings. With them they carried three of Matisse's paintings and many stories of life in Paris. These drew Alice Toklas to her destiny.

The next photograph is a full-length, head-on portrait, "Gertrude Stein in front of the atelier door." It properly initiates section two, "My Arrival in Paris," in which Gertrude Stein introduces Alice Toklas to the world of modern art. Gertrude Stein is placed directly in the middle of "the heroic age of cubism" (7). Picasso, Matisse, and she were all at work, changing the fundamental conceptions of the western world. Their success was summed up, she thought, in Braque's rueful remark: "How life has changed we all now have cooks who can make a soufflé" (8). Gertrude Stein's own and special revolutionary activity was symbolized by the notebooks she used. They were the kind "french children use, with pictures of earthquakes and explorations on the outside of them" (10).†

* To facilitate the exposition in the discussion that follows, Alice Toklas will normally be treated as if she were its narrator.
† In fact, the notebook covers represented a host of diverse subjects. Two of Gertrude Stein's compositions— "Dahomy or As Soft A Noise" and "A Bouquet" —were directly inspired by the cover of the notebook in which she was then writing.

Having arrived in Paris, Alice Toklas proposes to "describe what I saw when I came." It all commences with the Stein cook of that period, Hélène, because Alice Toklas first saw 27 rue de Fleurus when she was invited to dine there. Hélène in turn reminds her of Braque's soufflé remark. Her digressive manner permits a mix of time. She moves effortlessly back and forth along lines of association, reverting to the main subjects with variants of the phrase, "but to return to."

Alice Toklas's preliminary tour of the Stein atelier really constitutes a survey of modern art. She speaks for the novice: "Now I was confused and I looked and I looked and I was confused" (12). Her tone is at once respectful and jaunty. There is never any doubt expressed about the legitimacy of the modern school, yet its leaders are treated with a cheerful off-handedness. Alice Toklas recalls one habitué of the salon who would light matches in order to inspect portions of a Cézanne portrait more closely. When conventional painters regarded the painting dubiously, he would assure them that, of course it was finished—"You can can tell because it has a frame" (13).

Dinner with the Picassos follows this first inspection of the Stein collection. In the book, Picasso, the genius and intimate of Gertrude Stein, is placed at the center of the modern movement. While treated as a deep child, spontaneous, emotional, even silly at times, he is manifestly the leader. Alice Toklas discovers him "standing meditatively. Do you think, he said, that I really do look like your president Lincoln." Her reaction is, "I had thought a good many things that evening but I had not thought that" (18). The dinner flows without a break into a typical Saturday evening gathering at the Steins where the whole painting community assembles to gossip. Alice Toklas's initial exposure (and the reader's) is abbreviated, so that this private gathering can open out into a public occasion, the independents' vernissage. Here Alice Toklas differentiates French from American culture in a few words. She had never imagined "there could be so many kinds of men making and looking at pictures." In America she had been accustomed to seeing women and some men at exhibitions, "but here there were men, men, men . . ." (23).

By including more and more people from this new world, the second part of the *Autobiography* progressively enlarged its scope. After the vernissage, its focus narrows again. Alice Toklas is led to the painter's studio on a visit to Picasso in Montmartre. Her first reaction to his paintings was that they were "rather awful." This permits the enunciation of one of Gertrude Stein's main principles—that the efforts of those who do original work will invariably be ugly, so profound are the problems faced by the creator. Imitators, because they have been relieved of the struggle of conceiving afresh, can concentrate on making their art "pretty." This represented a modification of Gertrude Stein's position in "Composition as Explanation." There she had argued that the new artistic creation, although by definition beautiful, would be scorned, because its unfamiliarity irritated the viewers. The public judgment was a subjective one though, and could be counted upon to change. But now in the *Autobiography* and thereafter, Gertrude Stein argued that ugliness was an objective condition, inherent in anything original.

The second part of the *Autobiography* ends with a series of anecdotes about the wives and mistresses of various painters. These encounters prove the Stein-Toklas intimacy with the painters, and lead to the final sentence: "And now I will tell you how two americans happened to be in the heart of an art movement of which the outside world at that time knew nothing" (34). Section two has carried us to the very heart of the painters' domestic life to give a sense of the lively and complicated existence out of which modern art emerged.

If all of this is open to any criticism, it is that the painters are treated as inspired children. Picasso and Fernande, for example, compete jealously for the American comic sections featuring the Katzenjammer kids. At the same time, though, the stylized realism is refreshing. Van Dongen's young daughter, for example, is described as literally "terrific." "Van Dongen used to do acrobatics with her and swing her around his head by a leg. When she hugged Picasso of whom she was very fond she used almost to destroy him, he had a great fear of her" (33). It was out of this mélange of Sunday comic supplements, dogs, movies, spinach-eating, and powerful children that modern art came. The level of vision in the *Autobiography* is neither romantic and bohemian, nor sordid. Alice Toklas's history has a full measure of wildness, alarm, and despair, but is lightened by a pervasive hopefulness and even gaiety.

The third section, "Gertrude Stein in Paris 1903–1907," develops the intimate connection between Gertrude Stein and the modern movement. It starts with her and Leo making their first acquaintance with Cézanne's work at the dealer Vollard's, and concludes with the publication of *Three Lives*. Although Leo shared these years with his sister, he, like the other Steins, is never mentioned by name. He is merely "her brother." The *Autobiography* is a virtual address book of names, but only one Stein appears in it. According to the book, the Steins' education in Cézanne took place over the course of a long winter. After penetrating Vollard's skepticism, they first merely looked. Then they started to purchase, often taking pairs of paintings "because one of them usually liked one more than the other one did" (38). At last they decided to stop with the acquisition of one big Cézanne. After long consideration and discussion, they "narrowed the choice down to two, a portrait of a man and a portrait of a woman . . ." (40). They took the woman.

Whether the sex of the subject was important or not, Gertrude Stein firmly attached her own career to this portrait. It was "in looking and looking at this picture," she said, that she wrote *Three Lives* (40). While she does not amplify the use she made of Cézanne's example, she does underline the causal relationship.* Immediately following this important acquisition, Gertrude Stein describes their purchase of a second female portrait, Matisse's "La Femme au Chapeau" (41). Although it infuriated the general public (thereby certifying it to be in the vanguard of painting) the portrait seemed "perfectly natural" to her (42). This had not been the case with the Cézanne. "It had taken her some time to feel that it was natural" (42). Nor would it be true subsequently of the Steins' first Picasso, again a portrait of a female, this time, of "a nude girl with a basket of red flowers." Striking her as "rather appalling," the Picasso nude "repelled and shocked her" (52).

By means of her discussions of the three portraits of women, Gertrude Stein delicately established relationships and rankings. Cézanne was the source, Matisse the fellow artist sharing an era of major innovation with Gertrude Stein, and Picasso was the giant equal to her.

Matisse received equivocal treatment throughout the book. Gertrude Stein did not fail to acknowledge his importance as a painter, nor to affirm the pleasure that their friendship gave her. Nonetheless, the two were never close, and gradually Matisse's stature seems to diminish in the book and his force to weaken. According to her account, Matisse's relationship began with indebtedness to Gertrude Stein. By purchasing "La Femme au Chapeau" the Steins rescued Matisse from severe financial and psychological depression. When his qualities were assessed, he was implicitly placed with those whose skill is derived from a master's

* The painting was sold in 1940 to raise money during the crisis caused by the Nazi invasion of France (Brinnin, 370). See Chapter 3 for a discussion of Cézanne's importance for her. For the portrait, see Brinnin, 62, or *ABT*, facing 50.

creative toil. "Cezanne had come to his unfinishedness and distortion of necessity, Matisse did it by intention" (49). Alice Toklas made a further important distinction. Whereas Matisse possessed "an astonishing virility that always gave one an extraordinary pleasure . . . there was not much feeling of life in this virility" (44). That observation hangs oppressively over the history of Matisse's success. Ultimately, he became "irritated by the growing friendship between Picasso and Gertrude Stein" (80). Her response to his pique was "there is nothing within you that fights itself . . ." (80). In a moment a bland, deadly observation follows: "It was about this time that Matisse began his teaching" (81). The explanation for the gradual estrangement lies in the unstated assumption that Matisse, having lost his creative powers, had become, as Gertrude Stein teasingly called him, "The C. M. or cher maître" (83).*

Picasso's friendship with Gertrude Stein is developed through successive references to his painting of her portrait. Gertrude Stein claims that he had had no one pose for him for the past eight years, and that she had not commissioned the portrait, her implication being that the two were drawn together by the natural affinity of genius. Posing for him ninety times, she says, forged their friendship (55). During this period, she was at work on *Three Lives*. Then "one day Picasso painted out the whole head. I can't see you any longer when I look, he said irritably" (64-65). Both of them were undergoing artistic metamorphoses. That summer she traveled to Italy to work on *The Making of Americans*. When she returned, she was well launched into her ambitious new project. Picasso spent his vacation in Spain, independently experiencing a transformation as he moved from "the Harlequin . . . to the intensive struggle which was to end in cubism" (66). Their mutual evolution is symbolized by Picasso's completion of Gertrude Stein's portrait. "The day he returned from Spain Picasso sat down and out of his head painted the head in without having seen Gertrude Stein again" (70). Transcendent sympathies were in control.

While it would be mistaken to accept this as a literal historical account, its mythical truth is unimpeachable. Picasso's portrait of Gertrude Stein attests to the intimacy of the two prime innovators. At the same time Gertrude Stein was careful to establish her independence of his

* Juan Gris's letter in 1923 to D.-H. Kahnweiler concerning Matisse, is relevant here. "He wouldn't come and dine with Gertrude and myself when I invited him on Gertrude's behalf. He too has quite the air of a great master. There's no doubt, painters become quite unbearable when they are successful" (*Letters*, #232).

influence. Every detail informs the reader that the two worked congenially yet separately, advancing along parallel lines.

The third section concludes with the publication of *Three Lives*. Although Gertrude Stein's editor at the vanity press had been doubtful about her command of English, the chapter ends with a recantation. The director of the press "was very pleased that his firm had printed the book" (84). Up to this point then, the book is a good-humored success story, not without its obstacles and discouragements, but essentially observing an upward progress.

Section four, "Gertrude Stein Before She Came to Paris," completes the review of her life by means of a pleasant mixture of facts, opinions, and anecdotes. All of these enlarge the sense of Gertrude Stein's importance and provide credentials for her legitimacy. At one point she acknowledges that she has been accused of "inordinate pride" because "in english literature in her time she is the only one. She has always known it and now she says it" (94). If it does not infuriate the reader, such candor will disarm him. Gertrude Stein escapes becoming a complacent bore by meeting hostility and scepticism head-on and in a cheerful, determined way, dealing with it. She observes, for example, that although the newspapers consistently ridiculed her writing, "they always quote it and what is more, they quote it correctly, and those they say they admire they do not quote" (86–87). But for all her good humor, Gertrude Stein was serious. Her belief that she was not an amusing grotesque, but a serious artist was maintained steadily throughout the book in every possible way except by quoting examples of her work. Now, with an account of her education, she provided testimony concerning her ability in the traditional arenas.

Her self-portrait reveals a woman who was at once cosmopolitan and provincial. She had traveled widely, read omnivorously, and had been educated at Harvard and at the Johns Hopkins School of Medicine. She had worked under and received the approbation of men like William James and William Osler. Yet, for all her admiration of these eminent figures, she guarded her own independence. Throughout the section she selects the unpretentious, the normal, the common. It was essential for her to establish that she was not a freak, and therefore, despite appearances, she insisted that she had always been the champion of bourgeois moderation.

Considering that her career had received its support from a very specialized coterie of people, it was bold indeed for her to dismiss them in a bid for popular support. "It has always been rather ridiculous that she who is good friends with all the world and can know them and they can know her, has always been the admired of the precious" (86). Although Gertrude Stein was openly covetous of fame and fortune and enthusiastically accepted both when they finally came, she sought readers not for the material rewards they would bring, but because she truly believed in her art. Belief in its authenticity was crucial for her self-esteem.

The last task of this section devoted to Gertrude Stein's maturation was to establish her as a devoted writer of English, and no exotic expatriate or aesthetic hybrid. She insists that she never reads French. "There is for me only one language and that is english" (86). Since adolescence, she tells us, she has been indifferent to music. The theater too she found less satisfying than reading. "It goes too fast, the mixture of eye and ear bothers her and her emotion never keeps pace" (92). She could not draw, nor had she ever "been able or had any desire to indulge in any of the arts" (93). Most important, "Gertrude Stein never had subconscious reactions, nor was she a successful subject for automatic writing" (97).

All these specifications about her preferences insist that Gertrude Stein must be taken seriously. Her background established her competence. She voluntarily turned away from science, for her main interest had always been literature. "She is passionately addicted to what the french call métier . . . Her métier is writing and her language is english" (94). She was a healthy, middle-class American, born in Pennsylvania, raised in California, educated in Massachusetts and Maryland. In sum, the oddity of her writing could not be attributed to foreign corruption, to personal aberration, to the unconscious, or to some ill-considered imitation of modern painting. Her case was impressively and artfully made.

Until 1951 when *Things As They Are* finally appeared, no one save a few friends could have understood the conclusion of the fourth section of *The Autobiography of Alice B. Toklas.* Whereas the other sections concluded on a phrase of general significance, such as the end of the war, the fourth section described Gertrude Stein finding the manuscript of *Things As They Are.* Three times she insists that the book had been "completely forgotten," and that she had "never mentioned it" to Alice Toklas (104). Having recovered this account of youthful sexuality, she remained "very bashful and hesitant about it, did not really want to read it." The last sentence is: "Louis Bromfield was at the house that

226

evening and she handed him the manuscript and said to him, you read it" (104).*

This is a characteristic instance of concealed confession such as Gertrude Stein indulged in throughout her lifetime. Her usual strategy was to record the incident to which she wished to refer in an incomplete or indirect way. Or she would use a private vocabulary to render her meaning ambiguous. In the *Autobiography* however she had committed herself to clarity. In order to include her sexual orientation, she created this peculiar conclusion which would necessarily mystify the most attentive reader. No clue is furnished to the contents of *Things As They Are,* save that she felt bashful and hesitant about Bromfield's reading it. Even those feelings are more likely to be attributed to the embarrassment caused by apprentice work rather than by an illicit theme.†

After the brilliant strategies of the early part of the *Autobiography* Gertrude Stein's inventiveness flagged. The lines of characterization, formerly sharp and clear, now blurred. The wit dampened. The narrative became burdened by too many diary-like entries consisting merely of names and places. The early shrewdness flashed infrequently and the thematic purposefulness became obscured. The fifth section, "1907–1914," begins with Alice Toklas joining the household in the rue de Fleurus (a permanent alliance symbolized by a photograph of the two women before St. Mark's Cathedral in Venice) and concludes at the precipice of the first great war. Except for occasional notices of the progress of *The Making of Americans,* the narrative is virtually random. As Alice Toklas remarks, "It was an endless variety. And everybody came and no one made any difference" (151).

Whether a change in the conditions under which the book was created occurred at this point is not clear. In part, though, the problem is that Alice Toklas can no longer give a direct, personal account of either herself or of Gertrude Stein. The stages of her increasing intimacy with the writer, and the estrangement from Leo were both privileged information. These were memoirs, not confessions. A little of the stress and affection of the two women's friendship is made discreetly visible, but the passion, the quarreling, and the despair that churn through Gertrude Stein's other writing are absent.

* In the manuscript another sentence followed: "When we ["get home" cancelled] return to Paris this autumn ["we" cancelled] I will read it." The whole was cancelled with Alice Toklas's red pencil.
† As late as 1941 when R. B. Haas was preparing the *Yale Catalogue,* he inquired by mail: "What about the early novel. . . . Could it, should it, may it be included? Stein: No" ("Gertrude Stein Talking—A Transatlantic Interview," *UCLAN Review,* VIII [Summer 1962], 5).

The freshness of Alice's initial encounters with the Parisian art world was gone too. Now, although Picasso and Matisse still turned up, their personalities were obliged to compete with innumerable minor figures —Uhde, Manolo, Delaunay, Purrmann, Rönnebeck. At times the details were utterly pointless:

> Then there was the youngest of the cubists. I never knew his name. He was doing his military service and was destined for diplomacy. How he drifted in and whether he painted I do not know. All I know is that he was known as the youngest of the cubists. (135–6)

The technical analysis is also weak. To confirm her expertise, Gertrude Stein made some gestures at explaining the rationale of cubism as well as her own stylistic innovations. But her comments were too brief to be helpful and rarely illustrated with examples. She does tell of Picasso seeing camouflaged cannon for the first time. "Pablo stopped, he was spell-bound. C'est nous qui avons fait ca, he said, it is we that have created that, he said. And he was right, he had" (110). More often though she merely makes arbitrary assertions, as when she claims that Americans can understand cubists because "like spaniards, they are abstract and cruel" (111).

It could be argued that the looseness of the narrative at this point corresponds to the unsettled condition of Europe on the eve of the first World War, but that does not excuse its flat tone. Typically, we are told that on their trip to England, "We had an extremely good time" (156). That visit is expanded by such details as, "We went to Lady Otoline Morrell and met everybody" (156). They are introduced to Mrs. John Lane, "a Boston woman and very kind" (157). With Mabel Dodge, they have "a very amusing time" (158). The tedium of these idle memories may be a risk of the conversational style, but if so, Gertrude Stein forgot her own advice to Hemingway, twice repeated in this very book—"Remarks are not literature" (94, 270).

Still, to concentrate only on the disappointments of the fifth section of the *Autobiography* is misleading, for it is more entertaining than not. It still offers a good measure of anecdotes and aphorisms, such as the lament of one of the non-entities who swarm through this section: "A little artist has all the tragic unhappiness and the sorrows of a great artist and he is not a great artist" (140). New details expand the personalities of the two companions. Alice Toklas habitually breaks and loses things; when aroused, Gertrude Stein swears. Endearing eccentrics like Mildred Aldrich and Constance Fletcher are introduced, while in

228

the middle of the fifth section occurs the long, amusing account of the legendary banquet for the douanier Rousseau (125–32).

Toward the end of the section, the scene almost imperceptibly darkens. Avery Hopwood dies, Alvin Coburn disappears, Leo breaks with Gertrude and leaves for Italy. Picasso, now separated from Fernande, moves "a little further out to Montrouge" (173). Mildred Aldrich "was preparing to retire to the Hilltop on the Marne" (174). And finally, Hélène, the Stein cook, gives up her position. If not sombre, the tone is subdued, ambiguously autumnal. Picasso was not precisely melancholy; still, one no longer heard his "high whinnying spanish giggle" (173). Similarly, Mildred Aldrich after her move to the country found herself "not unhappy but rather sad" (174). All the old friends were retiring, instinctively hibernating before the long winter descended. No one explicitly recognized why, and indeed, it would be incorrect to ascribe the malaise only to the advent of the war. The passage of time had worn friendships thin, there was success and there was middle age. In combination it all signified that "in this spring and early summer of nineteen fourteen the old life was over" (175).

Because she wrote of human events in personal and often idiosyncratic terms, Gertrude Stein has sometimes been accused of trivializing existence. But she did not fail to respond to the convulsions of the first World War. Her reaction was that of the ordinary person. Inconvenienced by history, she was bewildered, sometimes frightened, and slow to grasp its meaning. Furthermore, as she points out at the beginning of the sixth section, "The War," Americans never really believed there would be a war. The signs were there, yet people continued to go about their daily business.

When the war came Gertrude Stein and Alice Toklas were staying with the Alfred North Whiteheads in England. Slight reverberations touched their country retreat. An editorial writer on one of the London papers complained, for example, that because of the war, he would not be able to eat figs in Provence. Then, when Belgium was invaded and Louvain destroyed, Gertrude Stein's isolationism yielded. "Gertrude Stein desperately unhappy said to me, where is Louvain. Don't you know, I said. No, she said, nor do I care, but where is it" (180–81). The German drive on Paris made her withdraw in distress to her room. "She loved Paris, she thought neither of manuscripts nor of pictures, she thought only of Paris and she was desolate" (183). Gertrude Stein did not ignore world events, but interpreted them in particular terms.

Since all things reside in the individual sensibility, she remained the advocate of the personal response.

The war enabled her to discover her Americanness. After her initial indifference to the war, followed by fear and then flight, the two women actively participated by going to work for the American Fund for the French Wounded. Their job was to deliver supplies to the military hospitals, but more importantly they served as surrogate mothers for the French soldiers and then later for their beloved doughboys. The experience was financially costly, although worth it. Gertrude Stein not only had to acquire a Ford truck from the United States, but then she had to learn to drive it. Once embarked, she had to commandeer fuel for it, crank and repair it, and struggle with the military bureaucracy. The war diversified her life and gave her the confidence of possessing practical knowledge. It was a sardonic veteran who referred to "one of the young men of the peace commission who was holding forth, as one who knew all about the war, he had been here ever since the peace" (234).

The war did bring Gertrude Stein back into contact with the stuff of American life. She discovered her secret and her justification in the American manner. America, she decided, shared her attraction for the ordinary and the abstract. Arguing with Bertrand Russell, she claimed to distinguish a "disembodied abstract quality" in the American character, a point she clinched by coupling automobiles and Emerson (187).

Gertrude Stein's resemblance to Walt Whitman was re-enforced during the war. Like Whitman she was a literary innovator, whose results were long ridiculed and deplored. Both writers early gained strong support from the English. Both were preoccupied with sex, had equivocal sexual identities, and therefore insisted all the more upon their normality. The careers of both were interrupted by a war that gave their energies and compassion a social outlet. They both affiliated themselves with hospitals, brought gifts to the invalided soldiers, and genuinely delighted in their immersion in common life.

After distributing clothes to Alsatian refugees following the armistice, the two women returned to "a changed Paris" (233). Their funds were depleted, household help was scarce and expensive, and everywhere they saw new faces. The "war" section of the *Autobiography* ends with the triumphant procession of the Allied troops down the Champs Elysées. After it was over, the crowds disappeared "and the piles of captured cannon that had made two pyramids were being taken away and peace was upon us" (236). That concluding note was just faintly foreboding. When the stage was cleared, an eerie emptiness named peace leapt on. Unlike the Allied victory, peace provided no evident cause for celebration. Rather it came almost like a ravager, or a plague.

A ravaged Paris may not be far from the truth, to judge by the seventh and last part of the *Autobiography*, "After the War—1919–1932." In spite of its hardships, the war had been therapeutic for Gertrude Stein. For all the crowds of faces, peace proved a barren gift. Before the war Gertrude Stein had been a young pioneer, associated with other vital young artists. After the war she found herself a middle-aged minor deity, visited by ambitious young men eager to use her influence. The post-war scene swarms with youth, while "the old crowd had disappeared" (237). Pages are devoted to men of little consequence or interest, but Gertrude Stein rose only to smite competitors of stature—Ezra Pound, T. S. Eliot, and most memorably, Ernest Hemingway. Photographers, musicians, sculptors but now mostly writers visited her. If sympathetic, they received her imprimatur. If they scoffed or rebelled, they were dismissed with the incisiveness of her judgment of Glenway Westcott: "He has a certain syrup but it does not pour" (269).

On the surface, the seventh section seems to bring this American success story to a climax. *The Making of Americans* finally appeared in print. Gertrude Stein lectured by invitation at the universities of Cambridge and Oxford, where her admirers strained for comparisons. "The lecture had been his greatest experience since he had read Kant's Critique of Pure Reason" (289). For all the indicators of success though, the specifics of Gertrude Stein's achievement never emerge convincingly. Whenever she undertook to state her views on art and literature, the results were usually equivocal, or if clear, contradictory.

With a revealing strenuousness, Gertrude Stein protested her dedication to the rational operation of the mind. She "has always been possessed" she wrote, "by the intellectual passion for exactitude in the description of inner and outer reality" (259). Her objective was the purgation of "associational emotion" from art (259). As a woman whose psychic well-being was frequently threatened by her turbulent emotions, and as one who experienced unremitting difficulty in accurately describing outer reality, Gertrude Stein was obliged to insist upon her objectivity. If her claim to descriptive exactitude was valid, then her literary efforts represented the record of a scientific investigation of reality. They would merit serious consideration. If, however, she failed to convince her readers of her objectivity, then she became vulnerable to the accusation of being a muddled thinker, incapable of communicating her ideas coherently.

If by "associational emotion" Gertrude Stein referred to the conditioned response of the reader to familiar verbal images—a daisy, a girl in a pinafore, a rattlesnake—then, insofar as she sought to purge her prose of those clichés that evoked an automatic emotional reaction, her position was sound. But if she substituted rambling gibberish for stereotypes, then claimed that the results were the product of an "intellectual passion for exactitude," she was guilty of a certain imposture.

Gertrude Stein's search for a new leader in painting provides the thematic thread for the concluding pages of *The Autobiography of Alice B. Toklas*. She does not explain why she should have been "very interested" in resolving this question of leadership, but it is not hard to see that her capacity for making independent aesthetic judgments required re-enforcement. She considered several candidates from the neo-romantic school, Tchelitchev, Christian Bérard, Genia Berman, but rejected each in turn. She was certain that somewhere there must be "a very dominating creative power," for in painting she detected "a distinctively new creative idea. Where had it come from" (279). She confessed herself bothered and then perplexed by her investigation.

In the midst of the search, she noticed "a painting of a hand by this young englishman." She did not like it, which had been precisely the case with the other true geniuses of painting, Cézanne and Picasso, but she did remember it (281). Having dropped this provocative reference, without further identification, she turned to other matters. Before long though, she came across "a picture of a poet sitting by a waterfall" (283). Now the young Englishman's name was mentioned. It seemed fated that not only did he portray the favorite subject of amiable Lucy Church, but that he should have been named Francis Rose. Gertrude Stein remarked that she was not interested in his work, then abruptly bought the picture "and we went away for the summer" (283). The following winter, although she continued to purchase Rose's paintings, she declined to meet their creator. Eventually, she asked her concierge to hang all thirty of the Rose canvases that she now owned. They "upset" her, "very much," but "she could not help it" (284).

None of these contradictory responses is accounted for. The sequence of events deliberately creates an impression of Gertrude Stein being moved by some mysterious compulsion. Finally, one page from the *Autobiography's* conclusion, she agrees to meet Rose. Picasso was invited to confer his blessing. Upon first viewing Rose's work, he indirectly pronounced it superior to that of Rose's contemporaries: "At least they are less bêtes than the others." Since then, he always repaired to a corner to examine the canvasses in private—"but he says nothing" (308).

The situation is left diplomatically ambiguous. Picasso's silence may be regarded as contempt, jealousy, or awe. Although never openly identified as the new artistic messiah, Rose seems destined for the role. Until the last though, Gertrude Stein persists in her equivocation. Rose painted her portrait, but she is not sure whether she likes it—"perhaps she does" (308). She did use two of Rose's paintings to illustrate the *Autobiography*.

Although the art world has evidently confirmed Gertrude Stein's wisdom in remaining evasive in her judgment of Rose, she actually acquired some one hundred and thirty of his paintings by the end of her life. Art historians have not missed the notable diminution in merit of the painters Gertrude Stein patronized in her life. She began by purchasing Cézanne, then supported Matisse, Picasso, and Juan Gris, followed by Francis Picabia, and at last Francis Rose and Riba-Rovira. Her remark that after the cubist highpoint painting had lapsed into a secondary form of expression in part indicates her realization of this (277). But naturally, her taste rendered her vulnerable too, so that her ambiguous public support of Rose must be read as a self-protective gesture as well.

In spite of the tedium of portions of *The Autobiography of Alice B. Toklas*, over-all the book is a triumph. Gertrude Stein had not yet comprehended the meaning of some of the incidents, nor had she fully absorbed the character of some of the persons she described. When that happened, or when she was less than candid, the book does flag. As she herself put it, "when the vision is not complete the words are flat" (263). On balance though, the *Autobiography* is a wise and entertaining piece of cultural history, not unlike Henry Adams's *Education*, save that the theorizing is less pretentious and the tone considerably more humane.

The portrait of Gertrude Stein, built up through hundreds of incidents and statements, finally becomes more substantial than the woman herself. The character she created is unique—varied, believable, coherent, and utterly underivative. Whatever Gertrude Stein herself may have been, in the *Autobiography*, she appears cheerful, competent, and certain of herself. In spite of pessimistic moments and explosions of frustration and anger, serenity prevails. Alice Toklas recalled that after a long conversation with Picasso, Gertrude Stein said, "Pablo has been persuading me that I am as unhappy as he is. He insists that I am and with as much cause. But are you, I ask. Well I don't think I look it, do I, and she laughs" (95).

As presented, her character is far from ideal. Her judgments were often abrasive and her temper volatile. She could be mulishly obstinate. But the most reassuring aspect of her self-portrait is that her weaknesses enhance her attractiveness. Once while out driving, Alice Toklas volunteered the opinion that they were on the wrong road. "Wrong or right, said Gertrude Stein, we are going on" (214).

She never concealed her ambition. When Elliot Paul was trying to decide whether to become editor of *transition*, "Gertrude Stein was naturally all for it. After all, as she said, we do want to be printed" (295). Later, when she sees one of her books displayed in store windows, we are told of her "childish delight amounting almost to ecstacy" (299). Such details are reassuring in their very openness. She clearly understood her relish for praise. "After all, as she always contends, no artist needs criticism, he only needs appreciation" (289). But she mainly wished to be widely circulated because she genuinely believed herself in the vanguard of modern literature. That being the case, it was essential that she be read. It irked her that the rarity of her books made them collectors' items. "She wants her books read not owned" (301).

The cumulative impression of Gertrude Stein in the book is of a person of sanity, good humor, and vigorous common sense. Gertrude Stein herself no doubt differed from her verbal creations, but her "Gertrude Stein" like Whitman's "Walt Whitman" is a memorable one, which has happily survived its maker.

By her own account, the success of *The Autobiography of Alice B. Toklas* traumatized Gertrude Stein. It temporarily blocked her ability to write, and it affected her identity.

Success was both pleasurable and enlightening for her. Having received a sizable advance on the royalties for the book, she enthusiastically commenced to spend the money. But the irony of the situation did not escape her. She was exhibiting the same reactions that other newly successful writers had, and for which she had always reprimanded them. "Once they had made a success they became sterile, they could not go on. And I blamed them. . . . Now I know better. It does cut off your flow" ("And Now," *Vanity Fair*, [September 1934], 35; reprinted in the anthology, *Vanity Fair*, ed. Cleveland Amory and Frederic Bradlee [New York, 1960], 280–81).

Unexpected celebrity also shook her conception of herself. "All of a sudden I was not just I because so many people did know me. . . . I was I no longer" ("And Now," 35). This disturbance of her identity is not easy to account for. Gertrude Stein was hardly an unknown suddenly thrust into prominence. She had a reputation, several of them in fact, and had long listened to her merits and deficiencies being debated in public. Furthermore, she was accustomed to entertaining the famous of every rank, so that their society could hardly turn her head. Whatever the cause of the trauma, it directly affected her creativity. For the first time in her life, she could not write. "I began to think about how my writing would sound to others, how could I make them understand, I who had always lived within myself and my writing" ("And Now," 35).

This was a puzzling ailment; self-consciousness had never afflicted Gertrude Stein before. She had appeared in magazines of wide circulation without becoming tongue-tied. She had certainly never suffered over how to make an audience understand her. On the face of it, she had been oblivious of her readers for the greater part of her literary life, and then when she decided to communicate with them directly, she did so with brilliant ease, writing her classic autobiography in a month and a half.

Gertrude Stein's writing block would make more sense had Alice Toklas had a hand in the writing of the *Autobiography*. Were that the case, then Gertrude Stein might well feel her identity had been usurped and that she need be concerned about what her subsequent writing would sound like in comparison.

If her comparison of herself to young writers paralyzed by success is not convincing, equally unconvincing is her version of how the spell was broken. Financial apprehensions did it. When "the dollar fell," "somehow I got frightened," and—"the fright has made me write" ("And Now," 35). Her explanation is almost impossible to accept. Virtually nothing that she produced in 1933 and 1934 was printed until well after her death. What did appear was published in little magazines and catalogues for art exhibitions. Her financial recompense must have been infinitesimal; yet we are asked to believe that it stimulated her into production again.

As for the nature of her renewed efforts—"I have changed," she noted. "I write the way I used to write in *The Making of Americans,* I wander around." The witty concision of the memoirs was no longer useful to her, she asserted. "I have come back to write the way I used to write . . . because now everything that is happening is once more happening inside, there is no use in the outside . . ." ("And Now," 65).

"And Now," the piece explaining her silence and stylistic regression, appeared about two years after the composition of *The Autobiography of Alice B. Toklas.* What had Gertrude Stein been writing in the interim? The chronology is less clear than one would wish. "And Now," itself, dated 1934, says, "Just at present I write about American religion and Grant . . ." (65). The first part of *Four In America* treats U. S. Grant as a religious leader. Aside from *Four In America,* Gertrude Stein's mind was filled with mysteries, puzzles, and crimes, the solutions of which were known to intimates, although they were kept secret from outsiders. These preoccupations emerged in a group of writings clustered around a short narrative entitled *Blood On The Dining-Room Floor.**

This reasonably comprehensible meditation drew upon the actual death in 1933 of one Madame Pernollet. She, with her husband, owned the hotel in Belley where Gertrude Stein and Alice Toklas had stayed when summering in the Bugey. The two women therefore had known the Pernollets for seven years. Madame Pernollet fell to her death from a window that opened onto a cement courtyard. Gertrude Stein was impressed by the rapidity with which her body was removed, so that the hotel guests would be undisturbed by the tragedy. "It was wonderful the way they covered it up and went on" (19).

The intricate personal relationships in the provinces fascinated Gertrude Stein. She devoted a good deal of time in *Blood* to developing the various families' problems, parental histories, physical infirmities, and eccentricities. In particular she was struck that so intimate was

---

* "A Waterfall and A Piano" and "Is Dead" concern the same tragedy, while "Why I Like Detective Stories" reflects upon the weakness of *Blood.* ". . . it was all very clear in my head but it did not get natural . . ." (*Harper's Bazaar* [London], XVII [November 1937], 104). She also acknowledged in this piece that *Blood* lacked an ending, which she regretted "because it came so near to being a detective story and it did have a good title" (106).

this microcosmic society that, even though everyone knew what had happened to Madame Pernollet, no one openly discussed it. "There are no secrets about what everybody knows." Therefore, "everybody knows and they need not say" (78). There was some question whether the death had been an accident, a suicide, or a murder. A man—Gertrude Stein, like the townspeople, is purposely ambiguous—witnessed the event. "And now, he had been there, when the lady fell, very well" (73).

The melodrama of the event did not touch *Blood On The Dining-Room Floor.* What did intrigue Gertrude Stein was the discreet continuity of a number of not very satisfactory lives. Somehow everyone seemed to adjust, or die. The piece ended with an appeal for understanding. "It has to be that holding all together, there must be a family . . ." Then, "Oh do you see how aided to be by and by. Aided by aided by which they may not die" (79). At the very end, Gertrude Stein connects the cautionary tale to herself. "Do you understand anything. How do we do. . . . Thank you for anxiously. No one is amiss after servants are changed. Are they" (80).

If the death of her friend, Madame Pernollet, affected her, Gertrude Stein did not show it. Rather, she twisted the violent episode into an oblique presentation of her own concerns. She sought to show why understanding and assistance were required, why no one was finally hurt by what had happened, and why discretion was wisdom. All this she did, "anxiously" however, and even she had second thoughts about the lack of consequences. "No one is amiss after servants are changed. Are they."

Similar confessional moods occur in other short pieces written soon after *The Autobiography of Alice B. Toklas.* "Afterwards," for example, begins: "Why should she refuse to go on which she does not. What else does she remember. She says she never forgets anything" (*SIM,* 290). "First Page" contains the lines: "I have made a vow that I will admit everything. I have wished for success and I have it . . ." Then shortly, "Do not disguise what has happened . . ." (*SIM,* 283). The tensions she felt in this period are evident in the open-ended conclusion of another of these pieces. "Nobody was dead and it was all over. / Or. And then silence" ("Or. And Then Silence," *P&P,* 245). With a "crime" in the background and clues scattered everywhere, Gertrude Stein's preoccupation with the detective story is understandable.

12

☞. "I mean to be human nature's daily food. I mean to be."

("Didn't Nelly and Lilly Love You")

Four in America is one of several of Gertrude Stein's lengthy works accorded that measure of cautious respect due an unread book. It originated as a tribute to the unexceptional man who through sheer determination makes his mark on history; specifically, Ulysses S. Grant.* Gertrude Stein's imagination was kindled by the fact that Grant had changed his name as a young man. This alteration, she argued, necessarily affected his social role. Had he kept the name Hiram Ulysses, Gertrude Stein believed Grant would have become "a religious leader or saint" (3). That notion was expanded to provide the conceptual model for the whole book. Her plan was to consider Grant as a religious leader, Wilbur Wright as a painter, Henry James as a general, and George Washington as a novelist. A promising conceit, it was left unfulfilled.

Four in America's ambitious analysis of the American character was probably inspired by Bernard Faÿ's lectures on "Franco-American things" (*LIA*, 205). In the main, Gertrude Stein's comments on American existence are based on her assumption that it has no context, no organizing boundaries. Lacking a substantial, limited environment, Americans find themselves free-floating. Therefore, they are Gertrude Steins all, perpetual pioneers, ever building, never completing (10).

* As early as 1927 Grant had entered Gertrude Stein's prose. (See "A Diary," *A&B*, 211; and "Regular Regularly," *HTW*, 244) The date of *Four in America*'s composition is still unclear. Gertrude Stein said "just before" *ABT* (*EA*, 91). In a letter of September (?) 1935 to Thornton Wilder, she said, "it was all written 4 years ago . . ." (YCAL) A portion of it, "Scenery and George Washington," was published in the July–September 1932 issue of *Hound and Horn*. The *Yale Catalogue* dates it 1933. In "And Now" written in 1934, Gertrude Stein said she was presently working on "American religion and Grant" (*Vanity Fair*, [September 1934], 65). Several versions of the manuscript are at Yale.

238

They have no home, they even lack a sky. All Americans have is air (30). "There is no all, there is no over all" (32).

The infinite openness of America produced a people who, if they did not lack emotion altogether, learned to conceal what they had. Grant becomes the exemplar of this restraint. "He never said I like, out loud" (58). No despair, no humility, no human contact of any kind is ever displayed in American life. "Thank you for all your kindness, was never said by Grant" (62). At bottom, "he had no interest, that is the way it was" (31).

These sentiments preceded her six-month tour of America, which by and large simply washed them out of her life. But the impression given by *Four In America* and other contemporaneous pieces is that Gertrude Stein admired this ideal of reserve—or at least had had it prescribed for her. In "First Page" she wrote, "and now I will always do what I do without any emotion . . . as there is . . . not . . . anything . . . that is better" (*SIM*, 289). The upshot of this stoical restraint, according to Gertrude Stein, was that Americans can neither make a living nor can they die (16, 80). They can be killed, but the full experience of death is denied them, for they have never lived.

The vision of the inhibited Grant elicited strong feelings in her. "I cannot think of Ulysses Simpson Grant without tears" (81). Gertrude Stein was questing for her self once more, but if she correctly understood the American character, her own prognosis was gloomy, for she realized "I am an American . . ." (81). In the same breath though, she drew back from the consequences of that identification, saying, truthfully, "but I do not sit and stand in that way . . ." (81).

Not having seen her homeland for almost thirty years, Gertrude Stein's assessments were too fragmentary to be more than suggestive. Moreover, there is a certain loose craziness to the prose of *Four In America*. In the book Gertrude Stein runs frantically from topic to topic, stops to pick up a previously abandoned idea, finds she still cannot develop it, drops it again and, muttering to herself, rushes on. "I lose myself in thoughts" (36). Having indulged in the luxury of candor, the next moment she reverted to a posture of defensive assertiveness. "I know so well what I mean. They say not but I do" (98).

Gertrude Stein's choice of Wilbur Wright as her second subject was virtually fortuitous. In part she chose him because Orville was still living, in part because by chance she saw a French monument dedicated to him (104, 84). She knew virtually nothing about the inventor and had only a mild interest in airplanes at that time. But since flying was an action that she identified with the modern world, Wilbur Wright followed easily.*

Again she opened the section on Wright by ruminating on names— on liking, fearing, changing them. Shortly though she embarked upon an abortive attempt to relate actors, painters, and flyers with one another. If Gertrude Stein meant motion picture actors, the first two professions do share resemblances. Both actors and painters see the results of their work, she argued. A writer "can be alone because he may have nothing to look at," but "not an actor or painter." She continued, "Oh no or a flyer oh no. / Now you do see what I mean" (86). But she never succeeded in clarifying how a flyer shared the experiences of actors and painters. Rather, as was her wont in times of confusion, she relied upon exhortation. "Oh yes without my saying it . . . you do know what I mean" (91). Her tone was all imperatives —"Listen to me"—and exclamations—"How I love to explain"—substituting for accomplishment.

Toward the end of the Wright section, Gertrude Stein had abandoned specifically American considerations for personal ones. She defined suffering as "being certain that some time later . . . if it is difficult to go on nobody will join in" (115). Then, without explanation, the Wright section concludes on sadness and tears. "I could be careful not to cry." "Make it that I am not to try to cry." "I have no reason to cry" (117).

While critical ingenuity might be capable of expanding the meaning of the Wilbur Wright section of *Four In America,* its author could not. She evidently had some inchoate analogies in mind, but her exposition lurched along until it lapsed into insufficiently explained expressions of private feeling.

A series of dualities formed the framework for the Henry James section: accident and coincidence, Shakespeare's plays and Shakespeare's sonnets, lively sound and smooth sound. All of these were dedicated to defining two types of writing. The first, spontaneous and natural with a lively sound, was represented by Shakespeare's plays. They were "written as they were written." Contrasted to the plays were his sonnets which "were written as they were going to be written" (120; see also *Narration,* 51–52). To extrapolate a little from Gertrude Stein's

* Picasso admired Wilbur Wright too. He once signed "a note to Braque with the name 'Vilbure' (his French attempt at Wilbur) to testify that they, too, were brother pioneers . . . exploring space" (*Life* [27 December 1968], 56).

fragmentary notations, the sonnets were compositions planned in advance. Hence, their effects were artificial and their sound, smooth.

Gertrude Stein asserted that Henry James used both approaches to literature (as did she), but not at separate times. "I did not choose to use either one of two ways but two ways as one way" (123). That was her complicated way of summarizing the creative amalgam of intention and accident. Gertrude Stein was coming round to valuing artfulness in her work, including revision. Her prolonged meditations finally led to a consideration of Henry James as a general. Like a writer, the general must first plan for a battle, then once in it, improvise. The military observations run precisely counter to what Gertrude Stein had said about battles in the Grant section. There she had declared that the outcome of a war was decided before the actual engagement took place. Like a bridge hand after concession, battles were carried out merely to demonstrate conclusively an issue already decided. "The war is always won before the war," but "most everybody wants to be shown" (26, 27).

The latter part of the Henry James section contemplates him as a poignant figure. Tears again threaten, for Henry James struck Gertrude Stein as a vulnerable and sensitive boy, burdened by the responsibilities of his father's name and the responsibilities of leadership. "Henry James was was was a young thing" (151). As both son and grandson of "generals," he automatically had a status such that "they may say to him you cannot be afraid." To this, his rejoinder was passionately honest. "But I am I am afraid, I am often afraid" (154). His heritage oppressed him. "Henry James was a name, and weeping he wept" (149). Nonetheless, he prevailed until the war was won. His career, however painful to contemplate, was inspirational, Gertrude Stein thought, for it said, "Do what there is or is not to do. Some do" (159).

In the course of the Henry James section, Gertrude Stein interjected a proposition that subsequently would become a motto of the greatest significance to her.

I am I not any longer when I see.
This sentence is at the bottom of all creative activity.
It is just the opposite of I am I because my little dog knows me.
(119)

At this point Gertrude Stein failed to expand her meaning, but it is clear that the first sentence says, when my eyes are functioning truly, I lose my sense of identity, while the second says, my dog's recogniton of me supplies my identity. That the former "is at the bottom of all creative activity" may be taken to mean that only as we transcend the subjective self, do we become creative. "Seeing" represents a concentration upon something so complete that it excludes personal feelings. This squares with Gertrude Stein's accounts of how she created her still lifes and portraits. "I am I because my little dog knows me" refers to an existence dependent upon recognition from the world outside. Such an identity is unreliable, capricious, and finally, intolerable. In a later piece, "Identity A Poem," Gertrude Stein added to "I am I because my little dog knows me," the line, "The figure wanders on alone" (*WAM*, 71).* She also said later that as she worried at the problem of identity, she remembered the little dog verse from "the Mother Goose," but "was not sure but that only proved the dog was he and not that I was I" (*EA*, 297).†

The introductory portion of the George Washington section of *Four In America*, separately published in 1932, is quite different in mood from the book in which it is embedded. A brief, pleasant interlude, it associates Washington with harvest time, with morning mists followed by warm days, with walnuts and a few birds still singing. "An autumn landscape pleases" (164). After the long stretches of stuttering thought, the lyricism comes as a relief.

Gertrude Stein never attempts to imagine Washington as a novelist. What seemed to motivate her assignment of that role to him was her notion of America as a fountain of novelty. In this sense, Washington as father of his country was equivalent to Washington, the author of a novel. Because Washington knew "the United States of America is not surrounded," he "began a novel, the novel, the great American novel" (169). Again using the analogy of creativity, she says, "every day he wrote a piece of his novel" (176). No teller of fairy tales, "he never began a novel with Once upon a time." His subject was reality. "He always began it with what happened" (180). An early Gertrude Stein, in short.

While the analogy is plausible enough, Gertrude Stein's use of it was uninspired. As had happened before, she had little else to say

---

* "Identity A Poem" is drawn for the most part from GHA, pp. 62–78.
† Gertrude Stein would have encountered the "little dog" verse in one of her assigned texts at Radcliffe, Josiah Royce's *The Spirit of Modern Philosophy*. Royce used the verse to illustrate Kant's contention that the phenomena of the sense-world "recognize the authority of my thought-forms, or categories" (128). Gertrude Stein's first use of the line was in 1929: "What is a sentence for if I am I then my little dog knows me. Even if it is all tenderness ("Saving The Sentence," *HTW*, 19).

about her subject, and the Washington section soon lapsed into tedious maundering. She strung out her verbal responses to the stimulus of his name, pausing once to remark, "It is all mine, coming too fluently" (210). Whereas her efforts at genuine exposition required protracted struggle—and even then her ideas often evaded verbalization—this kind of writing cost her little. Who could not continue effortlessly in this vein? "George Washington was young and as young. / He was not begun. / He was as he is. / It is always less as a use. / Or however clouded" (211). At last Gertrude Stein ran down. Her final line affirmed Washington's wisdom. His creation had endured until the present. Because he knew what a novel was, it had come "through to you" (221).

On balance, the idea of *Four In America* was far superior to its execution. The notion of gaining perspective on representative Americans by assigning them improbable professions was an engaging one. But two of Gertrude Stein's subjects—Washington and Wright—failed to stimulate her imagination. Furthermore, there is no cumulative force or developing enlightenment in the order in whch they are treated. The pattern of the book is altogether characteristic of Gertrude Stein's mind: brief enthusiasm followed by a diminishing interest in the material until at last it trails off to an arbitrary conclusion.

The years 1934 and 1935 constituted Gertrude Stein's most active period of theorizing. In successive books she tried to clarify her intentions as an experimental artist without compromising her principles. This ambition required that, without abandoning her stylistic habits, she advance comprehensible propositions about her art and her world. In the two years following *The Autobiography of Alice B. Toklas,* she finished *Four in America,* and composed *Lectures in America, Narration, The Geographical History of America,* and two short but important pieces, "What Are Master-Pieces" and "How Writing Is Written."

The lectures Gertrude Stein prepared for the triumphal tour of her homeland might well have been entitled *Six in America* to indicate their refinement of the ideas tentatively advanced in the preceding book. *Lectures in America* also profited substantially from Gertrude Stein's return to the one subject she knew well, herself.

Lectures in America turned from anecdotes about others to a consideration of the modern movement in art as Gertrude Stein perceived and practiced it. In other words, she undertook to expand those few sentences in *The Autobiography of Alice B. Toklas* which had pretended to summarize her theories. The resulting defense of her art was much more satisfactory. To be sure, it remade Gertrude Stein's artistic past as the *Autobiography* had remade her personal past. For this reason, the *Lectures* must be used cautiously. Critics have heretofore relied too heavily upon its explanations in order to clarify the huge splatter of Gertrude Stein's career. Not that the *Lectures* are a deliberate falsification. If their generalizations do not actually fit the material they purport to explain, that is because Gertrude Stein's literary career was too varied and random to yield a simple pattern. She suggested the disparity between her exposition and her practice in the *Lectures* themselves. "Will you see it as clearly when I read you some of the portraits that I have written," she asked her audience. "Maybe you will but I doubt it" (184). In fact, the *Lectures* often furnish valuable clues to her methods and intentions. Their objective reliability is perhaps equivalent to that of Holy Writ.

Sometimes Gertrude Stein gives the impression of being a bright child who has pondered aesthetic matters deeply, but lacks the vocabulary necessary to communicate her conclusions.* She habitually left major terms undefined and crucial lines of thought undeveloped. When she discovered herself in intellectual trouble, the confidence of her tone expanded. "So the history of English literature is beginning to be clear," she informed her audience ten pages into the first lecture (21). The remark was as much a reassurance of self as a statement of reality. It was generally the case that the more aggressively Gertrude Stein insisted upon her success, the more resistant were the problems she was struggling to resolve. After an arabesque of words that ended, "which being practically everything could be called anything and everything," she stepped forward and prodded her readers:

> Oh yes you do see.
> You do see that. (34)

Some of her other moments of rhetorical persuasion were less scrupulous. When she asserted that "that anybody can understand," her implication was that if one did *not* understand, then one possessed something less than average intelligence (35). Similarly, after inquiring

---

* Twice she referred to something "effecting" something else, when she meant "affecting" (28, 211). She also had difficulty making subject and verb agree, as in "the next thing I remember . . . were the advent . . . of two . . . paintings" (65). These errors make no visible contribution, not even a humorous one. Gertrude Stein had not markedly improved her knowledge of grammar since her troubled themes at Radcliffe. No doubt this accounts for her confident remark: "English grammar is interesting because it is so simple" (146).

"Do you understand," she continued, "if not it is perhaps because after all you have not read all English nineteenth century litrature . . ." (41). That undertaking she claimed to have completed long ago. Hence, one was implicitly obliged to cede to her expert judgment. At another point, dealing with the idea that "the essence of the completed thing is completion," she paused to remark that since she had already said "a very great deal" about that subject in *Four In America* (which, even if that work could have helped, would not become publicly available until 1947), "I am not going to say any more about this now." Having evaded offering a fuller explanation, she then waved the carrot tantalizingly, at the same time taking a firm grip upon the stick. "But slowly you will see what I mean. If not why not" (24).

In effect, Gertrude Stein began her lectures with a history of English literature and ended them with a critique of the comma. But her own career was always regarded as the very point of culture's spear. As an American, a modern, and a woman she regarded herself as inevitably leading the thrust of innovation.

To the question in the title of her first lecture, "What Is English Literature," Gertrude Stein provided a schematic answer. She assigned distinctive characteristics to the various centuries. The literary manifestations she designated for each period were related to the political history of the country and its geographical features, then translated into a concern for verbal units of various sizes.

The key phrase for England was "the daily island life." Gertrude Stein assigned great significance to the insularity of the English. Their isolation produced a homogenous population with shared ideals. Therefore, they were interested in simple descriptions of what existed around them. So stable and homely was their existence, they preferred realism —"birds beasts woods flowers, roses, violets and fishes" (49). But history shook the English preference for domestic realism. At first, according to Gertrude Stein's myth, words came to the English poets as naturally as a bird song. Chaucer offered "a sound that gently sings . . . because the words are there, they are not chosen as words, they are already there" (30). By the Renaissance however, the Englishman was obliged to choose among words. With verbal alternatives, much of his art depended upon his skill at selection. The Renaissance offered lyricism which "was no longer just a song it was a song of words that were chosen to make a song" (30).

It was after the "confusion" of the civil wars, Gertrude Stein argued, that English literature's basic unit became the sentence. Clarity was the writer's goal, "the choosing of a completed thing" (33). Eighteenth-century sentences were built out of approved formulations. In the meantime, the British Empire had begun to grow. This expansion out from the island until "they owned everything outside" necessarily changed the literary needs of this formerly insular nation (34). "The time now had come when they began to explain" (37). While the English writer continued "describing your daily life which is all yours," he naturally began to "explain how you own everything besides" (41). In short, the Empire brought self-consciousness.

Explanation was not possible, however, in "completed sentences" (43). If something were completed, it did not require explanation. "Anybody can see that, anybody can" (43). Introspection was a fragmented activity. "If you think about what you are thinking you are not thinking about a whole thing" (43–44). Gertrude Stein furnished one of her few illustrations by asking her audience to compare *Clarissa* to the work of Dickens. "One lives by its whole the eighteenth century thing and the nineteenth century thing lives by its parts" (44).

By the end of the nineteenth century when Gertrude Stein came to literary consciousness, the British Empire had begun to contract again, and the stability of its domestic life was diminishing. "The daily life was less daily and the owning everything outside was less owning" (46). At that point, phrases were no longer sufficient. "A phrase no longer soothed, suggested or convinced, they needed a whole paragraph" (49). By this time though, the English writers were debilitated. "The young generation were doing the second class writing of the past generation, Wells, Galsworthy, Bennett, etc." (46–47). New energy was required. America furnished it.

The formulaic nature of Gertrude Stein's conception of English literary history is evident in her summation of it from Chaucer through the nineteenth century. "One century has words, another century chooses words, another century uses words and then another century using words no longer has them" (27). Fanciful as this was, it enabled Gertrude Stein to fix her own position more clearly, and thereby defend her practice. From the outset she insisted upon the subjectivity, or at the very least, on the personal quality of knowledge. The keynote of the whole series was sounded in the first sentence. "One cannot come back too often to the question what is knowledge and to the answer knowledge is what one knows" (11). What followed was neither "The history of English literature" nor "the English people's history of their

English literature" (13). It was her own. "Knowledge is what one knows."

With the decline of English literary energies, the Americans entered. Gertrude Stein continued to utilize her view of America as a disembodied country whose people "do not live every day" (50). Because her ideas were still in the process of being formed, the audience was exposed to a monstrous proposition about American literature:

> There is inside it as separation, a separation from what is chosen to what it is that from which it has been chosen. (51)

Clarity came slowly for Gertrude Stein. But she was at pains to emphasize that Americans were identifiable by their "lack of connection" (53). By this she seemed to mean that they use systems of communication not in relation to their daily lives, but abstractly and for their own sake. She did not go further into this idea. "This is another story" (54). But she did identify herself directly as the heir of the tradition she had been describing. She took over the paragraph from the enervated English writers and began to tinker with it. The lectures that followed detailed the stages of her dismantlement and then reconstitution of the verbal mechanism.

The goal she set herself was the creation of something free of historical bonds, free of programmatic design, free of representational function. One of her early queries was, "can one serve god and mammon" followed by its corollary, "if one can should one" (12). She gave *god* and *mammon* special meanings that had nothing to do with either religion or success. For a writer to serve mammon meant to her that he generated words in the full consciousness that they would be heard by someone. When the writer shaped his words to produce a particular effect upon his audience, the purity of the relationship between "the thing done and the doer" was spoiled. This compromised method was what Gertrude Stein called writing "indirectly," or writing "the way it has already been written" (54). It partook both of calculation and of imitation. But known methods produced predictable results, hardly a worthy ambition for a leader.

"Serving god" however meant writing "as you are to be writing" (54). Gertrude Stein was still trying to clarify for herself those creative absolutes by which in *Four In America* she first attempted to differentiate Shakespeare's sonnets from his plays. "Serving god" meant writing "directly." The subject matter was of no importance. What counted was the concentrated focus of the writer on his subject. "The relation between the thing done and the doer must be direct" (24). Succeeding lectures showed Gertrude Stein learning this lesson, and in the process simultaneously enlarging and obscuring it.

The second lecture, "Pictures," moves at the slow, flat-footed gait of a museum guard making his rounds. Nevertheless, along with its recollections of the paintings in Gertrude Stein's life, it does represent her fundamental thesis.

The first pictures she remembered were representations of social history—art as historical record in a panorama of Waterloo; art as literary illustration in the painting "of a scene from Scott's Marmion the nun being entombed in a wall as a punishment"; art as local color in Millet's "Man with a Hoe" (65). Following these instances of literal representation, Gertrude Stein's education in art became increasingly preoccupied with style. She moved through etchings to Japanese prints to a painting of a wheat field blowing in the wind. Its painter, Jean Charles Cazin (1841–1901), was "the commonplace end of the then still outlawed school of impressionists" (67). Her first actual purchase she said was a landscape by the American Alexander Shilling (1859–1937). "It looked like any piece of American country" (69).

Then she began to travel to Europe and to visit its museums. There she did two eccentric and inexplicable things. She looked out of museum windows for no more definite reason than that "it is more complete" (70). Obviously she meant to suggest that some process of comparison was taking place between the world of art and the world outside, framed by the windows. Secondly, she insisted that at this period in her life, she lay down on the long red benches of the Italian museums and "began to sleep and dream in front of oil paintings" (70). Gazing out of museum windows and sleeping in front of paintings prepared Gertrude Stein for modern art. "I really began to realize that an oil painting is an oil painting" (71). The autonomy of art had to be accepted in order to liberate it from the tyranny of representation. She had started her lecture by repeating her answer to the question, "What do you feel about modern art." "I like to look at it" (59). She insisted that a painting could hold her attention, however poor its quality, because "for me it has achieved an existence in and for itself . . ." (61). That was her goal in this lecture—to establish the work of art as independent of any practical function. Once something had been made, all that mattered was "how much vitality has it" (61).

She had argued the same point in *Four in America*, insisting there that "clarity is of no importance because nobody listens and nobody knows what you mean no matter what you mean . . ." As a defensive gesture, she located redemption in sheer presence. "But if you have vitality enough . . . somebody . . . will have to realise that you know what you mean . . ." (*FIA*, 127–8). She did not conceal the improvisational nature of her work. "I wonder if you know what I mean," she inquired of her audience. "I do not quite know whether I do myself" (*LIA*, 172).

Gertrude Stein's education in oil painting culminated with Cézanne. "I came to Cezanne and there you were, at least there I was . . ." (76). Quoting from her portrait of Cézanne, she concluded that his example had been such, that "I began my writing" (77).*

With the review of her education in art concluded, Gertrude Stein began to elaborate her basic principle that a painting was a painting and nothing more. She admitted that a relationship existed between the thing painted and the painting of it, but "that relation was so to speak nobody's business" (79). While she was contesting the criterion of verisimilitude for the judgment of art, she was not austere in her opinion. Personally, she said, resemblance gave her a "pleasurable sensation." She did not wish to outlaw likeness, but merely wished to remind her audience that the essential consideration was "the life in and for itself of an oil painting" (80). If she could gain assent to that proposition for painting, then it would obviously be easier for her to argue the same case for literature.

The weakest of the six lectures is also the most poorly placed. "Plays" would fit better after "Portraits and Repetition" since it is at that point in her career that her interest in plays developed. The lecture's ideas are chaotically expressed, for the normal theatrical experience upset Gertrude Stein. Even though many of her pieces were ostensibly "plays," she wrote them not out of a love of the theater, but rather in an attempt to refashion the dramatic experience.

Her memories of the stage from her youth are strangely trivial and incongruous. She mixed drama and opera together, remembering *Uncle Tom's Cabin* and *Faust*, Buffalo Bill and *Lohengrin* from early childhood, then later melodramas starring William Gillette. After drenching

* The quotation from "Cezanne" included in the lecture is incomplete. A portion was omitted from the center, with no warning of the editing. Gertrude Stein was oddly cavalier about the integrity of her own work. Abridgement hardly seemed to trouble her.

herself in opera during her college days, she said she concluded that music was for adolescents, so she gave it up. As for the theater and the motion pictures, she rarely attended as an adult.

In her dismissal of the theater, she attempted to elevate a nervous indisposition into universal law. Her critique of the theater centered upon an insistence that there was inevitably a gap between the action depicted on the stage and the emotion felt by the person watching in the audience. This caused what she call "syncopated time" (93). Even before the curtain went up, she anticipated that "one is not going to have the same tempo as the thing that is there behind the curtain." Her apprehension was translated into a nervousness that she defined as "needing to go faster or to go slower so as to get together" (95). But the pace of the play invariably outstripped her own. While the action moved inexorably on, Gertrude Stein was left behind, still trying to absorb the players' voices and costumes. It frustrated her that in the theater she could never "begin over again" as she could with a book (115).

Gertrude Stein's reason for dismissing the theater is of revelatory importance for understanding her personality. Her torpor was everywhere evident. She moved and changed intellectually, but very slowly. In her writing, ideas heaved ponderously into view and only after interminably rolling about did their crude, heavy forms finally stabilize themselves. It is no wonder that the lively pace of the theater was generally too demanding for Gertrude Stein's nervous system. The tensions created by the theater could not be relieved at will, unlike those experienced in reading where "one can always look at the end of the book and so quiet down one's excitement" (100). She created plays lacking a plot, partly to relieve this idiosyncratic condition of nervousness, partly to do in the theater what she had been doing in portraits and lyrics: that is, to make them an experience of essences. "The business of Art" she insisted firmly "is to live in the actual present . . ." (104).

Plays for her were group portraits. She offered the essences of several individuals as perceived by her sensibility in some active relationship to one another. That activity was not a plot. Her intention was "without telling what happened . . . to make a play the essence of what happened" (119). By eliminating visible action and concentrating the intensity in the evocation of essences, she believed she had solved the problem of emotions in the audience lagging behind stage action. For her a play seemed "exactly like a landscape" (122). The principals

in her plays need not be acquainted, save in the author's mind. Therefore, the "action" could mix historical and fictional personages with
intimate friends, as in "Lynn and the College De France." Two of the
play's characters appear in its title, and they are joined by Madame
Rose, Marcelle Mariot, and Henry Clay (*O&P*, 249). The author's conception of the essential character of each furnished their common meet-
ing-ground.

While the theory made reasonably good sense, when it was imple-
mented, Gertrude Stein's results necessarily were virtually indistin-
guishable from her other work. The following example, cited approv-
ingly by her, might well be drawn from the still lifes of *Tender Buttons*.

> A wide oak a wide enough oak, a very wide cake, a lightning
> cooky, a single wide open and exchanged box filled with the same
> little sac that shines. ("What Happened," *LIA*, 120; see also *G&P*,
> 206.)

The only real distinction she could provide was a negative one. "Anything that was not a story could be a play" (119).

Lecture four, "The Gradual Making of The Making of Americans,"
is fitfully useful. Its ideas were imperfectly conceived because too many
diverse energies had invaded that monstrous book as it was being written to permit lucid analysis. Only when the book was viewed as part
of a continuum of development (as it was in the next lecture, "Portraits
and Repetition" could Gertrude Stein discuss it coherently. Although
she designated it as her entry in the race for literary eminence, in the
lecture she merely invoked its presence.

Still, the several motives she invented for abandoning the book are
of interest. Feeling "livelier just then," she said she preferred to turn
to *A Long Gay Book* which, instead of describing individuals, sought
to describe how "any one feels acts and does in relation to any other
one" (150). Although Gertrude Stein could not say it directly, this
can be translated as her recognition that Alice Toklas liberated her
from the scientific pretensions of *The Making of Americans*. A second
explanation offered was that after the terrible struggle to put down her
"complete conception . . . of an individual," one day "in 1908 I just
did not go on any more" (147–8). A third was that she had finally
learned William James's lesson that science's job was complete description. So, "if it can be done why do it" (157). Even though these

motives were at cross-purposes, they indicate Gertrude Stein's need to explain and justify her career.

She could not, however, clarify the meaning of the stylistic metamorphosis that had taken place in *A Long Gay Book,* so was reduced to reading samples from it which she pretended would explain how she had changed. Or, she created grotesque sentences such as the following:

> And so the Long Gay Book little by little changed from a description of any one of any one and everything there was to be known about any one, to what if not was not not to be not known about any one about anything. (158)

Whenever Gertrude Stein insisted that her audience must or would understand her, or attempted to ingratiate herself with them—"I hope you like what I say"—or threw out a contorted sentence like the one just quoted, it signalled unresolved bewilderment in her (157).

At the end of the lecture, she embarked on yet another attempt to characterize her countrymen. They had a unique sense of "a space of time" (160). Americans regarded time as a dimension in which to accomplish something. Time was not merely lived in, nor did it subjectively change its dimensions for them. Rather it had fixed limits, established according to its productive potential. Every American knows, she asserted, "just how many seconds minutes or hours it is going to take to do a whole thing" (160). Since Americans were always active, "a space of time" "is a natural thing for an American to always have inside them as something in which they are continuously moving" (160–61).

Imperfectly related to the composition of *The Making of Americans,* the best Gertrude Stein could do in concluding this inchoate argument was to say that the big book had been her "first real effort to express this thing . . ." (161).

Attempting definition of her aesthetic once more in the fifth lecture, "Portraits and Repetition," Gertrude Stein finally hit the mark. This defense of innovation was the most reasonable and sustained summary of her career she had ever managed.

Its expositional success can be attributed to the fact that she began by recapitulating the argument of her 1926 lecture, "Composition as Explanation." She had ruminated on its ideas for at least a decade, and the luxury of time had increased her lucidity. She herself recognized the lecture's superiority, telling a friend before she sailed for

America that she preferred it over the rest (W. G. Rogers, *When This You See*, 118).*

"Portraits and Repetition" again argued the case that each age needs art forms appropriate to its "composition." Change was established by contrast, as when one realizes that a train is moving when it passes something fixed (165). However, she believed that, as free agents in the world, Americans were destined for the task of creating movement through sheer internal vitality. Conventional description would not do the job, for it was imitative or repetitious in an inert way. She devoted considerable time to arguing that her writing was not repetitive but "insistent." It always contained variations, as each new hop of a frog, trill of a bird, or detective story does (167). She had been strongly impressed by the differences in similarity, especially in listening to her Baltimore aunts telling the same stories over and over, but each time differently (169).

Her portraits were independent of any imitations of the subject's activities or speech. Her clue to a person was "the rhythm of anybody's personality," which had "nothing to do with remembering any one" (174, 175).

Gertrude Stein remained in flight from "remembering." Memory was the jailer that imprisoned her in the nightmares of the past. Under certain circumstances it could be soothing, but even so it was lifeless (181). She had always had a poor memory and commented upon it numerous times. "It is difficult to remember anything oh how difficult," she exclaimed in 1930 ("Parlor," *O&P*, 325). Alice Toklas recalled that Gertrude Stein disliked "unpleasant things—things that she didn't like, she didn't remember, really, because it was the only way to get rid of the embarrassment of them" (Duncan, 85–86). Her argument incorporated her actual condition. "We in this period have not lived in remembering, we have living in moving . . ." (*LIA*, 182). Her goal was accurate self-expression, "making what I know come out as I know it" (181). She called the capacity to listen and to talk simultaneously "the essence of genius," by which she evidently meant the ability to concentrate on a subject (listening) and at the same time to respond to it (talking or writing). When "the two in one" existed, there was "no element of remembering" (180).

Her shift to the still lifes of *Tender Buttons* she now regarded as a

* On the other hand, in an unpublished manuscript, "Pathe," written while she was in the United States, Gertrude Stein characterized the last lecture, "Poetry and Grammar," as "the most xciting thing I have ever done . . ." (YCAL).

means of weakening memory's grip. With them she was "trying to live in looking" free of memory (189). She recalled her excitement when she discovered that the words she used were not descriptive, and indeed often had nothing whatever to do with the thing being represented (191–2). In time, however, she realized that she had become intoxicated with the "beauty of the sounds as they came from me as I made them" (196). Preferring sobriety, she drew back from lyricism and again sought essences (199). Her goal once more became the creation of "something out of something without adding anything" (204).

The most popular of Gertrude Stein's lectures has been the last, "Poetry and Grammar." Her discussion of parts of speech and marks of punctuation is relaxed and amusing, yet pointed to a serious end.

Insofar as her goal was to evoke the reality of anything without naming or describing it, nouns and adjectives antagonized her. She started the lecture by dismissing nouns as unnecessary, although she ended by identifying them with poetry. Initially she stated her preference for verbs and adverbs. They were "on the move" (212). Articles and pronouns received her blessing because of their vagueness, prepositions were praised because they could be "mistaken," and conjunctions because they were colorless drudges. The dominant quality in her impressionistic evaluation of parts of speech was the vitality each possessed.

Punctuation, on the other hand, she assessed on the basis of rhythm. If a sentence has been correctly phrased, it will be clear if it is a question or an exclamation. Therefore, such marks of punctuation are extraneous. She felt the same way about quotation marks, adding "they are ugly, they spoil the line of the writing or the printing . . ." (215). Colons and semi-colons she refused to employ because "writing should go on" and not be interrupted by pauses. Periods she accepted though, because one had to stop sometime. Commas, she simply slandered in an amusingly high-handed way, using them at the very instant that she condemned their use: ". . . to me for many years and I still do feel that way about it only now I do not pay as much attention to them, the use of them was positively degrading" (220).

All these opinions were preliminary to a more esoteric extension of her basic principle that "sentences are not emotional but paragraphs are" (223). She apparently meant that a paragraph makes a cumulative effect which is not available in its individual sentences. To test the proposition out, she had tried in *The Making of Americans* to write

"enormously long sentences that would be as long as the longest paragraph" (223). This was one instance where she now felt "dimly" that
she had made an error. Why lose two effects in order to achieve one?
(224). That would only diminish the variety of writing. In any case,
the experiment was based upon a false premise: namely, that the paragraph possesses fixed limits of size.

Still, she claimed that in *How To Write* she had tried to achieve "the
unemotional balance of a sentence" and "the emotional balance of a
paragraph." "Even in a short sentence" she sought to make "the two
things come to be one" (226). Her illustrations resemble Zen aphorisms:

He looks like a young man grown old.

A dog which you have never had before has sighed. (226) *

The problem she was grappling with was how to achieve emotion in
writing without relying upon logical effects built up sequentially.

At long last she came to her definitions of prose and poetry. Prose
she identified as "balance" attained by using dynamic parts of speech.
Prose deals with "movement in space" (245). Poetry, however, is based
on vocabulary, specifically upon the noun. For her, prose moves and
does, while poetry is.

When she turned to writing "very short things" following *The Making of Americans,* she decided to meet the question of nouns head-on,
"to refuse them by using them" (228). To reconcile her earlier rejection of nouns, she reminded her audience that "you can love a name"
and want to call it out passionately. So poetry was essentially lyric for
her—"really loving the name of anything" (232). Because poetry was
a series of love-cries, its lines were short and repetitive. So subjective
was this that Gertrude Stein felt compelled to instruct her listeners—
"Think about it and you will see what I mean by what you feel" (234).

Tender Buttons served for illustration. Yet it was perverse of Gertrude Stein to claim that in that book she called out "the names of
things" with passion, for in its still lifes she precisely did not use names,
but indirection. She pushed on though, saying that she then wondered
if there were not a "way of naming things . . . without naming them"

* She used the first sentence quoted to exemplify successful writing in "Genuine
Creative Ability," a piece inspired by "the Guggenheim prize" and known in the
Yale Catalogue as "Letter to Henry McBride." Her negative example was, "It was
my fault that my wife did not have a cow" (*Creative Art*, VI [February 1930],
Supplement p. 41).

(236). Her efforts in this sounded surprisingly like automatic writing. "I remember . . . looking at anything until something that was not the name of that thing but was in a way that actual thing would come to be written" (237). The decisive element in poetry was intensity of feeling. If it were sufficient, she could compose an independent entity without resorting to naming her subject (242).

"Something" that was "in a way that actual thing." The secret of Gertrude Stein's esoteric writing is locked in those phrases. Her determination of what the "actual thing" might be was wholly subjective. Her desire to escape from staleness was commendable. "We who had known the names so long did not get a thrill from just knowing them" (237). But the actual creation was arbitrary and really only approximate—"in a way" the actual thing.

Such dissociated naming constituted Gertrude Stein's solution for keeping poetry based on the noun, while at the same time liberating it from "the rigid form of the noun" (237). She employed nouns, but broke their hold on poetry by detaching them from their normal referents. It was all very neat, very ingenious, and very suspect.

Summary of Gertrude Stein's account of her own career at this length and with a minimum of interruptions was necessary to bring into prominence its salient features and problems. In the lectures themselves these features and problems are severely obscured by the eccentricities of her prose. The lectures were Gertrude Stein's earnest effort to explain and justify the perplexing sprawl of her literary evolution. While in them she confessed to moments of doubt and confusion, on the whole she presented that career as if it had been systematically and rationally conceived. Needing the assurance of continuity and stability in her life, she created her own myth of order. Provided with the trappings of logical exposition, the lectures have a surface plausibility to them. But underneath, they swarm with wandering, disconnected pronouncements. A mixture of the banal, the keen, the improbable, the silly, the fresh, and the wise, if they are approached with a measure of scepticism, the American lectures deserve a more careful and sympathetic reading than they have yet received.

In March of 1935 Gertrude Stein was invited back to the University of Chicago to deliver four more lectures, later collected as *Narration*. These represented her latest ideas on a subject she had been steadily closing in upon, for she felt "something else is going to happen about narrative" (*LIA*, 233). The problem of narrative was "bothering" her.

Throughout Gertrude Stein's account of her evolution as an artist, she was repeatedly driven by psychological uneasiness to tackle certain problems. She was "concerned" to the point that she undertook experiments, she was "irritated" into action, she was "bothered" until she had effected a change. Art functioned as a form of therapy. "What's the use of portraiture, to tranquilise your mind" ("Possessive Case," *AFAM*, 130).

Depending upon which direction Gertrude Stein was facing, *Narration* can be judged a success or a failure. When she was groping after new concepts, her expression was tentative and confused, but when she was presenting ideas she had already verbalized, her meaning took on a sharp focus.

The first two lectures are unusually helpful in establishing just what Gertrude Stein had been trying to say about American writing and its relationship to English literature. In them English stability was contrasted with American mobility: the English don't move, even when they are travelling, while the Americans move even when they're still (11). The verbal consequence was that in England words "expressed arrested motion or a very slow succession," whereas in America, words were detached "from the solidity of anything" and were in motion (10). The awkward consequence of these distinctions was that the Americans inherited a language alien to their style of life. This was an unprecedented situation, "two nations having the same words . . . telling things that have nothing whatever in common" (7). The question then of how Americans might adapt this language to their lives was a crucial one. Gertrude Stein thought the answer was to change the emphasis put upon words in order to alter the rhythm of the language, "the pressure being put upon the same words to make them move in an entirely different way" (7). This was accomplished by rethinking the use of grammar and punctuation as she had in *Lectures In America*, by "shoving" the English language around (12).

In her second *Narration* lecture, Gertrude Stein probed further into the modern mind, which she believed was exemplified by America, since it was the country that had practiced twentieth-century methods longest. Here she centered upon narrative. It used to be defined, she said, as "a telling of what is happening in successive moments of its happening" (17). But people were no longer certain that things did happen in a coherent sequence. "Moving is in every direction" (19). If that were the case, then narrative writing had to adjust to it. She illustrated the new condition by recalling the American soldiers she observed in

France during the war, "standing, standing and doing nothing standing for a long time not even talking but just standing and being watched by the whole French population" (19). That, she declared, symbolized "narrative as it is now" (20). There was no action, no progress through a sequence of events to reach a desired end. There was only "being something existing" (20). It was to that vital state that narrative should aspire. "Knowledge is not succession but an immediate existing" (20).

She now believed that sentences had some merit for embodying such a condition, for they were "contained within themselves" unlike paragraphs that were "a succession of sentences" (20). This was a variation of her dictum that sentences were not emotional. "A thing balanced within itself does not give out nor have within any emotion" (22). Nor did it require a beginning, middle, or end. All that was required to provide balance to a sentence was that each part be in place (22–23). Although Gertrude Stein did not repudiate the paragraph outright, she did implicitly reject it as being of no further expressive use.

That was really the limit of her thought at this point concerning narrative structure. She defined what it had been and indicated its inadequacy for dealing with the modern world. But she remained uncertain how narrative might be transformed or whether it should be abandoned altogether. She did speculate at the conclusion of the second lecture that "perhaps narrative and poetry and prose have all come where they do not have to be considered as being there" (29).

The second pair of lectures veered off in other directions. Some of Gertrude Stein's notions are of random interest, while others are abortive efforts to clarify clouded issues she had previously raised. Her puzzlement and indecisiveness are particularly visible in the slow beginning of the third lecture. While threatening to say something, she killed time by stating the obvious in contorted and repetitive ways.

> Anyway anybody everybody can say anything about narrative their own or anybody else's narrative but one thing is certain and sure that anybody telling everything even if it is nothing that they are telling or is either telling what they want to tell what they have to tell what they like to tell or what they will tell they tell a narrative. (32).

Again, mannered prose was substituting surface complication for the rigors of thought.

Most of the third lecture was devoted to journalism. The newspaper story intrigued Gertrude Stein because it sought to give the impression that the events it reported had just happened. Obviously the newspaper was an attempt to cater to the needs of immediate experience. So, to meet the public's longing to feel alive now, newspapers "have to deceive the reader into feeling that yesterday is to-day" (37). Headlines, she thought, were invented to assist them in performing this function (43). By filling the days of their readers with events, newspapers provided them with the assurance that they existed. If nothing happens, "that makes anybody feel that you cannot call a day a day . . ." (36).

Gertrude Stein was drawing together evidence for her contention that the modern reader desired immediacy in his literature, a need that the newspapers could not meet. In repudiating journalism, she argued that it dealt only with surfaces, keeping the outside life outside without ever internalizing it (39). Consequently, all that newspapers could offer was "real life with the reality left out" (40).

Improvising freely, Gertrude Stein was far from being in control of her argument, as proved by an abrupt, bizarre interruption. Newspapers were on her mind because she had contributed a piece on the subject to the New York *Herald Tribune* during the very month she delivered the lecture. As she meandered on about them, suddenly she remarked, "I love my love with a b because she is peculiar." After adding, "One can say this," she went on to comment that this was why newspapers have "nothing to do with anything that is living" (37). The sentence turned up once more in the piece, this time merely inserted with no explanation whatsoever. It is notable that this eerie eruption came at a moment in the lecture when Gertrude Stein's ideas were decidedly inchoate.*

Having attempted more than she could manage, by the fourth lecture of *Narration,* Gertrude Stein had abandoned almost all pretense of cohesive exposition. All the odds and ends of her argument were thrown into this refuse heap of a lecture. Her ideas grew so muddled that she observed desperately, "I can almost cry about it" (51). At its conclusion she defended her failure, saying that she knew all the reasons that something could not be done and yet that she regarded falling short of accomplishment as much more interesting than easy success (62).

Her subject in this fourth lecture was why some literature which appears to be creative is actually not. Gertrude Stein suspected that the

* Gertrude Stein had been using that formula for several years. It was based on a child's game, in which each player must complete a line, using all the letters of the alphabet in turn. See *The Annotated Mother Goose,* 265. Also see "The Lion and the Unicorn" section in Lewis Carroll's *Through The Looking-Glass.*

crucial determinant was how the author related himself to his audience. But she could not quite make out the connections. Literature she defined as "the telling of anything." But to whom? Who listens? "Where is the audience" (60). Although through personal experience she could distinguish the audience to whom a letter was written and the one to whom lectures were delivered, she regarded an audience as an imperative futility, necessary but illusory. Gertrude Stein believed that even though no one really understands what another person has told him—the solipsistic misery—it was nonetheless necessary for human existence that one try to communicate (55–56). At one point she fell back upon "mysticism" to explain how it was that, in spite of her "absolute conviction" that no one can ever share what he is feeling, still union was still possible. The Trinity was one example, she said, and marriage another in which "after all after all three are one and two are one" (57).

The point she was fumbling after was that the writer is affected by his awareness of his audience. For her though, the true and omnipresent audience was oneself. Because "the writer writing knows what he is writing . . . he is an audience" (56). In lecturing, however, she had found that the ability to audit oneself disappeared. Having an audience directly in one's presence "in a way destroys the physical something that a writer is while he is writing" (56).

To the question, "What is anybody to do about writing," Gertrude Stein's response was a sane one. One must "amuse himself with anything" and not expect to "recognize"—that is, to possess imaginatively—anything other than the very act of "playing with what he is playing with as he is writing" (58–59).

Much of *Narration* was conceived as an indirect defense of the method of *The Autobiography of Alice B. Toklas*. It had already come under attack not only as historically inaccurate and ignorant, but as a betrayal of her principles, a deliberate act of venal popularization. Gertrude Stein was naturally eager to respond. At the end of the third lecture, brooding over the lack of intensity in journalistic writing, she exclaimed: "Why is it. / Oh why is it," then asked her audience to think of her model for the *Autobiography*, Daniel Defoe, who had "tried to write Robinson Crusoe as if it were exactly what did happen" (45). But although she kept "getting nearer and nearer" to discussing the autobiographical genre, she recognized the appropriateness of the inquiry, "Am I really near enough" (43).

She approached autobiography through history. The problem historians faced, she thought, was a glut of material. "In history you have everything" (54). To "recognize" it, to achieve a personal, actual awareness of any of it, was a complex challenge. Rarely do either history or biography succeed, although one instance of success did occur to Gertrude Stein, one which paralleled the relationship of herself and Alice Toklas. "Boswell conceived himself as an audience," she said, and by "the intensity of his merging himself in the immediacy of Johnson achieved recognition as Johnson himself was doing" (60). The necessary elements were the intimacy and reverence of a disciple for a great literary figure. She believed that the *Autobiography* had made a contribution. By using Alice Toklas as the medium, she was able to feel the events they had lived through afresh, could "recognize" their history in Alice Toklas's living presence (62). Normally, however, the biographer and historian lacked this intimacy with their subjects, and lacking it, how could their work be literature? "Well I am sure I do not know" (61). But the problem intrigued Gertrude Stein sufficiently for her to observe, "I almost would like to be an historian myself to perhaps do something" (62). The remark was prophetic. Her next full-length work was entitled *The Geographical History of America or The Relation of Human Nature to The Human Mind*.

The actual contents of *The Geographical History of America or The Relation of Human Nature to The Human Mind* reverse the title and subtitle. Relatively little attention is devoted to the "geographical history," while the two psychological conditions of "human nature" and "human mind" pre-empt the book. Possessed of one of those dualities that invariably stimulated her imagination, Gertrude Stein opened with some sixty strong and coherent pages of distinctions. But then her prose grew increasingly prolix until at last the expositional fabric unravelled altogether and concluded on a wavering note. "I am not sure that is not the end" (207).*

At this time Gertrude Stein chose to regard the human mind as in every way superior to human nature. Human mind was pure and objective, whereas human nature was trapped in the messiness of emotional existence. "If perfection is good more perfection is better" (29). Her goal was to partake of the values of existence in the condition of essence. One did not attain the human mind by rising through levels of

---

* Alice Toklas was openly sceptical about the book's pretensions. "Alice makes fun of me, but I think it is pretty good" (GS to Thornton Wilder, 10 July 1935, YCAL; see also *EA*, 123).

increasing abstraction until one entered some realm of ideal Platonic essences. Human mind exists absolutely in the immediate. To reach that condition though, one must "renounce because and become," for human mind has no aspirations for the future, no belief in causality, no memory of the past (156). Consequently, it is never disappointed, for it has neither illusions about progress, nor does it suffer from nostalgia. It is unremittingly affirmative, an Eden of innocence from which human beings are expelled after they fall into self-consciousness. As Emerson remarked in "Experience," "it is very unhappy but too late to be helped the discovery we have made that we exist. That discovery is called the Fall of Man." However, Gertrude Stein believed it possible to regain paradise. Human nature was only the benighted condition in which suffering occurs, whereas human mind, liberated from fear, jealousy, and sex, serenely recognizes and accepts things as they are.

Once more Gertrude Stein was trying to locate the means of an untroubled life. As the storms of sexuality subsided, the fear of death was moving in to replace them. Although the book opens with a mechanistic justification of death, she would later acknowledge in *Wars I Have Seen* that it failed to satisfy her (23–24). If people did not die, went the argument, there would be no room on earth for new life. Human nature cannot accept the bleak consolation of that fact, Gertrude Stein said, but human mind can. At once a fundamental distinction had been established. The materialistic egotism of human nature blocks it from the truth, whereas human mind has a selfless, lucid objectivity. By accepting the given, it frees itself from negative emotions.

Human mind provides intimations of immortality in a timeless present. Time and identity are burdens that human nature must bear, but not human mind. The persistent question—"one cannot say it too often"—of the early part of *The Geographical History* is, "What is the use of being a little boy if you are going to grow up to be a man" (25). The answer was absorption in the present moment with no regret for what is past, and neither hope nor fear of what is to come. For when it comes, it will be accepted. The liberating formula was: "Not solve it but be in it" (155).

Existing in the human mind also exempted Gertrude Stein from the problem of identity. I may be I because my little dog knows me, but personal security can hardly depend upon such external recognition. "The question of identity has nothing to do with the human mind . . ." (106). When in the human mind, one was out of oneself. "Identity is history and history is not true because history is dependent upon an audience" (111).

It seemed obvious to Gertrude Stein that human mind was the appropriate place to be when creating. She frequently reiterated that human nature was no longer interesting (35). Literature that was dedicated to fighting, remembering, sorrow, and age, to all the turmoil of mundane existence, was no longer relevant. Therefore, her second reason for championing the human mind was that it justified her own literary career. Whereas "human nature is just the same as any animal nature," "human mind is the mind that writes . . ." (80). Its subject-matter "does not consist in messages or in events." Messages assume a recipient who can be affected and events presuppose forms created by causal relationships. Liberated from such assumptions, the human mind will offer writing that "consists only in writing down what is written and therefore it has no relation to human nature" (80).

Gertrude Stein intended this bloodless abstraction of the human mind. She associated both numbers and money with it because of their abstract nature. Newspapers she again dismissed as the products of human nature. "The newspapers tell about events but what have events to do with anything nothing I tell you" (67). Inasmuch as continuity had proved illusory, the literary art must change. "There is no reason why chapters should succeed each other since nothing succeeds another, not now any more" (54).

In her view, vitality was conferred upon literature to the extent that the writer had escaped from human nature at the moment of composition. In the proper condition of serenity, "there is no such thing . . . as remember" (36). The masterpiece was exempt from criticism of its ideas, since thinking was not involved in it. Nor could it be right. "Write and right" she asserted "have nothing to do with one another" (199). In any case, like human nature she found being right "not interesting" and asked, "do you not get tired of always being right." Much more pleasing than correctness was "what is what. And what is what is what is what" (201–2). This dazzling proposition conferred an absolute value upon existence. "Anything is what it is" (47). It freed writing from inhibiting systems of order and handily exempted *The Autobiography of Alice B. Toklas* from such corrective criticism as had recently appeared in *Testimony Against Gertrude Stein*. Human mind was superior to such cavilling. "There are no witnesses to the autobiography of any one that has a human mind" (54).

Toward the end of *The Geographical History* Gertrude Stein meditated with wonder upon her uniqueness in the world of literature. Her self-admiration followed logically enough. If her theory about the proper role of the writer in the twentieth century were sound, and if she were practicing that theory while no one else was, then she could justifiably ask, "Why is it that in this epoch the only real literary thinking has been done by a woman" (182). Although she did not directly say as much in this book, a portion of her answer would be that she had assumed creative leadership because she was an American. For Gertrude Stein championed the human mind because it reflected the American continent as she saw it during her visit to the United States. "A great deal of flat land is connected with the human mind and so America is connected with the human mind" (51). The flatness of much of the American continent fused with an impression she had derived from the modern novelty of flying. Gertrude Stein had been impressed by the cubist appearance of the landscape when seen from an airplane. "When there was a sea the world was round but now that there is air the world is flat" (95–96). Analogically, it could be expected that modern writing would come from a mind formed in a modern nation, flat, abstract, and lacking a history. She even found supporting evidence in the national anthem. She was confident that "if you announce what you see nobody can say no." Therefore, "Oh say can you see" (134, 135).

Franklin Roosevelt, communism, and propaganda were mixed with the theorizing of *The Geographical History*. So were at least three suicides (34–35, 59, 121–2). As had happened in *Four In America*, distress and grief threatened to bring on tears in the early portion of the book. But they dried up as Gertrude Stein convinced herself of her own argument: that she was a great writer who had at last secured herself from anguish by entering the inviolate regions of the human mind.

Gertrude Stein's American justification of her career concluded with two short, lucid statements, "How Writing Is Written" and "What Are Master-Pieces and Why Are There So Few Of Them." While both are useful places to commence a study of Gertrude Stein, if taken uncritically they can wrench one's understanding of her literary work askew. As with the *Lectures In America* the actual record is much more dishevelled than Gertrude Stein's retrospective accounts would suggest. She ignored all that did not fit her scheme, or claimed that certain of her works illustrated that scheme when they manifestly did not. Because

264

she was perpetually engaged in a search for self-knowledge, her statements were generally incomplete, contradictory, and clouded. Reading her in chronological order then is tantamount to retrieving all of a writer's rough drafts from his wastebasket. Since she usually chose to regard her trial statements as true to the moment, even those which turned out to be wrong possessed a validity for her equal to any conceived in certainty. So, if those ideas about identity which she murkily advanced in *The Geographical History of America* became clarified in "What Are Master-Pieces," it is important not to forget the tentativeness of her original articulation of those ideas. And, the reader must remain armed against the temptation to filter and accentuate meanings in the obscurer work in light of subsequent knowledge.

Rather than step back to appraise her accomplishments with the objectivity of a craftsman, Gertrude Stein assessed her writing subjectively. Her state of mind when composing was what was evaluated. If she were wholly absorbed in the subject at hand, she was existing in that superior condition of the human mind. Then anything that emanated from her was certified good.

The peculiar consequence of this position was that as she explained why masterpieces were exempt from necessity and relation, she apologized for the confusion of her argument. She explained that she had been writing on the subject all summer and therefore could not help "remembering" what she thought, rather than confronting the problem afresh. This meant her ideas were couched in "secondary writing" which she believed could never be clear. The argument turned everything upside down. At the very moment that, from a benighted point of view, she was profiting from her previous considerations of the problem and therefore producing the clearest presentation of her ideas yet, she apologized for her confusion. And, as for the earlier and ambiguous versions in *The Geographical History of America,* she insisted upon their clarity. "If you do not remember while you are writing, it may seem confused to others but actually it is clear" (*WAM,* 89).

The primeval disorder of her subjective consciousness was closer to reality for Gertrude Stein than any revised and polished version. It is of course conceivable that sometime in the future her unpremeditated associations *will* be accepted as manifestly more psychologically accurate and even clearer than those statements that have been shaped to conform to conventional demands.

"How Writing Is Written" is the transcript of a rather casual and self-assured talk Gertrude Stein gave to the students of the Choate

265

School.* It was something of a valedictory. She again argued her case that the artist expresses the contemporary time-sense in a way that will inevitably be ugly and for the most part rejected by his generation. She did not regard herself as exempt from this critical blindness. "If you kids started in to write, I wouldn't be a good judge of you . . . What you are going to do I don't know any more than anyone else" (*Oxford Anthology of American Literature*, 1447). She left them with two problems to consider: first, that there was now no essential difference between prose and poetry; second, that literature must now produce excitement without relying upon the crutch of events. Their solution, she concluded, "is up to you" (1451).

"How Writing Is Written" does illustrate Gertrude Stein's contention that familiarity deadens expression. None of the intensity and involvement normally present in Gertrude Stein's work can be felt in it. Such is not the case with "What Are Master-Pieces" and Gertrude Stein explained why. Originally she had intended to "talk" this lecture rather than write it, but then decided not to because "talking essentially has nothing to do with creation" (84). Therefore, she prepared her ideas in advance of delivering them, even though she admitted that some of its ideas were still "remembered."

Her central proposition remained that masterpieces were less important than their creator. Never had it been clearer than in this lecture that Gertrude Stein was now defending her art by referring to an unverifiable state of being. If all people could escape identity and exist perpetually in the human mind, the number of masterpieces was potentially infinite. It was identity, which she translated as existence verified and affected by other beings or by the past, that ruined creativity. "Before there is an audience anything written is as important as any other thing . . ." (*WAM*, 94). Identity was a manifestation of human nature. The two key sentences of *The Geographical History of America*, "I am I because my little dog knows me" and "What is the use of being a boy if you are going to grow up to be a man" were brought forward again. Each represented a form of tyranny over the self. When the little dog knows you are you, and you *realize* that he knows, "that is what makes school" and "that is what destroys creation" (*WAM*, 84–85).

---

* The talk is not an altogether trustworthy example of Gertrude Stein's actual style. It was recorded by a stenographer who "had difficulties" in transcribing it (Dudley Fitts to GS, 18 January 1935, YCAL). Fitts wrote her, "I had to 'restore' a great deal of the lecture from memory . . . Sorry to have missed entirely what you said about the noun; but the text was so corrupt that I couldn't do anything with it" (5 February 1935, YCAL).

266

Your awareness of something outside conferring reality on you makes it impossible for you to concentrate upon your subject. In correspondence, for example, "the letter writes what the other person is to hear and so . . . there are two present instead of one and so once again creation breaks down" (86). Audience had a truly fearsome power. "After the audience begins, naturally they create something that is they create you . . ." (95).

Her ideal she now designated "entity," or the concentrated self. "Identity" contained her objection to it in its root: the word assumes similarity, repetition. But for Gertrude Stein repetition signified morbidity. The only time repetition occurred, she declared, was when something was learned ("How Writing Is Written," *Oxford Anthology of American Literature*, 1451). So, if the artist was attentive to the expectation of his audience, then he was lured into repetition by trying to fulfill expectations already conceived. The cost was betrayal of the self's vitality. If this position was remote from that of the young woman who sent her messages to the world in *The Making of Americans*, Gertrude Stein now felt it necessary to repudiate the past, saying it was "merely a literary formalism for if I did write for myself and strangers . . . then identity would take the place of entity" (86).

The other threat to entity was memory. It chained one to time. Boy and man were unrelated except through identity, through birth certificates and aunts (external recognition) and memory (internal recognition). If the adult accepted his connection with the child he had once been, he yielded to human nature, to continuity, and to necessity (93). That was a condition Gertrude Stein could not accept at sixty-one. A genius was "eternally young" (90).

The experience of reading the same lectures to unknown faces in unfamiliar auditoriums and of answering the same questions for scores of interviewers made Gertrude Stein aware of the destructiveness of public recognition. After years of seeking fame, she realized the need to protect her private self lest it be engulfed by the crowd. Her personal condition of threatened independence seemed magnified in the United States as a whole. In a series of six Saturday essays commissioned by the New York *Herald Tribune*, Gertrude Stein revealed her conservatism. She tentatively speculated in them that perhaps the apathy of college students was attributable to their having had too much freedom before they left home. For young people of her own day, she remembered, going away to college represented liberation. Further, she wondered if governments were not too big, and if the voters really wanted everything to be easy ("American Education and Colleges," *NYHT*, 16 March 1935, 15; and "The Capital and Capitals of the United States of America," *NYHT*, 9 March 1935, 11).

Her concern centered upon Franklin Roosevelt whom she regarded as not truly American because he failed to keep in mind that the United States was a vast country in which one could wander more or less indifferent to the government. Both he and his cousin Teddy "feel it to be a little country which they can govern" ("A Political Series," *PL*, 74). She suspected Roosevelt of spending money lavishly in order to secure his re-election (72). She believed he threatened private life, even though she defined private life as "when not everybody is being fed" (76). By taking away their initiative, welfare was weakening the American people. When applied, her transcendental notions of the human mind turned instantly into rugged individualism. In part, Gertrude Stein attributed the people's attraction to strong national leadership to the habit of obedience they had acquired during the first World War. In that time of crisis, they had been conditioned to obey. "The difficulty about Hitlerism and Fascism and Rooseveltism is that everybody is used to it even before they really hear what they are told to do" (76).

Although these particular opinions about the New Deal remained unpublished in Gertrude Stein's lifetime, they can be detected in "What Are Master-Pieces." There, however, "identity" is made the culprit. "If there was no identity no one could be governed" (*WAM*, 94). But regrettably, people were governed by the expectations of others. Governments were omnipresent, but still, they were not interesting, "because master-pieces are exactly what they are not" (94). Dismayed by what she had observed while touring the United States, Gertrude Stein extended her political sympathies not to radical experimentation but to the moderate conservatism of the century in which she grew up.

13

꼭. "Look facts in the face look facts in the face look facts in the face."

("Nest of Dishes")

When Gertrude Stein was planning *Everybody's Autobiography,* she anticipated it would be more sombre than its predecessor. The first auto-biography had been "gay" she wrote in 1934, but her new one would be "rather sad" ("And Now," *Vanity Fair* [September 1934], 35). After *Everybody's Autobiography* failed to sell particularly well follow-ing its publication in 1937, she told her publisher that she believed "the reviewers did it harm . . . it is not a reviewers book but it is a people's book . . ." (GS to Bennett Cerf, January 1938, YCAL). Later that same year she reiterated her sense of its peculiar quality: ". . . it is a funny book, it seems to bite very deeply much more so than the Auto-biography . . ." (GS to Bennett Cerf, 24 August 1938, YCAL). She felt so because throughout this very personal book she had wrestled with the newly resurrected spectre of death.

With its cast of established celebrities and plentiful stock of bon mots, *The Autobiography of Alice B. Toklas* was the more conservative book of the two. In *Everybody's Autobiography* the witty precision of Miss Toklas's mind gave way to the garrulousness of Miss Stein's. But Ger-trude Stein had evidently learned something, for that garrulousness was no longer pointless as it occasionally was in the latter parts of the *Auto-biography.* She had discovered how to carry the reader to a satisfying conclusion on its low-keyed charm. As this is difficult to convey ab-stractly, here is an example. In it, she reports a Southerner's response to her opinion that Robert E. Lee was not heroic for the reason that he had *knowingly* led his people to defeat.

> I said this one day down in Charleston, I was talking to some man who had a Southern wife and a Southern father-in-law, who was an important Southern newspaper editor and he said that is interesting

because my father-in-law one day it was a rainy Sunday and some
body said something about Lee and my father-in-law said yes he
was a great man a great great man and we all love him and I
sometimes think that if he had been here of a rainy Sunday well yes
I would not want him here all day of a rainy Sunday. (247)

That single sentence contains evidence aplenty of independent historical judgment, a deadpan wit, a good ear for colloquial speech, and
a strong feeling for rhetorical climax. It amply fulfills the requirement
of telling something simply and despite its apparent rambling, the
passage cannot be reduced without loss. In order to reach the concord
of opinion between Gertrude Stein and the editor, all the details are
essential. Or rather, to reach not concord but agreement sufficient for
peace. She says Lee was a moral coward, the man says that Lee was a
bore, and both express themselves in that steady, forward-moving style
that adjusts and repeats when necessary, but keeps heading for the
compact conclusion that will validate the route taken.

As she composed *Everybody's Autobiography* Gertrude Stein worried
about its quality. "I am telling it now so simply," she mused part way
through, "that perhaps it is not anything" (107). She recognized the
danger she ran in recording her apparently guileless reflections on how
the success of the *Autobiography* had affected her. But it was a risk she
was willing to take in order to achieve a narrative that would tell what
was happening, something she thought the first autobiography had
failed to do, for it had merely described what *had* happened (302–3).
In her Chicago lectures on narration she had announced the need for
narrative to adjust to new conceptions of the world, in particular to the
loss of belief in causality. *Everybody's Autobiography* explicitly represented her attempt to carry out her ideas. Even before she had left for
the United States, she had informed Thornton Wilder that narrative
worried her. "No one in our time had really been able to tell anything
without anything but just telling that thing" she declared, a judgment
that just pricked Hemingway in passing (107). For not only had *In
Our Time* been the title of his first important collection of stories, but
in 1935 he had published *Green Hills of Africa*. In the foreword to this
first-person account of his African hunting safari, Hemingway had said
that his goal had been to see if "an absolutely true book" could have
the imaginative impact of fiction. Gertrude Stein was indirectly pronouncing his enterprise a failure, while at the same time declaring her
own entry into the competition. "I was going to try once more to try
to simply tell something" (107).

That try, *Everybody's Autobiography*, began with the writing of *The Autobiography of Alice B. Toklas,* then moved steadily forward in time until it reached the present, that is, April 1937, when Gertrude Stein flew to London to see her play, "They Must. Be Wedded. To Their Wife," performed as a ballet under the title of "A Wedding Bouquet" by the Sadler's Wells Company. Having caught up with itself at this point, the book took on the contemporaneity of a diary. "Next Friday we go to London . . ." (314). Gertrude Stein captured the impression of time contained within itself. After announcing that the premiere would be tomorrow, she began her next paragraph, "It was tomorrow which was yesterday and it was exciting . . ." (317).

It was within the chronological framework that experimentation with narrative technique took place. Gertrude Stein achieved mobility by means of digressions that purposefully followed the paths of association. This not only allowed flashbacks in time, but it also permitted the connection of subjects that would normally be separated in a continuous narrative, even though they were actually linked in the author's mind. The resulting mix of time, free of strict historical channeling, produced "everybody's" autobiography.

The "Introduction" provides a model of how the associative method works in *Everybody's Autobiography.* It consists of five anecdotes, each pegged to a specific person, and each carrying a thematic burden.

After announcing that, Alice Toklas having done her autobiography, "anybody" will now do "theirs," Gertrude Stein is immediately reminded, she tells us, of Dashiell Hammett. But first, arbitrarily, she wants "to say that just today I met Miss Hennessy and she was carrying, she did not have it with her, but she usually carried a wooden umbrella" (3). Consideration of Hammett is therefore postponed so that Miss Hennessy can make her one and only appearance in the book. Through her, Gertrude Stein suggests the commingling of time in the mind. Because Miss Hennessy had been encountered this day, the memory of her was fresh. For the consciousness, it was true to say that Miss Hennessy did and did not have her wooden umbrella with her. She could be said to have had it because that was always her principal identifying feature, even though this particular day she did not happen to have it with her.

The umbrella is an exact replica of a real one, but when it rains it cannot be opened, which does make Miss Hennessy look "a little foolish." That does not bother her, however, inasmuch as hers is the only wooden umbrella in Paris. Should the reader balk at the logic of eccentricity, Gertrude Stein makes the necessary extension. Even if there were innumerable wooden umbrellas in Paris, she says, "it would not make any difference" to Miss Hennessy (3). Her umbrella is an artifact, of no practical use but pleasing nonetheless. Miss Hennessy stands for fidelity to one's own values, whether they are unique or commonplace. Her quirky independence is an appropriate starting-point for this universal autobiography.

This anecdote has reminded Gertrude Stein of one David Edstrom, but since Dashiell Hammett has precedence, she takes him next. At her request she had dined with the author of that recent success, *The Thin Man* (1934). In the course of their conversation, she told Hammett that it puzzled her that in the nineteenth century male novelists could create numerous and different male characters, whereas the female novelists could only create versions of themselves. Now, in the twentieth century, the situation was reversed. "The men all write about themselves" (5). Why? The creator of the cynical and urbane private detective thought he knew the answer: modern male writers lacked confidence and consequently they devoted all their efforts to creating a superior image of themselves.

This anecdote would seem to be another indirect hit at Hemingway, the epitome of those hyper-masculine authors who write about themselves "as strong or weak or mysterious or passionate or drunk or controlled but always themselves" (5). There is the additional implication that if the male writers have lost confidence, then females may replace them. Gertrude Stein does not say as much, but her first remark after the Hammett episode is, "Anyway autobiography is easy like it or not . . ." (6).

Before Gertrude Stein can take up David Edstrom, he reminds her of yet another person. This time though, she deals with Edstrom first. "But what reminded me of David Edstrom was that he used to complain so that I liked everybody in character" (6). Miss Hennessy's peculiarity had originally stimulated this association. Gertrude Stein recalled that when she was young she "thought everybody had a character" and therefore she had indeed "liked everybody in character" (6). But now, indifferent to the security of permanent classification, Gertrude Stein found it a matter of indifference whether people were in character or not. "Anything that is is quite enough if it is" (6).

Edstrom's wish to be photographed with Gertrude Stein during her American trip stirred up yet another memory, an incident involving

Mary Pickford—"a short little woman with a large head and there were curls . . ." (7). Mary Pickford had proposed a joint photograph, but when Gertrude Stein agreed at once, the cinema queen's suspicions were aroused and she disappeared. Gertrude Stein's friends explained that "if I were enthusiastic it meant that I thought it would do me more good than it would do her and so she melted away . . ." (8). The problems of a public identity were very much on Gertrude Stein's mind. Later, she wrote that "it always did bother me that the American public were more interested in me than in my work" (50).

The fifth anecdote brings the "Introduction" to a close by describing recognition, true because it is selfless. Two Negroes exemplify its practice. One, an elderly man Gertrude Stein encountered on a stairs, identified himself as the music teacher of one of the leading singers in *Four Saints in Three Acts.* "I wanted to say how do you do to you." The other, "a young colored woman," met Gertrude Stein as she passed a bookstore in which *Portraits and Prayers* was displayed with her photograph on the cover. The young woman's gesture was mysteriously benign, that of a protective spirit. She "smiled and slowly pointed . . . and she smiled and went away" (8). Gertrude Stein's lesson is that, unlike the pretentious and dishonest, "anybody" is real. "Anybody" has confidence, is unmotivated by ulterior motives, is courteous and loving, recognizes the genuine article, and does not trouble others. Miss Hennessy, the Negroes, herself: these were the models.

The "Introduction" gives an instructive sample of the associative logic that is to guide the book's movement; at the same time it establishes Gertrude Stein's ideal of actuality—unique, eccentric, and true to self.

Close analysis cannot capture the rich concision of the original, every detail of which is tellingly used. For example, the commercial orientation of the sculptor David Edstrom is suggested by the casual comment that when they met he "was doing a statue of some benefactor was it Jenny Lind or Grace Darling or Florence Nightingale, well anyway . . ." (6). Similarly, the venal hospitality a celebrity must endure appears, without rancor, in the observation: "In New York a great many places wanted us to come that was natural enough but we did not go . . ." (6–7). "Places" sought her, not people.

Although *Everybody's Autobiography* concerns two unusual years in the life of a specific person, its conclusions transcend her particular experience. For example, the social unrest pervading France in 1934 impressed Gertrude Stein. There were threats of civil war, poster battles, street skirmishes, and general public apprehension over what was taking place in Spain. Much of this Gertrude Stein observed while walking her dog. So she used Basket as a focal point through which she could indicate the class conflict as well as the common humanity beneath it. The banal, somewhat comic, core of man is expressed in the conversations which she said inevitably took place concerning her poodle:

> . . . they say I have not seen one before and is he sweet and I say yes very sweet and they say and he must have cost a lot of money and I say he was given to me and they say but what a care to take care of him . . . (97)

More follows in the same vein. As Gertrude Stein observed, "this is always the conversation and to everybody it is pleasing" (97). Indeed, she believed the book's appeal was "to serious hard-working men . . ." (GS to Bennett Cerf, 24 August 1938, YCAL). Throughout the book she used casual exchanges to express the kindness and shrewdness of the common man. Gertrude Stein was especially skillful at recording the laconic dialogue of the American Laborer. For example, in Chicago she went to rent a car:

> . . . I said to the man but this garage is too far away, when I come home in the evening I would not want to come all this way to put it away. Why he said where are you living, in a little street off the Midway I said, well he said, well I said, well he said what is the matter with it . . . and I said you mean I can leave it there all night I said and he said why not . . . (261)

This solid, commonsensical world prevails throughout *Eeverybody's Autobiography*, exemplified by French peasant, noblewoman and American garage mechanic alike. Around and over it swirl the disturbances of the era. So, in addition to the inevitable conversation concerning Basket, Gertrude Stein also reported the responses her poodle evoked from particular persons. Once when he was enclosed in her car, another dog sought unsuccessfully to join him. His mistress lugubriously lamented, "My poor dog you had wanted to play with a rich dog but it was not to be no my poor dog" (97). Another evening, hostility came boiling weirdly out of a man who "said in a song as he was walking, Piss you dog piss against the side of a house in passing, if it was my house I would take a gun and shoot you . . ." (97).

The social unrest resulting from the depressed economy frequently erupts in *Everybody's Autobiography*. "All the time that I am writing,"

274

Gertrude Stein remarked, "the Spanish revolution obtrudes itself" (88). When the civil war began, it frightened her French neighbors, "really scared them, scared them because it was so near . . ." (307). She felt safest in making local specific observations. She was willing to hazard an opinion, as when she was telephoned from America about the possibility of war. She did not think there would be one, "but as I am most generally always wrong perhaps there is" (40).

Although the sensibility through which this turbulent world was viewed was that of a woman in her later middle age, the scene is varied, for she was a woman with a lively curiosity. Her experiences extend from taking tea at the White House to viewing the Chicago ghetto in a police car. She may talk with Braque at one moment and in the next, quote her cook. At times she is fearful and admits it. Lecturing, flying, and driving in the mountains all alarmed her at first, although in each instance she quickly recovered her normal appreciative cheerfulness. The one emotion she lacked in her writing was indignation. Her capacity for tolerance is most remarkably expressed in an incident that concerned some corn seed sent to her by a liberal American friend. He asked her not to give any to the local fascists. Gertrude Stein's response was, "Why not if the fascists like it, and we liked the fascists, so I said please send us unpolitical corn" (309).

She did have a conservative bias in political and economic matters, but not in human terms, although the sheer number of people living in the world did worry her. Her long odyssey through dozens of lecture halls and receptions contributed to her remark that "the only thing that really bothers me is that the earth now is all covered over with people . . ." (101). The volume of humanity reduced the possibilities of individualism, while encouraging mass movements. "Generally speaking when a population gets large they cannot do their own thinking . . . organization is what they do . . ." (205). (In a personal attempt to reduce the dehumanizing effect of masses of people, she refused ever to lecture to more than five hundred people [176].) The Roosevelt administration continued to worry her, because she feared its ideology would stifle individualism. She was certain its monetary policy was unsound. Her characteristically homely way of expressing her scepticism was that while the budget was always planned in round numbers, the taxes collected to meet that budget were always taken in uneven numbers. How, she asked, "could so many uneven sums make an even one and how could that even sum be paid out again into uneven ones and not leave something the matter" (307–8).

In five articles on money, she had already aired her economic opinions in *The Saturday Evening Post,* and realized that her views made younger people call her "reactionary" (310–11). With her crackerbarrel shrewdness, her nostalgia for individualism and the joys of dirt-farming, and her suspicions of the New Deal Congress, she proved unexpectedly suitable for the *Post* audience.*

Money intrigued her because like celebrity it had changed both her and her writing. But even though she wanted to be rich, she insisted, "I never want to do what there is to do to get rich" (128). And she added impishly, "There are some things a girl cannot do" (129). However, the acquisition of money striking her as an antidote to socialism, "just at present my passion is avarice." This notion ran counter to the modern tide, she realized, for "the Americanization of everything has driven avarice out of every one and I do not like it" (128). Wealth was a reality to her, but a metaphor too for the concentration of one's inner resources.

Knowing that she now possessed a commercial value had affected her writing. "As long as the outside does not put a value on you it remains outside," she said, thinking of her long career as an unpublished writer, "but when it does put a value on you then . . . all your inside gets to be outside" (47). Private meditations then become, at least potentially, public property, and that knowledge blocked her creativity. "There was no word inside me. And I was not writing" (64).

Her identity was shaken and undergoing a transformation. "Everything in living is made up of finding out what you are . . ." (92). Gertrude Stein now distinguished three stages in her career: knowing self through recognition by the outer world (one's dog); being known for one's work by a public that refused to purchase it; and having the public pay for what one created. Each stage had affected her identity—"you are not the same you" (45). Since Gertrude Stein's theory of composition depended upon an integrated self, the disturbance was devastating. A name was not sufficient in itself to hold an identity together she had discovered. Names, she now suspected, were unimportant. She had noticed that her Indochinese servants sometimes went under pseudonyms and "they seem to be there or not there as well with any name" (10).

The American trip furnished her more clues to the enigma of self. She had to confront all the sophisticated means of exploiting a "person-

* See issues of 13 June, 11 July, 25 July, 22 August, and 10 October 1936.

ality." One protective measure she took was to refuse to be introduced to audiences. Hearing another person speak of her only unnerved her (177). Even the audiences lured her outside herself. "You were yourself," however, only when "you were there to you inside you . . ." (298). She now suspected that being known by one's dog "only proved the dog was he and not that I was I" (297).

At the same time that Gertrude Stein was describing the effect of her new celebrity upon her, she moved back into the past, probing, explaining, justifying it. She returned to her childhood, then followed her friendship with Leo up to its final rupture when he expressed his scepticism about her early literary efforts. Leo was confident that his sister had not found a way to reflect her age. Gertrude Stein expressed the memory of his cruelly negative opinion in one concentrated and stylized outburst:

> He said it was not it it was I. If I was not there to be there with what I did then what I did would not be what it was. (76)

Leo's doubts "destroyed him for me" (77).

That strange figure, the author William Seabrook, had stimulated this exploration of the past. The unnaturalness of the summer of 1933 when he visited her in Bilignin continued to obsess her. Following immediately upon the success of the *Autobiography,* it had been accompanied by the disturbing consequences of fame. She had described that summer in *Blood On The Dining-Room Floor* and now in *Everybody's Autobiography,* she returned to it. Three circumstances distinguished that "queer" season. First, she and Alice were obliged to endure a series of unsatisfactory servants. The anomaly was that in periods of general unemployment, it proved especially difficult to get anyone to work. Gertrude Stein thought she understood why. "If everybody is unemployed everybody loses the habit of work and work like revolutions is a habit . . ." (54). The two women expended prodigious energy in locating, interviewing, and trying out four sets of servants. The household confusion only augmented her impression that success was shaking her world to pieces.

Next, she suffered sabotage, an open expression of malice. One day neither her car nor that of a visitor would start. Moreover, the telephone was discovered to be out of order. When the garage mechanic arrived, he found water in her gas tank, a piece of cloth in the distributor, and broken spark plugs. The culprit appeared to be their valet de chambre, so he was dismissed. What motivated his ill-will is never explained, if indeed it was known.

Finally, two women acquaintances of her age died violently. In each instance, the official verdict was suicide, but the deaths were equivocal, especially that of the English woman who lived with a French woman, Madame Caesar, in the neighborhood. "They both wore trousers and raised chickens and turkeys" (61). Debts and jealousy were involved. The result was the demise of the English woman in a ravine with two bullets in her head. "Doctors said no one ever shoots themselves twice," Gertrude Stein noted thoughtfully. Therefore, "any one was frightened" of Madame Caesar, and they stopped seeing her (83).*

In the midst of this eerie summer during which the worst she could imagine came into being, William Seabrook arrived. While Gertrude Stein does not specify Seabrook's behavior during his visit, it was very probably irregular since he was then drinking so heavily that before the year was out he had voluntarily committed himself to a mental hospital.† Although Gertrude Stein never saw him again, it was he who drew out her recollections of herself and her brother. Her relationship to Leo was an important psychological fact in her life that she had largely evaded in the earlier autobiography. His loss obviously troubled her still, "We always had been together and now we were never at all together" (77). As she recounts it to Seabrook in the book, the estrangement was inevitable and the responsibility of neither. Her tone is conciliatory and yet, since she evidently regarded the separation as permanent, tinged with melancholy.

The next time that Gertrude Stein mentioned her youth at any length,

---

* Whether Madame Caesar is an actual name, and whether the name is related to the "Caesars" that appear frequently in Gertrude Stein's erotic prose of 1915–25 is at best still a matter of conjecture. Gertrude Stein reviewed the suspicious deaths in two short pieces also composed in 1936, some of whose sentences were drawn from *Blood On The Dining-Room Floor*. (See, for example, "Is Dead," *Occident* [April 1937], 6; and *Blood*, 12–13.) "A Water-Fall And a Piano" adds the information that Mme. Caesar's original companion, Mme. Steiner, was an orphan, whose mother had been insane, and whose father permitted himself to be killed in the war because of his wife's illness. This new information increases the possibility that Mme. Steiner might have committed a crime of passion against her successor (*New Directions* [1936], n.p.). "Is Dead' tells us that Mme. Pernollet died after five days of a broken back, and that some five years earlier her husband had been unfaithful to her. It directly questions whether she could have died while sleepwalking (*Occident*, 6–8).

† In *Asylum* (1935), Seabrook does not refer to the Bilignin visit. He does indicate that he regarded Gertrude Stein's literary eccentricities as "deliberate and intentional" (96).

it was to describe her childish alarm at realizing the finiteness of man, and, more specifically, her own vulnerability. A play on words was the cue for this section of reminiscence. When someone made money from the sale of her autobiography, the mother of two friends commented mordantly, "and when I think how often you tell the history of your lives for nothing" (114).

At its second level, the sardonic parental remark speaks for the meaninglessness of human life. With that, Gertrude Stein then recalled her surprise when at "about eight" she discovered that the Old Testament had a God, but made no reference to either "a future life or eternity" (114). This first awareness of her mortality was supplemented by reading about "the excavations of Nineveh." These made her realize that other civilizations had passed and been buried. At the same time, an even more comprehensive awareness came over her, that "the stars were worlds and the earth only one of them . . ." (115). To these cosmic traumas was added a fear of dying, or even more devastating, of never having been born, a threat that had become actualized for Gertrude Stein when she accidentally overheard that her parents had set a limit of five children for the family. Therefore, "if two little ones had not died there would be no Gertrude Stein" (115).

After long suppressing these morbid thoughts, now at sixty-two, Gertrude Stein reported that one morning she found herself drumming the rhythm of a tune she used to hear bands play in San Francisco— the Chopin funeral march (116). Other people seemed to her to have diverted themselves from the idea of death with numbers. "Counting" she thought "is all there is of religion for them" (118). She could sympathize with that strategy for relief, having herself been attracted by the self-contained abstraction of numbers during her short-lived enthusiasm for existence in the "human mind" (see GHA, 90). But it had proved inadequate for her. Nor did she suppose that she had found a solution. Gertrude Stein's merit was that she retained a sombre view of life, without losing courage. Candid enough to admit her moments of foolishness, belligerence, and fear, she nonetheless maintained her equanimity for the most part. Even though the vacancy of the universe appalled her, she did her best to proclaim the adequacy of the present moment.

As a therapeutic verbalization of her most perplexing problems, *Everybody's Autobiography* also reconsidered Gertrude Stein's father, and authoritarian figures in general. The topic emerged without warning, unleashed by the deceptively casual note: "Thornton Wilder writes to us these days and says he is shamelessly happy and now he has no father" (132). Gertrude Stein's thematic line was that "fathers are depressing" (132). After her own experience of years under the irritable, capricious tyranny of Daniel Stein, she preferred freedom. She professed herself a student of French families that had lost a parent. Her conclusion was that "when the father dies or the mother and it is a large family and the children are all old enough," then the children relish their new freedom as orphans"—just as the Stein children had found their life without father "a very pleasant one" (142).

Gertrude Stein remained a loyal partisan of freedom. She was as disturbed by the seductive winning of assent as by its tyrannical enforcement. Her visit to the Choate School made her wonder if the students would "ever come to be themselves." The sweet reasonableness of the teachers made believers of the boys too soon (241). She now feared certainty, not least because it deadened human responsiveness. "The only thing that does make anybody older is that they cannot be surprised" (40). American schools and colleges however graduated products that were all too predictable. That realization led her to ask herself, "Well what had I been" (242). Gertrude Stein's answer constitutes the philosophic heart of *Everybody's Autobiography*.

When her ideas were being formed in college, Gertrude Stein said, neither religion nor philosophy were of interest, because they represented nothing more than "satisfaction in a solution" (242). It was the idea of evolution and the methods of science that attracted the allegiance of young people then, for they were both open-ended. "Science meant that a solution was a way to a problem" (242). This belief was undermined for her by William James though, when he informed her that science was neither a solution nor a problem but merely "a statement of the observation of things observed and perhaps therefore not interesting perhaps therefore only abjectly true" (242).

Gertrude Stein added William James's opinion to her long-standing awareness that civilizations disappear and are replaced by new ones. Then wasn't one as good as the next? If so, of what interest could either science or progress be? The validity of the argument was of less importance than its attraction for Gertrude Stein. It drove her inside herself to find an escape from the fear of death. Science erected paper laws "to keep everyone from knowing that they are not going on living" (243). But these could not dissolve Gertrude Stein's anguish—"I had always been afraid always would be afraid . . ." (243). So she chose the course of the "completely wise," of the "genius." That meant "existing without any internal recognition of time," even while one lived in time (243).

Gertrude Stein tried to distinguish her position from James's notion of the will to live. She was not proposing an innate urge for survival that manifested itself in an irresistible, frantic engagement with the outer world. By existing, she meant internal, concentrated receptivity. The alert openness of this posture bore upon her critique of formal education. Answers were predictable completions of formulae, whereas questions opened out into infinite possibility. The first was the mechanical way of causality, the second of immortality. "Listening to an answer makes you know that time is existing but asking a question makes you think that perhaps it does not" (244). "Perhaps"—she was aware that this strategy for eliminating the fear of death by temporarily blanking out the movement of time was illusory. Still, for the moment it was effective.

Gertrude Stein's own experience however had proved the tentativeness of her solution. Her self-possession had been severely shaken during that "strange year" of 1933, and as she wrote things continued to seem strange—"the blue of the sky looks rather black to the eye" (65). Her preparations for the trip to the United States, to which she devoted a long chapter in *Everybody's Autobiography*, involved thinking about herself, her writing, her country of domicile, and her country of birth. She felt the need to compose her mind to meet the shock of fame.

The actual American tour is described sequentially. Whatever occurred, wherever Gertrude Stein went, she reported her feelings. The experiences were varied, ranging from a Yale-Dartmouth football game to following the trial of Bruno Hauptmann in the newspapers. The two women first visited New York, then the midwest, then New England, then the South and southwestern United States, and finally reached California which each had left some thirty years before. California appropriately culminated their experience of revisiting the past, even as it concluded Gertrude Stein's account of the American journey.

Gertrude Stein discovered that visiting places she had frequented as a girl was not pleasant. She toured them with reluctance and "did not like anything that was happening," for the environment of her youth reminded her of the passage of time, and by extension, of death (291). The Yosemite redwoods alone kindled her enthusiasm. By exaggerating the shallowness of their root systems, she could assert that they had "no roots," thereby proving that "the oldest and the solidest and the biggest tree that could be grown had no foundation . . ." (287). Nature had provided her proof that eminence and endurance were possible without history.

Gertrude Stein believed that the need to escape the consciousness of time's passage drove men to drink and to war. Only the genius could be aware of time yet escape it, "accept it and deny it by creating it" (281). The basic paradox was built into human experience. "You live on this earth and . . . yet there is a space where the stars are which is unlimited and that contradiction is there in every man and every woman and so nothing ever does get settled" (308). Incapable of synthesizing the knowledge of the finite and the infinite as the genius does, people oscillate discontentedly from one pole to the other. In peace they want war; in war, peace. Americans prided themselves on their superiority to Europe, yet they visited Europe to see what it had.

Her objection to repetition was that it permitted the mind to slide away from concentrating upon its work, so that it became aware of itself. She realized the seductiveness of repetition for the artist, who has achieved a fresh statement at great cost. But it was deadening. "If you do it again then you know you are doing it again and it is not interesting" (28). It was for that reason that she had given up diagramming human character types in *The Making of Americans*. "Since it could be done what was the use of doing it" (266). Painters rejected repetition too when they abandoned using models. Since Picasso, "they paint with what is inside them . . . and the only thing that is outside them is the painting" (29). The dynamism of the painting came not from reproducing "a thing moving" but from "the thing painted having inside it the existence of moving" (311).

The novel she now pronounced dead. Because of the impersonality created by the crowded conditions of this world, fictional characters were no longer of interest to readers. It was time for meditations (102). The only kind of fiction still possible, she thought, was the detective story, for the enigmatic reason that "the only person of any importance is dead" (102). She also liked the unpredictability of the detective story. "The great point" about truly creative work, she argued, "is that it really holds your attention" (263). The virtue of held attention was that it prevented one from brooding on death, something that people had previously found everyday existence sufficient for, since they believed that immortality awaited them. However, "hardly any one is really con-

vinced now that if they live every day that they will go on living . . ."
(263). So to relieve their anxiety, people needed something that would
thoroughly engage their attention.

Ultimately, she was obliged to rely upon intuition for certitude.
Understanding, rationality, mechanism she associated with "organization." A machine was "the only thing that says the same thing to any
and every one" (290). Lucid and complete explanation could be more
misleading than hints. "If you have dim lights and you add another,"
she said, "perhaps it makes less light to your feeling than if you only
have one dim one . . ." The full paradox then followed—"if you have
enough of them then you are in total darkness anyway to your feeling . . ." (308). It was a point that she would dramatize shortly in
Doctor Faustus Lights the Lights. The more life was ordered, the more
oppressive it became. "Feeling" resides under thought. One of her
favorite illustrations of the stultifying effect of civilization concerned
dogs. Formerly, they howled at the moon, but now, with streetlights and
automobile headlights, dogs are no longer excited by the moon appearing out of the darkness, and do not bark (92, 283).

Her human models of pure being were saints. They do nothing, she
insisted, for "a saint existing was everything" (283). These were not
ascetics or martyrs, for Gertrude Stein focused upon the sanctified
qualities of self-possession and cheerfulness, upon that imperturbability
that emanated from pure faith. She showed a momentary but undeveloped interest in Eastern culture. With the possibility that "Europe
is finished," she hinted that the "peaceful penetration" of Asian influence might bring calm and intuitive grace into western lives. Something was needed. "Everybody knows if you are too careful . . . you
are sure to stumble . . ." (11).

The book concludes with a springtime prothalamion, "A Wedding
Bouquet." The conclusion starts in a festively redemptive mood. The
flight to England was pleasant with the airplane's "peaceful hum" and
"unequal rocking" (315). London was cheerful, and the production
of her play as a ballet was well-received. The purpose of the trip made
Gertrude Stein recall the first play she ever wrote. Its title was, suitably,
"Snatched From Death," but its subtitle, "The Sundered Sisters," was
less serene. Its menacing undertones build against the melody of contentment, and climax in Gertrude Stein's account of her curtain calls
after the performance. It is a complex gathering of reiterated actions

283

going nowhere, of facing and saluting the void, and then of falling back. The sentence deserves careful reading to appreciate the degree of pessimism present in her memory of this auspicious occasion.

> And then gradually it was ending and we went out and on to the stage and there where I never had been with everything in front all dark and we bowing and all of them coming and going and bowing, and then again not only bowing but coming again and then as if it was everything, it was all over and we went back to sit down. (318)

"As if it was everything"! No wonder the next sentence is the equivocal, "I guess it was a great success."

On the flight back to Paris, Gertrude Stein saw the only frightening sight she had ever seen from an airplane, although she said she did not know why it frightened her. Her precise description of the phenomenon reads: "a wide layer of fog close to the water that went right down the middle of the Channel . . ." (318). The English Channel was split in half, obscurely. On the one side, "cheerful" London; on the other, "depressing" Paris. Although for the moment above the fog, Gertrude Stein sensed the symbolic aptness for her own life of that middle swath of mystery, that blankness that threatened to divide her every enterprise.

Her response to it was characteristically practical. "We gathered everything together and left for Bilignin." Then she reflected, "perhaps I am not I even if my little dog knows me . . ." Her identity remained in doubt, ". . . but anyway I like what I have and now it is today" (318). That was the end of everybody's autobiography—a declaration of acceptance and an affirmation of the present.

It is understandable that in her own day, with stories about Gertrude Stein having filled the newspapers and magazines for several years with the impression that she was a diverting eccentric, the book should have been taken as a casual production, conceived for profit and exhibiting an egotism so inflated that it could not distinguish the line between prattle and ideas meriting public attention. Today, though, it is clear that *Everybody's Autobiography* is one of her major successes. In it Gertrude Stein took up the most desperate problems she was then suffering from and managed to convey them without diminishing their complexity. With her unguarded style she produced moments of wit and illumination in the pedestrian ruck of existence. The cost was tenuousness at times and irritating confusion. But there are unappreciated depths to this book, in which humor and optimism are never allowed to discount the magnitude of human despair.

284

Near the end of *Everybody's Autobiography*, Gertrude Stein expressed the hope that someone might produce one of her plays as a play some day. *Four Saints* had appeared as an opera, "Identity" as a marionette show, and "A Wedding Bouquet" as a ballet. But no one had yet had confidence in the sufficiency of Gertrude Stein's words to carry a performance unassisted. Even she herself was uncertain. "I wonder can they" (318). Nonetheless, she wrote two plays in 1936, each based on material handled more directly in *Everybody's Autobiography*.

"A Play Called Not and Now" was derived from a Hollywood dinner party at which Gertrude Stein had met Dashiell Hammett, Charlie Chaplin, and Anita Loos. To them she added persons she had recently been introduced to, like Gertrude Atherton, or whom she already knew, like Picasso. The play represents another of Gertrude Stein's studies of the effect of celebrity. It displays famous public images circling warily around one another, exchanging trivialities. The disparity between the public and private selves is expressed in a repeated locution— "The one that looked like . . ." as in, "The one that looked like Dr. Gidon said that the one that looked like Charlie Chaplin was gone" (*LO&P*, 425). The technique is so strenuously used however, that the play as a whole is very dull.

"Listen To Me" on the other hand is one of the best plays Gertrude Stein ever created. Too long perhaps for staging, it strikes just the right balance between provocative mystery and communicative assertion. At first perplexing, it is lively enough to carry the listener along until it begins to make sense.

Its subject is the difficulty of living in a world so crowded and artificial that naturalness and individuality are virtually eliminated. Gertrude Stein used her familiar example of dogs no longer barking at the moon to prove that technology has eradicated natural mysteries. "The moon shines and no dog barks" (*LO&P*, 402). Moon madness is gone too. "Luna now . . . has nothing to do with lunatic" (404). On an earth swarming with masses of people, no one cares about developing or sustaining his uniqueness. The number of characters expands and contracts accordingly without warning, and the inquiry, "Does anybody know for certain how many characters are they" is dismissed. "There is no use counting them" (395).

Through the play moves Gertrude Stein's friend, Sir Robert Abdy, here known as "Sweet William." He is a person who is "never discouraged" but "never encouraged" either. His secret for enduring the human turmoil is to blot it out with pleasurable occupations—"because I like it there is no one there there is no earth and there are not people everywhere on it" (411, 412). Like Gertrude Stein, he relies principally upon nature for consolation. "Sweet William prepared verdure and fountains and he admired what he did" (399). But if absorption in rural pursuits permits him to forget that the earth is covered with people, as the play opens, one character remarks: "For has nothing to do with get" (387). Sweet William may never weep, but then neither does he ever express himself. His limits are patent.

Gertrude Stein's consciousness could not be satisfied by the diversion of gardening. As she revealed in a little "novel" also written in 1936 called "What Does She See When She Shuts Her Eyes," Bilignin did not protect her from her thoughts. Depending upon the inner eye had its hazards. In *Everybody's Autobiography* she had reported that "when you have been digging in the garden . . . when you close your eyes you see what you have been seeing . . . a peaceful thing" (88). The little "novel" initially says the same. "She sees the green things among which she has been working" (*MR*, 375). But at night when she closes her eyes to sleep, that vision proliferates disturbingly. "The green things then have black roots and the black roots have red stems and then she is exhausted" (375). Wherever testimony is taken in the thirties, evidence is obtained of her mental suffering. It was more bluff than truth for her to claim that "any life you look at seems unhappy but any life lived fully is fairly cheerful and whatever happens it goes on being so" (*EA*, 101).

The characters of "Listen To Me" engage in a long fourth-act discussion which begins with people's indifference to fundamental values. "The earth is all covered over with people and they do not care about it any more" (*LO&P*, 409). But, protest the characters, they have known nothing else, for they have never been here before. In fact— "Nobody knows before" (409). They simply cannot conceive of a line that has a beginning somewhere. "How can there be another end when the earth is round" (409). Everything is enclosed within itself and exists absolutely in the present. That observation momentarily puts "all the characters in tears" (409).

The characters are questing after the unity represented by a single syllable. In one syllable "there is no after or before." In *Everybody's Autobiography* Gertrude Stein had already identified one-syllable words with America. The laconic American says "everything in two words and mostly in words of one syllable" (*EA*, 203). One-syllable words have a positive value then in the play. After the sentence, "The air is there which is where it is," she suggests, "Kindly notice that is all one syllable and therefore useful" (*LO&P*, 414). Yet, there are exceptions. "War" is one syllable, and "silence," two (405, 410). It is impossible to resolve the human dilemma by enforcing the use of only one-syllable words. Opposition is built into human existence, "syllables have to be" (410). When the inevitability of this hits the characters, they laugh. "There is no argument that makes anything better" (410).

Gardening is one solution offered for survival in the play. Gallows humor is another, and eating is a third. Because "eating has nothing to do with yesterday or to-morrow . . ." one scene is set aside for baking (404). Eating would not be necessary "if anything is to happen after but oh so necessary if nothing is to happen after" and nothing is (404).

The conclusion of "Listen To Me" reduces human life to its fundamentals of action and character, existence and essence. Both will be eradicated at the end, that much is assured, that and the loneliness of man. The conclusion is exceedingly desolate.

> Acts
> Curtain
> Characters
> Characters
> Curtain
> Acts
> There is no one and one
> Nobody has met any one
> > Curtain Can Come.
> > *Curtain.* (421)

Baroness Pierlot exemplified the pessimistic stoicism that runs through "Listen To Me." In a short tribute to her Bilignin neighbor, Gertrude Stein quotes her philosophic witticisms. When someone spoke of something as natural, "No she said it is nature but it is not natural" ("La Baronne Pierlot," *PL*, 316). The conflict between the human ideal of harmony and the actual grotesqueries of this world could be endured by the Baroness and even relished, but she refused to blink at the realities. "I have enjoyed my life all the time," she said, "but there is no pleasure in it because there is so much pain" (316). In her own way, Gertrude Stein spent the rest of her life trying to approximate that position, for the disharmonies of her existence demanded resolution. She continued to try to make them sing, and in the suspension of art, sometimes succeeded.

The splendid destruction of the modern world is one of the few new

287

conceptions to be found in *Picasso,* a short study of her friend, first written in 1938, first in French, then in English. On the whole the book is a compact restatement of Gertrude Stein's ideas on art and on Picasso. She had said most of it before, so profited by her familiarity with the ideas in the ease with which she exposed them. The struggle was almost over. Except that it demanded her first sustained effort at composing in the French language, this was an unadventurous book.*

Instances of her former eloquent obscurity appear in *Picasso* only when she tries to explain why he stopped painting in the thirties and why his style changed. These were new and difficult problems and her prose contorted accordingly. She regarded Picasso as having been strongly tempted because of his sensitivity and tenderness, to share the common vision rather than remain faithful to his own. The temptation, which she well understood, was that of a saint: "to see things as he does not see them," to create forms "not seen but conceived" (42, 47). Her sympathy for Picasso was strong, for she knew the temptation to betray one's self out of kindness.

The book ends by describing the shattered modern world and yet finding splendor in it. The twentieth century "is a time when everything cracks, where everything is destroyed, everything isolates itself . . ." But for all of its chaos, Gertrude Stein found the century "more splendid" than "a period where everything follows itself" (49). Picasso's ability to perceive and render this was his glory.

She hoped the same was true for her. More convinced than ever of an irrational destructiveness abroad in the world, with her own identity threatening to splinter, and the knowledge of its eventual permanent annihilation haunting her, Gertrude Stein tried to maintain the capacity of recording the truth, and, harder still, of accepting it.

* Gertrude Stein really did compose her own French, but painfully—"never did I think that anything could be so difficult never" (GS to W. G. Rogers, December 1937, YCAL). She habitually depended upon Alice Toklas though "to reduce tenses grammar spelling and genders into some kind of order . . ." (GS to T. Wilder, 8 December 1937, YCAL). She was far from illiterate in French, even if her errors were often gross. For example, in the *Picasso* manuscript, Alice Toklas was obliged to change "ciecle" to "siècle" and "son splendeur" to "sa splendeur" (YCAL). Gertrude Stein rarely used French in her English prose, and when once she did, she immediately added: "Excuse me for introducing French it is not my custom but it seemed a choice thanks so much" ("To Kitty Or Kate Buss," *P&P,* 104).

14

ʻ᷈. "Fear can be in three places
Fear of yes
Fear of not yet
Fear of felt it as fear."
      ("Byron A Play")

Gertrude Stein's bravery is a conspicuous feature of her career. Although timorous in many respects, and far from the regally imperturbable figure she is sometimes supposed to be, Gertrude Stein did attempt to understand and put into words what disturbed her. As Europe darkened in the late thirties and private fears swooped and circled around her, she resolutely faced the menace. In several imaginative pieces that stayed within the range of a broad audience, she addressed herself to these personal anxieties.

Of these compositions, the most atypical by far was the libretto, *Doctor Faustus Lights The Lights,* written in 1938 in the expectation that Gerald Berners, who had composed the music for *A Wedding Bouquet* and thereafter commissioned this new piece from her, would do the same for it. But, demoralized by the onset of the second World War, Lord Berners found himself incapable of meeting his artistic obligations.*

Neither Marlowe's nor Goethe's version of the Faust legend seems to have been in Gertrude Stein's mind as she wrote. More likely her most direct experience with the story had been through Gounod's opera, for she still recalled *Faust* from her childhood (*LIA,* 113). Whatever the case, only the three principals remain: Faust, Mephistopheles, and Marguerite.†

---

* *Doctor Faustus* was produced as a play in 1951 at the Cherry Lane Theater in New York, with incidental music by Richard Banks.
† Allegra Stewart, noting that Gertrude Stein calls her main character by several names—Faust, Doctor Faustus, and Faustus—argues that the play is a "monodrama" taking place in the psyche of a single man, Faust. In this reading, Faustus

Doctor Faustus's problem is that he is the dissatisfied inventor of the electric light, which, since the American trip, had been on Gertrude Stein's mind. In fact, even before that visit, Carl Van Vechten had sent her photographs of her name in electric lights on Broadway. Then when she arrived in New York, "we saw an electric sign moving around a building and it said Gertrude Stein has come and that was upsetting" (*EA*, 112, 175). American technology and the threat of success to her personal identity coalesced for her in the phenomenon of electric lights to make Doctor Faustus a disgruntled Edison. Electric lights stood for the sometimes useful but never ultimately satisfying, true, or illuminating function of reason. Not that Doctor Faustus is deceived by the illusory brilliance. "I keep on having so much light that light is not bright," he complains, "and what after all is the use of light, you can see just as well without it . . ." (*LO&P*, 89–90).

More recently, in *Picasso*, Gertrude Stein, acclaiming the twentieth century as "a splendid period, not a reasonable one in the scientific sense, but splendid," had added, "reasonableness does not make for splendor" (49). Her play then chronicled the displacement of the scientific ethos in which she had been trained. Electric lighting was not only unsatisfying; it also destroyed natural responses. Doctor Faustus is accompanied by a dog and a boy, each of whom enunciates one of Gertrude Stein's favorite observations. The dog points out that because of artificial illumination, he no longer bays at the moon, while the boy attributes the disappearance of craziness to the loss of the moon (*LO&P*, 111). Both complainants speak on behalf of the superiority of instinct and intuition.

Doctor Faustus's invention is brilliant therefore but, in Gertrude Stein's stern dismissal, "not interesting in my sight" (115). Unfortunately, he has sold his soul to achieve this unsatisfactory illumination. As a consequence, in Gertrude Stein's version, he cannot go to Hell. That he is blocked from that aspiration makes Hell seem a desirable and consuming darkness rather than a feared place of punishment.

Doctor Faustus's existential vision of the world accords with Gertrude Stein's. He sees existence as limited to the present situation and

---

is his ego, his conscious will, while Doctor Faustus is his persona or social personality. (See Stewart, *Gertrude Stein*, 160–62.) Even though casualness and inconsistency in nomenclature is an identifying feature of Gertrude Stein, the reading is plausible. There are moments though, as in the first scene, when both Faustus and Doctor Faustus speak, without any evident psychic distinctions being present in their lines. Also, the antagonist is known as both Methistopheles and Mephisto.

time. "There is no hope there is no death there is no life there is no breath, there is just every day all day and when there is no day there is no day . . ." (90). As the play opens, he is irritable, chagrined by the mess of pottage he has received at the cost of his soul—if he has one. But still independent, he contemptuously kicks the ingratiating Mephisto away.

A blaze of electric lights surrounding him represents Doctor Faustus's consciousness. The play follows his release from their hard illumination. In spite of his disgust with his fate, that escape is not easy, for Doctor Faustus is a proud and intelligent man. The equivalence of the electric lights and his state of being is demonstrated early. Doctor Faustus is seated, surrounded by his lights when the dog enters and speaks what will be his theme line throughout the play, "Thank you." Instantly one of the electric lights goes out. When the dog repeats his expression of gratitude the light turns into a glow (91). The dog, like his species, perpetually expresses his thanks, which first reduces one portion of Doctor Faustus's total intellectuality, then temporarily softens its harshness.

A similar but stronger effect is made by the entrance of the little boy. Awaiting something, anticipating an "it," Doctor Faustus sings a duet with the dog: "Will it be it / Just it" (92). At that moment the lights pale and "shocked," Doctor Faustus says, "It is it." Thereupon the little boy enters to play with the dog. He announces that both the day and the moon begin this day. In other words, he heralds the present existence and the dominance of the imagination (93). The two—dog and boy—may be regarded as components of Doctor Faustus's being. The animal represents an instinctual acceptance of things as they are, and the child, the capacity for living uncritically in the present. Both run counter to the demands of the intellect. In consequence, Doctor Faustus resists their company, singing an aria, "Let me alone" (93). He seeks not adjustment but total change. "Night is better than day so please go away." To this, the boy replies that life goes on, even though that process necessarily threatens the soul. "When the hay has to be cut every day then there is the devil to pay" (94).

Doctor Faustus's psychic change, if not rehabilitation, is underway. The principal agent in that change is now mentioned for the first time. She is a woman who will simultaneously be Doctor Faustus's patient and antagonist. Doctor Faustus is understandably ambivalent toward her, both affirming and denying her powers and even her name. She is multiply known as "Marguerite Ida and Helena Annabel" (96). The two pairs of names suggest the split felt in the roles played by the woman.

When she first appears, this woman fears the "wild" world in which she finds herself. She yearns for a chair and a carpet, for that would make her feel secure, would make her feel that "there is there" (96). But even when she closes her eyes, she sees "the wild woods everywhere" (96). For all her desire to be elsewhere and to see other things, she was here and could not avoid seeing things "it is not well that I could tell" (96). At the very instant that she has made her distress clear, she is stung by a viper.

The viper sting, or "bite" as she subsequently calls it, is not a traumatic one. In fact, Marguerite—to use a shortened version of her full name—is forced to examine it more closely to be sure that a bee was not responsible. She finds that the bite does not really hurt. But a country woman carrying a sickle confirms that she has been bitten. She therefore advises Marguerite to see Doctor Faustus "to kill the poison" (97). In an uncertain frame of mind, Marguerite goes to him, singing and puzzling over whether she is Marguerite Ida or Helena Annabel and over what the mysterious doctor can do for her.

The meaning of the viper remains ambiguous. The serpent's sting was not incurred because Marguerite committed a forbidden act, nor was it instantly and dramatically dangerous. It might either represent an inadvertent encounter with a degree of adult experience, possibly sexual, or the ego-shaking result of success. While not painful, both deserved treatment.*

Ironically, the man she consults is himself in the throes of his own psychical crisis. Doctor Faustus finds himself unable to cry, and disturbed, asks himself, "Oh what am I" (98). But Marguerite's arrival causes his lights to glow softly again, and although he cannot actually see his female patient, he does confirm her split personality—"you you are the two" (101). Since the poison is now passing up through her body, Marguerite fears that she will die and implores the doctor to save her.

> He can but he will not
> And she says he must and he will
> And the dog says thank you
> And the boy says very well (102)

* Gertrude Stein was "bitten by a serpent" in 1933, and described it as "a very xciting xperience, quite biblical, it made me want to reread Elsie Venner, it is a curious experience" (GS to Lindley Hubbell, 4 November 1933). A letter from W. A. Bradley, 11 October 1933, also refers to the incident (YCAL).

While his lights flicker, Doctor Faustus finally helps her by confirming her identity. "You have said you are you / Enough said. / You are not dead" (103). The dog, the boy, and the country woman all join in chanting this refrain until Marguerite too repeats it. The scene ends there, the assumption being that the cure has taken place. Although not visible to the rationalist, the poisoned young woman can be cured by him.

Allegra Stewart has devoted a long chapter of her *Gertrude Stein and the Present* to a Jungian interpretation of this play. Although it is often impossible to assent to her conclusions because of the difficulties of accepting or fathoming the terminology, her psychological classification of the characters as well as her interpretation of the action is useful and stimulating. The play is sufficiently suggestive to bear several interpretations. Beyond its possible biographical relevance, the play's action fits the historic shift in alignments and priorities in the twentieth century, and at the most general level, it describes the eternal contest between the "logical" man and the "intuitive" woman.

Following a choral revival of the mystery surrounding the action as the second act opens, Marguerite is discovered in a sanctified pose, one that would be repeated in *The World Is Round* and *The Mother Of Us All*. Crowned with a halo of candlelight, she is seated with her back to the sun and an artificial viper at her side. After the chorus emphasizes her presence, she herself sings a declaration of pure being, "I am there is no not" (108). Everyone now comes to view her, for "she has everything" (106).

One of her band of admirers is severally designated. He is a man who "comes from over the seas," is a "man from over seas," is "the man of the seas" (107, 108). He possesses some of the attributes of a romantic lover. His shifting identity carries over into the action, for the man claims to have "been bitten by her"—that is, by Marguerite—just as she had been by the viper (107). He asserts that he was "won," that he is her sun, and that she should throw away viper, sun, and all, for he is the only one (108).

Marguerite finds herself irresolute in his presence, and at first turns back on him. When she inquires whether he is Doctor Faustus, his only response is a laugh. During his impassioned wooing, she momentarily drops her artificial viper, but picks it up again, saying in a distress so severe that she then faints, "You are not one you are two" (108). Someone does literally stand behind the man of the seas: Mephistopheles accompanied by a boy and a girl. The romantic lover is equivocally associated with the great hypocrite. Furthermore, the boy and girl play the same roles as those attributed by the man of the seas to Marguerite and himself—that is, the elemental male and female. They address him as "Mr. Viper" and implore him to confirm that he is in fact Mr. Viper.

Turning back a moment in the action will assist an understanding of it. Irritated by Marguerite's candlelight, Mephisto had stormed at her until she raised her artificial viper and said: "Lights are all right but the viper is my might" (109). The artificial viper clearly represents experience transformed into the intuitive forms of art. But art turns out to be relatively impotent. Not only does the man of the seas momentarily succeed in getting Marguerite to drop it, but now when she gestures toward Mephisto with it, he responds contemptuously, "Pooh . . . I despise a viper, the viper tries but the viper lies" (109). While we are not encouraged to believe Mephisto, in fact the artificial viper has no visible effect upon anybody.

On the other hand, since the man of the seas is addressed as "Mr. Viper," he would appear to be a physical embodiment of experience. The Satanic overtones in his name are re-enforced by his proximity to Mephisto. When the boy and girl plead with him to confirm that he is Mr. Viper, his smiling response is, "It is lovely to be at ease" (110). The answer is no less enigmatic than his laughter when Marguerite asked if he were Doctor Faustus. Nothing in the play ever conclusively affirms the worth of this mysterious figure.

In the third and last act, the main characters achieve a resolution. Doctor Faustus begins it, again complaining of his lack of feeling and his isolation. He is oppressed by his own egotism. "Ah I do not like that word me" (111). But then, that very egotism is appealed to by a chorus which reports that he now has a rival also capable of turning night into day. After discovering that Marguerite is the possessor of this power, he eagerly sets out to confront her, for "if she can turn night into day then I can go to hell . . . never again will I be alone" (113). Meanwhile Marguerite has informed the man of the seas that "it is not there well anywhere." Nonetheless, "who hears me knows me . . . and here I am, yes here I am" (114). Her position remains unchanged. Given the sickness of the world, the one effective action available to the individual is a declaration of existence.

Doctor Faustus now entreats Mephisto to tell him how he can be well again and so go to Hell, for according to his logic, going to Hell will prove he has a soul. Even though Mephisto had assured him at the beginning of the opera, "Yes dear Doctor Faustus yes of course you have a soul," his spiritual dryness continued to trouble him. Mephisto's solution is a brusque one. "Commit a sin." Asked how this might be done, Mephisto is again abrupt. "Kill anything" (116). Turning to the dog and the boy, Doctor Faustus resolves to destroy them, saying, "The viper will kill you but it will be I who did it, you will die" (116). That is precisely what happens. Scientific reason sacrifices instinctual enjoyment and the ability to live fully in the present in order to prove (or gain) by sinning, his spirituality.

As Doctor Faustus prepares then to descend into hell, Mephisto deceives him one last time. With the doctor's assent, Mephisto makes him young again, so that he can convince Marguerite to accompany him to Hell. But she rejects him, denying that he is Doctor Faustus. The doctor is old, she says, and this tempter is young. "You think you are so clever you think you can deceive . . . but never never . . . I can be anything and everything and it is always always alright" (117–18). Marguerite's outburst cannot inspire unreserved admiration. On the evidence available, her indignation is misplaced. Doctor Faustus is still Doctor Faustus. He has not attempted to trick her, but has identified himself forthrightly and explained how he was made young again. So while Marguerite may sensibly reject his offer to accompany him to Hell, the specific grounds for her refusal are in error. The effort this act of rejection requires is extreme enough to cause her to fall, fainting, into the arms of the man of the seas, who comforts her as Mephisto calls Doctor Faustus to come to Hell. For the last time the doctor sings "Leave me alone," then "sinks into the darkness and it is all dark and the little boy and the little girl sing / Please Mr. Viper listen to me . . . / *Curtain*" (118).

The ending leaves some crucial questions unanswered. Does Doctor Faustus disappear into the darkness with Mephistopheles? If he does, he appears to go willingly and in the same isolated condition in which he started. Although the darkness of Hell may be desirable, at the last moment Doctor Faustus still wished to relieve his loneliness, a wish denied by Marguerite's topmost effort. When "it is all dark," does Gertrude Stein mean that darkness has fallen on the whole world? The last mention of Doctor Faustus's electric lights occurred at the opening of the third act—"the electric lights are right but the room is dark" (110). Taken as literally as possible, the final tableau finds the stage in darkness, Marguerite unconscious in the arms of a faintly unsavory lover, and two children pleading to no apparent avail with Mr. Viper.

The impression left by this ending is grim. Doctor Faustus's misanthropy has not changed, Marguerite's lover retains his sinister equanimity, Mephisto is left unaccounted for, and the plaintive voices of the children come from a darkened stage, pleading for assurance. Given these gloomy facts, it is simply impossible to accept Allegra Stewart's conclusion that at the end the psyche is brought into healthy balance. While Professor Stewart admits that the psychological condensation of the ending "makes summary very difficult," she still makes certain unwarranted assumptions, particularly that Marguerite is now "wedded" to the man of the seas to create "the real self," now that the ego, Faustus, has surrendered "its position as the center of the psyche" (Stewart, 179, 181). While her interpretation is not implausible, the details of character and action refuse to accommodate themselves to it. Far from achieving "self-realization or individuation" in this psychic drama, the main characters are silenced and lost in darkness at the end (Stewart, 142).

Doctor Faustus Lights The Lights is unusual for Gertrude Stein in that she used a traditional plot and developed reasonably consistent characters. The problems treated were deeply personal, but this strong, imaginative drama extended them into general availability. The central symbol of the play is light, the light cast by various sources—electricity, the moon, the sun, and candles. Gertrude Stein's attitude toward the electric light is clearest. For all its brilliance, it casts no light at all. Daylight is minimally used, except that Marguerite sits with her back to the sun. It apparently stands for quotidian perceptions and the common-sense philosophy derived from them. Moonlight is associated with a more primitive world, representing social intuitions, genuine but now largely lost. Finally, there is the individual and romantic vision of candlelight. Whatever the merits of these several sources of illumination though, it is indisputable that darkness overwhelms all at the end of the play.

In 1939 Gertrude Stein turned away from intensely felt personal concerns to prepare a small book extolling her second country. Entitled *Paris France* it has little to do with the French capital. Its real subject is the French character, especially as represented by the solid virtues of the agricultural provinces.

The woman who four years earlier in *The Geographical History of America* had made an effort to champion the American propensity for abstractions and for idealism in the guise of the "human mind," now offered France as a model, France where "life is tradition and human nature" (8). She now praised the French adherence to tradition, to private life, and to the soil. True enough, the twentieth century was driven by new conceptions. Its painters liberated themselves by accepting the notion that painting should be subjective, "that thoughts should be painted and not things seen" (61). Equally true, the modern movement had received its impetus from the realization of infinity, from that disquieting news from the theoretical physicists that the world was round and space illimitable (61). But now in her role as a conservative, Gertrude Stein argued that throughout all this the French never dissociated themselves from the earth. Even though the world was round, "there it still is the ground, it is still there" (62).

Freedom was rooted in stability, she thought (38). Respect for tradition and the observation of formal amenities permitted a person to go about his business free from interference. Such an evironment was ideal for the artist. Not only did it spare him the hostility generated when demands for democratic conformity were not met, but it actually respected his profession. Artistic boldness thrived therefore in this congenial atmosphere. Gertrude Stein's sunny account hardly accords with the furious controversies that arose among spectators when Matisse's paintings were first exhibited or when Stravinsky's *Le Sacre du Printemps* was first performed, but in trying to locate some preserve of safety in the dangerous thirties, she was obliged to invent a mythical civilization. "The essence of being civilised," she wrote, "is to possess yourself as you are" (56). For her France now epitomized that ideal order.

While Gertrude Stein's realignment was being forced by history and by the fact that she was now in her middle sixties, her conservatism was not the timorous egotism of the aged. She had always been a good bourgeois. In fact, the goal of her first novel re-emerged in her approving description of the French people. "They naturally saw things as they were, and accepted life as it is . . ." (17).

In part, the book sought to rationalize away Gertrude Stein's apprehensions about the imminent war. She had already expressed her opinion that Europe was not ready for another conflict. When *Partisan Review* asked her in 1939 what she thought the writers' responsibilities would be, should a war come, she responded with some exasperation: "It does not seem possible for any of you to realize that most probably there will not be another general European war . . ." But should the worst happen, she was in no doubt about the writers' role. They "would have to fight too like anybody else, some will like it and some will not" (*Partisan Review*, VI [Summer 1939], 41).

In *Paris France*, her opinions had lost some of their fire. Because French cats "do not fight much" and because French chickens "do not get flustered running across the road," and because the French people dislike crises, it was her hope that "all this may be only a fire drill, by all this I mean war and thought of war . . ." (1, 29, 30). By the winter of 1939, she was searching for the positive side of conflict. Detained with other refugees in the provinces, she said "war comes and it has its advantages, it does make a concentration of isolation . . ." (65).

These gestures of optimism were accompanied by despair, which Gertrude Stein assigned to the village women. One wondered if anyone would ever really laugh again, and when the local men were called into service, a second woman observed that "now once again it is evening" (41, 33). But when the men returned on leave, their large, healthy fatness renewed Gertrude Stein's hope. She resuscitated her primitive theory that centuries had lifetimes like men. If so, the twentieth century being about forty years of age, she concluded that it should be ready "to settle down to middle age and a pleasant life and the enjoyment of ordinary living" (119). On that pitifully unrealistic note, she dedicated her little book to France and to England (119).

When Gertrude Stein was as wrong as she was at this point, it was less from political naïveté than it was from a reluctance to accept a future as grim as all the signs indicated it would be. But even amidst the rationalizations of *Paris France* Gertrude Stein inserted the enigmatic adventures of one Helen Button, precisely in order to give vent to her true apprehensions.* Two of Helen Button's experiences symbolize the otherwise unnameable dread Gertrude Stein felt. In the first, while walking her dog, Helen Button comes upon a bottle standing upright in the road. It contained something, something dark green, or blue, or black. She neither touched it, nor turned to look back at it. "That is war-time" (82). The second incident Helen herself did not actually see (we are informed after it has been recounted), "but she told herself about it" (90). Helen sees a horse pulling a wagon with a dead animal on it, one that nobody had ever seen before. It had neither a tail nor ears. "It was an enormous animal and it was war-time" (90). If Gertrude

* The Helen Button section runs from 80–92 and is shown as a separate item in the *Yale Catalogue*, indicating that it was independently composed. "Lady Helen Button" also appears in *Ida*, 86.

Stein's reason refused to believe what was in store for Europe, her imagination could not fail to express it.*

Toward the end of 1936 Gertrude Stein had written a third "autobiography," "The Autobiography of Rose." By itself it resists interpretation, save that it concerns the character of a seven-year-old girl named Rose. However, two years later Gertrude Stein wrote a long story for children entitled *The World Is Round* in which the same girl, now nine, played a leading part.† In *The World Is Round* Gertrude Stein expanded some of the abbreviated references found in "The Autobiography of Rose" so that they make more sense, especially an incident where, during a rainstorm, water is dammed on a hillside by hay piled there. Suddenly the hay slides down the hill, and the released water nearly drowns Rose's family as they pass in their car. (See *World*, 14–15.)

Essentially, in the first, arcane version, Gertrude Stein was puzzling over a child's sense of herself. Was her nature determined by her name? When she looked at herself, "she could see that perhaps her name was not Rose" (*Partisan Review* [Winter 1939], 62). But had she an autobiography—that is, a history of which she was conscious—at so young an age? "Can she remember Rose. Can she. I am wondering" (63). On that speculative note, Gertrude Stein ended this brief meditation on a child's self-awareness.

When she returned to Rose in *The World Is Round*, Gertrude Stein put her in the midst of certain arbitrary, mysterious actions, interspersed with songs. Rose is a rather willful, disturbed girl who now questions for herself who she is. Particularly depressed to discover that everything goes round, when she sings, she cries. Her cousin Willie is

---

* In "Observations on *Paris France*," after calling the Helen Button sequence "the best thing in her book," Kemp Malone contented himself with quoting the bottle in the road incident. The rest of his long paper is devoted to summarizing the book and objecting to its grammar and logic. Throughout his article, Malone resists the only two questions worth asking—Is Gertrude Stein worth reading in spite of her obvious flaws; and if so, why? See *Papers on Language and Literature*, III (Spring 1967), 159–78.

† The book was dedicated to "A French Rose," specifically to "Rose Lucy Renée Anne d'Aiguy" evidently the daughter of the Baron and Baroness Robert d'Aiguy, Bilignin friends. The Baroness had translated *Paris France* into French.

The World Is Round was abridged for publication in *Harper's Bazaar* [New York] (June 1939), 46–47, 92, 94–96. Twenty-one chapters, those describing Rose's ascent of the blue mountain, were eliminated—that is from "A Chair on the Mountain" to "A Light." The concluding marriage chapter was retained at the cost of some continuity. The magazine text also shows minor changes in spelling and paragraphing, as well as a few lines dropped and a few added.

an adventurous boy who becomes excited when he sings. At the conclusion of their adventures, they are revealed to be unrelated, which permits them to marry, have children, and live happily ever after. But before that traditional close, they undergo several enigmatic experiences, the first involving a lion, the second, the climbing of a mountain. The conquering of fears, self-exploration, aspiration, and success are all components of the story.

The world's roundness is the given from which everything proceeds. That feature of the physical world stood for a basic fact of life. Roundness means perpetual continuation, the serpent with his tail in his mouth. "You could go on it around and around" (*World*, 7). The round earth bespeaks unity too, whereas flatness suggests infinite change, no return ever to an original point, only endless novelty and diversity. The linked circle was used for the famous rose device on Gertrude Stein's stationery and also on the cover of *The Autobiography of Alice B. Toklas.**

The first part of *The World Is Round* develops the oppressiveness of circularity. Willie almost drowns in a round lake, and sleeping after the experience, he murmurs, *"Round drowned"* (17). If everything does turn perpetually, then the individual self loses its meaning, its uniqueness swallowed in a sea of eternal return.

Rose is more depressed than she is actually threatened by roundness. When she went to school,

> The teachers taught her
> That the world was round
> That the sun was round
> That the moon was round
> That the stars were round
> And that they were all going around and around
> And not a sound
> It was so sad it almost made her cry. (21)

Rose's response to the huge, mechanically circling, silent universe was similar to Gertrude Stein's when she discovered there were other solar systems. Rose's makeshift defense was to "remember the mountains were so high they could stop anything" (22).

Willie is the first to try actively to solve the problem of retaining his individuality. He is confident of his being. "I would be Willie what-

---

* Much depends upon the phrasing and punctuation of the rose sentence. If there is a period—as there is on the *ABT* cover—then the sentence is not continuous, but affords relief.

300

ever arose" (15). Still, the natural world questions and threatens him through the agency of the owl. *"Who are you who are you"* (16). Willie's answer is to acquire a lion which "looked like Rose's dog Love only the Lion was terrifying" (30). However, the moment that he had selected a lion, he began to cry, for he realized this made him *"just like my cousin Rose"* (31). He therefore resolves to give the lion to her.

Both children eventually rid themselves of the Lion, which seems to represent all the diverse things nature throws up to terrorize mankind. The scenes of exorcism are imaginatively perplexing.

Long before she had been given the lion, Rose had brooded about wild animals. Her poodle had not barked when a puppy, causing some concern lest he had no voice. But one day in the country, coming upon a circus truck that carried lions, tigers, bears, and monkeys, Love barked for the first time. Rose's apprehensive questions ensued: *"How does Love know how wild they are,"* and *"Why are they wild oh why"* (35, 36). The apparent fixedness of the world troubled her. The mechanism of the world determined that wild animals shall be wild and that their wildness shall be instinctively recognized. However unjust it seemed to a child, their wildness appeared to be a permanent fact.

Rose's torment over the inevitability of the world's constitution was related to her distress at the world's roundness. In fact, when Willie asks himself why wild animals abound, his answer is because the world is round (31). Everywhere Rose looked she discovered signs that told her life was determined. Moreover, schools taught the ordained articulation of natural law. Faced with this universal denial of free will, Rose then feels threatened by Willie's lion, which he has attempted to pass along to her.

Her crisis over the lion comes to a climax at school when a fearful representative of mechanicalness and roundness appears, "a man with a drum, he was on a bicycle and the drum was on a bicycle and he was drumming . . ." (41). The man calls out with all the insistence of a nightmare figure, *"either or either or either there is a lion here or there is no lion here, either or, either or"* (41). Rose counters him with two articles of faith. First, she knows that she would not be permitted to keep a lion at school. Second, she would hardly keep a lion anyway, since a lion is yellow-brown whereas blue was her favorite color. Fortified by her logic, Rose sings a counter-tune: *"Neither nor, he is neither here nor there, no no lion is here, no lion is there, neither nor"* (42).

With that, the man with the round drum, the round wheels on his bicycle, and his round mouth draws away until at last there was "no more drumming" and he has disappeared.

The episode would seem to describe a mental crisis. The lion and the representative of roundness have been driven off by an effort of will, supported by faith in the supremacy of the individual's subjective consciousness. "*No lion is blue / So there is no lion for me . . .*" (43). Rose passes sobbing through a door, "and never any more . . . would she remember that it had been a lion that she saw, either or" (43). With that, the lion becomes Willie's problem again. His solution is easier and more expeditious. Hearing a bell ring, he discovers that Billie the lion is back. But then he asks himself, was Billie a lion? No. A kitten? No. A rat? No. What then? "He was a twin . . . that is what Billie was when he got back." Having so concluded, Willie begins to laugh, and the lion "was never there any more anywhere . . ." (44–45).

Although Willie's response is less clear than Rose's, as used here "twin" evidently means an illusion of some sort. Perhaps Gertrude Stein's meaning was that once a problem has been solved, it is useless to fret over it when it reappears. It can be laughed away. It is possible, of course, given the similarity of their names that Willie accepts Billie the lion as so closely resembling himself that he need not exist. That is, Willie recognizes himself as a wild animal like the lion. But the story offers no other evidence to support this interpretation. The best one can say is that as the first part of the story ends, Willie and Rose are free of the lion.

The second half of *The World Is Round* described an ascent through adversity. One day Rose decided to climb a mountain with a meadow at the top and sit there in a chair where she could see everywhere (49). "Full of alarms," she sets out, protected only by her refusal to be discouraged (55). "All a Rose with a chair can dare is just not stare but keep on going up there" (57). Rolling rocks, stinging twigs, the glowing eyes of animals all menace her, but carrying a blue garden chair, she keeps climbing. An aura of unspeakable threats surrounds her. Once she falls. "What did Rose see close, that is what she never can tell and perhaps it is just as well . . ." (66). At one point she enters a cave behind a waterfall. There, in the utter darkness, she saw with perfect clarity "*Devil Devil Devil . . . in large writing*" (68–69). While Gertrude Stein was emphatic in asserting "of course . . . there is no devil anywhere," that did not reduce the ominousness of the incident.

302

Setting out in the early morning, Rose climbed all day and all night. At dawn the following day, she carved *"Rose is a Rose is a Rose is a Rose"* on a tree-trunk. As she finished she noticed carved on another tree: "Rose and under Rose was Willie and under Willie was Billie. / It made Rose feel very funny it really did" (77). The three, boy, girl, and lion form some unalterable union. (If a hierarchy is intended, the female is at the top.)

Rose climbs until she hears the same sound Willie heard when his lion was returned to him, the ringing of a bell. She has almost reached her goal. "All around the sun was shining and the bell was ringing and the woods were thinning and the green was shining" (79). In spite of these propitious signs though, she now feels "a little lonesome" (79). At last she emerges from the trees to see the meadow on the mountain-top. In it she perceives a small black dog, shaking himself. Even though "it is hard to go on when you are nearly there," Rose persists, hot, stumbling, the garden chair heavy in her arms. Suddenly, the "green became blue and she knew that one would become two and three would become four and never again no never again would there ever be a door for her to go through" (85).

This climactic moment demands careful attention. Blue was Rose's favorite color. Even before the climb began, the reader had been told that "when mountains are really true they are blue" (46). Later on, he learned that "nothing green ever has anything to say. / Rose knew that that is why she always did prefer blue" (82). Therefore, one would normally anticipate that the metamorphosis of green into blue would be a favorable moment, a sign of reality yielding to the persistence of the private will. That is not the case, however. Perceiving the change, Rose's "eyes were round with fright." To keep from "stumbling" and then "tumbling," she institutes corrective therapy (85). She closes her eyes and begins to count *"one two one two."* When she opens them again, she sees a rainbow through which she then moves to the mountain-top and at last seats herself.

The crisis Rose survived just before reaching her goal is one in which her identity threatened to disintegrate. If green can become blue, then one could become two, and three, four. Her ability to control her imagination would be lost. Rose knew very well that if you look down at the ground, "you see that the world is not round" (39). But that was only a part of what she knew. The subjective expedient was useful if employed at strategic times, but dangerous if mistaken for the only truth. Fantasy must be voluntarily entered. If not, there would never be a door for her to pass through again. All would fall to pieces, multiplying infinitely. That was the danger Rose's mind ran in making this arduous climb. Only her determination to concentrate saved her.

Once atop the mountain, Rose seated herself and for the first time began to sing. The song started, "Here I am," and it concerned the nature of reality—is it an objective, imagined, or dreamed world? (87). *"Once when five apples were red, / They never were / It was my head / No said she / No it was not my head / It was my bed"* (88). As Rose sings it grows darker and darker, alarming her. "Here I am all alone all night and I am in a most awful fright" (91). Satisfying as it had been, her achievement had not made her, any more than success had made Gertrude Stein, impervious to fear.

Her relief comes in the form of light. A search-light, operated by her cousin from another mountain, sweeps all around Rose, brightening the sky and ground. Interestingly enough, in this single scene, her cousin is named "Will" instead of "Willie," even though Rose continues to refer to him as "a little boy" (93). Although she had climbed the mountain without any assistance from him, and remains still separated from him, the circling brightness of his Faustian light comforts her. She feels "warm right through to her back" (93). But the conclusion is neither triumphant nor peaceful. "And she sang *oh Will oh Will* and she cried and cried and cried and cried and the search light went round and round and round and round" (93).

Rose may have prevailed, but she is weeping at the end as the light does what had always oppressed her—goes round. The mingled note of success and despair, of warmth and sadness is one heard repeatedly in Gertrude Stein's work in the thirties. In *Doctor Faustus Lights The Lights,* a threatened girl who, like Rose, worries over "why woods are wild why animals are wild why I am I, why I can cry," is transformed into an enthroned figure (*LO&P*, 95). She undergoes an ordeal, resists temptation at the cost of her consciousness, and is ambiguously supported by a male lover. Although she has survived her trial, at the end the mood is dark and sad. The last chapter of *The World Is Round* in which Willie and Rose marry betrays the book's fundamental mood.

Doctor Faustus, "The Autobiography of Rose," and *The World Is Round* all concern the transformation of identity by experience. Other work Gertrude Stein did in the same period indicates the centrality of the subject for her. One short, distraught piece entitled "Lucretia Borgia A Play" picks up the situation in which Willie the boy rid himself of

304

Billie the lion by pronouncing him a "twin." Lucretia, who goes under various names, suffers from a lack of cousins. As Jenny, she makes herself a twin named Winnie, whereupon she "began to sit and write." Later though, she kills Winnie and is called "a murderess." This one-page play concludes, "If you made her can you kill her. / One one one" (*Creative Writing* I [October 1938], 15).

These cloudy references to writing, to multiple identities, and to murder can be interpreted as referring to the creation of the persona of Alice B. Toklas, through whom she wrote her first successful book, but whose voice she never used again, thereby, in effect, murdering her. Or, they might refer to the several psychological roles Gertrude Stein detected within herself over the years.

In the latter part of Gertrude Stein's career, the image of a woman enthroned, usually insecurely, is as prominent a feature as twins. Marguerite with her halo of candlelight and artificial viper is one instance, Rose atop her mountain is another. A third, who also possesses a dual identity, is the heroine of "Ida," a short sketch composed in 1937.*

Even though she has had two husbands, a son, and "two sets of children," Ida comes very close to sharing Gertrude Stein's experience (*The Boudoir Companion*, 34). A person who busied herself by doing nothing, she worried whether one should "do what they tell you" (33). Sometimes she would sit and ask herself "am I one or am I two" (34–35). In time, she straightened out her double personality for herself, so that she could play either role easily. However, other people remained confused—"they did not know which was which but Ida did . . ." (35). When she tells the story of her life, "every one wanted it." Being desired in this way unified her again. "Ida was no longer two she was one . . ." (36). When "just like that they were all pleased," she found it an "exciting" time (37, 36). But eventually the public lapsed into their former habit of condescending affection. "So you see now again they say dear Ida" (38). No longer the prevailing oracle, she found herself assimilated. "Stored and adored. / Bored and reward . . ." (38). Again she became merely a harmless, endearing eccentric. "Of course it does happen . . . Once more dear Ida" (38). The public fickleness not only disconcerted her; it brought her vitality into question. "Somebody says she is dead now and adored," but "she was

* The novel *Ida* was not completed until 1940.

thinking about life. . . . she never did want to leave it" (31). This brief history reveals quite clearly the kinds of stress that Gertrude Stein's personality underwent in the thirties.

The longer *Ida*, published in 1941, faintly resembles the original sketch. Gertrude Stein first conceived it in 1937 as "a novel about publicity . . . a novel where a person is so publicized that there isn't any personality left. I want to write about the effect on people of the Hollywood cinema kind of publicity that takes away all identity" (Rogers, *When This You See*, 168).* By 1940, her concern and manner of attack had changed so drastically that this thematic statement no longer described the finished result.

The book originally took the Duchess of Windsor as its heroine.† The finished relationship is only tangential, although the Duchess had a special claim on Gertrude Stein's attention, having lived in Baltimore at 212 East Biddle St., directly across the street from the flat Gertrude and Leo had shared at 215 East Biddle. After moving as a young woman in the company of military officers, Wallis Warfield had contracted her first marriage with a naval lieutenant, Earl Winfield Spencer. Ida too moves a good deal about the United States, marries a succession of army officers, and remains "good friends" with them after their separation. She finally settles down with one Andrew who, like the Duke of Windsor, has many names (136, 139). (In *To Do*, Gertrude Stein would offer a sketch of an "Ivy" who "fell in love with a pretty king" [*A&B*, 19–20].)

More than any other single composition, *Ida* incorporates a variety of material from Gertrude Stein's other pieces. The cannibalism ranges from mere references, such as an encounter with Madame Pernollet and the walking marathon first described in *Everybody's Autobiography*, to Ida calling herself a suicide blonde and saying that she will be accused of being a murderess for killing her twin, as in "Lucretia Borgia" (18, 45, 11). Superstititions concerning spiders and dwarfs

* On 11 May 1938, Gertrude Stein wrote Thornton Wilder, "Ida has become an opera . . . an opera about Faust. . . . Some day she will be a novel too, she is getting ready for that . . ." On 27 June?1938, she told Wilder, "Now once more I am going to do the novel Ida, I am beginning all over again just as if it never had been done" (YCAL).
† ". . . about three years ago I told you I was doing a novel about the Duchess of Windsor and it was to be called Ida . . . I have written it over almost three times completely . . ." (GS to Carl Van Vechten, 21 April 1940, YCAL). When *Ida* was published, Gertrude Stein asked Bennett Cerf to send a copy to the Duchess, who later replied, "I hope to emerge from this literary labyrinth with some idea of Ida's thoughts and ways!" (Cerf to GS, 14 May and 13 June 1941, YCAL).

306

that were merely touched upon in *The World Is Round* are expanded in *Ida* into a prolonged dramatic debate. Two anecdotes about dogs that appeared in *Paris France* were taken over almost verbatim (*Paris,* 34; *Ida,* 36, 65). The line, "Come firefly light up baby's nose" first appeared in "A Lyrical Opera" (*O&P,* 49). The whole plot of "Film," the scenario that contained a laundress, two ladies in an automobile, and a white poodle, written eleven years earlier, was now recast as an incident in the life of Ida (21–22).

Ida drew upon conceptions that had originated much further back than 1929 though. It contains a rebellious girl with a broken arm like Melanctha, and Ida's mother, like Melanctha's, is a sweet, gentle woman who does not wish Ida to be born, and who soon fades away, leaving her daughter in the care of a series of relatives. One astonishing episode was derived from an experience Gertrude Stein had first put into words forty-five years before. Drawn from her last college theme, "The Temptation," prepared in 1895 for her Radcliffe composition course, it concerns Ida (originally Hortense) attending a crowded church service in the company of some relatives. Separated from them, Ida "stayed close against one or two" people in the hot, dark church, deliberately not looking at them, but "she felt something, all right . . ." (13). This episode of illicit eroticism, which had brought family disapproval down upon her, remained vivid in Gertrude Stein's memory.

The first twenty pages of *Ida* contain as eerie a set of incidents as Gertrude Stein ever imagined. For a time, she ventured down into a world of "funny things" that happened to Ida (12). Most of these involved men in roles of faintly threatening sexuality. An early encounter sets the pattern. A man follows Ida, sufficiently alarming her for her to cry. Yet, "some time after it was a comfort to her that this had happened to her" (9). Another time, two men jump out from behind some trees, but when Ida turns to look back at them, they are gone (13). An Arab rolls in a road, his legs kicking. Then, like the two men, "suddenly, he went away" (17). These occurrences all have the arbitrary irrationality of hallucinations and dreams. One evening Ida looks through the fence of a public park and perceives a policeman "bending down and looking at her" (15). As she puzzles over his behavior, she notices a very old woman standing next to her, although her sex is ambiguous—"she had so much clothing on and so many things hanging from her and she was carrying so many things she might have been anything" (16). With that comment, Ida departs for home, bringing the enigmatic incident to an end.

In the midst of these disturbing encounters, Ida at the age of eighteen conceives the wish to have a twin (18). A twin, Ida-Ida, had been born at the same time as she, but was never mentioned again. The new twin is an imaginary one. "Ida often wrote letters to herself that is to say she wrote to her twin" (18). The twin is explicitly conceived for the purpose of protection. Ida explains that the reason she wants a twin is so that if she gets into trouble, people will not know which of them is at fault (11).

After her twin is awarded first prize in a beauty contest, Ida names her "Winnie" (23). One day though, she suddenly felt that she had lost something, what, she did not know, but she "felt or rather she heard" voices call to her, "Ida is that you Ida" (27). Soon after, she repudiates Winnie. An army officer having remarked pleasantly to her, "Winnie is your name and that is what you mean by your not being here," Ida feels very faint, "Her name was not Winnie it was Ida, there was no Winnie" (29). Therefore, she carefully informs the officer that he is mistaken. In effect, that is the end of her twin. As she had foreseen, she had made her and she had killed her (11).

Although this description has left out certain contributory incidents as well as relevant minor details, one can see in all this the lonely, spirited girl who is simultaneously frightened, puzzled, and attracted by the masculine mystery. As an alter ego who will permit her to talk and write to herself, she invents a beauty queen. But when she realizes that this invented personality threatens to take over her real self, she quickly drops it. This part of *Ida* is a variant of the story of Rose in *The World Is Round*.

After the elimination of Winnie, *Ida* becomes a very different and increasingly tedious book. Ida's principal activities are moving from place to place, marrying, and resting, none of them accomplished with much energy. Sporadically though, the complicated young woman of the beginning reappears, superstitious and eccentric. As a girl, "she was very careful about Tuesday" (9). When she grows up, she acquires the "funny habit" of bowing "to anything she liked," having learned that albatrosses "always bowed before they did anything" (131). Hats, dresses, jewels all received her secret homage. Although attracted to two professions of special interest to the author, that of a nurse and a nun, Ida does not pursue them because both require early rising (94).

Locales shift arbitrarily in *Ida*, from Oakland (Ida's house atop a hill [11]) to Paris to Bilignin to Baltimore. Once, late in the novel,

Gertrude Stein crudely inserted the memory of having been taught to swim by a young man at the Lurline Baths in San Francisco. He stood next to her in the water, holding her chin, "and he said kick and she kicked again and he was standing very close to her and she kicked hard and she kicked him. He let go her he called out Jesus Christ my balls and he went under . . ." (113).

Coming without warning, such anecdotes make no contribution to the development of the ostensibly fictional character, Ida. However, only if their meaning for Ida is sought are they problems. If it is accepted that Ida is a peg on which Gertrude Stein can hang her obsessions, particularly those involving men, then these disconnected stories fall into place.*

The Autobiography of Alice B. Toklas stands behind a debate in *Ida* that erupts among a spider, a cuckoo, a goldfish, and a male and female dwarf. Supposedly, if one hears the first cuckoo in the spring with money in one's pocket, one will be rich all that year. For proof, the case of a woman who wrote "a lovely book" is cited. But nobody purchased the book, despite the fact that she and her lover needed money. "So she wrote and she hoped and she wrote and she sighed and she wanted money money money . . ." (124). Finally, one spring day she hears a cuckoo singing and "knew that it was true and that she would be rich and love would not leave her . . ." (125).

Gertrude Stein's acceptance of the efficacy of signs was summed up for her by the dwarfs, who declared, "We believe in everything" (128). However, the potency of various folk superstitions was predominantly negative. Cuckoos brought misery as well as money, and both a goldfish and a female dwarf meant bad, bad luck. Gertrude Stein's anxiety was beginning its resurgence. Two anecdotes from *Ida* suggest her negative mood at the time.

> Once upon a time there was a meadow and in this meadow was a tree and on this tree there were nuts. The nuts fell and then they plowed the ground and the nuts were plowed into the ground but they never grew out. (60)

* Equally arbitrary is the ten-page section introduced by the remark, "And sitting she thought about her life with dogs and this was it" (96). In the *Yale Catalogue,* the item "My Life With Dogs" is keyed to *Ida,* indicating that this separately written meditation was inserted later. This explains why, although Ida had possessed dogs as a child, notably, one born blind and given the same name as Rose's dog, Love, in this review of Ida's dogs, Love is never mentioned (10–11, 21–22). But Gertrude Stein's Mallorcan hound, Polybe, as well as Basket I and Basket II do appear (102–3; 105, 106). Gertrude Stein made no attempt to conceal her patchwork.

The barrenness of that parable is matched by the nihilism of this:

> Once upon a time there was a shotgun and there were wooden guinea hens and they moved around electrically, electricity made them move around and as they moved around if you shot them their heads fell off them. (61)

Yet, like her creator, Ida tried to remain a yea-sayer (132). She held trouble at arm's length by living from day to day and "never took on yesterday or tomorrow . . ." (135). Her allegiance to the present was expressed in physical terms: she disliked passing through doors (134). As the book approached its conclusion though, something happened, but just what was uncertain. Even to her "it is all very confused . . ." (153). But the book gives evidence everywhere that Gertrude Stein's mind was reverting to her youth. The memories and problems of that tumultuous time were crowding out those abstractions that had occupied the front of her mind for the past several years. The change in her had become evident even to others. "Everybody began to miss something . . ." (148). The change began slowly, then quickened, or rather, it did both. "It was little by little and it was all of a sudden" (151). The past was overtaking her. "Little by little she was not there she was elsewhere" (151). After all the years of resolutely keeping her mind on the present, Gertrude Stein now yielded to the unresolved enigmas of the past.

The cause of her introspection appears to have been disappointment in the inadequacy of her social life. Women visited her, but now their interchange was superficial. "They had not really come nor had they said Thank you my dear. That is really the reason that Ida ran away not ran away or went away but something in between" (152). Gertrude Stein was trying very hard to communicate precisely what change had taken place in her. "For a little time she did not say yes." Then, when the crisis was passed, everything was—"well not as it had been." And there were still times when she did not say yes (153).

The novel ends in this minor key. "Ida was resting but not resting enough." She had less to say; if she spoke, she said yes, but otherwise, not. "She dresses, well perhaps in black why not . . ." (154). Ida's serenity is troubled and her activity mechanical as the novel ends. A medical prognosis might read: Depression incipient. Keep under observation.

While writing *Ida,* Gertrude Stein conceived her second children's book, *To Do: A Book of Alphabets and Birthdays.* In it, her mood of tempered pessimism continued. She composed it, in May and June of 1940, she said, to keep her mind off the German invasion of France, and the task so thoroughly engrossed her, she even "went to sleep making up stories" ("The Winner Loses," *SW*, 620). *To Do* contains numerous short fantasies, each built around characters whose names begin with a particular letter of the alphabet. Even though portions of it are inflated beyond the patience of a child, *To Do* is a strange and captivating book. In it, Gertrude Stein permitted her imagination to call up words in the form of rhymes, near-rhymes, and alliteration, producing original results that could be easily accommodated in an atmosphere of serious play.

> She asked her way and she asked every way and she could not find out and at last she saw a man who was stout sitting in a boat and she commenced to tell him what it was all about. (*A&B*, 60)

Although the associative method of creation was a familiar one for Gertrude Stein, its novelty in *To Do* was that she retained control over the structure of her sentences so that they did not unravel into confusion. Only at selected points did she permit sound cues to take over. The man is "stout" and sits in a "boat" and is told what it is "all about."

Normally in *To Do*, Gertrude Stein offered four names for each letter of the alphabet, then involved them in situations that concerned their birthdays. The characters were not always people, but might be animals or even the letters themselves. D, for example, is said to dislike being followed by E. "Sometimes D says bad words to E says don't come tagging after me, I have had enough of E, let me be" (8). Similarly, the birthdays are often treated as objects that can be lost, stolen, or bartered.

While a few of the episodes reach happy conclusions, the greater part are dominated by acts of agression and disaster. Characters are bitten, burned, drowned, and eaten, and yet the over-all effect is not morbid, for the fantasy distances the violence and cruelty. There is occasional evidence of justice at work. A rich boy, fishing illegally with a light, drowns. "And the fish could rest every night" (6). A faithful horse returns from being mobilized in the war to find that his job of pulling a milk wagon has been rendered obsolete by mechanization. So, without fuss or explanation, he becomes an automobile (4–5).* The most im-

---

* This horse, called "Active" in *To Do*, also appears—as "Kiki"—in *Paris France*, 66–68.

pressive thing about *To Do* though, is that Gertrude Stein found another means of imaginatively embodying her vision of the inexplicable calamity in the world.

The Quiets, for example, own a very large rabbit which "had the habit of always eating a little rabbit on his birthday . . ." (43). In an effort to prevent this, the Quiets take his birthday away from him. But the large rabbit responds by eating a rabbit a day "just to be sure" (43). The Quiets's next move is to give away the rest of their rabbits, which infuriates the cannibal. His pink eyes grow redder and redder until at last they burst into flame and burn the large rabbit up until all that is left is a glowing cinder, "and that Mr. and Mrs. Quiet put out by dropping tears on him" (44). The savagery typified by the large rabbit is neither explained nor permanently eliminated. The Quiets merely do their best, which includes, incidentally, expressing compassion for the furious aggressor.

Birthdays—one's particular anchor in the world of time—do strange things to the characters of *To Do*. They may make them ferocious, devouring monsters like the large rabbit, or they may fatally curse them. Xantippe and Xenophon, for example, feel themselves to be unreal. It occurs to them that perhaps the X's that begin their names are responsible. But after they have discarded their initial letters, their anxiety is unrelieved. Meanwhile, they have discovered five men and ten women walking behind them. The group's presence alarms Xantippe and Xenophon, who fear that "if the X's frightened them they might try to kill them" (72). The two try various maneuvers to change their identities, but the ominous band remains just behind them. Then, "all of a sudden"—as catastrophes happened in those days for Gertrude Stein—"the five men and ten women . . . walked right into Xenophon and Xantippe . . . the women opened their mouths as if they were yawning and just then Xenophon and Xantippe disappeared down the mouths of them . . . and the ten women and five men went away" (73).

Examining the story of the doomed pair carefully, one sees that through no fault of their own they were born with a disturbing feature, that they tried desperately to free themselves from its stigma, and that suddenly and without explanation, they were swallowed up. That disturbing pattern characterizes most of *To Do*, which concludes by praising Zero. His merit is that nullity generates numbers. Without him, "there would not be a million of them there would be only one" (85). Therefore, "thanks to Zero the hero Zero we all have a birthday. /

Hurray" (86). But since the prevailing impression *To Do* has given is that birthdays are dangerous possessions which more often than not bring misery and destruction upon their owners, that concluding single cheer for Zero is not without its irony.

Not long after *To Do,* Gertrude Stein composed a set of twenty lessons which were published posthumously as *The Gertrude Stein First Reader.* Its undercurrent of trouble and despair is equally notable. There are frightened children, predatory birds, disappearing flowers and several drownings throughout. The oppressive mood is lightened by examples of kindness, good humor, and even a measure of success. But in the main, the lessons of the *First Reader* are epitomized by the little boy who learns a new word—"anxious" (16). The *First Reader's* world is enigmatic and menacing. Its last lesson is an earnest series of admonitions to children: "be very careful . . . as careful as you can be" (56).

15

Shortly after Hitler invaded Poland on the first of September 1939, Gertrude Stein and Alice Toklas returned briefly to Paris to secure their winter clothing and a few paintings, then retreated once more to Bilignin. From that provincial vantage point they observed the subsequent invasion of France by the Nazis, followed by Pétain's capitulation. Indeed, they did not see Paris again until the middle of December 1944, well after they had been liberated by American troops.

The war's advent shocked Gertrude Stein. "I was terribly frightened," she said in "The Winner Loses: A Picture of Occupied France." "I had been so sure there was not going to be war and here it was, it was war, and I made quite a scene" (*SW*, 615).* Alarmed as Gertrude Stein was, she remained in France, trying to keep her mind off the situation by inventing the bizarre stories of *To Do*. Nightly she read in "the Bible," her name for Leonardo Blake's book of astrological predictions, *The Last Year of War—and after* (1940) (616). When nearby Italy entered the war, the two women momentarily panicked, "because—well, here we were right in everybody's path" (622–623). Various people gave them contradictory advice, until ultimately Gertrude Stein decided to rely upon the familiar. In spite of being "completely scared," in spite of her Jewish birth, in spite of the opportunity to return to the United States where security and fame awaited her, she chose to stay where she was. In her version, it was the counsel of an old friend that settled it. Here in Bilignin, he argued, she was known and liked. " 'Why risk yourself among strangers?' / 'Thank you,' we said, 'that is all we need.

* "Sundays and Tuesdays," the original title of this article, referred to the fact that France declared war on Sunday and Germany invaded Poland on Sunday, to precipitate the full European conflict, but a popular book of prophecy predicted disaster for the Nazis on a series of Tuesdays.

We stay' " (624). A local farmer confirmed her decision by pointing out that in this little corner of the world, she was *en famille*. If she left, where could she go? (625). That fatalistic analysis of her situation impressed her. She was too settled to move again, and at any rate, one could not escape the world. The decision may have been as foolhardy as the American consul in Lyons believed it to be. But it made sense to Gertrude Stein and it produced some of her most moving accounts of human life.

Gertrude Stein's friends have been at some pains to suggest the danger that she and Alice Toklas ran as elderly Jews under the thumb of the Nazis. She herself never encouraged such notions, and the most that Alice ever made of it was an oblique reference to "a possible danger one refused to face" (*The Alice B. Toklas Cook Book*, 227). In *Wars I Have Seen*, Gertrude Stein did recall that they were warned in 1943 to cross into Switzerland immediately. "Otherwise they will be put into a concentration camp." But they decided again not to flee, and nothing came of the threat. What struck Gertrude Stein most about "the whole affair was its unreality" (50–51).

While on the surface it might seem that the two women were unusually vulnerable, it should be remembered that among her friends were figures of some regional prominence, the wealthy nobility and royalists who supported the Vichy government. Like them, she longed for social stability, and regarded the various political movements of social reform with scepticism. In 1936, she wrote a friend that "nobody thinks you can live or be quiet under communism, nor under constitutional government as made to-day . . ." (GS to W. G. Rogers, November 1936, YCAL). By "nobody" she had in mind "all our French friends . . . who are all Croix de feu . . ." (GS to W. G. Rogers, ? late November, 1936, YCAL). The Croix de Feu was a nationalistic and anti-parliamentarian organization originally founded by veterans of the first world war. "Belley has become its center," Gertrude Stein reported in 1936, "and so everybody is terribly interested" (GS to Mrs. C. Goodspeed, 24 October 1936, YCAL). While acknowledging that dictatorships habitually repressed artists, she observed that not only did Russia "want nothing advanced at all," but moreover, "I guess it would have taken me just about as long to be published anywhere as anywhere" (GS to W. G. Rogers, December 1936, YCAL). In *Paris France*, she underlined her views. "I cannot write too much upon how necessary it is to be completely conservative that is particularly traditional in order to be free" (38).

She never seems to have referred to the Nazi party or Hitler's treatment of the Jews in her correspondence. However, Bernard Faÿ showed no hesitation in informing her on Halloween, 1938, of the apparent fate of the man who had recently organized and printed the attack upon her, *Testimony Against Gertrude Stein*. "The American newspapers say that Hitler has arrested Eugene Jolas—I did not think that Hitler had so much sense or Jolas so much luck. At last he has found his 'place' and a good one too. He may achieve some thing" (YCAL).

During the occupation, Faÿ, a professor of American culture at the College de France, was appointed director of the Bibliothèque Nationale in Paris. In that capacity, he conferred monthly in Vichy with Marshal Pétain. He visited Gertrude Stein on several occasions during the war, corresponded regularly with her, and on at least one occasion, sent her extra bread tickets (Gallup, *Flowers*, 356, 363). Also, after the Gestapo had made one visit to Gertrude Stein's apartment in Paris, Faÿ "arranged" that her "pictures and manuscripts would not be harmed" (Donald Gallup, "The Gertrude Stein Collection," *The Yale University Library Gazette*, XXII [October 1947], 24). Therefore, the two women were unlikely to be harmed as long as they kept silent and neutral, which they did.*

Against the usual accounts of derring-do in the Resistance, Gertrude Stein's defense of the French capitulation may seem tame and perhaps even craven. But the world is not made up of rebellious males alone, and her position was true to her conservative, common-sense philoso-

---

* Although there is no other substantiation for it, and one should be cautious about accepting its veracity, Francis Rose, who had been an intimate of the Nazi leaders—"I loved Ernest Rohm and he loved me"—claimed that just before he left Germany, he exacted a promise from Goering "that should anything happen to France, he would see that Gertrude Stein and Alice Toklas would be safe and never be in financial need" (*Saying Life*, 235, 401). As late as December 1945, Gertrude Stein was telling Rose, "you are the most important young painter painting today here or there and I have never doubted it . . ." (GS to Francis Rose, copy by Leon Katz, YCAL).

After the war, Bernard Faÿ was sentenced to life imprisonment at hard labor as a collaborator. To her credit, Gertrude Stein defended him, saying "he certainly did certain things that he should not have done, but that he ever denounced any body, no, that I do not believe" (GS to Francis Rose [?1946], copy by Leon Katz, YCAL). Faÿ later escaped from the prison hospital at Angers (30 September 1951), and went into exile in Switzerland, after which he accepted a Chair of History at the University of Madrid. In a long defense of his wartime activities, Faÿ said: "I obtained from Pétain that the Préfet and the Sous-Préfet should help them [i.e., Gertrude Stein and Alice Toklas], watch over them . . ." (Faÿ to François Monahan, 22 July 1955, YCAL). There is a note, apparently in the hand of Gertrude Stein, on the back of an otherwise unmarked envelope in YCAL that reads: "10 IX 40 de prie M. Faÿ Administrateur de la B. N. de conserver toute ma collection pour toute la durée de la guerre."

phy. During their brief, initial stay in the Rhone Valley, the feared and despised Germans turned out to be polite with low, slightly sad voices, she recalled. They bothered no one, except for one threatening flare-up over securing fuel. Gertrude Stein understood the ignominious peace: the country people were not Hotspurs. The paramount fact for them was that the armistice kept the death toll to a minimum. "It was not like the last war, when all the men were dead or badly wounded . . ." (*SW*, 633). Pétain's decision to capitulate seemed eminently rational to most people. They soon forgot about the defeat and set to "accommodating themselves to everything," which meant securing butter, gasoline and firewood ("The Winner Loses," 636). Gertrude Stein concluded her 1940 article by asserting that France had been revitalized by defeat. The loser was winning. It was her hope that soon perhaps everyone would turn to "the business of daily living," and "that will be enough" (637).

It was not enough. In comparison to the sinister energy of the Nazis, her hope proved pitifully inadequate. Over the long course of the war, Gertrude Stein shifted her point of view, although it always remained limited. She lacked a global imagination, and it was this provinciality that laid her vulnerable to charges of callousness and stupidity. When Russia entered the war and "smashed" Poland, Gertrude Stein said candidly, "I did not care about Poland, but it did frighten me about France . . ." (*SW*, 615). Poland had no more reality to her than the Philippines or Italian Somaliland. She remained invincibly local, so that her emotion was reserved for those whose immediate existence possessed reality for her.

In 1941, Alice Toklas believed that Marshal Pétain might be France's George Washington, "first in peace and first in war and first in the hearts of his countrymen . . ." (GS to T. Wilder, 13 January 1941, YCAL). A year and a half later, Gertrude Stein had "about decided" to translate Pétain's *Paroles Aux Français, Messages et Écrits, 1934–1941*, "for America" (GS to W. G. Rogers, I September 1942, YCAL). That she translated 180 pages—the bulk of Pétain's book—attests to the seriousness of her commitment.*

In the introduction she prepared for the volume, Gertrude Stein offered Pétain as the savior of France, first at the battle of Verdun and

* Alice Toklas corrected and revised Gertrude Stein's literal version. For example, "Politique Éxterieure," Gertrude Stein translated as "Foreign politics" until Alice Toklas changed it to "Foreign policy." Similarly, "ses entraves actuelles" she rendered "its actual fetters," changed by Alice Toklas to "its present fetters" (MS, vol. 2, YCAL).

now in restoring the faith of the French people. She believed that Pearl Harbor had made it possible for Americans to comprehend now "so convincing and so moving a story." Before that debacle, "we in the United States . . . have been spoiled children." Until they became familiar with defeat, Americans could not understand Pétain's patriotism. Pétain's evocation of traditional French values accorded precisely with the views Gertrude Stein had recently expressed in *Paris France*. In her translation of one of his appeals to the people—"The soil does not lie. It remains your resource. It is your country stuff. A field left uncultivated is a part of France which dies" (MS, vol. 2, YCAL). At the time, Gertrude Stein's gratitude for Pétain's restoration of order in French life overrode all other considerations. In this, she reflected the bulk of local opinion, which regarded Pétain's armistice as a reasonable act. "Being vanquished was a sadness and a sorrow and a weakness and a woe but it was not a horror" (*WIHS*, 33). On the other hand, she was surprised and even indignant at first that so many of the French "were not sure that they did not want the Germans to win" (81). Then a banker explained it to her. A single person could entertain several points of view simultaneously, he said. A man could wish an English victory so that his business would be secure. And yet that same man, if he had a son who was a prisoner, might want the Germans to win so that his son would be returned to him as quickly as possible. Still, at the time that France sued for peace with the Germans, the Germans were allied with the Russians; therefore, that same businessman might, out of fear of communism, prefer the English. And yet, the French prefer order, which was precisely what Pétain promised them. So, when the armistice was signed, "we were all glad in a way and completely sad in a way and we had so many opinions" (81, 87).*

"The Winner Loses," like *Paris France*, was an independent assessment of life in the provinces at the beginning of the war. Gertrude Stein's most intricate reaction to those years was *Mrs. Reynolds*, a long novel in which she reverted to the monotonous discontinuities and obscurity of her earlier career. *Mrs. Reynolds* cannot be advanced as a pleasurable reading experience. Its record of pointless and apparently repetitive experiences is often irritating. Nonetheless, the book manages to convey the shifting feelings of an unexceptional person menaced by events over which she has absolutely no control. Both in individual mo-

* The explanation of mixed French reactions first appeared in Gertrude Stein's introduction to Pétain's *Paroles* (MS pp. 12–14, YCAL).

ments and cumulatively it has more substance than her public pieces. Gertrude Stein needed the bewildering depths of her intuition to create the psychic reality of wartime in the country.

Mrs. Reynolds records the daily domestic life of a couple living in some unspecified place during a war. Although most of the characters have Anglo-Saxon names, the subject is obviously life in unoccupied France. Its menace, whose career at first runs parallel with Mrs. Reynolds's, then toward the middle of the book, becomes the clock by which the passage of time is measured, is one Angel Harper. He is clearly a version of Adolf Hitler, treated as if he were originally a member of the community who then departed. While Mrs. Reynolds never knew him, the neighbors recall his childhood and people occasionally arrive with fresh news about him. In the early part of the novel, another strange figure, Joseph Lane, receives almost as much attention as Angel Harper. More self-confident and calm than the troubled Angel Harper, he was intended to represent Joseph Stalin, although Gertrude Stein finally made little effective use of him. Reports about Lane turn up so infrequently that his character never coalesces, nor does he ever enter actively into the plot, such as it is.*

Angel Harper is described as having been a corporal at twenty-five, then later a "dictator" who made everyone go to war and suffer (83, 17, 33). Still, his portrait is not a hostile one. Gertrude Stein creates his character in two ways. She provides a series of reports of what he has done or is doing, or how he feels. These are often enigmatic. For example, "as he grew older he grew fonder and fonder of potatoes. Besides eating them he liked to rub raw ones over his hands and arms and face. / He liked it better than soap" (21). About the time he turns fifty, Angel Harper's unseen presence begins to dominate the narrative. (Hitler having been born 20 April 1889, this would make the time 1939, the year the war began.)

Angel Harper's character also expands in a series of incidents, each of which he associates with a particular age of his youth. The incidents suggest a lonely and disturbed development. At nine "he asked the others to build him a little room that would be like a prison and in that he sat . . ." (221). At twelve, "he was in a very strange costume, a hat of a girl and an apron of his mother and he was playing with water, he remembered the water was coming out of a faucet . . ." (223).† In

* See Gertrude Stein's letter to W. G. Rogers, 24 November 1940 for an overt identification of Harper and Lane as Hitler and Stalin (YCAL).
† Neither *Mein Kampf*, nor the several specialized studies of Hitler's youth give any indication that Gertrude Stein based these incidents on recorded fact.

providing such bizarre details, Gertrude Stein did not seem to intend to ridicule or expose Angel Harper. They are offered with a sleepwalking intensity not easy to account for. The over-all impression made by these scraps of information is of a nervous, insecure, and sexually disordered man. Yet, while Angel Harper is not regarded with hostility, neither is he the subject of sympathy, although near the opening of the novel, Mrs. Reynolds is said to have prayed "not against Angel Harper but she prayed for his opponent and she prayed against his friends" (33). Possibly the reason for this selective animus was that Francis Rose had described Hitler to her, if not sympathetically, at least as a human being of complex motives. Later, however, as the war and its tensions persist, Mrs. Reynolds passionately longs for Angel Harper's death.

Mrs. Reynolds is not altogether an autobiographical figure, even though she is "heavy" and "quite plump," has dogs, meditates on George Washington, reads detective stories, takes walks, gardens, talks with the neighbors, and generally engages in those activities that Alice Toklas and Gertrude Stein did when they were in the country, including contemplating flight, then deciding against it (44, 165, 265, 41, 42, 99, and passim).* Mr. and Mrs. Reynolds seem to be composites of Gertrude Stein and Alice Toklas. She and her husband form a sympathetic union. With his calm irony, he serves as a solid contrast to her excitable, superstitious, and emotional nature. On a characteristic day Mrs. Reynolds goes out where she sees or hears something that arouses her feelings, then returns to the house to tell Mr. Reynolds about it. He responds to her account with short, bemused answers, then suggests that it is time to go to bed. He is her ballast, her keel. As Mrs. Reynolds moves through her "ups and downs," his unruffled adherence to the quiet life stabilizes her moods (170). He has a rational fatalism that Mrs. Reynolds often shares, but which she cannot consistently maintain. For example, in response to her reliance upon prophetic signs, "Mr. Reynolds said that if the weather was set to be fair all the signs that look like rain do not count and if the weather is set for rain all the signs that look like clearing do not count. And he was right. It was the same about war and about victories" (59–60). When her charitable nature veers toward forgiveness of the enemy, Mr. Reynolds

* Her birthday is designated as just 10 days after Angel Harper's, which detail happens to fit Alice Toklas, for Hitler was born April 20, she April 30. Gertrude Stein wrote W. G. Rogers that with that birthdate, Alice Toklas "comes right in with the king of Spain and Hitler and Daisy Fellowes, horoscopically speaking it's a mixed bag, of which we have the Pearl" (*When This You See*, 23).

instructs her firmly, "Do not in any way whatever happens to them do not pity them." She comprehends the justice of this. When men are really bad, "they must end" (131).

Their conversations reveal a woman sensitive to nuance, subtle, ever probing for the meaning of gestures, and a man, courteous but sceptical.

> Mrs. Reynolds suddenly woke up she heard herself saying if he is fifty and he is how old is everybody, and Mr. Reynolds woke up too and said he did not know. How could he know how old everybody is, even Mrs. Reynolds now that she was really awake knew that she could not know how old anybody is. . . . Why then said Mr. Reynolds do you bother and Mrs. Reynolds began to laugh and cry. . . . Mr. Reynolds said go to sleep and they went to sleep . . . (159)

Mrs. Reynolds depends upon her husband's strength. Invariably pleasant and never visibly worried, he believes in the restorative of sleep. Even though the external world is in a state of perpetual change, the one thing that remains the same is sleep—"even if they dreamed well it was all right because dreams go by contraries or else they do not and so the night was all right" (183, 187, 183). Mr. Reynolds then is the solid home post around which Mrs. Reynolds's feelings revolve.

The theme of the book appears in the first sentence. "It takes courage to be courageous said Mrs. Reynolds" (1). Even as ordinary life proceeds, the peril that requires courage envelops them. "Claudia ate cheese with her knife and slowly it was enormous not the cheese but everything and they were all of it" (35). Portents of literal danger appear. Thinking of the black market in food, Mrs. Reynolds foresees the time when purchase will be a matter not of money but of personality. "If you are popular you can buy if you are not popular you can die" (22).*

The danger she encounters is rarely dramatic or immediate. Rather, inner doubts awaken fear and wrap a pall of uncertainty about otherwise harmless external incidents. Without actually revealing their source or dimension, those doubts penetrate her dreams and make her uneasy at night as well. She had ominous daytime visions such as "three very very large dark red slugs climbing a tree" and moving "very very slowly" (12). Another day Mrs. Reynolds came upon some children piling dirt on "a terrible big beetle . . . and the more they covered him with dust the more he worked his way out. / Oh yes said Mrs. Reynolds" (65). The crisis recorded in *Mrs. Reynolds* is low-keyed and continuous, never resolved but never fatal either.

* The observation is attributed to Madame Pierlot in *WIHS*, 45, and *WIR*, 163.

The war was not the sole source of Mrs. Reynolds's malaise. As it happened, the coming of the European catastrophe coincided with Gertrude Stein's renewed brooding over her mortality. Her wistful versions of apotheosis in the enthronements and worship of Rose, Marguerite, and Ida were incapable of permanently dissipating the idea of death. "Every day Mrs. Reynolds remembered yesterday. . . . I never did before, I used to just remember today but said she I always remember yesterday" (154). Yesterday signified how far she had come and how close she was to being superseded. As soon as Mrs. Reynolds announces her new propensity for reminiscence, we learn that no children had come that day, that Mrs. Reynolds had never had a child, and indeed, that she was not very fond of them. Nonetheless, she begins to cry, although for what reason she does not know (154). Symptoms of the grand climacteric were upon her. After years of resolutely shoving the past away and denying its legitimacy, she found it crowding irresistibly in upon her. "The past was never past enough" (253).

Not all her encounters were ominous. More often the incidents she observed were banal but slightly askew. She encounters a total stranger from Hudson's Bay whose name turns out to be Hudson (171–2). She meets a colonel dressed in his best clothes. He salutes her "with a very pretty motion" (186). Her dog is frightened by soldiers firing guns (144). A lamb dies of hunger (145). There is a windstorm but no rain accompanies it (228). All these incidents contribute to her uneasiness. "There is no use blinding oneself to it," says Mrs. Reynolds, "all these things are happening" (144). For a time she inquires of everybody she meets what *is* happening (69). But the military and political situations are utterly confused. Yet Mrs. Reynolds cannot bring herself to accept an existential dictum: "What is going to happen now is what is happening now" (196). She objects to this as too parochial. "I do not mean that I mean everything" (196). Gertrude Stein's whole aesthetic, if not practice, had long been based upon the assumption that reality consisted precisely in "what is happening now." But the international clamor at this point in time made her leading character yearn for a comprehensive understanding.

Sometimes her dreams were clear instances of wish fulfillment. "Mrs. Reynolds dreamed about two very large slices of ham upon a silver salver" (205–6).* Or, she dreams that Mr. Reynolds has said to her, "My love my love, I love my love." Awakened and informed of the dream, his response is comically compassionate. "He said, if you

* The ham dream is Alice Toklas's. See *ABT Cook Book*, 218, and *WIR*, 164.

dreamed it then I did say it, and he went to sleep" (92). Another time, Mrs. Reynolds dreams that Angel Harper is "over" (66). Some of her dreams are more surrealistic, as the one of a wild rabbit that followed her, wanting to be tame, and of the friend with a frog inside her that a doctor had to remove (64, 84). Once she frightens herself by dreaming that "nobody had a name." Mr. Reynolds thought that this might actually come about. Mrs. Reynolds replied that she would dislike it if it did. "And Mr. Reynolds said her liking it or not would not stop it" (150).

Mrs. Reynolds places a great deal of credence in prophetic books, especially those of saints. In the swirl of uncontrollable international events, the hope that prophecy offered was her buttress against total depression. Saint Odile and Saint Godfrey offered just enough detail to gain Mrs. Reynolds's assent (33, 39). The fact that they were saints reassured her, for "she preferred that a man should be a holy man if he was to predict coming events . . ." (23).

The saints' predictions of eventual victory for France and the Lord were occasionally challenged. When asked about the future, one "very pleasant" man had a stock answer. "He always said there was nothing to look forward to except ruin. Ruin was inevitable" (20). Two women sum up man's fate even more bleakly. "They said, when you ring nobody answers and when you do not ring nobody answers" (60). Although Mrs. Reynolds is too good-natured to accept these gloomy assessments for long, Angel Harper's continuing success does dampen her normally ebullient spirits. She regarded little birds as optimistic, because they sang in the rain. But when one of these birds sought recognition in the very formula Gertrude Stein had long employed, Mrs. Reynolds was no longer responsive.

> When this you see remember me sang a little bird.
> But what was the use. . . .
> Mrs. Reynolds said she preferred potatoes.
> And she was right. (58)

Eventually, as the war persisted and as it got "darker in the morning and in the evening," Mrs. Reynolds realized "there was no use wishing . . . it was quieter when there was no use wishing . . ." (137). She still asked everyone she met if there was anything to do, but she knew there was not (171). One day, late in the book, when she suddenly finds herself bereft of hope, she feels the better for it (231).

The distress Mrs. Reynolds must endure is primarily psychological, although of no great force. Its principal manifestation is unmotivated weeping. But her anguish is no less wearing for being muted, for it is persistent. Gertrude Stein conveys the effect of day-to-day worrying, of fluctuations of moods, of the slim props against which hope leans, and the silent, unseen forces that knock them away. Like her creator, Mrs. Reynolds is buffetted by contradictory feelings. An incident in the garden dramatizes her ambivalence. Seeing some mice run under the raspberry bushes, she calls a gardener to capture them. He catches two, which he then kills by squeezing them between his thumb and fore-finger. One mouse escapes though. "Mrs. Reynolds did not know how she felt about it" (200). The mice could not be permitted to eat precious food. Yet their elimination, for which Mrs. Reynolds was indirectly responsible, was cruel. The conflict within her could be reconciled only in the exclamation, "Yes life is strife, dear life, dear life" (156).

Mrs. Reynolds's basic solution for incertitude is bed. But that does not solve the following day. Once she comes home with "an underground happy feeling that it is all the same . . ." She seeks Mr. Reynolds's agreement—"yes or no." His reply reveals how he sustains his equilibrium. "Mr. Reynolds said yes yes, and no no, or if you like it better yes no or no yes." Undaunted by her husband's formulaic responses, Mrs. Reynolds asserts the essential acceptance she feels. "Yes said Mrs. Reynolds, yes and nevertheless makes it just the same . . ." (236). In that statement, "nevertheless" balances "yes," although the positive is emphasized.

The Yale editors have dated *Mrs. Reynolds* 1940–42, but the eleventh section refers to 23 December 1942, and the twelfth and thirteenth sections were almost certainly written more than a year later (232). For these concluding sections have references in them to the springing up of the Resistance, the German debacle in Russia, rumors of the Nazis weakening, and the comforting hum of bombers on their way to Italy (246–7, 252, 263, 264; for the bombers, see also *WIHS*, 22). Holding on till the end makes the populace uncomfortable and irritable—"it is very hard to wait that last day" (260). Then suddenly in the autumn, not because of any specific event, "It is finished said Mrs. Reynolds, it is not ended yet but it is finished" (265). The book concludes on a note of subdued victory. "Saint Odile had not been mistaken. Angel Harper was not fifty-five alive" (266). But even though Mr. and Mrs. Reynolds go to sleep at the end "very happily," the general mood is hardly celebrative.

In an epilogue Gertrude Stein noted, "There is nothing historical about this book except the state of mind" (267). That is assuredly accurate and it is its excellence. *Mrs. Reynolds* contains a credible history of a mind existing from day to day under wearing circumstances. The book never sentimentalizes wartime conditions in the provinces. Daily life goes on with its usual incidence of monotony, a good deal of inconvenience, some drama, and much psychological anxiety. The region still experiences adultery, assaults, suicide, and accidental deaths, often by drowning. But over it all hangs the oppressive cloud of Angel Harper.

Through it all, and with the assistance of her husband, Mrs. Reynolds gives a demonstration of survival techniques. She has the considerable advantage of a grateful nature. "When she went to sleep she said thank you for the pillow" (38). She easily absorbs the wry truth that "it is very convenient to like what you have" (211). Her own experience taught her to believe that the world will provide, or destroy. "If it rains on one day there will be no hay, if it rains the next day there will be no wheat, and if it rains the next day there will be no wine. But all the same there is hay and wheat and wine, all the time" (56). *Mrs. Reynolds* is a chronicle of secular faith, troubled and wavering, but finally in its quiet, unexceptional way, justified.

The circling narrative of Mrs. Reynolds might have done for a short war, but it would not suffice for the seemingly endless conflict Europe was obliged to endure.* Some time in early 1943 therefore, Gertrude Stein started a kind of daybook which she kept until the end of August 1944, when the American army finally reached her neighborhood. Published as *Wars I Have Seen*, the book records her experience during the last fifteen months of the war. It runs as a consecutive monologue with no formal stopping-places, save paragraphing. After the first forty pages or so, she begins to announce the first of each month as she proceeds, as well as other significant dates such as Easter and Bastille Day.†

* Gertrude Stein believed *Mrs. Reynolds* was "almost done" as Angel Harper entered his fifty-first year (ca. p. 161), but she squeezed out another hundred pages before actually putting an end to the book (GS to Carl Van Vechten, 23 March 1942, and GS to W. G. Rogers, 26 March 1942, YCAL).
† A few dates are out of sequence. For example, on p. 31 Gertrude Stein refers first to "now in 1943" and then to "Now in 1942 in April 1942 . . ." And on p. 105, "it is the first of December 1943," then on 106, "now November 1943." These may be misprints, as is the case in the first instance cited. In the MS Gertrude Stein wrote, "Now in 1943 in May 1943 . . ." In red pencil, Alice Toklas noted, "perhaps you'd like to make it April." The month was changed in the printed text—but so was the year (*WIHS* MS, vol. 2, YCAL). In other cases, Gertrude

On the whole, *Wars I Have Seen* reads easily, although there are spots, especially in the early pages, when without warning or explanation, personal feelings well up to interrupt the exposition. "Today we were at Aix-les-Bains, end of June 1943 when this you see remember me, and in a kind of way it was different . . ." (46). At another moment as she prepared to discuss anti-semitism, she suddenly interjected, apropos of nothing identifiable—"He can read acasias, hands and faces" (55). Some difficulty is also caused by exceedingly long sentences which were rendered more complicated by her refusal to use commas: ". . . this question of realism was becoming the vital question for Americans who having a land with a clear light manufacturing light and resistant steel, their life needed a clear and resistant realism . . ." (48). But the first part, where these stylistic oddities congregate is quite different from the balance of the book. It evidently constitutes what she first regarded as "An Emotional Autobiography," for the early pages turn inward and back in time.

Gertrude Stein had long ago proposed that great social upheavals represent the death throes of a certain style of living, which she believed last about a century. She now believed she could distinguish definite periods in human life. The two she discussed before tiring of her theory were from "babyhood" to fourteen, and from fourteen to twenty-four. The first she designated as the "legendary" period, the second, as the "medieval" or "pioneer" period (20, 26). She could detect a legendary quality to childhood because every event in it was sanctified by its consummate importance to the child. "They can become a legend if they hold a flower in each hand, they can become a legend if they had an accident and lost a finger . . ." In time though, self-consciousness intruded; then "the legend is not so pure because you mix yourself up with it" (20).

Her account alternates between idealizing her childhood and invoking its bitter psychological conflicts. "Such wars as there were were inside me, and naturally although I was a very happy child there were quite a number of such wars" (6). Her father was the prime agent for her misery. He imposed the responsibility for her illnesses upon her, reproaching her "whenever I had anything the matter with me" by reminding her that after all she had been born "a perfect baby." Child-

---

Stein may have been playing with dates, although that is very unlikely. Her mood was far from mischievous at this time. She may have been deliberately crossing back and forth in time, but if she was, the point of the exercise is not clear. Finally, it is possible that in arranging the manuscript, she may have inadvertently joined certain parts out of sequence.

hood then was a time of legendary perfection for her, but also one of growing anger, fear, guilt, and remorse, negative emotions that peaked in adolescence.

It was particularly necessary to struggle, she said, "not to know that death is there . . ." (21). Death haunted her childhood. "Death starts history and fears. And that begins very soon and dies out little by little or not at all or all" (9). She remembered being "very worried" when as a girl she read of someone dying, for if this person had no children, then there would be no continuity. This bothered her "from that time on until just now" (15). When she encountered Swift's Struldbruggs, she wondered why it was necessary to live eternally as an old person— why not eternal youth? But later she realized that if no one died, then there would be no room in the world for her—"I could not have come to be." Being excluded from life would have bothered her "as much as anything," she said, and yet when she tried that logic on herself now as she approached her seventieth birthday, she found the idea of dying in order to make room for new life "not a thing to be liking" (24).

These dramatic and disconnected notes were all that Gertrude Stein could produce after rummaging in her formative years. Seeking to account for the war by finding an analogy for it in her personal life, and at the same time trying to reconcile herself to the certainty of her impending death, she could resolve neither the outer military conflict nor the inner psychological one. She was temporarily reduced to pronouncing life meaningless and unreal. Events now struck her as without purpose, as utterly coincidental. She was then reading Shakespeare's history plays, and they confirmed for her that "nothing was anything," and worse, "that human beings had no meaning" (13). She sank into an apathy where "it does seem that the future is not important any more," and where the world "does not mean much and there is no love interest in it . . ." (15–16). Soon though, she turned these depressing notions to positive ends. "The meaningless of why makes all the nothingness so real" (13). No answers were sufficient to explain the war. All she could be certain of was that this war had ended the nineteenth century once and for all. The war "kills it dead, dead, dead" (79).

That conclusion salvaged Gertrude Stein's spirits, and she turned with relief to asserting what she found possible to accept: that this dreary, bewildering, brutal war validated her career. No one could possibly believe in progress any longer. Human affairs were too chaotic for anyone to accept the existence of natural laws—not even the law of chance. "Coincidences are real again, they recreate faith, they make a future, and they will make the twentieth century. Everybody, wait and see" (21). She herself had been brought up to believe that "everything was being understood," that there would be no more wars, and that "if death and life were not understood and eternity and beginning was not understood," then it was the better part of wisdom not to think about them. Now she was positive that there was no genuine progress (62). Nothing was to be discovered from facts; accordingly, the nineteenth-century enthusiasm for literary realism was terminated in 1938. "There is no realism now, life is not real it is not earnest, it is strange . . ." (44). Its strangeness shows up in its unpredictability, its chanciness. The first World War had been a simple one, but this—"oh it is all so complicated." Still, "I must say I like it" (70). She liked it, or could bring herself to say that she did, because she had devised a means by which the confusions and alarms of war would confirm her interpretation of the twentieth century.

In the middle of 1943, shortly after she had begun *Wars I Have Seen,* several events shifted Gertrude Stein's attention from the past to the present. For a time, the monotony of rural isolation had encouraged introspection. Vegetable gardens symbolized her boredom. How happy were the days, she remarked, "when vegetables grew not in the ground but in tins" (39). But then the Germans commenced to clamp down upon the French. They began taking young men away as hostages, and to work in the munitions factories in Germany. At the same time, Gertrude Stein became concerned lest her new servant, Olympe, might denounce Alice and herself (41). And then, after some unsuccessful legal action, she was obliged to give up her home in Bilignin to her landlord who needed a place for his family. Just as she moved to nearby Culoz, the warning came to flee instantly to Switzerland (49–50). Since they did not, very soon German and then Italian soldiers were billeted in their new house. By the time this series of crises had passed, Gertrude Stein's attention was fixed upon the present again.

The main strength of *Wars I Have Seen* lies in its dramatization of the complexity of the actual. "The mental workings of people in a time like this are so simple and natural that they are completely surprising" (180). "Thinking agriculturally," Gertrude Stein recorded the mundane life of the country (184). An example of her ability to seize the logic of surface illogicality occurred in 1944. After two years during which everyone wore shoes with wooden soles, suddenly leather shoes appeared. Noticing this, Gertrude Stein sought an explanation. The one she uncovered was that the provident French had stored away their best shoes until the war gave signs of coming to an end, then brought them out. At the same time, the shopkeepers, having hoarded their stock of pre-war shoes, now released them "at big prices before prices became normal" (123). She was similarly bemused at the absurdity of "the motorised German army being carried around by French taixs" (103).

As "rather favored strangers," she and Alice did not suffer deprivation during the war (114). From friendly local officials and tradesmen they quickly learned the "system D, debrouillez-vous, that is look around and find the way" (163). For them, this meant discreet use of the black market in food.

Nonetheless, the occupation became increasingly stifling. Petty officialdom aroused Gertrude Stein's animus. The disparity between the judgment of government employees and that of the man in the street particularly struck her. Rankled by continual restraints, she decided that the bureaucrats' occupational security put them out of touch with "the business of living," where they were free to concentrate on believing what they were told to believe (54). Their detachment from ordinary life coupled with their zeal on behalf of their employer, the government, was in large part responsible for wars. Lacking independence themselves, they attempted to impose their servitude on others. Thoroughly chafed by regulation, Gertrude Stein burst into a long appreciation of independence. The one thing anyone wanted, she said, was to be free. "Even if they are not free they want to feel free . . . and not to be managed, threatened, directed, restrained, obliged, fearful, administered . . ." (75). When she made her first broadcast after being liberated, the strength of her passion remained undiminished. "I can tell you that liberty is the most important thing in the world more important than food and clothes more important than anything on this mortal earth . . ." (Eric Sevareid, *Not So Wild A Dream*, 462).

Gertrude Stein's growing admiration for the maquis counterbalanced her conservatism. The signs of French resistance appeared slowly. Informers were threatened by being sent small wooden coffins (42). Trains were blown up—"nobody just knows why they do it, but they do . . ." (67). The son of a count, an escaped prisoner, was shot as he emerged from church on the grounds that he was in the pay of the Germans. The charge was denied. He "seems to have been a gentle and defeated soul." All Gertrude Stein can say at this point is "it is all so mixed" (91). On several occasions she said that Fenimore

Cooper's *The Spy* closely approximated the situation of conflicting loyalties and judgments based on equivocal evidence that the French were obliged to endure. As in the American Revolution, there were patriots and false patriots, denunciations and deceptions. "Anybody could be an enemy and anybody not" (164, 170).

Originally, the "mountain boys" were young men who had fled to avoid being taken by the Germans. Gertrude Stein sometimes encountered them during her walks at night as they descended from the mountains for dinner and a warm bed. At first they rarely did much against the Germans, nor were they much harassed (98–99). But in 1944, "just like Robin Hood," they started to confiscate supplies from unpopular farmers (133). Now their behavior appealed to Gertrude Stein. They were, after all, the children of acquaintances and seemed "so young so gay so disciplined" (133). She recognized the hard choice the local young men had to make when they came of age. "Shall you betake yourself to the mountains, shall you stay at home and risk it, shall you go to Germany and hate it . . ." (143). Without underestimating the difficulty of the decision, Gertrude Stein refused to moralize the individual's choice. For her, it was a matter of the boy deciding "which he has the strength for" (144).

As the war approached its climax, the fearful Germans grew alternately more vicious and more polite, while the maquis became increasingly daring. Gertrude Stein mentions that "some charming neighbors" who were "firm reactionaries" regarded all the maquis as plain terrorists. Their opinion worried her, for she feared that an angry populace might harm them "and we are very fond of them" (206). She took equal note of the false maquis, those roving bands who capitalized on the temporary sanction of marauders, and frightened the local residents. Even the true resistance forces alarmed them, for when the maquis descended from the mountains to clash with the Germans, then withdrew again, the Germans were likely to retaliate with indiscriminate burning and killing (218).

Gertrude Stein's tone changed perceptibly in this quasi-diary of *Wars I Have Seen* as the Germans departed. She accepted the resistance as the necessary response of the young, who were a generation without futures (190). Her adaptability came dangerously close to sycophancy. She now reported her quarrels with the local "old grumblers," "decayed aristocrats," and "decayed bourgeoisie, who feel sure that everybody but themselves should be disciplined" (227). As the "suffocating cloud" of the occupation was lifted, "honneur aux maquis, one cannot say it too often" (236, 243).

The very last pages of the book describing Gertrude Stein's search for the Americans in the neighborhood, also border on the unpleasant. Just before the American army arrived, a friend drove to Switzerland. "We have asked him to bring back with him a newspaper man or a newspaper woman, or two of them, if he did that would be nice" (242). When Gertrude Stein encountered her first soldiers, "I told them who we were and they knew" (245). Her reception of the Americans was openly affectionate. There was something, she observed, "in this native land business" (250). She patted and kissed the soldiers, questioned them about their backgrounds, and concluded the book as a passionate patriot.

On the face of it, her hunger for her countrymen is attractive. What spoils it is her unconcealed and ravening need for recognition. The experience of being cut off from public appreciation for almost five years had been a severe trial for her. Three one-act dramatic fantasies composed during the war years suggest the state of her imagination when turned away from the war. Briefly, "In A Garden" concerns a woman who is wooed by two kings. Although aware that she is herself uncrowned, she insists, "I know I am a queen . . ." (*GSFR*, 61). After the men kill one another contesting for her hand, she crowns herself with their two crowns. "Look and Long" features an apparition who makes one person so thin he can slip through a ring; who turns a boy named Silly into Willy and then obliges him to sit on Susy who is turned into a bad egg; and finally who splits Oliver in two, except that he manages to hold himself together with string and sticking plaster. In the last play, "Three Sisters Who Are Not Sisters," five children decide to perform a play of murder. When all but Jenny have been slain, she takes poison, up come the lights, and the children go off to bed. Regal ambition, dangerous transformations, murder, and sleep— these were the fantasies that churned behind Gertrude Stein's anxiety to be recognized again.*

In *Wars I Have Seen* Gertrude Stein had introduced a long and seemingly trivial description of a train trip. But in its two major incidents, Gertrude Stein first slurred the writer whom she regarded as her chief rival, then recorded proof of her continuing fame. In the first

---

* With the assistance of Pierre Balmain, these plays were performed by local children. See "From Dark to Day," *Vogue* (November 1945), 52.

episode she recalled seeing a German soldier—or worse, "a Czech or something" in a German uniform (in other words, a traitor)—who resembled Hemingway when he was young. By forcing the proprietress of a bar to shake hands with him when he leaves, he humiliates her. "To sell and take money is one thing but to shake hands is another . . ." (118). In the second incident, she discovers a French translation of *The Autobiography of Alice B. Toklas* on sale in the train station. "Very excited," Gertrude Stein is then asked by a ticket seller to autograph the book (119–20). It was small wonder that in the ecstatic moments of the liberation, she identified completely with the democratic vitality of the "G. I. Joes" (259). Their poise and confidence impressed her. In "dominating their language" they had "become men" (259). Like magicians they had transformed the long desolation of war during which everyone had been a refugee or a prisoner into a casual festival of freedom. Equally important, they lifted their compatriot out of obscurity into the light of recognition again.

Around the beginning of 1944, Gertrude Stein noted in *Wars I Have Seen* that she had as a neighbor a "very charming oldish lady who lives in a castle" with her children. One of her daughters, Claude, had given birth to a baby. Gertrude Stein added that she was "just now writing a novel about them Castles in Which We Live" (123). The piece survives, perhaps incomplete, at Yale under the title of "Castles they live in. Castles on the wall." Its importance is that the same family figures centrally in the first straight dramatic play of Gertrude Stein's ever to be staged. The original title, *In Savoy* (and so published in England), was later changed to *Yes Is For A Very Young Man*.* The daughter Claude is one of the four principals of the play, although sometime after the first version was completed she was renamed Denise. A castle-dweller, she is married to Henry, a member of the Resistance. In five scenes, the play chronicles the fortunes of this pairing, from the armistice of 1940 through the liberation in 1944.

Gertrude Stein was unusually sensitive to the tensions caused by conflicting loyalties. Not only did she compare the French experience to that of the Americans during the Revolutionary War, but upon later

---

* Information about the first four stagings of *Yes*—in Pasadena, London, and twice in Princeton—appears in Carl Van Vechten's introduction to *Last Operas and Plays*, pp. xii–xvi. It also includes Gertrude Stein's program notes for the Pasadena production. The evidence is conclusive that the play was revised, but details about when it was started are scanty. Donald Gallup remembers having read the first complete version in MS on 12 January 1945 (*LO&P*, xiv).

reflection, she also recalled stories her mother told her about life in Baltimore during the Civil War—"the divided families, the bitterness, the quarrels and sometimes the denunciations . . ." In spite of the rancor though, she said that these people—and by implication, all people—realized "the natural necessity of their all continuing to live their daily life together, because after all that was all the life they had, besides they were after all the same family or their neighbors, and in the country neighbors are neighbors" (Program notes for *Yes, LO&P,* xv).

The compromise of an armed truce seemed to her the civilized solution. Life and war were synonymous to her (*WIHS,* 15). There was always a struggle in progress, and an unjust one at that. No hope existed for ultimate survival, yet she believed one must hope. When one of the characters in *Yes Is For A Very Young Man* objects that, "Yes can be said too often," the response is firm. "What is there to say but yes, no does not mean anything" (*LO&P,* 8–9). Without yielding their awareness of the bleak truth, Gertrude Stein and her characters tried to practice optimism.

The characters at odds over the use of the word "yes" are Ferdinand, Henry's younger brother, and Constance, an American woman, described in the stage directions as "A Young Woman in white." In a letter, Gertrude Stein said that "Constance in a kind of a way is a woman if you know what I mean like Claire [*sic*] Luce" possessing "a certain kind of virginity even if married and having children." It was a condition that Gertrude Stein regarded as typically American (GS to Mr. and Mrs. Lamont Johnson and Mr. and Mrs. Robert Claiborne, January 1946, YCAL). Mrs. Luce had visited her at Bilignin in the summer of 1939, so she was at least minimally associated with the region and the time (Brinnin, 364). Constance has opinions about American men such as might be expected from the author of the recent comedy, *The Women* (a copy of which she presented to Gertrude Stein). Asked if American men are "attractive and passionate" like the French, she responds, "Perhaps not, perhaps they ask less and they give more . . ." (12). When wooed by the youthful Ferdinand in the first scene of the play, she turns him away with a gentle world-weariness, for he is still only a yea-saying youngster.* Their incipient affair re-

---

* Like Gertrude Stein, Constance is an American living in wartime France with two servants named Olympe and Clothilde. Other personal details, drawn from *WIHS,* such as the wish that vegetables would grow in tins again, are distributed among the other characters.

mains undeveloped. This must be one of the rarest situations in stage history: a lovers' disagreement in the first act that fails to be resolved in the last.

Ferdinand must make several difficult decisions during the four years covered by the play. Because he shares Gertrude Stein's range of tolerance, they are especially trying. His first speech reveals his anguish. "I take everybody's side. Don't keep at me, you make me cry" (3). Ferdinand is the sober, rational spokesman for the French viewpoint that regards Pétain's armistice as wise. "An armistice is not peace, it is a truce and as long as there is no peace we are at war with Germany even if we are not fighting" (7).

When ordered by the Germans to join their labor force, Ferdinand first goes to the mountains to consider whether he wishes to join the maquis. He is troubled, because most of them are "a pretty lawless lot, gutter snipes you know." What bothers him even more is "anything awful they order you to do you got to do. I don't blame them but could I do it . . ." (21). His trepidation, coupled with a fear of reprisals that might be taken against his parents or his two brothers imprisoned in Germany, determine his decision to obey the order to go to Germany. Once there, he becomes not only the foreman of the factory, but also representative of the French workers to the Germans. He returns to France for the Liberation (just how he manages this is left vague), but at the end of the play, he shakes hands with Constance, the woman for whose affection he had earlier pleaded, and returns to Germany to organize the workers' resistance there.

Ferdinand's thoughtful courage contrasts with that of his more explosive and sardonic older brother. Henry suffers under the goad of his reactionary wife and her family. His brother-in-law, Achille, although never on stage, is referred to frequently. He is one of those who give their allegiance unquestioningly to authority. Before the armistice, he shoots down six German planes, then enlists in Marshal Pétain's army. When the Marshal is deposed, he anticipates joining the Americans in the war against Japan. Loathing such expedient behavior, Henry throws himself into the Resistance. Constance joins him in this effort, and in the most improbable part of the play is discovered passing messages about German supply trains.

Yes Is For A Very Young Man is poor, crude theater. Its language is often ludicrously stiff, as when Henry announces his father's murder by crying, "Those loathly birds, they have killed my father" (42). On several occasions, characters stop to deliver long set speeches drawn from the pages of *Wars I Have Seen.** The action is loose, often improbable and insufficiently developed, and rarely dramatic. The few successful moments come when Gertrude Stein deals with the tensions that wrung French men and women of good will.

One such moment occurs when Henry learns by a telegram from his mother that the Germans have executed his father. He realizes that his mother specified the perpetrators of the murder "so Denise and her damned family could not say that it was terrorists and maquis who shot him." But then, churning with grief and anger, Henry's emotions swerve unexpectedly and he bursts out: "Oh my God, oh my God. I love my wife, I adore my baby" (42). In that single line, Gertrude Stein dramatized what it meant for a feeling man to be racked by contesting loyalties.

"Living in an occupied country is very complicated and that is what I have tried to make people understand in my play Yes is for a very young man," Gertrude Stein wrote Francis Rose (? 1946 Copy by Leon Katz, YCAL). Before she returned to Paris in December 1944, she had taken time to prepare this sincere but maladroit defense of the behavior of herself and her friends.† Now she became the enthusiastic partisan of a new generation of American liberators. The experience she accumulated while listening to the soldiers she poured into what was to be her last book, *Brewsie and Willie* (1946).‡

Brewsie and Willie records a series of conversations carried on by American soldiers and nurses. They are overheard, as it were, in long sessions of talk. Where these informal discussions take place is never certain. Sometimes they are outside, walking; mostly, however, they seem to be indoors, but whether at camp, or at Gertrude Stein's apartment, or somewhere else is not specified, nor need it be. The voices, arguing and worrying over the future, dominate the book. These are the new Americans talking about the faults they see in the world they have inherited, and how to improve it.

Gertrude Stein had recently expressed her preference for the ordinary soldier, saying that "anybody interested in art or literature almost automatically does not become an officer." She believed that even those

---

* For example, the murdered count, *Yes*, 30–31, *Wars*, 91; the German interpreter, Yes, 33–34, *Wars*, 223–5; the French war prisoner, *Yes*, 39, Wars, 136–7.
† The trip back to Paris is described in an interesting piece, "Raoul Dufy," *Harper's Bazaar* [New York] (December 1949), 93, 148, 154–7).
‡ In a New York *Times* dispatch, 24 August 1945, C. L. Sulzberger noted that Gertrude Stein had begun *Brewsie and Willie* "two weeks ago."

soldiers who were indifferent to the arts had freer minds than officers. Therefore "I gravitate naturally to the society of the enlisted men" (*Life* [6 August 1945], 56).

Although the speakers in *Brewsie and Willie* ostensibly come from various parts of the United States and from different social levels as well, they employ a common idiom. Gertrude Stein made no efforts to distinguish her Southern farmer from her Californian. The soldiers do seem members of that broad segment of American society that includes the lower and lower-middle classes. Most of the speakers use "ain't" and some military slang such as "flack" and "sucking up" to the Germans (10, 76). Their sentences are either very short, or very long with numerous independent clauses loosely connected with co-ordinating conjunctions. Despite a few dated and incongruous idioms—referring to a woman as a "wench" or as a "Jane"—on the whole the dialogue gives the impression of stylized authenticity (4, 53).

Because it exempted her from the need to develop her positions fully, dialogue was a particularly attractive way for Gertrude Stein to convey her ideas. She was constitutionally incapable of sustained exposition, for her mind rapidly clogged with qualifications and objections as she proceeded. Dialogue though permitted her to interject disagreements and illustrative anecdotes. And it sanctioned the abrupt change of subject. Concerned about the uniformity of American thought, Gertrude Stein warned, "You have to really learn to express complication" (114). The dialogue form was her means of doing that.

The two characters who give the book its title are friendly opposites. Their styles of living are complementary, even though they agree on fundamental matters. Both feel strongly and both must resist powerful undercurrents of pessimism. Willie is the dominant male of the book, however, and represents more closely than Brewsie the enlisted man's viewpoint. Loud, hard-headed, sceptical, sardonic, his characteristic response to a fanciful proposition is, "Oh get the hell out of here" (20). At the beginning of the book he is a hot-tempered bellower, but gradually, without losing its humorous and exaggerated edge, his character enlarges so that it may serve as a counter-weight to that of Brewsie.

Brewsie is the group's contemplative, who proposes the issues that the others debate. He talks to himself, fears he will cry, and sometimes absents himself from the group without explanation. Admittedly "kind of foggy in the head," he nonetheless wishes to be clear (11). That he is Gertrude Stein's spokesman is verified in a brief address "To Americans" appended to the book. In it, Gertrude Stein, speaking in her own voice, exhorts her countrymen to pursue the goals that Brewsie earlier espoused.

After all the objections to character inconsistencies, flawed idioms, confusing argument, and fallacious economic theory have been noted, *Brewise and Willie* remains a remarkable achievement. Gertrude Stein encountered her countrymen at a crucial juncture in their history—as they moved to the center of the world stage—and she listened carefully to them. Their talk ranged from the trivial to the momentous, from the Gallup poll, baby carriages and peanut butter, to the French, the Germans, sex, money, jobs, Negroes, food, and the atomic bomb. All of it was directed to understanding themselves.

Gertrude Stein's portrait of the American male was not flattering. Soon after completing *Wars I Have Seen*, she felt obliged to revise her initially ecstatic opinion of the G.I.'s. In June 1945, she toured army bases in occupied Germany under the auspices of *Life* magazine. During the course of the trip, she found herself engaged in "very excited" talk with the soldiers, causing one sergeant to complain "that I confused the minds of his men." But it angered her, she said, when she heard the men express their preference for the Germans "Of course you do, I said, they flatter you and they obey you . . ." That the soldiers could be so readily seduced by German sycophancy disturbed her. She realized that they were put off by the independence and cultural strangeness of "the Latins . . . the Arabs . . . the Wops . . . the British." Significantly, when she left the next day, the sergeant presented her with a card inscribed, "To Gertie, another Radical" ("Off We All Went To See Germany," *Life* [6 August 1945], 58). His somewhat cryptic assessment was accurate enough. In *Brewsie and Willie*, Gertrude Stein came within an ace of counselling the overthrow of capitalism in the United States.

Her hostility to the American economic system was partially derived from her belief that it was responsible for the immaturity of the bulk of Americans she met. It often pampered them materially—but only on the condition that they forfeit the independence of their thought. They seemed "spoiled babies" to her, loving sweets and soft foods and living in a world of illusion (94). "American soldiers think life is a movie . . ." (44). They sustained their fantasies by collecting pin-up pictures and getting drunk. Real women frightened them, with the possible exception of the German woman, for "they do all the work" (16). The soldiers she had recently praised in *Wars I Have Seen* for having "ceased to be adolescents" were now mocked as an army of "E. T. O.

[i.e., European Theater of Operations] Virgins" (*WIHS*, 259; *B&W*, 17).

A fortunate few of the soldiers were aware of this national infirmity. These men and women were afforded a brief period in their lives during which they could debate the problems of their society. As they drifted from one subject to the next, the villain began to emerge. Its name was "Industrialism." In a long description of its history and motivations, Brewsie places upon industrialism the responsibility for all the pernicious conditions about which the Americans complain (34–37). The worker who must first worry about securing a job, once he has one, hates it. But industrialism turns people into automatons who perpetuate the system by laboring for it, then purchasing its products from it. "Industrialism which produces more than anybody can buy and makes employees out of free men makes 'em stop thinking, stop feeling, makes 'em all feel alike" (55). Its greed brings on depressions and creates wars to secure new markets (36).*

"Industrialism" served as a catch-all for Gertrude Stein's attack against the whole complex of modern technological life in a capitalistic democracy. The vigor of her indictment was impressive. Americans were squandering their raw materials to make gadgets they did not need and which they could afford only by purchasing them on the installment plan. "That is what you call a high standard of living. Hell of a high standard of living, said Jo, which is on top of you all the whole time" (33). The only truly active people Gertrude Stein could see were the Negroes. They were doing "the only real pioneering there is in America these days . . ." (65).

The Gallup poll symbolized this standardization of judgment in America. The need to answer yes or no troubles Brewsie. "Thinking is funnier and more mixed than that" (102). At this point Gertrude Stein's personal concerns intersected with those of her country. Brewsie flatly concludes that Americans have lost the capacity to think. They only "articulate." That is, they standardize their responses to meet the demands of "their bosses" and "their unions." Although perhaps still feeling differently, "when you begin to articulate alike, you got to drop thinking out . . ." (103–4). Of their group, one lone Southerner from a poor, rural area is still capable of listening to the ideas of others. In the "job chasers," the ability has atrophied (109).

* In an interview with C. L. Sulzberger, Gertrude Stein went even further, saying, "We haven't a Gestapo but we have a financial Gestapo which amounts to the same thing in the sense of freedom" (New York *Times* [25 August 1945], 13).

Gertrude Stein offered no panacea for these urgent problems. Like all her books, *Brewsie and Willie* insisted upon the need to try to ameliorate conditions, while remaining deeply pessimistic. The group agrees that they are "ruled by tired middle-aged people, tired business men, the kind who need pin-ups, you know the kind, only they can afford the originals . . ." (89). Therefore, it was this generation's responsibility to protest. But when one soldier dramatically asks, "Have we the guts to make a noise while we are still young," Willie answers: "No we haven't, and you know it . . ." (90). His sceptical voice also comments upon the need to pioneer. Brewsie has put pioneering forth as an appropriately American antidote to the lazy but worried life now prevailing in the United States. "How can you pioneer when there aint no wilderness any more," asks Willie (82). A nurse believes she has an answer—"you got to break down what has been built up, that's pioneering." To which Willie responds:

> Well I don't want to say all I think because I was brought up to be nice to a lady but what do you want do you want us to drop our atomic bombs on ourselves, is that what you want, so we can go out and pioneer, is that the idea. Well yes kind of, said Janet. I get you, said Willie. (83)

Willie's practicality counterbalances the improving fervor of his friends. He does believe in the durability of mankind. Man seems to him capable of surviving anything from the atom bomb to potato bugs, and concentration camps to a lack of education.* But underneath Willie's coarse, scoffing manner, he feels that "nothing's funny nothing, not even the comics . . ." (52). Provoked once, he bursts out—"I just tell you and though I don't sound like it I've got plenty of sense, there ain't any answer, there aint going to be any answer, there never has been an answer, that's the answer" (30). The impact of this negative appraisal is never fully dissipated in the book.

Willie's sentiments closely resemble Gertrude Stein's last words, spoken to Alice Toklas just before she was operated upon. In Alice's version:

---

* Elsewhere, the soldiers have an exchange over the atom bomb. It is proposed as the one thing Americans have that "nobody else has got." The fragility of that ownership is expressed in the wry rejoinder—"not so got" (82). Gertrude Stein's last composition was "Reflection on The Atomic Bomb." In it she declared her lack of interest in the weapon on the grounds that if it were totally destructive, then "there is nothing left" and therefore "nothing to be interested about." But if it were not totally destructive, then it became one more mechanical means of killing, about which one could do nothing. Other matters were more worthy of attention (*Yale Poetry Review* [*Decem*ber 1947], 3).

By this time Gertrude Stein was in a sad state of indecision and worry. I sat next to her and she said to me early in the afternoon, What is the answer? I was silent. In that case, she said, what is the question? Then the whole afternoon was troubled, confused and very uncertain, and later in the afternoon they took her away on a wheeled stretcher to the operating room and I never saw her again. (*WIR*, 173) *

The one positive proposal made in the *Brewsie and Willie* discussions is resistance. Gertrude Stein's prudence restrained her from openly advocating revolution, which in any case would not be to her taste. She herself was unclear what actual measures might be employed against the repressive and dehumanizing economic system she saw shackling America. Positive that neither communism nor socialism was appropriate for the United States, all she could suggest in her own voice was "to fight a spiritual pioneer fight" (113). But her soldier spokesmen could be more direct. The proposals they advanced were all aimed at overturning the system. Brewsie advises a work stoppage. With the factories closed down, the movement of money would slow and soon "the chain stores and mail-order places go bust." After that, the small businesses that had been squeezed out by large combines could start up again (73). More revolutionary was the group's agreement that "You got to break down what has been built up." "We have got to get on top of industrialism and not have it on top of us." The means? "First you got to break it off you, said Jo. Oh dear, said Pauline, fighting is so natural" (83, 70).

Just that mixture of forthright iconoclasm and compassionate distress caused the original reviewers to treat *Brewsie and Willie* as a serious accomplishment. Although the book has since been ignored and even designated "probably her least" work, it has lost none of its force (Brinnin, 391). Its solutions to social problems may be naïve and its idiom faulty; still, passionately and with good humor, in *Brewsie and Willie* Gertrude Stein managed to give voice to the foot soldiers' concern for their country's future, without, however, minimizing in the slightest the sombre realities of human existence.

As her last full-length composition, Gertrude Stein prepared another libretto for Virgil Thomson, although *The Mother of Us All* was not

* As early as 1930, Gertrude Stein had written, "Now the whole question of questions and not answer is very interesting" ("Sentences and Paragraphs," *HTW*, 35). And in the shipboard interview she held upon arriving in the United States in 1934, she said, "Suppose no one asked a question. What would the answer be?" (*Time*, [15 November 1934], 15).

340

performed until 7 May 1947 at Columbia University, almost a year after Gertrude Stein's death on 27 July 1946 following surgery for cancer. She completed the text in March 1946, several months after she had begun to experience abdominal pain. *The Mother of Us All* gives every indication of being a valedictory.

Although Gertrude Stein had never publicly advocated female emancipation, for this opera she chose to dramatize the life of Susan B. Anthony, America's leading nineteenth-century champion of women's rights. Susan B. Anthony's specific attractions for Gertrude Stein were personal. She was a woman of courage who had carried on a vigorous struggle for her principles until her death in 1906. Although she was maligned and ridiculed in her lifetime, the merit of her cause was legislatively ratified in 1920, the centennial of her birth, when women finally attained the right to vote.

What in *Brewsie and Willie* had been, at worst, contempt for the childish American male now in *The Mother of Us All* became outright hostility, as Susan B. Anthony ticked off a list of masculine failings. Men were conservative, selfish, boring, ugly, gullible, unchanging, and bullies. Viewed as a sex, men were "poor things," pitiful, blustering, fearful creatures—and yet, they had the power (*LO&P*, 60–61). In order to be "a bigger man than a big man," Andrew Jackson advises drunkenness, counsel that is echoed by an all male chorus (65). And a trio of "V.I.P.s"—very important persons—sings proudly of their "special rights" (68–69). But through the person of Susan B. Anthony, Gertrude Stein asserts the over-all superiority of women. Disgust at heterosexual coupling goes undisguised. "If there are men and women, it is rather horrible, and if it is rather horrible, then there are children . . ." (85). The only possible justification for marriage is that it produces women for the guidance of men. "They do not know that two and two make four if women do not tell them so" (73).

The chief representative of masculine pomposity is Daniel Webster. That conservative advocate of New England mercantile interests is faced off against the compassionate strength of Susan B. Anthony. Gertrude Stein had employed Webster before in an unusually opaque play mixed with commentary, entitled "Daniel Webster, Eighteen in America" (1937). In it, she took the historical figures of *Four in America*—Grant, Washington, Henry James, and Wilbur Wright—and added to them a surprisingly mild Thoreau, as well as some women.* In his play, Web-

* Some of the women in "Daniel Webster" have names Gertrude Stein commonly used, like Jenny and Ida, while some are drawn from history, and others are

341

ster is a bit of a fustian orator, dedicated to his flag, his country, and monetary solvency. But in *The Mother of Us All,* he is an out-and-out windbag, in collusion with the monied classes to keep women and the Negro suppressed. The male tyranny he represents was directly related in Gertrude Stein's mind with the abstract cruelty of wealth. To be rich, says Susan B. Anthony, "is to be so rich . . . that they do not listen and when they do they do not hear . . ." (69). Daniel Webster's paternalistic control reminds the character "G. S." that "My father's name was Daniel he had a black beard he was not tall not at all tall . . ." (53). Daniel Stein still fixed his daughter's course.

Susan B. Anthony had first turned up in *Brewsie and Willie* when one of the nurses read a book about her. The emphasis at that point was upon the fact that her struggle had started under conditions similar to those existing just after the second World War. Susan B. Anthony undertook her campaign following the depression of 1838 when "nobody had any money to buy just like now" (89). In *Brewsie and Willie* she was offered as a model of self-liberation, who proved that if an individual made sufficient "noise" he would be heard.

The Mother of Us All takes a broader and less optimistic view. Unlike *Brewsie and Willie,* it is not a call to action but a sober consideration of the rewards of a life of moral action. Attaining a goal is of minimal importance compared to the struggle for that goal. Since women's suffrage became a reality only after Susan B. Anthony's death, her last words as a living person in the play savor the ironic success she had achieved on 21 July 1868 with the ratification of the Fourteenth Amendment to the Constitution. Establishing the Negro's right to vote meant that "for the first time the word male has been written into the constitution of the United States concerning suffrage" (80). Therefore, when a full chorus of men and women carols her triumph, she can only respond—"so successful" (83). And, when reassured by her companion that one day the vote for women would be won, Susan B. Anthony replies, "By that time it will do them no good because having the vote they will become like men . . ." (81). Her prediction of a compromised victory is so phrased as to suggest that women will be changed both by the very process of securing the vote and then, by possessing it. But the profound irony in her perception fails to diminish her determination to "fight for the right" (81).

Added to Susan B. Anthony's belief that people are changed in the

unidentified, although probably taken from either American history or Gertrude Stein's own experience. "Dolene," for example, is very likely named after an old Baltimore acquaintance, Dolene Block (Katz, 235).

very process of reaching long-range goals is her scepticism about their vision. She cannot overcome the inertia of the crowd, nor its blind, stampeding force once it does begin to move, nor its penchant for imitation rather than originality. As "Chris the Citizen" remarks, "I always repeat everything I hear" (71). People typically arranged themselves into an anonymous mass. At one public meeting, Susan B. Anthony insists that the audience enter as individuals—"A crowd is never allowed but each one of you can come in" (70). By the end of this meeting though, the whole audience has pushed up onto the platform with her in a mood of belligerent, democratic egotism. "We are the head we have all the bread." Susan B. Anthony is obliged to advance to the front of the platform and address the vacancy. "I speak to those below who are not there . . ." (72).* Her experience of being repeatedly frustrated, even by the best-intentioned people, contributes to the ironic edge of the play. Once, for example, upon encountering a Negro couple, she asks the man if he would vote even if the woman were denied the right. His response is an immediate "You bet" (67). In just this way had Frederick Douglass backed away from the issue of female emancipation in America when he feared it would compromise the Negro's quest for the vote.

With Susan B. Anthony and Daniel Webster as prototypes of the female secular saint and the male persecutor, other characters fill representative sexual roles. John Adams, for no evident reason, is the mannered lover who incessantly makes declarations of love. The essential egotism of his indulgent verbal displays is openly manifested when he asks the woman he courts, "Do you not admire me" (73). The object of his attentions is a female counterpart, Constance Fletcher. Essentially incapable of perceiving anyone but herself, she showers endearments indiscriminately wherever she goes. "I am blind and therefore I dream" (75).† While a congenial enough person, Constance Fletcher's sentimentality adds to the problem of securing the liberty of women. When she bows obsequiously to Daniel Webster, "this dear great man," Susan B. Anthony is short with her. "Hush, this is slush. Hush" (70).

The play contains other unattached representatives of their sexes, such as Anthony Comstock, the ferret of vice—"caution and curiosity,

---

* A mob in Syracuse, New York, did take possession of a platform from Susan B. Anthony. See R. Dorr, *Susan B. Anthony*, 148.

† In the libretto of *The Mother of Us All*, published in 1947, Adams is identified without further explanation, as "presumably John Quincy Adams" (15). Constance Fletcher was the nearly blind author of *Kismet* about whom Gertrude Stein had written in *ABT*, 158–62.

oil and obligation . . ." and Lillian Russell, the great stage beauty (55). Daniel Webster woos a woman of unearthly passivity, Angel More. A "mouse" and a "martyr," she is obliged to "darn and wash and patch, darn and wash and patch." In this she is very like Webster's first wife, the modest Grace Fletcher who, in a letter to her husband lamenting her inferiority, described herself as one who "all the early part of her life passed in obscurity, toiling with hands not 'fair' for subsistence" (R. Current, *Daniel Webster*, 49). As Webster epitomizes the masculine ego, so Angel More does feminine servitude. Ulysses S. Grant's role is that of the man who prizes silence above all else (74–75). Although a chorus decries "naughty men naughty men, they are always always quarreling," Grant is specifically exempted from the charge. "Ulysses S. Grant was not the most earnest nor the most noble of men, but he was not always quarreling" (63–64). He signals for silence in an exceedingly noisy way, however—by pounding his chair on the platform.

In the end, Susan B. Anthony realizes that she has failed to generate individualism. Again and again the evidence has indicated the absurdity of her efforts. As she remarks when entreated to come out of retirement and participate in the struggle once more, "You will never vote my laws even if I do come but if I do not come you will never vote my laws . . ." (78). She cannot manage to make people see that "they are alone to live and die," nor that their duty is "to struggle and thirst to do everything first, because until it is done there is no other one" (72).

Recognition that the mother of us all has proved sterile determines the concluding scene of the play. In it, all the characters gather in the presence of a sculpture memorializing Susan B. Anthony and two other leaders of the suffrage movement, Elizabeth Cady Stanton and Lucretia Mott. When they have all assembled, the voice of Susan B. Anthony is heard from behind the statue and beyond the grave, well past irony. Six times in the course of her brief restatement of her convictions, she lapses into a pensive silence. What she feels can scarcely be communicated, so that the silences most eloquently convey the meaning of her experience.

Numbly, she began by stating what Gertrude Stein had long believed, that "we cannot retrace our steps" (87). But the difference was that now the future was no longer open-ended, but irrevocably terminated. Life offered no second chances. But, she went on, if we cannot go back, neither do we seem to advance. "Going forward may be the same as going backwards." As the characters of the play approached Susan

344

B. Anthony's memorial statue, each had reacted in a way that proved him unchanged by temporal events. Their creator, who had never successfully negotiated a permanent truce with herself, knew the persistence of character traits.

So far as she could tell, her strife-filled life ended in this cold memorial—"here we are here, in marble and gold," and "here" was the sum of it. Her dedication may have produced results that were enduring and valuable—

> it will stay it will pay but
> (A long silence)
> But do I want what we have got . . .

When the prize was won, vitality seemed to drain out of it. "What made it live, has it not gone because now it is had."

She could affirm the martyrdom of her life, but not its purpose. Even the possibility of communicating her unique experience to another had always seemed remote at best to Gertrude Stein, save when she became her own listener, so that no answer was anticipated to her final question. "Do you know because I tell you so, or do you know, do you know." Following a last meditative pause, she withdrew into herself to concentrate all she knew with certainty into a phrase that had run like a refrain throughout this last public meditation. What she could never adequately analyze or justify or represent, she could name, and that would have to suffice:

> My long life, my long life.

That was the bleak sum of mother's wisdom.

CONCLUSION

⤳. "I master pieces of it."
　　　("Saints and Singing")

Persuaded that she owed her conception to the death of another Stein child, Gertrude Stein regarded her very existence as precarious from the start; according to her accounts, her parents offered little security, for she represented herself as virtually motherless, while in her father she saw a model of blustering male injustice; so that she emerged into young womanhood anxious, mesmerized by the sexual mystery, and fantasizing incoherently of intimacies with men; but after long endeavoring to submerge her yearnings for closeness in the camaraderie of intellectual life, she responded with gratitude to the sensual overtures of more experienced women; and presently quit her censorious homeland in a cloud of defiance and guilt to take sanctuary with her already expatriated brother; who, although he served as her protector and brought her to the leading edge of modern art, withered her self-esteem with his neurotic condescension; so that, driven both to understand her unhappy condition and to be recognized as an independent human being, she martyred herself to extended exercises in the analysis of human character; which gradually turned inward to representations of her own consciousness, until, possessed of a reader whose devotion sanctioned her erratic perceptions, she began to record the pleasurable tensions of domesticity in her subjective shorthand; involuted experiments which were challenged by a war that initially panicked her into flight, then furnished her the opportunity of exerting a provincial leadership, which brought her out of the war with a new confidence; finding herself regarded now as a mentor of the literary avant-garde, she undertook to examine more carefully the bases of her art, at the same time defending herself against the first encroachments of time by cultivating serenity in the rural sun; until her memoirs transformed her into a

346

celebrity, a role she accepted with enthusiasm, although at some cost to her inner stability; and as she sought to reconcile her public and private personalities, the pervasive social unrest surrounding her revived long-subdued anxieties, which the second world war confirmed by marooning her in an uneasy atmosphere of threat; over its long course, she managed to enlarge her fatalism to meet the dimensions of her despair, but although she endured until the liberation, like all conditions in her life, that happy event proved brief and perhaps even illusory, for she soon discovered herself fatally occupied by that implacable reality that she had dreaded all her life.

When assembled, so her story goes. She never told it directly, however, but offered it obscured, askew, incomplete, in pieces.

In pieces, because Gertrude Stein saw parts but no whole. Dedicated to discovering a comprehensive order in the bewildering tumult of her existence, she hoped for concord and often proclaimed its reign, as if assertion were sufficient to establish it. But what she perceived changed incessantly, tempting her with signs of apparent relationship, then mocking her with the unique and unexpected detail. All her attempts at classification failed. Abandoning received notions of objective exactitude, she sought consistency in the faithful registration of her verbal reactions to the immediate moment.

In pieces, then, because Gertrude Stein's prose echoed the cacophony of feelings, associations, and memories she distinguished in her mind. More than once she acknowledged her fear of suffering some irreparable split or lapse into incapacity. But her oblique and disconnected prose apparently saved her by furnishing an outlet for the tumbling, shifting cargo of her consciousness. It provided the means by which she could express otherwise ineffable inner states. The verbal crazy-quilts she fashioned from her musings constituted her truest approximation of unity.

So, in pieces, because no term more accurately describes Gertrude Stein's unit of literary expression. Her compositions memorialize that daily half-hour when she gathered what came to mind and randomly, incidentally, shaped it into a prose that was part free association, part mechanical variation, part revelation only partially revealed. Her strength resides in those unpremeditated moments. Whatever else she may have been, she has proved herself master of the telling phrase, of the memorable and haunting assessment reached when the tide of her persistence carried her to a spontaneous height.

A SELECTED BIBLIOGRAPHY

PRINCIPAL VOLUMES AND COLLECTIONS OF GERTRUDE STEIN

Three Lives. New York, 1909.

Tender Buttons. New York, 1914.

Geography and Plays. Boston, 1922. Foreword by Sherwood Anderson.

The Making of Americans. Paris, 1925.

Composition As Explanation. London, 1926.

Useful Knowledge. New York, 1928.

Lucy Church Amiably. Paris, 1930.

Before The Flowers of Friendship Faded, Friendship Faded. Paris, 1931.

How To Write. Paris, 1931.

Operas and Plays. Paris, 1932.

Matisse Picasso and Gertrude Stein With Two Shorter Stories. Paris, 1933.

The Autobiography of Alice B. Toklas. New York, 1933.

Four Saints in Three Acts. New York, 1934.

Portraits and Prayers. New York, 1934.

Lectures in America. New York, 1935.

Narration. Chicago, 1935. Introduction by Thornton Wilder.

The Geographical History of America. New York, 1936. Introduction by Thornton Wilder.

Everybody's Autobiography. New York, 1937.

Picasso. London, 1938.

The World Is Round. New York, 1939.

Paris France. London, 1940.

What Are Masterpieces. Los Angeles, 1940. Foreword by Robert Bartlett Haas.

Ida, A Novel. New York, 1941.

Wars I Have Seen. New York, 1945.

Brewsie and Willie. New York, 1946.

Four in America. New Haven, 1947. Introduction by Thornton Wilder.

The Gertrude Stein First Reader and Three Plays. Boston, 1948.

Blood On the Dining-Room Floor. Pawlet, Vermont, 1948. Foreword by Donald Gallup.

Last Operas and Plays. New York, 1949. Introduction by Carl Van Vechten.

Things As They Are. Pawlet, Vermont, 1950.

THE YALE EDITION OF THE UNPUBLISHED WRITINGS OF GERTRUDE STEIN (under the general editorship of Carl Van Vechten, with an advisory committee of Donald Gallup, Donald Sutherland, and Thornton Wilder.) :

Two: Gertrude Stein and Her Brother and Other Early Portraits (1908–1912). New Haven, 1951. Foreword by Janet Flanner.

Mrs. Reynolds and Five Earlier Novelettes (1931–1942). New Haven, 1952. Foreword by Lloyd Frankenberg.

Bee Time Vine and Other Pieces (1913–1927). New Haven, 1953. Preface and notes by Virgil Thomson.

As Fine As Melanctha (1914–1930). New Haven, 1954. Foreword by Natalie Clifford Barney.

Painted Lace and Other Pieces (1914–1937). New Haven, 1955. Introduction by Daniel-Henry Kahnweiler.

Stanzas in Meditation and Other Poems (1929–1933). New Haven, 1956. Preface by Donald Sutherland.

Alphabets and Birthdays. New Haven, 1957. Introduction by Donald Gallup.

A Novel of Thank You. New Haven, 1958. Introduction by Carl Van Vechten.

Selected Writings of Gertrude Stein. (Modern Library), New York, 1962. Edited, with an Introduction and Notes by Carl Van Vechten; and with an essay by F. W. Dupee.

OTHER WORKS, CITED IN THE TEXT, OR OF SPECIAL INTEREST

The Annotated Mother Goose. Arranged and explained by William S. Baring-Gould and Ceil Baring-Gould. New York, 1962.

Aristotle. *The Ethics of Aristotle.* Translated by J. A. K. Thomson. London, 1953.

Baldanza, Frank. "Faulkner and Stein: A Study in Stylistic Intransigence." *Georgia Review,* XIII (Fall 1959), 274–86.

Barker, Lewellys F. *The Nervous System and Its Constituent Neurones.* New York, 1899.

Barlow, Samuel L. M. "Ave Dione a tribute." 20-page typescript at YCAL. An account of a day's trip through Provence with Gertrude Stein and Alice Toklas in 1918.

Barry, Naomi. "Paris à table. A Memory of Alice B. Toklas." *Gourmet,* (August 1967), 13, 28, 30.

Bergson, Henri. *An Introduction to Metaphysics.* Translated by T. E. Hulme with an introduction by Thomas A. Goudge. New York, 1955.

Bluemel, Elinor. *Florence Sabin: Colorado Woman of the Century.* Boulder, Colorado, 1959.

Bodenheim, Maxwell. "To Gertrude Stein." *Poetry,* LVII (December 1940), 193. A sonnet.

Braddy, Haldeen. "The Primitive in Gertrude Stein's 'Melanctha.' " *New Mexico Quarterly,* XX (Autumn 1950), 358–65.

Bridgman, Richard. "Gertrude Stein" in *The Colloquial Style in America.* New York, 1966.

———. "Melanctha," *American Literature,* XXXIII (November 1961), 350–59.

Brillat-Savarin, Jean. *The Physiology of Taste.* New York, 1948.

Brinnin, John Malcolm. *The Third Rose: Gertrude Stein and Her World.* Boston, 1959.

Brion, Marcel. "Le Contrepoint poétique de Gertrude Stein." *Echanges,* III (June 1930), 122–8.

Burke, Kenneth. "Engineering With Words." *Dial,* LXXIV (April 1923), 408–12.

Cargill, Oscar. "The Primitivists" in *Intellectual America.* New York, 1941.

Chamberlain, Dorothy. "Gertrude Stein, Amiably." A review of *Ida, A Novel. The New Republic,* CIV (7 April 1941), 477.

Chase, Mary E. "Five Literary Portraits." *Massachusetts Review,* III (Spring 1962), 511–16.

Church, Ralph. "A Note on the Writing of Gertrude Stein." *transition,* #14 (Fall 1928), 164–8.

Connolly, Cyril. *Previous Convictions.* New York, 1963.

Corcelle, M. J. *Livret-Guide Illustré: Des Pays de Bresse, Dombes, Bugey, Valromey, Pays de Gex.* Bellegarde, Ain, 1906.

Corbett, Scott. "Give Me Land." *Yank,* II (11 November 1945), 17. An interview with Gertrude Stein.

Corke, Hilary. "Reflections on A Great Stone Face." *The Kenyon Review*, XXIII (Summer 1961), 367–89. Impudent, wholly negative— save his grudging admission of taste for autobiographical writing. An exchange appears in the following issue (Autumn 1961, pp. 695– 7) between Donald Sutherland and Corke.

Current, Richard N. *Daniel Webster and the Rise of National Conservatism*. Boston, 1955.

Davies, Hugh Sykes. Review of *Narration* by Gertrude Stein. *The Criterion*, XV (July 1936), pp. 752–5.

Dodge, Mabel. See Luhan.

Dorr, Rheta Childe. *Susan B. Anthony: The Woman Who Changed the Mind of a Nation*. New York, 1928. Probably the biography which Gertrude Stein read.

Duncan, Roland E. An interview with Alice Toklas in Paris on 28–29 November 1952. Bancroft Library, University of California, Berkeley. Eight tapes and a transcript.

Eastman, Max. *Great Companions*. New York, 1959.

Finch, Edith. *Carey Thomas of Bryn Mawr*. New York, 1947.

Forster, E. M. *Aspects of the Novel*. New York, 1954.

Friedrich, Otto. "The Grave of Alice B. Toklas." *Esquire* (January 1968), 98–103; 121–4. See "The Sound and the Fury," the letters column of *Esquire* in April, 1968 for a correction.

Gallup, Donald. "Always Gertrude Stein." *Southwest Review*, XXXIV (Summer 1949), 254–8. A reprinting of 10 informal letters written to Mr. Gallup from 1941 to 1946.

———. "A Book Is a Book." *New Colophon*, I (January 1948), 67–80. Details of the publication and reception of *Three Lives*.

———. "Carl Van Vechten's Gertrude Stein." *Yale University Library Gazette*, XXVII (October 1952), 77–86.

———. "Gertrude Stein and the *Atlantic*." *Yale University Library Gazette*, XXVIII (January 1954), 109–28. Correspondence between Gertrude Stein and Ellery Sedwick, 1919–33, regarding publication of her work.

———. "The Gertrude Stein Collection." *Yale University Library Gazette*, XXII (October 1947), 21–32.

———. "The Making of *The Making of Americans*." *New Colophon*, III (1950), 54–74.

———. "The Weaving of a Pattern: Marsden Hartley and Gertrude Stein." *Magazine of Art*, XLI (November 1948), 256–61. Marsden Hartley's correspondence with Gertrude Stein—26 letters at Yale.

Gallup, Donald, ed. *The Flowers of Friendship: Letters Written to Gertrude Stein*. New York, 1953.

Garvin, Harry. "Gertrude Stein: A Study of Her Theory and Practice." Ph.D. dissertation, University of Michigan, 1949.

————. "Sound and Sense in *Four Saints in Three Acts*." *Bucknell Review*, V (December 1954), 1–11.

————. "Stein's 'Lipschitz.'" *Explicator*, XIV (December 1955), item 18.

Gass, W. H. "Gertrude Stein: Her Escape from Protective Language." *Accent*, XVIII (Autumn 1958), 233–44. Perceptive, eloquent dismissal of B. Reid's *Art by Subtraction*.

Gilot, Françoise and Lake, Carlton. *Life With Picasso*. New York, 1964.

Gilman, Charlotte P. Stetson, *Women and Economics*. Boston, 1898.

Gris, Juan. *Letters of Juan Gris*. Translated by Douglas Cooper. London, 1956.

Haas, Robert Bartlett and Donald Clifford Gallup. *A Catalogue of the Published and Unpublished Writings of Gertrude Stein*. New Haven, 1941.

Haas, Robert Bartlett. "Gertrude Stein Talking—A Transatlantic Interview" (1945). *Uclan Review*, VIII (Summer 1962), 3–11; IX (Spring 1963), 40–48; IX (Winter 1964), 44–48. Problematic because of distressing errors, such as "Hall, Rinehart and Livingstone" for Holt, Rinehart and Winston.

Haines, George, 4th. "Gertrude Stein and Composition." *Sewanee Review*, LVII (Summer 1949), 411–24.

Harrison, Gilbert A. "Gertrude Stein and the Nay-Sayers." *The New Republic*, CXXXVI (18 March 1957), 17–18. A negative review of Elizabeth Sprigge's biography of Gertrude Stein; the review was commended by Alice Toklas in a letter to Annette Rosenshine.

Herbst, Josephine. "Miss Porter and Miss Stein." *Partisan Review*, XV (May 1948), 568–72.

Heron, Michael. "A Note on Gertrude Stein." *Envoy*, IV (January 1951), 72–76.

Hoffman, Frederick J. *Gertrude Stein*. University of Minnesota Pamphlet on American Writers. Minneapolis, 1961.

Hoffman, Michael J. *The Development of Abstractionism in the Writings of Gertrude Stein*. Philadelphia, 1965.

Hoover, Kathleen and Cage, John. *Virgil Thomson: His Life and Music*. New York, 1959.

352

Imbs, Bravig. *Confessions of Another Young Man.* New York, 1936.

James, William. *Psychology: Briefer Course.* New York, 1892.

———. *The Varieties of Religious Experience.* New York, 1929.

Jelenko, Therese. "Reminiscences." Bancroft Library, University of California, Berkeley. A 10-page Xerox copy of a transcript from a tape recording.

Johns Hopkins Half-Century Directory (1876–1926). Compiled by W. Norman Brown. Baltimore, 1926. "Trustees, faculty . . . students, graduates and non-graduates."

Kahnweiler, Daniel-Henri. *Juan Gris.* Translated by Douglas Cooper. New York, 1947.

Katz, Leon. "The First Making of *The Making of Americans:* A Study Based on Gertrude Stein's Notebooks and Early Versions of her Novel (1902–8)." Ph.D. dissertation, Columbia University, 1963.

Kazin, Alfred. "The Mystery of Gertrude Stein" in *Contemporaries.* London, 1963.

Lachman, Arthur. "Gertrude Stein as I Knew Her." A 33-page typescript at YCAL.

Lemaitre, Georges. *From Cubism to Surrealism in French Literature.* Cambridge, Mass., 1947).

Levinson, Ronald. "Gertrude Stein, William James, and Grammar." *American Journal of Psychology,* LIV (January 1941), 124–8.

Lowe, Frederick W., Jr. "Gertrude's Web: A Study of Gertrude Stein's Literary Relationships." Ph.D. dissertation, Columbia University, 1956. Rounds up identification and dates of the various friends and visitors of Gertrude Stein.

Luhan, Mabel Dodge. *European Experiences.* New York, 1935. The second volume of *Intimate Memories.*

———. *Movers and Shakers.* New York, 1936. The third volume of *Intimate Memories.*

Lundell, William. An interview with Gertrude Stein on WJZ radio in New York on 12 November 1934. A 9-page typescript is at YCAL.

Malone, Kemp. "Observations on *Paris France.*" *Papers on Language and Literature,* III (Spring 1967), 159–78.

McMillan, Samuel H. "Gertrude Stein, The Cubists, and The Futurists." Ph.D. dissertation, University of Texas, 1964.

Miller, Rosalind. *Gertrude Stein: Form and Intelligibility.* New York, 1949.

Mitchell, David. *The Fighting Pankhursts.* London, 1967.

Moore, Marianne. "The Spare American Emotion." *Dial*, LXXX (February 1926), 153–6. An appreciative review of *The Making of Americans*.

Münsterberg, Margaret. *Hugo Münsterberg: His Life and Work*. New York, 1922.

"No Question and No Answer." *The Times Literary Supplement*, II (4 April 1952), 236.

Paul, Elliot. *Understanding the French*. New York, 1955.

Peers, E. Allison. *Saint Teresa of Jesus*. London, 1953.

Perry, Ralph Barton. *The Thought and Character of William James*. 2 vols. Boston, 1935.

Pétain, Le Maréchal. *Paroles aux Français: Messages et Écrits: 1934–1941*. With an introduction by G. L. Jaray. Lyon, France, 1941. Printed 30 September 1941; contains messages as late as 31 August 1941.

Pollack, Barbara. *The Collectors: Dr. Claribel and Miss Etta Cone*. New York, 1962.

Porter, Katharine Anne. *The Days Before*. New York, 1952. "Everybody is a Real One" is an eloquent appreciation of *MOA*; "Second Wind," a parody of *Useful Knowledge*; "The Wooden Umbrella," a long unsympathetic review of Gertrude Stein's career.

Rago, Henry. "Gertrude Stein." *Poetry*, LXIX (November 1946), 93–97.

Reid, Benjamin Lawrence. *Art By Subtraction*. Norman, Oklahoma, 1958.

Rogers, W. G. *When This You See Remember Me: Gertrude Stein in Person*. New York, 1948.

Rönnebeck, Arnold. "Gertrude Was Always Giggling." *Books Abroad*, XIX (Winter 1945), 3–7.

Rose, Francis. *Saying Life*. London, 1961.

Rosenshine, Annette. "Life's Not A Paragraph." Bancroft Library, University of California, Berkeley. An undated autobiographical typescript of approximately 70,000 words.

Royce, Josiah. *The Spirit of Modern Philosophy*. Boston, 1893.

Russell, Francis. *Three Studies in Twentieth Century Obscurity*. n.p., 1961.

Saarinen, Aline B. "The Steins in Paris." *The American Scholar*, XXVII (Autumn 1958), 437–48. Forms part of *The Proud Possessors*.

Santayana, George. *Persons and Places*. New York, 1944.

Sawyer, Julian, "Gertrude Stein: A Bibliography, 1941–1948. *Bulletin of Bibliography* XIX (May–Aug., Sept.–Dec. 1948), 152–6, 183–7.

Schmalhausen, Samuel D. "Gertrude Stein, Or, Light on the Literary Aspects of Enuresis." *The Modern Quarterly,* V, 3 (no date), 313–23. Sophomoric jeering that does however detect the sexual import of "Mildred's Thoughts."

Schneps, Maurice. "Gertrude Stein: A Brief Encounter" in *The Woman at St Lo.* Tokyo, 1959. A hard-breathing attempt to argue philosophy with Gertrude Stein in 1944.

Sevareid, Eric. *Not So Wild a Dream.* New York, 1946. An interview with Gertrude Stein upon her liberation in 1944.

Skinner, B. F. "Has Gertrude Stein a Secret?" *Atlantic Monthly,* CLIII (January 1934), 50–57.

Slemons, J. Morris. *John Whitridge Williams: Academic Aspects and Bibliography.* Baltimore, 1935. No reference to Gertrude Stein, but details on his character and teaching methods.

"Speaking of Pictures: Gertrude Stein Left a Hodgepodge Behind Her." *Life,* XXIII (18 August 1947), 14–16. Description of shipments that Yale Universty Library had been receiving from France since 1938.

Sprigge, Elizabeth. *Gertrude Stein: Her Life and Work.* New York, 1957.

———. "Gertrude Stein's American Years." *The Reporter,* (11 August 1955), 46–52. An impressionistic account of doing research for the biography, with some quotes and ideas not in the more formal book.

Steele, Oliver L., Jr. "Gertrude Stein and Ellen Glasgow: Memoir of a Meeting." *American Literature,* XXXIII (March 1961), 76–77.

Stein, Amelia (née Keyser). "Diary." Bancroft Library, University of California, Berkeley. 5 vols. From January 1878 through September 1886, although not continuous.

Stein, Leo. *Appreciation: Painting, Poetry and Prose.* New York, 1947.

———. *Journey Into the Self.* Edited by Edmund Fuller. New York, 1950.

Stewart, Allegra. *Gertrude Stein and the Present.* Cambridge, Mass., 1967.

———. "The Quality of Gertrude Stein's Creativity," *American Literature, XXVIII* (January 1957), 488–506.

Sutherland, Donald. *Gertrude Stein: A Biography of Her Work.* New Haven, 1951. Although mannered and partisan, a remarkable critical study.

355

———. "Ole Woman River: A Correspondence with Katharine Anne Porter." *Sewanee Review*, LXXIV (Summer 1966), 754–67. Concerning "The Wooden Umbrella," and Miss Porter's nephew's encounter with Gertrude Stein.

Sypher, Wylie, *Rococo to Cubism In Art and Literature*. New York, 1963.

Testimony Against Gertrude Stein. Supplement to *Transition* (February 1935).

Thompson, Francis. *Saint Ignatius Loyola*. London, 1909.

Thomson, Virgil. Liner notes, RCA Victor Red Seal recording of *Four Saints in Three Acts*, LM2756, 1964.

———. *Virgil Thomson*. New York, 1966.

Toklas, Alice B. *The Alice B. Toklas Cook Book*. New York, 1960.

———. *What Is Remembered*. New York, 1963.

Troy, William. "A Note on Gertrude Stein," *The Nation*, CXXXVII (6 Sept. 1933), 274–5. Review of *The Autobiography of Alice B. Toklas*.

Tufte, Virginia J. "Gertrude Stein's Prothalamium: A Unique Poem In A Classical Mode." *Yale University Library Gazette*, XLIII (July 1968), 17–23.

Van Ghent, Dorothy. "Gertrude Stein and the Solid World" in *American Stuff*. New York, 1937.

Walker, Franklin. *Frank Norris: A Biography*. New York, 1963.

Weininger, Otto. *Sex and Character*. London and New York, 1906.

Wilcox, Wendell. "A Note on Stein and Abstraction." *Poetry*, LV (February 1940), 254–7.

Wilder, Thornton. "Gertrude Stein Makes Sense." *47: the Magazine of the Year*, I (October 1947), 10–15. This precedes excerpts from *Four in America* and may be a version of Wilder's introduction.

Williams, William Carlos. "The Work of Gertrude Stein." *Pagany*, I (Winter 1930), 41–46.

Wilson, Edmund. *Axel's Castle*. New York, 1931.

———. "Gertrude Stein Old and Young" in *The Shores of Light*. New York, 1952.

Wright, George T. "Gertrude Stein and Her Ethic of Self-Containment." *Tennessee Studies in Literature*, VIII (1963), 17–23.

Yalden-Thomson, D. C. "Obscurity, Exhibitionism, and Gertrude Stein." *Virginia Quarterly Review*, XXXIV (Winter 1958), 133–7.

APPENDIXES

A. GERTRUDE STEIN'S ACADEMIC RECORD

Radcliffe College
(Where there are two grades in parenthesis, GS took the course twice, or received double credit for it. Starred courses are half-courses, lasting only one semester.)

1893–4
German 7 (B plus)
Philosophy 1 (A)
Philosophy 7 (A)
Economics 1 (B plus)
History 11 (A)

1894–5
Philosophy 9 (B plus)
Philosophy 20a (B) (B)
English 22 (C)
French 2 (C plus)
Philosophy 13 (A)

1895–6
Philosophy 20a (A)
* Philosophy 20b (A) (C)
* English C (A minus)
* Mathematics D (B)
* Mathematics E (C)
* Physics B (C)
* Zoology 1 (B)
* Zoology 2 (B)

1896–7
Philosophy 20a (A) (A)

Chemistry 1 (C minus)
Botany 3 (B)
Zoology 3 (B plus)
* Zoology 16 (B)
* Zoology 5 (A)

Johns Hopkins School of Medicine
(This data reproduces a copy of GS's transcript, made by Dr. Alan Chesney, former Archivist of the Medical Institutions.)

Grade Values:

1.0 = 10	2.0 = 8.0
1.25 = 9.5	2.75 = 7.5
1.5 = 9.0	2.5 = 7.0
1.75 = 8.5	2.75 = 6.5
	3.0 = 6.0

1897–8
Normal Histology (1.5)
Physiological Chemistry (2.5)
Anatomy (1)
Physiology (2)

1898–9
Pathology and Bacteriology (1.5)
Pharmacology and Toxicology (2)

1899–1900
Medicine (2)
Surgery (2.5)
Neurology (3)
Clinical Microscopy (3)
Obstetrics (3)

1900–1901
Medicine (3)
Surgery (2.5)
Gynecology (2)
Obstetrics (5)
Pediatrics (3)
Laryngoolgy and Rhinology (5)

Ophthamology and Otology (4)
Dermatology (4)
Psychiatry (2.5)

B. GERTRUDE STEIN CHRONOLOGY

Note: the items in the following chronology are selected principally for their bearing upon Gertrude Stein's writing. Therefore, her dogs and automobiles are included because they are frequently mentioned in her work.

In some instances the chronology is still uncertain. Whenever a date is central or conflicts with previous records, the source of information is cited.

1864   Daniel Stein and Amelia Keyser marry.

1865   March 26, Michael Stein born.

1867   Simon Stein born.

1870   October 11, Bertha Stein born.

1872   May 11, Leo Stein born.

1874   February 3, 8:00 a.m., Gertrude Stein born, Western Avenue., Allegheny, Pennsylvania (Brinnin, 5).

1875   Spring, Stein family at Gemünden and Vienna, Austria (Sprigge, 4).

1877   April 30, Alice Toklas born in San Francisco (Duncan, 50).

1878   Late November, Stein family moves to Passy, France. November 24: "Dan went to Paris with the boys." December 5: "At the garden of Plants . . ." (AS *Diary*, II).

1879   Family with Keyser grandparents in Baltimore (Brinnin, 7).

1880   Family comes west, lives in Tubb's Hotel in Oakland for a year (Brinnin, 8). Then at 461 East 12th Street, corner of 9th Avenue (AS *Diary*, III, "Memoranda").

1881   April 28, moved to "Old Stratton House," 25th Street and 13th Avenue in Oakland (AS *Diary*, III).

1883   Michael Stein student at Johns Hopkins. BA 1886.

1885   April 29, family moves to "Harrington House," 10th Avenue, Oakland (AS *Diary*, V, February 5, March 18, April 24). Amelia Stein ill with cancer.

1888   Amelia Stein dies. Gertrude and Leo at Oakland High School. (None of the Stein children's names appear in the records surviving at Oakland High School, which list members of a graduating class only. Alice Toklas said Gertrude attended high school only one year [Duncan, 36].)

1891   Early in year, Daniel Stein dies. With Michael Stein as head of family, they move to Turk Street, San Francisco.

1892   Family disperses. Gertrude and Bertha go to live with their mother's sister, Fannie Bachrach in Baltimore. Leo, having begun college at the University of California in Berkeley, transfers to Harvard (*Appreciation*, 137, 142).

1893   Winter, GS visits Leo at Cambridge, Mass. Fall, she enters Harvard Annex (which in 1894 would be renamed Radcliffe College).

1894   GS works under Münsterberg in Harvard Psychological Laboratory.

1895   Leo graduates from Harvard. Michael Stein and Sarah ("Sally") Samuels married. Leo makes round-the-world trip with his cousin Fred Stein (*Appreciation*, 145–6).

1896   September, GS's first publication, "Normal Motor Automatism" co-authored with Leon Solomons, published in *Psychological Review*. Summer, GS makes first trip as an adult to Europe, meeting Leo in Antwerp.

1897   Spring, GS fails Radcliffe Latin entrance examination, is not awarded her bachelor's degree. Summer, visits the Michael Steins in San Francisco (Gallup, *Flowers*, 14). Fall, GS enters Johns Hopkins School of Medicine. Lives with Leo, who is studying biology at Johns Hopkins University.

1898   Awarded her Harvard A.B.

1899   Again summers with the Michael Steins in San Francisco.

1900   Summers in Italy and France with Mabel Weeks and Leo. Leo has permanently quit Baltimore. Leon Solomons dies.

1901   Spring, last term at medical school. Fails four courses. Summers in Tangiers and Granada, then Paris with Leo (GS to Mabel Weeks, 10 July 1901, YCAL; Pollack, 40–51; Gallup, *Flowers*, 23). Returns to New York then (Katz, 24). Fall, GS doing research on the brain in Baltimore.

1902   Spring, GS joins Leo in Italy. Summer in England, in September they settle at 20 Bloomsbury Square, London (*Journey*, 10). GS reads in British Museum. December 24, Leo departs for Paris (*Appreciation*, 151).

1903 February, GS sails for New York (Katz, 13); spends the winter in "The White House," 100th Street and Riverside Drive, with Mabel Weeks, Estelle Rumbold Kohn, and Harriet Clark. Begins early versions of *The Making of Americans* and *Things As They Are* (Katz, 36). Leo living at 27 rue de Fleurus (*Journey*, 13). Summer, GS joins Leo in Europe for a trip to Rome, Florence, Siena (Katz, 53–56). Fall, both living in Paris at the rue de Fleurus. The Michael Steins also in Paris.

1904 Winter, GS returns to America. Sails from New York with Etta Cone in June (Pollack, 62–63). Summers with Leo in Fiesole, Italy. They see Charles Loeser collection of Cézannes in Florence. They begin purchasing paintings.

1905 February, GS begins *Three Lives*. Steins purchase *Matisse's La Femme au Chapeau* at Salon d'Automne. November, GS meets Picasso through the art dealer, Clovis Sagot.

1906 GS sits for Picasso portrait. Early February, *Three Lives* completed (Katz, 86). The Michael Steins return to San Francisco to assess damage of the April 18th earthquake and fire. Summer, GS and Leo in Italy, Villa Ricci, Fiesole, overlooking Florence; she again working on *The Making of Americans*.

1907 September, Alice Toklas and Harriet Levy arrive in Paris, meet GS (*WIR*, 19). (Pollack quotes letters from Etta Cone to GS in February 1907 referring to ABT's presence in Paris [90–91]. Rosenshine says she returned to Paris in December 1906 with the Michael Steins and corresponded with ABT, her old friend, during 1907 [65, 82]. But she also says ABT did not arrive until the spring of 1908, and she habitually refers to the "Rue de Fleurs" [82, 83].)

1908 Summer, Alice Toklas and Harriet Levy summer in Italy near GS and Leo (*WIR*, 48). Alice learns to type, begins to transcribe *The Making of Americans* (*WIR*, 54).

1909 Early, Alice Toklas joins the Stein household at the rue de Fleurus (*Flowers*, 48; Pollack says 1908, 98). *Three Lives* published, GS's first book in print.

1910 Leo meets Nina Auzias (*Journey*, 22). Summer, GS and Leo to Perugia (*Journey*, 34).

1911 October, GS finishes *The Making of Americans* (Katz, 247).

1912 Spring and summer, GS and ABT in Spain. August, Stieglitz publishes "Matisse" and "Picasso," in *Camera Work*, first periodical publication of GS's creative work. Fall, house guests of Mabel Dodge at Villa Curonia.

1913 January, trip to England to stimulate interest of publishers. February, Armory Show opens in New York, its publicity connecting GS with cubist painting. Leo and GS separate definitively. "One of the greatest changes that has become decisive in recent times is the fairly definite 'disaggregations' of Gertrude and myself" (7 February 1913, *Journey*, 52). "My brother has decided to stay in Italy and I decided to stay in Paris. . . . we have taken a place with very little balconies third story in the Palais Royal and its going to be very nice. we don't move until July . . ." (GS to Henry McBride, 29 December 1913, YCAL). August–September, GS at Alahambra, Granada (GS to Alvin Coburn, Henry McBride, YCAL).

1914 July, GS and ABT in London. June, *Tender Buttons* published. August, house guests of A. N. Whiteheads in Lockridge when war breaks out. October, with Mrs. Whitehead, they return to Paris.

1915 March, alarmed by zeppelin raids, GS and ABT leave for Barcelona; then, cross to 45 Calle de Dos de Mayo, Terreno, suburb of Palma, Mallorca. Breton servant, Jeanne Poule and hound Polybe, named after "Solomon Reinach who signed himself Polybe in the Figaro" (GS to Carl Van Vechten, 31 May 1923, YCAL). August, 5-day trip to Valencia to see bullfights, including Belmonte and Gallito.

1916 Heartened by outcome of Battle of Verdun, they return to Paris by way of Madrid.

1917 GS obtains Ford motor van from America, drives "Auntie" (named after Pauline [Mrs. Solomon] Stein) for American Fund for French Wounded as a supply truck. March 18, to Perpignan to open distribution depot. Back to Paris, then stationed in Nîmes.

1918 After November, back to Paris, then to Mulhouse in Alsace, providing relief for civilians.

1919 May, return to Paris. Leo, having spent war in U.S., returns to Italy.

1920 December, new Ford, "Godiva," purchased. ("I remarked that she was nude. There was nothing on her dashboard, neither clock nor ashbox, nor cigarette lighter. Godiva was Gertrude Stein's answer" [*ABT Cook Book*, 81].)

1921 March 5, Leo and Nina Auzias marry. Spring, Lipchitz's bronze of her head made. GS reconciled with Juan Gris. Summer, GS meets Sherwood Anderson.

1922   March, GS meets Ernest Hemingway. Awarded the Médaille de la Reconnaissance Française for war-time activities (Gallup, *Flowers*, 150). Late summer trip to Saint Rémy; December, *Geography and Plays* published.

1923   February, GS returns to Paris from St. Rémy. Fall, godmother to John Hadley Hemingway. Summer, first trip to Belley. "We have found this charming spot . . ." (postcard to Henry McBride, 8 September 1893, YCAL).

1924   April–December, part of *The Making of Americans* serialized in *transatlantic review*.

1925   September, *The Making of Americans* published by Contact Editions, Paris.

1926   May, GS delivers "Composition as Explanation" before the Literary Society of Cambridge University; also at Oxford. Late spring, to Belley, the Hotel Pernollet. Meets Bernard Faÿ. Fall, meets Virgil Thomson (Gallup, *Flowers*, 193).

1927   May 11, Juan Gris dies.

1928   Mildred Aldrich dies. Spring, new unnamed Ford purchased. Also Basket I acquired. "We named him Basket because I had said he should carry a basket of flowers in his mouth. Which he never did" (*WIR*, 124).

1929   Bilignin house leased. "We did have a beautiful summer, we got our home and we were so pleased . . ." (GS to Henry McBride, 18 November 1929, YCAL).

1930   GS meets Francis Rose.

1931   January 5, *Lucy Church Amiably*, first volume in Plain Edition published.

1932   Early summer, Byron, a Mexican Chihuahua acquired from Picabia (letter to Ellen Daniel, June 1932, YCAL). So named because "he was to have as a wife his sister or mother . . ." Soon dies, succeeded by Pépé, "named after Francis Picabia" (*EA*, 49). October–November, *The Autobiography of Alice B. Toklas* written at Bilignin.

1933   Summer, Madame Pernollet falls to death. August, *The Autobiography of Alice B. Toklas* published.

1934   February 8, first public performance of *Four Saints in Three Acts* at Avery Memorial Auditorium of Wadsworth Athenaeum in

Hartford, Conn. February 20, opens in New York. October 24, GS lands in New York City. Lectures in East, Midwest, and South. November, attends performance in Chicago of *Four Saints.*

1935   GS travels to far west, lecturing. May 4, departs for France. Summer, French soldiers billeted in Bilignin.

1936   GS lectures again at Oxford and Cambridge (Brinnin, 354). Visits Lord Berners in Berkshire, and Sir Robert and Lady Diana Abdy in Cornwall.

1937   April 27, attends premiere of *A Wedding Bouquet* at Sadler's Wells in London. Summer, visited by Thornton Wilder. Makes "sentimental journey" with W. G. Rogers and wife through Provence. Lease terminated at 27 rue de Fleurus by landlord.

1938   Ca. February 1, GS moves to 5 rue Christine. "We were tired of the present which also was the past because no servant would stand the kitchen, there was no air in the house, the garage they had built next door had made it uncomfortable . . ." (GS to W. G. Rogers, 19? November 1937, YCAL). They expected to move by January 15, but didn't. (See letters to F. Rose, W. G. Rogers, and Robert B. Haas)

1939   Summer in Bilignin. September, to Paris to close apartment, return to Bilignin.

1940   June 14, Paris occupied. Two trips to American consul in Lyons. "I think you were and you are very wise to stay in Bilignin for some time" (B. Faÿ. 18 July 1940; *Flowers*, 351).

1943   February, lease expires on Bilignin house. Dispossessed, GS moves to "Le Colombier," in nearby Culoz, where in August, a German officer and his orderly are billetted, and in September, Italian troops stay.

1944   August 31, GS sees American soldiers, marking end of the war for her. December 15, she returns to Paris.

1945   June, tours U.S. Army bases in occupied Germany. December, lectures in Brussels.

1946   March 13, *Yes Is For a Very Young Man* performed for first time at Pasadena Playhouse. July, GS sets out from Paris for Bernard Faÿ's country house, falls ill. July 19, admitted to American Hospital at Neuilly-sur-Seine. July 23, makes her will. July 27, dies following operation for cancer at 6:30 p.m. The final verbal dislocations occur on her gravestone, where her place of birth is shown as "Allfghany" and her date of death as "29 July 1946."

364

1947 July 29, Leo Stein dies in Florence.
1967 March 7, ABT dies.

C. KEY TO THE *Yale Catalogue*, PART 4

Note:

1. Titles are shown in their published form, which sometimes differs from the listing in the *Yale Catalogue*. Titles are taken from the book or periodical proper, since they have sometimes been abbreviated or otherwise altered in the table of contents.

2. Only the page on which the item begins is shown.

3. Items with no volume reference following have been published as independent volumes.

4. Items after 1940 are based on the Julian Sawyer extension of the Haas-Gallup chronological list in the *Yale Catalogue*. See *Bulletin of Bibliography*, XIX (May–August 1948), 152–6; and XIX (September–December 1948), 183–7.

5. The existence of items 464, 517, and 522 is in doubt. They may form parts of other pieces, or may be titles only.

1903

A. *Things As They Are*

1905–6

1. *Three Lives*

(1903)–1906–1911

2. *The Making of Americans*

1908–12

3. A Man. *TWO*, 235.
4. Five or Six Men. *TWO*, 253.
5. *Two Women.*
6. Italians. *G&P*, 46.
7. Orta or One Dancing. *TWO*, 286.
8. Four Protégés. *TWO*, 305.
9. Men. *TWO*, 310.

1911–12

42. G.M.P. *GMP*, 199.

1912

43. Jenny, Helen, Hannah, Paul and Peter. *TWO*, 143.
44. Mi-Careme. *P&P*, 173.
45. Monsieur Vollard et Cezanne. *P&P*, 37.

1913

46. A Portrait of One. Harry Phelan Gibb. *G&P*, 201.
47. Scenes. Actions And Dispositions of Relations And Positions. *G&P*, 97.
48. Publishers, The Portrait Gallery And The Manuscripts At The British Museum. *G&P*, 134.
49. A Portrait of F. B. *G&P*, 176.
50. Portrait of Prince B. D. *G&P*, 150.
51. England. *G&P*, 82.
52. What Happened. A Five Act Play. *G&P*, 205.
53. One. Carl Van Vechten. *G&P*, 199.
54. Article. YCAL.
55. White Wines. *G&P*, 210.
56. Braque. *G&P*, 144.
57. Marsden Hartley. *Marsden Hartley Exhibition*, Little Gallery of Photo-Secession, January–February 1914.
58. Old and Old. *O&P*, 219.
59. Susie Asado. *G&P*, 13.
60. Mrs. Th----y. *Soil*, I (December 1916), 15.
61. A Curtain Raiser. *G&P*, 202.
62. Miguel (Collusion). Guimpe. Candle. *BTV*, 36.
63. Simons a Bouquet. *O&P*, 203.
64. In General. YCAL.
65. Thank You. *BTV*, 43.
66. A Sweet Tail (Gypsies). *G&P*, 65.
67. Carnage. *BTV*, 41.
68. Yet Dish. *BTV*, 53.
69. Americans. *G&P*, 39.
70. In. *BTV*, 44.
71. In the Grass (On Spain). *G&P*, 75.
72. Guillaume Apollinaire. *P&P*, 26.
73. Carry. *BTV*, 41.

74. France. *G&P*, 27.

74a. Go in Green. *BTV*, 43.

75. Simon. YCAL.

76. Bee Time Vine. *BTV*, 35.

77. Irma. *P&P*, 96.

78. A Lide Close. The Story of a Spanish Morrison. *BTV*, 43.

79. Mrs. Edwardes. *P&P*, 97.

80. Preciosilla. *SW*, 550.

81. Sacred Emily. *G&P*, 178.

1914

82. Meal One. *BTV*, 147.

83. Emp Lace. *BTV*, 157.

84. Series. *BTV*, 173.

85. Tillie. *BTV*, 173.

86. Curtain Let Us. *PL*, 159.

87. Dates. *BTV*, 168.

88. Four. *BTV*, 167.

89. Finished One. *BTV*, 170.

90. Oval. *BTV*, 119.

91. One or Two. I've Finished. *BTV*, 179.

92. Crete. *BTV*, 172.

93. In One. *BTV*, 177.

94. Wear. *Broom*, IV (January 1923), 130.

95. Gentle Julia. *BTV*, 178.

96. Painted Lace. *PL*, 1.

97. At. *BTV*, 155.

98. A New Happiness. *PL*, 151.

99. Mrs. Whitehead. *G&P*, 154.

100. Lockeridge. *BTV*, 177.

101. Mrs. Emerson. *Close up*, 2 (August 1927), 23.

102. Tubene. *BTV*, 179.

103. Bird Jet. *BTV*, 179.

104. One Sentence. *AFAM*, 71.

1915

105. Not Slightly. A Play. *G&P*, 290.

106. Pink Melon Joy. *G&P*, 347.

107. Johnny Grey. *G&P*, 167.

108. Study Nature. *BTV*, 181.

109. Possessive Case. *AFAM*, 109.

110. No. *AFAM*, 33.

111. When We Went Away. *PL*, 19.

112. Farragut or A Husband's Recompense. *UK*, 5.

113. How Could They Marry Her. *Envoy*, IV (January 1951), 57.

114. If you Had Three Husbands. *G&P*, 377.

115. This One Is Serious. *PL*, 20.

116. He Didn't Light the Light. *PL*, 17.

117. David Daisy and Appolonia. *P&P*, 226.

118. Independent Embroidery. *PL*, 81.

119. I Have No Title To Be Successful. *PL*, 23.

120. He Said It. Monologue. *G&P*, 267.

1916

121. For the Country Entirely. A Play in Letters. *G&P*, 227.

122. What Does Cook Want To Do. *PL*, 31.

123. It Was An Accident. *PL*, 34.

124. Mr. Miranda and William. *PL*, 274.

125. Henry and I. *PL*, 273.

126. We Have Eaten Heartily and We Were Alarmed. *PL*, 39.

127. Letters and Parcels and Wool, *AFAM*, 163.

128. Water Pipe. *larus*, I (February 1927), 6.

129. Ladies Voices. Curtain Raiser. *G&P*, 203.

130. Every Afternoon. A Dialogue. *G&P*, 254.

131. Advertisements. *G&P*, 341.

132. Do Let Us Go Away. A Play. *G&P*, 215.

133. Let Us Be Easily Careful. *PL*, 35.

134. Bonne Annee. A Play. *G&P*, 302.

135. Captain William Edwards. *PL*, 272.

136. Captain Walter Arnold. A Play. *G&P*, 260.

137. In Memory (Polybe Silent). *PL*, 29.

138. Please Do Not Suffer. A Play. *G&P*, 262.

139. I Like It To Be A Play. A Play. *G&P*, 286.

140. A Very Good House. *PL*, 26.

141. Turkey and Bones and Eating and We Liked It. A Play. *G&P*, 239.

142. I Often Think About Another. *PL*, 32.

143. A Collection. *G&P*, 23.

144. I Must Try to Write the History of Belmonte. *G&P*, 70.

145. Universe or Hand-Reading. *PL*, 268.

146. Mallorcan Stories. *G&P*, 96.
147. Look At Us. *PL*, 259.
148. Mexico. A Play. *G&P*, 304.
149. Decorations. *BTV*, 185.
150. A Poem About Walberg. *G&P*, 166.
151. All Sunday. *A&B*, 87.

1917

152. Lifting Belly. *BTV*, 61.
153. Miss Cruttwell. *AFAM*, 173.
154. The King or Something. (The Public Is Invited To Dance). *G&P*, 122.
155. Marry Nettie. *PL*, 42.
156. Counting Her Dresses. A Play. *G&P*, 275.
157. Have They Attacked Mary. He Giggled. (A Political Caricature). *SW*, 533.
158. An Exercise In Analysis. A Play. *LO&P*, 119.
159. I Can Feel the Beauty. *PL*, 84.
160. Will We See Them Again. *PL*, 275.
161. Why Can Kipling Speak. *BTV*, 188.
162. The Great American Army. *Vanity Fair*, X (June 1918), 31.
163. Relief Work in France. *Life*, LXX (27 December 1917), 1076.

1918

164. One Has Not Lost One's Marguerite. *Black & Blue Jay*, VI (April 1926), 16.
165. Why Win Wings. On a Hat. *BTV*, 205.
166. In Their Play. *BTV*, 206.
167. Can You Behave Better. *BTV*, 207.
168. What is the Name of a Ring. *BTV*, 180.
169. In the Middle of the Day. *BTV*, 206.
170. Do You Like Your Suit. *BTV*, 183.
171. The Ford. *BTV*, 183.
172. Call it a Table. *BTV*, 183.
173. Third Day Not Thirsty. *BTV*, 183.
174. Can Call Us. *BTV*, 184.
175. Can You See the Name. *BTV*, 204.
176. Exceptional Conduct. *BTV*, 207.
177. Light Butter. *BTV*, 208.
178. James is Nervous. *BTV*, 208.

179. In This Shape Wood. *BTV*, 208.

180. Mirror. *BTV*, 207.

181. Can You Speak. *BTV*, 209.

182. Red Faces. *UK*, 78.

183. Can You Sit in a Tree. *BTV*, 209.

184. Selected Poems: *BTV*, 196.

      Amaryllis or The Prettiest of Legs
      An Incident
      What Is This
      A Lesson For Baby
      A Radical Expert
      America
      Your Own
      Let us Talk About Waxing
      In This Way, Kissing
      Can You Imitate Disaster
      In the Same Poem
      An Elegant Escape
      Can You Climb In Little Things
      We Cannot
      Why Cannot You Speak in Pieces
      Making Sense

185. Work Again. *G&P*, 392. ["Barrels" begins on page 399.]

186. Rich in the City. YCAL.

1918

187. Monday and Tuesday. YCAL.

188. J.R. *Vanity Fair*. XI (March 1919), 88b.

188a. J.R., II. *Vanity Fair*, XI (March 1919), 88b.

189. Accents in Alsace. A Reasonable Tragedy. *G&P*, 409.

190. Our Aid. *BTV*, 184.

191. The Meaning of the Bird. *Vanity Fair*, XI (March 1919), 88b.

192. A Deserter. *Vanity Fair*, XI (March 1919), 88b.

193. A Poetical Plea. *BTV*, 195.

194. Prim Roses. *BTV*, 211.

195. Scenes From the Door. *UK*, 78.

196. A Patriotic Leading. *UK*, 81.

197. White Wings. *BTV*, 210.

198. I Expressed My Opinion. *BTV*, 210.

199. Animated. *BTV*, 210.

200. Won. *BTV*, 187.

201. Left Poem. *BTV*, 211.

202. The Work. *BTV*, 189.

203. Old Dogs. *BTV*, 213.

204. Kicking. *BTV*, 213.

205. Then Steal. *BTV*, 214.

206. The Present: *BTV*, 212.

      The Present

      Italy

      The Liberty Loan

      Sacred Fountain of Bellows

      Say it Again

      Postal Cards

207. Tourty or Tourtebattre. A Story of The Great War. *G&P*, 401.

1920

---

208. Ireland. *Der Querschnitt* (March 1925), 224.

209. Wood. *BTV*, 216.

210. A Movie. *O&P*, 395.

211. Polish. *BTV*, 215.

212. The Reverie of the Zionist. *PL*, 94.

213. A League. *UK*, 84.

214. More League. *UK*, 84.

215. Events. *UK*, 84.

216. A Hymn. *BTV*, 215.

217. The Psychology of Nations or What Are You Looking At. *G&P*, 416.

218. Daughter. *UK*, 79.

219. Next. Life and Letters of Marcel Duchamp. *G&P*, 405.

220. Names of Flowers. *BTV*, 217.

221. Rich and Poor in English. To Subscribe In French And Other Latin Languages. *PL*, 95.

222. Photograph. *LO&P*, 152.

223. Scenery. *BTV*, 217.

224. Coal and Wood. *PL*, 3.

225. Land of Nations (Subtitle And Ask Asia). *G&P*, 407.

226. Develop Spanish. *BTV*, 217.

227. Land Rising. *PL*, 276.

228. A Circular Play. *LO&P*, 139.

229. Vacation in Britany King or Kangaroo King Or Yellow King Or

Marie Claire Suggests A Meadow. And The Use of Thought. *Little Review*, VIII (Spring 1922), 5.
230. Woodrow Wilson. *UK*, 104.

1921

231. B. B. or The Birthplace of Bonnes. *P&P*, 162.
232. Three Moral Tales. *NOTY*, 241.
233. Nest of Dishes. *PL*, 97.
234. Emily Chadbourne. *UK*, 88.
235. Not a Hole. *BTV*, 223.
236. Curtains Dream. *BTV*, 224.
237. Dinner. *Two Poems*.
238. Counting. *BTV*, 222.
239. Kites. *BTV*, 222.
240. Readings. [Published as *Kisses Can* (Pawlet, Vermont: Banyan Press, 1947).]
241. Separated. *BTV*, 221.
242. Attacks. *BTV*, 221.
243. Jokes for Jessie. *BTV*, 222.
244. Dolphin. *PL*, 160.
245. Little Pillows. *PL*, 162.
246. Singing to a Musician. *P&P*, 232.
247. Finish Constance. *PL*, 276.
248. A Sonatina Followed by Another. Dedicated by Request to D. D. *BTV*, 1.
249. Currents. *PL*, 233.
250. Mary. *BTV*, 223.
251. Capture Splinters. *BTV*, 218.
252. A Little Cream. *PL*, 161.
253. Think Again. *PL*, 107.
254. Read a New Currant. *PL*, 161.
255. Today We Have a Vacation. *Two Poems*.
256. Sonnets That Please. *BTV*, 220.
257. Reread Another. A Play. To be played indoors or out. I wish to be a school. *O&P*, 123.

1922

258. Objects Lie on a Table. A Play. *O&P*, 105.
259. As Fine As Melanctha. *AFAM*, 255.
260. I Feel a Really Anxious Moment Coming. *PL*, 236.

261. Mildred's Thoughts. *The American Caravan*, 648.

262. Didn't Nelly and Lilly Love You. *AFAM*, 219.

263. American Biography and Why Waste It. *UK*, 162.

264. Saints and Singing. A Play. *O&P*, 71.

265. An Instant Answer or A Hundred Prominent Men. *UK*, 144.

266. Jo Davidson. *P&P*, 194.

267. A Singular Addition. A Sequel To An Instant Answer Or One Hundred Prominent Men. *PL*, 277.

268. A Saint in Seven. *WAM*, 41.

269. Lend a Hand or Four Religions. *UK*, 170.

270. Why Are There Whites To Console. A History in Three Parts. *AFAM*, 198.

271. A Valentine To Sherwood Anderson. Idem The Same. *P&P*, 151.

272. Prudence Caution and Foresight. A Story of Avignon. *NOTY*, 253.

273. If He Thinks A Novelette of Desertion. *Transition*, 10 (January 1928), 9.

274. Lily Life. *PL*, 132.

275. Erik Satie. *P&P*, 27.

276. Talks to Saints Or Stories of Saint Remy. *PL*, 108.

277. Yes You Do. *PL*, 118.

1923

278. Procession. *Programme*, 8 (June 1935), 8.

279. For Ten: *PL*, 133.
    Very Prettily
    Chapter II
    Did She Read
    He Knows

280. Praises. *PL*, 123.

281. Harold Loeb. *P&P*, 208.

282. Fourteen Anonymous Portraits. *P&P*, 227.

283. Cezanne. *P&P*, 11.

284. An Indian Boy. *The Reviewer*, IV (January 1924), 104.

285. Precepts. *PL*, 128.

286. A List. *O&P*, 89.

287. Capital Capitals. *O&P*, 61.

288. Jonas Julian Caesar and Samuel. *PL*, 286.

289. An Elucidation. *P&P*, 246.

290. *A Village. Are You Ready Yet Not Yet. A Play in Four Acts.*

291. Practice Of Oratory. *PL*, 124.

292. Subject-cases: The Background Of A Detective Story. *AFAM*, 1.
293. Am I to Go or I'll Say So. *O&P*, 113.
294. He and They, Hemingway. *P&P*, 193.
295. A Book Concluding With As a Wife Has a Cow A Love Story. *SW*, 543.
296. Van or Twenty Years After. A Second Portrait of Carl Van Vechten. *P&P*, 157.
297. Are There Arithmetics. *Oxford 1927* (28 May 1927), 24.
298. New. *BTV*, 229.
299. If I Told Him. A Completed Portrait of Picasso. *P&P*, 21.
300. Geography. *PL*, 239.
301. As Eighty Or Numbered From One To Eighty-One, A Disputation. *BTV*, 224.
302. Are There Six or Another Question. *UK*, 83.
303. Studies in Conversation. *Transition*, 6 (September 1927), 75.
304. My Dear Coady and Brenner. *PL*, 291.
305. Equally So. A Description Of All The Incidents Which I Have Observed In Travelling And On My Return. *AFAM*, 269.

1924
---
306. Wherein the South Differs From the North. *UK*, 19.
307. A Birthday Book. *A&B*, 127.
308. In Which House Did he Live. *PL*, 58.
309. Wherein Iowa Differs from Kansas and Indiana. *UK*, 38.
310. Elected Again. *PL*, 48.
311. The Difference Between the Inhabitants of France and the Inhabitants of the United States of America. *UK*, 43.
312. Made a Mile Away. *Transition*, 8 (November 1927), 155.
313. Mildred Aldrich Saturday. *P&P*, 111.
314. And So. To Change So. (A Fantasy on Three Careers) Muriel Draper Yvonne Davidson Beatrice Locher. *P&P*, 143.
315. Birth and Marriage. *A&B*, 173.
316. Dahomy Or As Soft A Noise (A Serial). *A&B*, 155.
317. Pictures of Juan Gris. *P&P*, 46.
318. The Brazilian Admiral's Son. *P&P*, 216.
319. Emmet Addis the Doughboy; A Pastoral. *UK*, 97.
320. A Description Of The Fifteenth of November. A Portrait of T. S. Eliot. *P&P*, 68.
321. Colored as Colors. A Gift. *AFAM*, 381.
322. Descriptions of Literature. *Transition*, 13 (Summer 1928), 50.

323. Which One Will. *AFAM*, 384.

324. To Call It a Day. *PL*, 243.

325. Man Ray. *PL*, 292.

326. Near East or Chicago. A Description. *UK*, 51.

327. After At Once. *PL*, 50.

328. A Comedy Like That. *BTV*, 234.

329. A History Of Having A Great Many Times Not Continued To Be Friends. *AFAM*, 285.

1925

330. Sitwell Edith Sitwell. *P&P*, 92.

331. Early and Late. *BTV*, 241.

332. Or More (or War). *UK*, 115.

333. Business in Baltimore. *UK*, 63.

334. Among Negroes. *UK*, 60.

334a. A Stitch in time saves nine. birds of a feather flock together. chickens come home to roost. *Ex Libris*, II (March 1925), 177.

335. A Third. *AFAM*, 329.

335a. Review: Troubadour. *Ex Libris*, II (June 1925), 278.

336. A Novel of Thank You. *NOTY*, 1.

337. Natural Phenomena. *PL*, 167.

1926

338. Jean Cocteau. *P&P*, 80.

339. Composition as Explanation. *SW*, 511.

340. Edith Sitwell And Her Brothers The Sitwells And Also To Osbert Sitwell And to S. Sitwell. *PL*, 293.

341. Allen Tanner. *UK*, 86.

342. *An Acquaintance With Description.*

343. Pavlik Tchelitchef Or Adrian Arthur. *P&P*, 213.

344. Lipschitz. *P&P*, 63.

1927

345. Patriarchal Poetry. *BTV*, 249.

346. Regular Regularly in Narrative. *HTW*, 215.

347. Duchess de Rohan. A Writer. *PL*, 310.

348. A Diary. *A&B*, 199.

349. Four Saints in Three Acts. An Opera to be Sung. *O&P*, 11.

350. Felicity In Moon-light. A Traveler's Story. *PL*, 64.

351. Two Spaniards. *PL*, 309.

352. By the Way. *PL*, 135.

353. Hurlbut. *PL*, 308.

354. Relieve. *PL*, 308.

355. One Spaniard. *P&P*, 65.

356. Admit. *PL*, 136.

357. An Advantage. *PL*, 304.

358. Love A Delight. *PL*, 251.

359. With A Wife. *PL*, 301.

360. Three Sitting Here. *P&P*, 124.

361. The Life Of Juan Gris. The Life And Death of Juan Gris. *P&P*, 48.

362. *Lucy Church Amiably*.

362a. Advertisement. *LCA*.

363. A bouquet. YCAL.

1928
___

364. Finally George A Vocabulary Of Thinking. *HTW*, 271.

365. Dan Raffel A Nephew. *P&P*, 86.

366. To Virgil And Eugene. *PL*, 310.

367. A Lyrical Opera Made By Two To Be Sung. *O&P*, 49.

368. Arthur a Grammar. *HTW*, 37.

369. J. H. Jane Heap. *Little Review*, XII (May 1929), 9.

370. The d'Aiguys. *P&P*, 108.

371. Paisieu. *LO&P*, 155.

372. A Bouquet. Their wills. *O&P*, 195.

373. George Hugnet. *P&P*, 66.

374. Christian Berard. *P&P*, 73.

375. Virgil Thomson. *P&P*, 198.

376. Sentences. *HTW*, 113.

377. Answer: Why I Do Not Live in America. *Transition*, 14 (Fall 1928), 97.

378. Advertisement. *UK*, no page.

378a. Introducing. *UK*, 1.

1929
___

379. Bernard Faÿ. *P&P*, 41.

380. For-get-me-not. To Janet: *SIM*, 230.
    Left Alone. To Basket
    To The First Bird Which They Heard.
    They May be Said to be Ready

Orphans

Advice About Roses

A Bird

A Ball

Balls

To a View

A Desire

A Summer With Marcels

With Pleasure

Chosen

381. Basket. *P&P*, 181.

381a. Letter to *Little Review*. *Little Review*, XII (May 1929), 73.

382. Film. Deux Soeurs Qui Ne Sont Pas Soeurs. *O&P*, 399.

383. Five Words in a Line. *Pagany*, I (Winter 1930), 39.

384. More Grammar Genia Berman. *P&P*, 185.

385. Saving the Sentence. *HTW*, 11.

386. Kristians Tonny. *P&P*, 212.

387. G. Maratier. *P&P*, 183.

388. Paragraphs. #399.

389. Bibliography. *Transition*, 15 (February 1929), 47.

1930

390. Sentences and Paragraphs. *HTW*, 23.

391. The Return. *PL*, 66.

392. Evidence. *Modern Things*, ed. Parker Tyler (1934), 39.

393. Absolutely As Bob Brown Or Bobbed Brown. *PL*, 311.

394. Eric De Haulleville. *P&P*, 211.

395. Madame de Clermont-Tonnerre. *P&P*, 89.

396. Bravig Imbs. *P&P*, 210.

397. Madame Langlois. YCAL.

398. Parlor. *O&P*, 325.

399. More Grammar For A Sentence. *AFAM*, 359.

400. A Grammarian. *HTW*, 103.

401. At Present A Play. Nothing But Contemporaries Allowed. *O&P*, 315.

402. Grace, or Yves de Longevialle. YCAL.

403. Title, Sub-Title. *AFAM*, 386.

404. The Pilgrims. Thoughts about Master Pieces. *PL*, 145.

405. Why Willows. *Modern Things*, ed. Parker Tyler (1934), 40. [A part of #392.]

406. Pay Me. *PL*, 137.

407. How are Fears. *PL*, 139.

408. To Kitty Or Kate Buss. *P&P*, 103.

409. *Before the Flowers of Friendship Faded Friendship Faded.*

410. To Pierre De Massot. *PL*, 311.

[no 411.]

412. We Came a History. *Readies For Bob Brown's Machine* (1931), 99.

413. History Or Messages From History. *A&B*, 219.

414. A French Rooster. *A History. SIM*, 213.

415. Abel. *SIM*, 222.

416. Madame Recamier An Opera. *O&P*, 355.

417. They Weighed Weighed-Layed A Drama of Aphorisms. *O&P*, 231.

418. Narrative. *SIM*, 250.

419. To Help. In Case of Accident. *SIM*, 253.

419a. An Historic Drama In Memory of Winnie Elliot. *LO&P*, 182.

420. Will He Come Back Better. Second Historic Drama. In the Country. *LO&P*, 189.

421. Politeness. *PL*, 142.

422. Louis XI and Madame Giraud. *O&P*, 345.

423. Play I [–III]. *LO&P*, 200.

424. Genuine Creative Ability. *Creative Art*, VI (February 1930), supplement, 41.

1931

425. Say it With Flowers. A Play. *O&P*, 331.

426. The Five Georges. A Play. *O&P*, 293.

427. Left to Right. *Story*, III (November 1933), 17.

428. Hotel François Ier. *MR*, 301.

429. Forensics. *HTW*, 383.

430. Brim Beauvais, a Novelette. *MR*, 269.

431. She Bowed To Her Brother. *P&P*, 236.

432. Grant or Rutherford B. Hayes. *Americans Abroad* (1932), 419.

433. Poems. *SIM*, 267.

434. Winning His Way. A Narrative Poem of Poetry. *SIM*, 153.

435. Review: Yesterday's Burdens. YCAL.

436. Lynn And The College De France. *O&P*, 249.

437. They Must. Be Wedded. To Their Wife. A Play. *LO&P*, 204.

438. Civilization. A Play In Three Acts. *O&P*, 131.

439. A Ballad. *SIM*, 256.

440. Thoughts On An American Contemporary Feeling. *Creative Age*, X (February 1932), 129.

1932
___
441. A Play Without Roses Portrait of Eugene Jolas. *P&P*, 200.
442. A Play of Pounds. *LO&P*, 239.
443. Marguerite Or A Simple Novel of High Life. *MR*, 339.
444. Bartholemew Arnold or After The War Is Over. *MR*, 321.
445. A Manoir An Historic Play In Which They Are Approached More Often. *LO&P*, 277.
446. A Play A Lion for Max Jacob. *P&P*, 28.
447. Short Sentences. *LO&P*, 317.
448. A Little Love Of Life. *SIM*, 277.
449. Here. Actualities. *PL*, 11.
450. Margite Marguerite and Margherita. *SIM*, 269.
451. Stanzas In Meditation. *SIM*, 1.
452. *The Autobiography of Alice B. Toklas.*
453. Scenery and George Washington. See *Four in America*, #458.
453a. Preface. *Picabia, Chez Léonce Rosenberg* (Paris, December 1932).

1933
___
454. A Plan for Planting. *PL*, 14.
455. Byron A Play But Which They Say Byron A Play. *LO&P*, 333.
455a. A Poem. *SIM*, 289.
456. Letter to Bernard Faÿ. Kansas City *Star*, 20 January 1934, no page.
457. Story of a Book. *Wings*, VII (September 1933), 8.
458. *Four in America.*
459. Or a History of the United States of America. YCAL.
460. First Page. *SIM*, 282.
461. *Blood On The Dining-Room Floor.*
462. Lucy La Fontaine. *PL*, 315.
463. Afterwards. *SIM*, 290.
464. Detective Story.
464a. Or. And Then Silence A Portrait of a Frenchman. *P&P*, 241.
465. Answer to 'Metanthropological Crisis'. *Transition*, 21 (March 1932), 136.
465a. Page IX. *The Observor*, II, 1 (1933), 12.

1934.

466. And Now. *Vanity Fair*, XLIII (September 1934), 35.

467. The Superstitions of Fred Anneday, Annday, Anday; A Novel of Real Life. *Nassau Lit*, XCIV (December 1935), 6.

468. Qu'est-ce je pense de la France. *L'Intransigent*, 6 January, 1934, 1.

469. *Lectures In America*.

470. Plays and Landscapes. *Saturday Review of Literature*, XI (10 November 1934), 269. [Excerpts from "Plays," *LIA*, 93.]

471. Letter to *Vanity Fair. Vanity Fair*, XLIII (December 1934), 13.

472. Meditations On Being About To Visit My Native Land. *PL*, 254.

473. Sir Francis Rose. *Notice of Wildenstein & Co., Ltd.*, (London, February 1934); also *The Arts Club of Chicago* (Chicago, November 1934); and the *Marie Harriman Gallery* (New York, December 1934).

474. Stieglitz. *America and Alfred Stieglitz, A Collective Portrait*, ed. Waldo Frank *et al.* (New York, 1934), 280.

474a. Pathe. YCAL.

475. *Chicago Inscriptions*.

476. Preface. *Recent Paintings by Francis Picabia* (New York: Valentine Gallery, November 1934).

1935

476a. Gertrude Stein to Cousins in Baltimore. *Letters* (Spring 1935), 16.

477. I Came and Here I Am. *Cosmopolitan*, XCVIII (February 1935), 18.

478. The Capital and Capitals of the United States of America. New York *Herald Tribune*, 9 March 1935, 11.

479. American Newspapers. New York *Herald Tribune*, 23 March 1935, 15.

480. American Education and Colleges. New York *Herald Tribune*, 16 March 1935, 15.

481. American States and Cities and How They Differ From Each Other. New York *Herald Tribune*, 6 April 1935, 13.

482. American Crimes and How They Matter. New York *Herald Tribune*, 30 March 1934, 13.

483. American Food and American Houses. New York *Herald Tribune*, 13 April 1935, 13.

484. *Narration.*

484a. Review: Puzzled America. YCAL.

485. *The Geographical History Of America Or The Relation Of Human Nature To The Human Mind.*

485a. Letter to Freddy. *New Music* (April 1935), 12.

486. Identity a Poem. *WAM*, 71.

487. Identity a Tale. *PL*, 69.

487a. Identity a Poem a Story and a History. YCAL.

488. A Political Series. *PL*, 71.

489. *What Are Master-pieces and Why Are There So Few of Them.*

490. How Writing is Written. *Oxford Anthology of American Literature* (1938), 1446.

491. Paintings by Elie Lascaux. *The Arts Club of Chicago* (February–March 1936).

491a. Mark Twain Centenary. *PL*, 316.

1936
_____

492. An American and France. *WAM*, 61.

493. Listen to Me. A Play. *LO&P*, 387.

494. A Play Called Not and Now. *LO&P*, 422.

495. Review: Oscar Wilde Discovers America. Chicago *Daily Tribune*, 8 August 1936, 9.

496. *Everybody's Autobiography.*

497. A Waterfall and a Piano. *New Directions in Prose and Poetry* (1936), 16.

498. Is Dead. *Occident*, XXX (April 1937), 6.

499. Money. *Saturday Evening Post* (13 June 1936), 88.

500. More about Money. *Saturday Evening Post* (11 July 1936), 30.

501. Still More About Money. *Saturday Evening Post* (25 July 1936), 32.

502. All About Money. *Saturday Evening Post* (22 August 1936), 54.

503. My Last About Money. *Saturday Evening Post* (10 October 1936), 78.

504. Butter Will Melt. *Atlantic Monthly*, CLIX (February 1937), 156.

505. (Part of) Letter to the Atlantic. *Atlantic Monthly*, CLIX (February 1937), xvi.

506. What Does She See When She Shuts Her Eyes. *MR*, 375.

507. The Autobiography of Rose. *Partisan Review*, VI (Winter 1939), 61.

1937

508. Daniel Webster Eighteen In America A Play. *New Directions in Prose & Poetry* (1937), 162.

509. Quelques Oeuvres Récentes de Sir Francis Rose. *Galerie Pierre* (27 April 1937).

509a. Selections. *Academic Observor,* LI (February 1937), 6.

510. La Baronne Pierlot. *PL,* 316.

511. Why I Like Detective Stories. *Harper's Bazaar* [London], XVII (November 1937), 70.

512. Ida. *The Boudoir Companion,* ed. Page Cooper (1938), 31.

512a. Conversation à Belignin [*sic*]. *Peintures Dada* (Paris: Galeries De Beaune, Paris, November–December 1937).

1938

513. *Picasso* [In French].

514. *Picasso* [In English].

515. Doctor Faustus Lights the Lights. *LO&P,* 89.

516. *The World is Round.* [See also, *Harper's Bazaar* (New York) (June 1939), 46.]

517. Arthur and Jenny.

517a. Lucretia Borgia. A Play. *Creative Writing* (October 1938), 15.

1939

518. Catalogue of an Exhibition of Paintings by Francis Rose. *The Mayor Gallery* (London, January 1939).

518a. Excerpts from Gertrude Stein's Letters. *Press Book for . . . the World Is Round* (1939), 11.

519. My Debt to Books. *Books Abroad,* XIII (Summer 1939), 307.

520. Paris and English Painting. YCAL.

521. Les Superstitions. YCAL.

521a. Letter to Batsford. *Gertrude Stein, The World Is Round* (London, 1939), 4. [Prospectus for the English edition.]

522. Actually Writing.

523. Helen Button A Story of War-Time. *Paris France,* 80.

524. My Dear Miss Steloff. *We Moderns* (1939), 3.

525. *Paris France*

526. Answer to The Situation in American Writing. *Partisan Review,* VI (Summer 1939), 4.

527. *Prothalamium for Bobolink And His Louisa.*

1940

528. My Life with Dogs. *Ida*, 96.
529. To Do: A Book of Alphabets and Birthdays. *A&B*, 1.
530. *Ida A Novel.*
531. The Winner Loses, A Picture of Occupied France. *Atlantic Monthly*, CLXVI (November 1940), 571. Also, *SW*. 615.
532. Superstitions. YCAL.
533. Mrs. Reynolds A Novel. *MR*, 1.

1941

534. Francis Picabia. *Exposition Francis Picabia* (3 et 5 rue Commandant-Andre, Cannes, 11 April 1941).
535. La Langue Francaise. *Patrie*, 2 (August 1941), 36.
536. The United States of America. YCAL.
537. The Gertrude Stein First Reader. *GSFR*, 7.
538. Sherwood's Sweetness. *Story*, XIX (September–October 1941), 63.
539. Translation of and introduction to Pétain's *Paroles aux Français*. YCAL.

1942

540. Conference à Belley. YCAL.
1942–4
541. *Wars I Have Seen.*

1943

542. Castles they live in. Castles on the wall. YCAL.
543. In A Garden A Tragedy In One Act. *GSFR*, 59.
544. Three Sisters Who Are Not Sisters A Melodrama. *GSFR*, 63.
545. Look and Long. *GSFR*, 73.
546. Realism in novels. YCAL.
547. A Poem about the end of the war. YCAL.

1944

548. American language and literature. YCAL.
549. La Voix de L'Amérique. *Le Bugiste* (2 September 1944), 2.
550. What a day. *WIHS*, 244.
550a. Lyon broadcast. YCAL.
551. Broadcast at Voiron. Abridged in Eric Sevareid, *Not So Wild a Dream* (1946), 457.
552. L'Amérique est mon pays. *Life*, (16 April 1945), 14. [Extracts.]

1944–6

553. Yes is for a Very Young Man. *LO&P*, 1.
554. En Savoie. YCAL.

1945

555. We Are Back in Paris. *Transformation Three,* ed. Stefan Schimanski and Henry Treece (London, n.d.), 5.
556. Le Retour A Paris. *Fontaine,* VIII (April 1945), 135.
557. Decouverte D'Un Peintre. *Fontaine,* VIII (May 1945), 287.
557a. France-Amérique. *Harmonies* (May 1945), 11.
558. Off We All Went to See Germany. *Life,* (6 August 1945), 54.
559. The New Hope in Our 'Sad Young Men.' *The New York Times Magazine* (3 June 1945), 5.
560. *Brewsie and Willie.*
561. To Americans. *B&W*, 113.
562. From Dark to Day. *Vogue* [London], CI (November 1945), 52.
563. Introduction. YCAL.
564. Everything. YCAL.

1945–6

565. *The Mother of Us All.*

1946

566. Abstract painting. YCAL.
567. A Message From Gertrude Stein. *SW*, vii.
568. Raoul Dufy. *Harper's Bazaar* [New York] (December 1949), 93.
569. John Breon a novel or a play. YCAL.
570. Meditations. YCAL.
571. Reflection On The Atomic Bomb. *Yale Poetry Review,* 7 (December 1947), 3.

Leroy, George: EA 149-50.
Lewis, John L.: EA 133.
Lewis, Lloyd: EA 102, 235, 269-70.
  Myths After Lincoln: EA 270.
Lewis, Margaret: EA 145.
Lewis, Wyndham: ABT 150, 173.
Lincoln, Abraham: ABT 18-19, 303.
Lind, Jenny: EA 6.
Lindbergh, Charles A.: EA 185.
Lipschitz, Jacques: ABT 133, 249-50.
Loeb, Harold: ABT 245, 253, 267, 269.
Loeser, Charles: ABT 35, 37, 38.
Lohengrin: EA 212; LIA 113.
Long, Huey: EA 219, 258.
Longfellow, Henry W.: LIA 241.
Loos, Anita: EA 282.
Lounsbery, Grace: ABT 246.
Lovelace, Lord: ABT 159.
Loy, Mina: ABT 162, 245-6, 267.
Lutz, Mark: EA 132, 157, 158-9, 181.
Lynes, George: ABT 261.
Lyon, George: EA 81.

Machiavelli, Niccolo: ABT 161.
Maddalena: ABT 67, 106.
Maeterlinck, Maurice, *The Bluebird:* ABT 148.
Maillol, Aristide: ABT 51, 78.
Mall, Dr. Franklin: ABT 99-100.
Manet, Édouard: ABT 12, 38, 61.
Manolo: ABT 117-19, 136.
Manguin, Henri: ABT 12, 46.
Mantegna, Andrea: LIA 71.
Maratier, George: ABT 283; EA 19, 54-55, 166, 190, 296, 305-6.
Marie: ABT 204.
Marinetti, Emilio F. T.: ABT 153.
Mario: EA 50-51.
Mars, Ethel: ABT 16, 141.
Marchand, M.: ABT 201-2.
Marcoussis, Louis: ABT 136; EA 41-42.
Masson, Mr.: ABT 210-11.
Masson, André: ABT 258, 269; EA 28.
Matisse, Henri: ABT 5, 7, 8-9, 10, 12, 17-18, 20, 41-51, 58, 65-6, 70, 77-83, 98, 112-15, 121, 134, 140, 143, 148, 172, 184, 237, 251, 301; LIA 80-81; EA 29, 32, 311, 313, 314.
Matisse, Mme.: ABT 16, 42-44, 47-51, 66, 105, 114, 115, 184.
Matisse, Jean: ABT 44.

Matisse, Margot: ABT 44, 48-49.
Matisse, Pierre: ABT 44.
Matthews, Edward: EA 8.
Maurer, Alfred: ABT 13-14, 40, 66, 185, 191.
McAlmon, Robert: ABT 246, 261, 267, 269, 273, 276; EA 66.
McBride, Henry: ABT 36, 149, 210, 228; EA 32, 47, 187.
McClellan, General George: EA 236
McDougall, William: EA 265
McGrew, Tarn: ABT 221.
Meredith, George: LIA 47, 48, 52-53.
Merovingian, Alexander: EA 96.
Merovingian, Louis: EA 96.
Meryon, Charles: LIA 66.
Michaelangelo: ABT 303; EA 37.
Miller, Harlan: EA 311.
Miller, Joaquin: ABT 159.
Millet, Jean François: LIA 65-66, 68; EA 293.
Milton, John: ABT 57; LIA 32; EA 9, 301.
A Miner My Brother: EA 137.
Mirlees, Hope: ABT 172, 178.
Miro, Joan: EA 27, 28, 312.
Modigliani, Amedeo: EA 94, 313.
Mohammed: ABT 201.
Monnier, Adrienne: ABT 234, 240-41.
Monte Carlo, Bishop of: EA 220-21.
Moore, Cora: EA 117-18.
Moore, George: ABT 186.
Moore, Marianne: EA 187.
Moréas, Jean: ABT 119.
Morrell, Lady Ottoline: ABT 151, 154, 156.
Mother Goose: EA 297.
Muncie, Mrs.: EA 245.
Münsterberg, Hugo: ABT 95; EA 265.
Murphy, Hub: EA 113.
Mussolini, Benito: EA 133.

Napoleon: ABT 3, 71. LIA 36; EA 115, 123, 246, 306.
Nelson, Lester "Baby Face": EA 207.
Nevada, Emma: ABT 53.
Nightingale, Florence; EA 6.
Nijinsky, Vaslav: ABT 167.
Norton, Allan: ABT 141, 169, 192.
Norton, Louise: ABT 169.
Nyen: EA 155, 161-62.

INDEX

404

critically recognized, 205; bitten by serpent, 292n; unnatural summer following *The Autobiography of Alice B. Toklas*, 277-78, 281; suffers inability to write, 234-36, 276; lectures in U.S., 13-14, 243, 281; returns to California, 281-82; observes social unrest, 268, 273-75, 315; retreats from Nazis to Bilignin, 314-16; translates Pétain, 317-18; sympathizes with Resistance, 329-31; is liberated, 331; last words, 339-40; death, 341

OPINIONS

America, 63-64, 68, 238-39; its people, 68, 230, 247, 252, 257-58, 276; soldiers, 331-32, 335-38; language, 162, 286-87

childhood, 12-13, 326-27

fame, 112, 169, 205, 234

France, 296-97

history, 204, 260-61, 262-63

identity, 241-42, 260, 262, 266-67, 268, 304-5; shaken, 235, 276-77; split, 26-27, 83, 98, 291-92, 331; psychic crises in fiction, 301-2, 303-4, 310

"industrialism," 340

Judaism, 160-61, 314-15

liberty, 329

men, 341; fathers, 10-11, 16-17, 279-80, 341; male tyranny, 342; male aggression, 13, 17-18, 307

middle class, 24, 43-44

modern world, 288

money, 275-76

Negroes, 23, 49, 52, 181, 273, 338, 343

newspapers, 258-59, 263

pregnancy, 77-78; obstetrics, 36; on giving birth, 99, 341

saints, 162, 165, 283

the South, 23

teachers, 130

women, 15, 36-37, 78, 104; mothers, 10, 16; the sensualist, 45, 68; image of enthroned female, 293, 305, 331

WRITING

abridged works, *The Making of Americans*, 59-60; "George Hugnet," 194n; "Cezanne," 249; *The World Is Round*, 299n

aesthetic: cultivates subjectivity, 66, 70, 71, 79, 84-85, 89-90, 174, 265; immediacy, 123, 128-29, 131, 258, 259, 261ff.; spontaneity, 55; intuition, 283, 290, 294; indirection, 131; randomness, 100, 174; inconsistency, 70, 93, 130; no revision, 50, 101-2; rejects compositional centrality, 132

associative process, 85, 143, 163, 167

audience, GS tries to dominate, 240, 244-45, 252, 255; as a threat, 247, 260, 266

authorial presence in writing, 89, 103, 122-23, 153

autobiographical details in writing: 8, 9-11, 15, 16n, 18-19, 23-24, 28-29, 40, 49, 61-62, 65, 68, 76, 80-81, 82, 84, 112-14, 144, 146, 149, 150, 172, 175, 191, 199-200, 203, 204, 305, 320, 333n

automatic writing, 31-32, 135-36, 226, 256

censors self: **sexual** euphemisms, 27, 54, 56-57, 78, 94, 105, 106, 119n, 129-30, 145, 151-53, 202, 227; name-changing, 106, 148, 149-50, 166-67, 192, 238, 255-56; overt verbal

Three Lives, 46-58, 71, 100, 112, 218, 224, 225; "The Good Anna," 47, 49-50; "The Gentle Lena," 50-52; "Melanctha," 16, 44, 49, 52-58, 168, 307; composition, 45, 64, 110; Cézanne portrait, 223; as *Three Histories,* 46; GS in it, 49; key word, "certainly," 126; quoted, 157

"Three Sisters Who Are Not Sisters," 331

To Do, 306, 310-13, 314

"To Kitty or Kate Buss," quoted 200, 288n

Toklas, Alice, 8, 12, 19, 41, 107n, 108-11, 125n, 205-6, 322n; *What Is Remembered,* 109, 213, 219

    birthday, 320n; personality, 109; resemblance to GS, 108; meets GS, 109; moves to rue de Fleurus, 110, 227; closeness to GS, 105, 106, 150, 151, 163; jealousy, 40, 121; as "Pussy," 150, 151, 209; as little jew," 151, 161; as "St. Therese," 177; as Boswell to GS' Johnson, 261; as cook, 130; as typist, 84; admires Henry James, 220; Pétain, 317; Avila, Spain, 177; participates in GS' compositions: editing, 210, 227n, 325n; writing, 93n, 209-17; in *The Autobiography of Alice B. Toklas,* 209-10, 212-13, 235, 305; corrects GS' French, 288n, 317n; criticizes, 145; *The Making of Americans,* 84, 212-13; "A Sonatina," 151n; *Lucy Church Amiably,* 190; *The Geographical History of America,* 261n; in "Ada," 93; Mallorcan pieces, 145-46; *Stanzas in Meditation,* 214

"Tourty or Tourtebattre," 156n, 158-59

Troy, William, 217

Twain, Mark, *Adventures of Huckleberry Finn,* 219n

Two, 88, 91, 107, 112-14; quoted, 57

Two Poems, quoted, 152

"Two Spaniards," 187

"Tubene," quoted, 143

Tzara, Tristan, 218

"Universe or Hand-Reading," quoted, 149

Useful Knowledge, xiii, 200

"The Value of College Education for Women," 36-37

Van Dongen, Kees, 222

Van Vechten, Carl, 14, 41, 95, 138, 171, 172

Verne, Jules, 12

"A Very Good House," quoted, 141

"A Village Are You Ready Yet Not Yet," 171

Vollard, Ambroise, 222-23

Wars I Have Seen, 158n, 324, 325-32, 337; quoted, 8, 11, 12, 13, 75, 315, 318, 333

Washington, George, 176, 242-43

"Water Pipe," quoted, 147

"A Waterfall and a Piano," 236n, 278n

Webster, Daniel, 341ff.

"A Wedding Bouquet," 271, 283-84, 289

"We Have Eaten Heartily . . . ," quoted, 150

Wells, H.G., 246

Westcott, Glenway, 231

What Are Master-Pieces, 264, 268; quoted, 242